Big Bend's Ancient and Modern Past

Big Bend's Ancient & Modern Past

EDITED BY

Bruce A. Glasrud and Robert J. Mallouf

Foreword by Lonn Taylor

Texas A&M University Press | *College Station, Texas*

Copyright© 2013 by Texas A&M University Press
Manufactured in the United States of America
All rights reserved
First edition

This paper meets the requirements
of ANSI/NISO Z39.48<H>1992
(Permanence of Paper).
Binding materials have been chosen for durability.

Library of Congress Cataloging-in-Publication Data
 Big Bend's ancient and modern past / edited by Bruce A. Glasrud and
Robert J. Mallouf; foreword by Lonn Taylor.—1st ed.
     p. cm.
 Compilation of articles originally published in the Journal of Big Bend studies.
 Includes bibliographical references and index.
 ISBN 978-1-62349-022-5 (book/pbk. : alk. paper)
 ISBN 978-1-62349-105-5 (e-book)
 1. Big Bend Region (Tex.)—History. 2. Prehistoric peoples—Texas—
Big Bend Region. 3. Ethnology—Texas—Big Bend Region.
I. Glasrud, Bruce A. II. Mallouf, Robert J.
 F392.B54B54 2013
 976.4'93—dc23
 2013017820

Contents

Foreword, *Lonn Taylor*   VII
Acknowledgments   IX
Introduction: Big Bend History and Prehistory   1
   Bruce A. Glasrud and Robert J. Mallouf

PART I: PREHISTORY MEETS HISTORY

1. Cradles, Cribs, and Mattresses: Prehistoric Sleeping Accommodations in the Chihuahuan Desert   19
   Solveig A. Turpin
2. Comments on the Prehistory of Far Northeastern Chihuahua, the La Junta District, and the Cielo Complex   34
   Robert J. Mallouf
3. The Rough Run Burial: A Semisubterranean Cairn Burial from Brewster County, Texas   69
   William A. Cloud
4. The Río Conchos Drainage: History, Archaeology, Significance   106
   J. Charles Kelley

PART II: HISTORY MEETS NATIVE AMERICANS

5. Native American and Mestizo Farming at La Junta de los Ríos   119
   Enrique R. Madrid
6. The Peyote Religion and Mescalero Apaches: An Ethnohistorical View from West Texas   132
   Stacy B. Schaefer
7. Spanish-Indian Relations in the Big Bend Region during the Eighteenth and Early Nineteenth Centuries   147
   Elizabeth A. H. John
8. New Light on Chisos Apache Indian Chief Alsate   157
   Franklin W. Daugherty and Luis López Elizondo

PART III: SETTLERS AND SETTLEMENTS

9. Settlements and Settlers at La Junta de los Ríos, 1759–1822   177
   Oakah L. Jones

10. Mexican American Traditional Foodways at La Junta de los Ríos
    Joe S. Graham   196
11. Naming Practices among the Black Seminole of the Texas-Mexico Border Region   218
    Mischa B. Adams
12. Transient Clergy in the Trans-Pecos Area, 1848–1892   238
    Robert E. Wright
13. William Rufus Shafter with the Frontier Army in the Big Bend   276
    Paul H. Carlson
14. Acculturation on the Rio Grande Frontier: The Founding of San José del Polvo and the Family of Lucia Rede Madrid   288
    Earl H. Elam

Glossary of Archaeological Terms   301
   Robert J. Mallouf
Suggested Readings   305
   Bruce A. Glasrud and Robert J. Mallouf
Contributors   311
Index 315

Foreword

The Big Bend of Texas is one of those places that exist more vividly in the imagination than in reality. Everyone in Texas has a story about it, even though there is not total agreement among Texans about exactly where it is. The region takes its name from the big bend in the Rio Grande, which starts to deflect southward from its southeast course just at the point where the western tip of Jeff Davis County touches it, then flows south-southeast fifty miles to Presidio, then eastward about eighty miles, and then, between Santa Elena Canyon and Boquillas Canyon, turns sharply north until it reaches a point about twenty-five miles south of Sanderson. From there it runs almost due east until the Pecos flows into it just west of Del Rio, and then it resumes its southeast course to the Gulf of Mexico. On a map the river forms the bottom of a cupped hand supporting the state of New Mexico.

There are purists who will tell you that the true Big Bend encompasses only the area within the sharpest bend of the river, the 1,250 or so square miles that make up Big Bend National Park. Others more generously place everything south of Interstate 10, west of the Pecos River, and east of Van Horn within the Big Bend. I know an old gentleman in Alpine who makes an intermediate distinction. He says that there is a line running east to west from Sanderson through Alpine and Marfa to Van Horn, south of which the country is so poor that everyone who lives there has had to do something illegal to get by. That, he says, is the Big Bend. It is certainly true that proximity to Mexico has made smuggling a rewarding enterprise in the Big Bend for a century and a half, and that some land titles there were obtained by means not entirely in conformity with the law.

The Big Bend is not exactly a Garden of Eden. The late Elmer Kelton used to tell about a man who was trying to sell his father some land south of Sanderson. "What's it like?" his father asked. "Well, it's sorry as hell," the man replied, "but it's pretty good." That is as good a definition of the Big Bend as any: sorry as hell, but pretty good.

A large part of the Big Bend is unquestionably desert. High desert and beautiful desert, but still desert. However, within that desert are flowing springs that create lush oases shaded by cottonwood trees, and narrow canyons filled with ferns, and, in the Davis Mountains, stands of

Ponderosa pines and even aspens. The aspens are on Mount Livermore, which at 8,378 feet above sea level is the second-highest peak in Texas. Senator Tom Love of Dallas, who was an early promoter of tourism in the Big Bend, liked to say that it was the second-tallest mountain between the Rockies and the Swiss Alps. The Big Bend lends itself to that kind of hyperbole.

The history of human occupation in the Big Bend goes back at least ten thousand years. When Spanish explorers arrived in the 1500s, they found flourishing villages of farmers at the junction of the Rio Grande and the Conchos, where the cities of Presidio, Texas, and Ojinaga, Chihuahua, now stand, a place the Spanish called La Junta de los Ríos. The ancestors of the people the Spanish encountered there had been planting and harvesting crops at La Junta since about 1200 AD, and the ancestors of those ancestors had been hunting game and gathering food there, and on the flats and in the mountains to the north and the south, for thousands of years before that.

Since its founding in 1982, the Center for Big Bend Studies at Sul Ross State University has been studying the human occupants of the Big Bend and recording their activities back through time. The center has an outstanding record, perhaps unique among southwestern archaeological institutions, of publishing the results of its investigations promptly and distributing them widely. One of the center's vehicles of publication, but by no means the only one, is the *Journal of Big Bend Studies*, a very handsome annual publication that has been appearing regularly for the past twenty years. Each of the articles in this volume, selected from the journal by Bruce Glasrud and Robert Mallouf, tells a portion of the Big Bend's story, and each represents a part of the center's work.

No two people could be better qualified to make these selections. Bruce Glasrud, who served as dean of Arts and Sciences and professor of history at Sul Ross from 1995 to 2003 and was a member of the center's advisory board during those years, is a well-known bibliographer of Texas history. Robert Mallouf, a living legend among Texas archaeologists, was director of the center from 1995 until his retirement in 2008.

—Lonn Taylor

Acknowledgments

We received considerable help in preparing and publishing this book. For that assistance we wish to thank a number of people. We are of course grateful for the cooperation of the authors whose studies are featured. We are indebted to members of the staff at the Center for Big Bend Studies who aided and supported us. Particularly helpful were the late Ellen Kelley, administrative assistant Susan Chisholm, director William A. (Andy) Cloud, and scientific illustrator Avram Dumitrescu. Since all of the articles in this anthology originally were published in the *Journal of Big Bend Studies,* we especially thank the center for granting us permission to use them. Two readers asked pertinent questions, made suggestions, and supported publication. As always, Mary Lenn Dixon, editor in chief at Texas A&M University Press, provided initial acceptance and encouragement for our proposal. Pearlene Vestal Glasrud read, edited, and improved our writing. For the rest we remain responsible.

—Bruce A. Glasrud
—Robert J. Mallouf

BIG BEND'S ANCIENT AND MODERN PAST

Introduction: Big Bend History and Prehistory

Bruce A. Glasrud and Robert J. Mallouf

The Big Bend region of Texas, sometimes referred to as El Despoblado or "the uninhabited land," and sometimes as a land of contrasts, as Texas' last frontier, or as a part of the Trans-Pecos, has had a long, colorful, and eventful history, a history that began before written records were maintained. This study, *Big Bend's Ancient and Modern Past,* reviews the unique past of the Big Bend area from the earliest habitation to 1900, the early modern era. Students of the region have investigated not only the peoples who successively inhabited the area, but also the nature of the environment and the inhabitants' responses to it. To a great extent the physical character of the Big Bend has dictated its history.

The Big Bend's name is derived from the substantial curve of the Rio Grande River. In Mexico, it includes the provinces of Coahuila and Chihuahua. In Texas, the Big Bend/Trans-Pecos includes the counties of Val Verde, Terrell, Pecos, Brewster, Presidio, Jeff Davis, Reeves, Culberson, perhaps Crockett, and, even though they are located east of the Pecos River, Loving, Winkler, Ward, and Crane. Since Hudspeth and El Paso counties are also west of the Pecos, their influence and importance cannot be ignored; the city of El Paso is the largest in the region. Other communities of importance include La Junta de los Ríos (historically), Del Rio, Alpine, and Pecos. The educational center of the Big Bend today is Sul Ross State University in Alpine, although the larger University of Texas at El Paso serves the region even beyond the Trans-Pecos. The Big Bend National Park, containing over eight hundred thousand acres, offers research, environmental protection and maintenance, and pure tourist enjoyment. So, too, do the state parks, including Big Bend State Park and Davis Mountains State Park.

The region is a geologic wonderland. Two geologic ages evident in the Big Bend are the Mesozoic Era, extending from 135 million to 63 million years ago, which produced Big Bend's marvelous peaks and mountains, and the present Cenozoic Era, beginning 63 million years ago, which produced the striking volcanic formations. The rugged terrain is dominated by towering mountains, precipitous canyons, and the parched, flat Chihuahuan Desert. During the summer the sun beats down mercilessly, but its effects are at least somewhat mitigated by a little rainfall, a small number of springs, and a few rivers and creeks. Without the competition of city lights and with its clear, dry air, Big Bend presents superb views. At night the skies are brilliant with stars seldom visible in more settled areas. Animals are rife; the Big Bend is the home of deer and antelopes, javelinas, bears, coyotes, and elks. Rattlesnakes, too, share the deserts and mountains and plains. And it is a bird-watcher's paradise, abounding in yellow-headed blackbirds, roadrunners, turkey vultures, songbirds, and hawks.

This magnificent country, with its spectacular environment, open distances, and dry climate, has produced numerous studies. Ron. C. Tyler's *The Big Bend: A History of the Last Texas Frontier,* originally published in 1975 by the National Park Service, provides a first-rate introduction to the history and peoples of the Big Bend.[1] This excellent offering was reprinted by Texas A&M University Press in 1996. Ross A. Maxwell's ambitious 1968 study, *The Big Bend of the Rio Grande: A Guide to the Rocks, Landscape, Geologic History, and Settlers of the Area of the Big Bend National Park* is somewhat dated but remains a useful resource. Two other works published by Texas A&M University Press, Dennis Blagg's *Big Bend Landscapes,* with its photorealistic images, and Gary Clark and Kathy Adams Clark's *Enjoying Big Bend National Park,* both suggest many reasons to visit the area.

For a readable, knowledgeable account of the geology of Big Bend, see William MacLeod, *Big Bend Vistas: A Geological Exploration of the Big Bend.* Carlysle Graham Raht, in *The Romance of Davis Mountains and Big Bend Country,* first published in 1919, helps the reader acquire a sense of the place. So, too, do the works of Elton Miles, who in *Tales of the Big Bend* and *More Tales of the Big Bend* explores the area through folk stories and lore. Virginia Madison tells tales of the Big Bend in her popular 1955 account, *The Big Bend Country of Texas.* And Patrick Dearen leads readers through his firsthand experience of the Trans-Pecos in his *Portraits of the Pecos Frontier.*

The late Sul Ross State University history professor Clifford B. Casey contributed substantially to our knowledge of Big Bend's past. His *Mirages, Mysteries, and Reality: Brewster County Texas, the Big Bend of the Rio Grande; Soldiers, Ranchers, and Miners in the Big Bend;* and *Sul Ross State University: The Cultural Center of Trans-Pecos Texas, 1917–1975* are valuable studies of the region, its institutions, and its people. Sul Ross State University biologist A. Michael Powell explored important topics enabling greater appreciation and understanding of the Big Bend area through his *Trees and Shrubs of the Trans-Pecos and Adjacent Areas, Grasses of the Trans-Pecos and Adjacent Areas* (with Patricia R. Manning), *Cacti of the Trans-Pecos and Adjacent Areas* (with James F. Weedin), and *Ferns and Fern Allies of the Trans-Pecos and Adjacent Areas* (with Sharon C. Yarborough). Roland Wauer introduces native birds in *A Field Guide to Birds of the Big Bend*. And spectacular photographs as well as insight into the environment, geography, and peoples of the Big Bend are to be found in George Wuerthner's *Texas' Big Bend Country*.

Settlement of the Big Bend was often sporadic until the US military established a presence there in the mid- and late nineteenth century. Arthur R. Gómez discusses earlier settlement by Europeans in *A Most Singular Country: A History of Occupation in the Big Bend,* and James M. Daniel in his PhD dissertation, "The Advance of the Spanish Frontier and the Despoblado," gives us a thorough account of the Spanish invasion. An incentive for tackling the Big Bend's hostile environment, both in Mexico and the United States, was silver mining, which Kenneth B. Ragsdale explores in *Quicksilver: Terlingua and the Chisos Mining Company*. As Glenn Justice noted in an article published in the *Journal of Big Bend History,* "Englishmen, Railroads, and the San Carlos Coal Mine," coal mining also played a vital role in settlement and development. And for the life of an early and prominent settler, see J. O. Langford (with Fred Gipson), *Big Bend: A Homesteader's Story.*

Much of the military's prominent role in the settlement and occupation of the Big Bend and Trans-Pecos was played out at one of the best-known US forts in Texas, Fort Davis, which was established in the 1850s. Robert Wooster, in *Fort Davis: Outpost on the Texas Frontier* and again in *Frontier Crossroads: Fort Davis and the West,* thoroughly and engagingly demonstrated the contribution of Fort Davis to military history. An important part of that contribution was in affording African Americans a military experience not often available to them elsewhere. During much of its existence, Fort Davis housed African American soldiers; for the black soldiers' stories see Harold Ray Sayre, *Warriors of Color.* Two other notable sources for exploring the history and peoples of the Big Bend region include the pathbreaking publications of the Center for Big Bend Studies and the twenty volumes produced by the West Texas Historical and Scientific Society; they offer additional research and comment on this singular region.

All of the essays in this volume were first published (some in very slightly different form) in the *Journal of Big Bend Studies (JBBS)*. From a wide range of useful articles, the editors have selected these for chronological and topical balance, interdisciplinary scholarship, and subject matter covering the years preceding 1900. We sought articles that were readable, informative, and well researched. *Big Bend's Ancient and Modern Past* is meant to supply some of the information generally lacking about the Big Bend, especially in comparison with the rest of the state. The *Journal of Big Bend Studies* is not widely disseminated and is often overlooked by students of Texas history. This book is meant to help to set right that deficiency and in so doing to offer an introduction to many readers unfamiliar with the Big Bend's fascinating story. It is intended for a wide-ranging audience—Big Bend enthusiasts and aficionados, students and teachers, scholars and lay readers, tourists and residents. It will prove a particularly valuable tool, we hope, for the classroom teacher—not least, perhaps, as a study in multiculturalism.

The book's three parts emphasize prehistory, Native Americans, and settlers, respectively; and the articles in each part are arranged in a generally chronological order, from prehistoric times to 1900. We stop at 1900 only because it would take another volume to explore Big Bend history from 1900 to the present. Perhaps one will be forthcoming.

Renewed interest in the relevance of border study and history means that the Big Bend deserves more extensive examination, for the study of Big Bend history is the study of borderlands history. This book will help ensure that the binational history of the region remains central to the historiography of the US-Mexico borderlands. Studying and researching across borders or boundaries be they national, state, or regional, requires a focus on the factors that often both bind and divide the inhabitants. The dual nature of citizenship, of landholding, of legal procedures and remedies, of education, and of history permeates the life and being of the residents of the Big Bend. The region offers a historical workshop for a new and growing group of scholars who study cross-cultural attributes in this place of sometimes shifting alignments. Among such scholars, including a number writing for *Big Bend's Ancient and Modern Past,* are James F. Brooks, *Confounding the Color Line: The Indian-Black Experience in North America* and *Captives and Cousins: Slavery, Kinship, and Community in the Southwest Borderlands;* Timothy K. Perttula, *The Prehistory of Texas;* Brian DeLay, *War of a Thousand Deserts: Indian Raids and the US-Mexican War;* Pekka Hämäläinen, *The Comanche Empire;* Gary Clayton Anderson, *The Conquest of Texas: Ethnic Cleansing in the Promised Land;* Ross Frank, "From Settler to Citizen: New Mexico Economic Development and the

Creation of Vecino Society, 1750–1820" (dissertation); and Andrés Reséndez, *Changing National Identities at the Frontier: Texas and New Mexico, 1800–1850*. These authors have followed in the steps of such predecessors as Elizabeth A. H. John, David J. Weber, and Oakah L. Jones.

The history and prehistory of the Big Bend has been the focus and strength of the Center for Big Bend Studies, located on the campus of Sul Ross State University in Alpine, Texas. The center is not alone in its historical pursuits at Sul Ross; affiliated with it and its mission is the Museum of the Big Bend and the Archives of the Big Bend. Each resource in its turn borrowed from the West Texas Historical and Scientific Society (WTHSS), which, organized in 1925, obtained a charter the following year. The Society published its twentieth and final *Bulletin* in 1964. In 1972 folklorist Joe S. Graham was elected president; in 1975 he was succeeded by the Trans-Pecos pioneering stalwart, Hallie Stilwell.

The WTHSS successor, the Center for Big Bend Studies, was established by Sul Ross State University in 1982 and approved by the board of regents in 1987. The principal purpose of the center is to support and promote programs and scholarly activities for the cultural and historical development of the Trans-Pecos/Big Bend region of Texas and Mexico. Leadership of the newly established center began with Earl Elam, former vice president for academic affairs at Sul Ross and a Texas Tech University PhD. Elam now lives in East Texas, where he is director of the Hill Country Press. Elam was followed in 1995 by Robert J. Mallouf, who had previously served as Texas state archaeologist. Mallouf conducted research and explorations in the Big Bend before becoming director of the center at Sul Ross, and he welcomed the opportunity to learn more about the region as well as to lead the center in fostering its mission for the Big Bend/Trans-Pecos area of Texas and northern Mexico. During Mallouf's tenure as director, the center grew significantly. It branched into conducting anthropological and archaeological research in the Big Bend for many organizations, including the National Parks Service and Texas Parks and Wildlife. Mallouf retired in 2008; he was followed as director by William A. "Andy" Cloud, who had worked with him at the center for the previous thirteen years.

For further dissemination of its scholarly projects, the Center for Big Bend Studies sponsors the *Journal of Big Bend Studies* (which recently completed its twenty-second volume) and publishes a newsletter, *La Vista de la Frontera*, which discusses events and undertakings at the center. The center also publishes occasional papers of special interest. These have included, among many others, Bruce A. Glasrud's *African Americans in the West: A Bibliography of Secondary Sources,* as well as *Rock Art of the Chihuahuan Desert Borderlands,* edited by Sheron Smith-Savage and Robert J. Mallouf, and *Bosque Bonito,* Robert Keil's intriguing firsthand account of, among other events, the Texas Ranger massacre at Porvenir. Two series, Reports in Contract Archeology and Papers of the Trans-Pecos Archaeological Program, focus on specializations of the Center for Big Bend Studies. And a few other publications, such as Russell Ashton Scogin's *The Sanderson Flood of 1965,* comment on events in the region.

An important adjunct of the center is its annual meeting, at which scholars, students, laypeople, and other guests from the US Southwest and Mexican North, and sometimes beyond, gather to learn about this exciting region, to roam around the book exhibits, to conduct research in the Archives of the Big Bend, or to peruse the Museum of the Big Bend. Most attendees manage to visit Big Bend National Park, view the Marfa lights, or travel to the mountains in Fort Davis while in Alpine. Sessions are held, papers are presented, and over the course of the conference a host of small unofficial discussions occur about facets of Big Bend history, culture, and environment.

In its publications, meetings, membership, and focus, the Center for Big Bend Studies takes the multidisciplinary approach to the history and prehistory of Big Bend that is apparent in the articles selected for this book. Anthropologists such as Robert J. Mallouf, historians such as Elizabeth A. H. John and Oakah L. Jones, and archaeologists such as J. Charles Kelley are featured here, as are geologist Franklin W. Daugherty, folklorist Joe S. Graham, and ethnohistorian Stacy B. Schaefer. They are not alone. Those who have published in the *Journal* or made presentations at one or more annual meetings include Paul Wright, a geographer; Paul Cool, an attorney; Gloria Duarte, a linguist; Chuck Parsons, a retired education administrator; William McLeod, a geologist; Barney Nelson, an English professor; and Jay Downing, a psychologist. Other disciplines represented at the meetings or in the published literature of the Center for Big Bend Studies include art, biology, economics, business, education, criminal justice, and drama. Participants at sessions of the Center may include Judge Tom Crum, business executive Thomas Alexander, or rancher Clifton Caldwell. Vital strengths of the Center are its multidisciplinary nature, its varied participants, and the character of the Big Bend/Trans-Pecos region itself.

The efforts of these and other scholars and investigators have provided information about the successive waves of incomers to the Big Bend. European knowledge of and engagement with the Trans-Pecos began in 1535 when Cabeza de Vaca wandered through the area on his circuitous route to Mexico. Traveling with de Vaca was Esteban, the first African American to set foot in the Big Bend. Subsequent Spanish excursions of note into the region took place in 1583 (Espejo), a century later in 1683 (Mendoza), and finally in 1747 (Ydoiaga, Terán, Vidurre). Historically, however, Native Americans, named Indians by the European settlers, preceded the Europeans by thousands of years.

The entry of Native Americans into the Big Bend actually began some thirteen thousand years ago with the arrival of Paleoindians, often characterized as highly mobile, wide-ranging big game hunters of mammoths, mastodons, giant bison, and other large Pleistocene-epoch animals. Practicing a basically hunting-gathering lifeway that included use of open-air campsites, the Paleoindians in the region appear to have had a rather sporadic presence, possibly linked to the availability of high-quality stone for making tools and to other highly desirable resources.

A much more pronounced and persistent Native American presence in the region is revealed by the innumerable archaeological sites of subsequent Archaic peoples. Beginning as early as 6500 BC, the Big Bend became home to hundreds of generations of atlatl-wielding nomadic hunters and gatherers who traveled in small groups or bands and who, of necessity, had intimate knowledge of the Big Bend's geological, hydrological, and biological resources. The Early Archaic period, from roughly 6500 to 2500 BC, saw the expansion of tool kits with a stronger emphasis on plant-processing implements such as metates and manos, the beginnings of more restricted territorial ranges, and the occasional use of rock-shelters and caves as well as open-air campsites—all adaptations to a slowly advancing aridity that had its beginnings in the earlier Paleoindian period.

The succeeding Middle Archaic (2500–1000 BC) and Late Archaic (1000 BC–AD 700) periods witnessed a continuing trend toward greater use of wild plant foods, which is reflected in rock ovens and middens throughout the Big Bend. As attested by their innumerable campsite and rock-shelter remains, Middle Archaic peoples appear to have successfully maneuvered through a particularly long, pronounced drying trend, referred to in scientific circles as the Altithermal, while succeeding Late Archaic inhabitants experienced a temporary climatic reprieve of increased moisture around 500 BC. This climatic episode is evidenced archaeologically by the appearance in the region of bison hunters and by an increasing overall population density. However, by the end of the Late Archaic period, a trend of increasing aridity through time was again entrenched, requiring adaptational adjustments on the part of Big Bend populations.

By the advent of late prehistory, or what is termed archaeologically the Late Prehistoric period (AD 700–1535), the region's inhabitants were still maintaining successful hunting-gathering lifeways that differed little from their Archaic predecessors'. Even the introduction of three major innovations into the Big Bend early in this period—agriculture, pottery, and the bow and arrow—seems not to have greatly altered the basic hunting-gathering mode of existence. By AD 1200, however, the Big Bend's first and only indigenous, semisedentary agriculturalists appeared along the Rio Grande and Río Conchos in what is known historically as La Junta de los Ríos, and symbiotic trade relationships between farmers and surrounding nomadic groups were quick to follow.

It was the entry of Europeans into the Big Bend in the sixteenth century that gave rise to abrupt and permanent change among Native American populations, regardless of their mode of existence. The region's nomadic groups were quick to adopt tangible European imports, including the horse and the gun, which were easily integrated into their existing cultural frameworks, but would ultimately have far-reaching effects on their social systems due to the greatly increased mobility and significantly enhanced firepower they provided. On the other hand, European ideological offerings, such as the Spanish economic system and Christianity, would prove much less palatable to Native Americans, who had long been entrenched in successful subsistence and cosmological systems of their own making.

The fascinating interplay of Spanish culture (which was dominant) with that of Native Americans in the Big Bend is probably best exemplified in William B. Griffen's *Culture Change and Shifting Populations in Central Northern Mexico,* which tells a story of changing social orders, long-lived hostilities with brief periods of harmony, and shifting Spanish priorities and policies. But ultimately, many of the nomadic cultures early encountered by the Spanish in the Big Bend of Texas and northeastern Chihuahua were essentially extinct by 1750, including those of some larger tribal groups such as the Tobosos, Chisos, and Jumanos.

As the focal point of Spanish economic and religious ambitions in the region, the farming Indians of La Junta de los Ríos fared only somewhat better than the nomads. Repeated circumvention of Spanish economic goals by the farmers led eventually to frustration and contempt on the part of Spanish administrators. Spanish missionaries, meanwhile, tackled the onerous task of changing the farmers' worldviews, although with little success. In the end, the mosaic of Indian groups and various cultures that historically composed La Junta, including the Abriaches, Julimes, Mesquites, Conchos, Pescados, Puliques, and others, suffered irreversible breakdown in their socioeconomic systems. The process of deterioration was only quickened by the arrival of a new and formidable Native American presence at La Junta by the end of the seventeenth century—the Apache.

The unheralded arrival of Mescalero and Lipan Apaches in the Big Bend between 1650 and 1700 effectively placed the indigenous nomadic and farming Indians, who were already under pressure from the Comanches to the north, in a pincer between two dominant and immovable forces. Nomadic groups such as the Jumanos and Cibolos were summarily overwhelmed and by 1725 were absorbed into the Apache sphere. Left with no tolerable recourse, the farmers of La Junta endeavored to cater to both the Spanish and the Apaches in a futile attempt at cultural survival. During the nineteenth century, the "Apache problem" was passed first from the Spanish to the Mexican military (1821) and at last to the US military (1848). It would take the US military over thirty years more to finally remove the Apache (and Comanche) presence from the Big Bend.

These and many other eventful episodes in the history of the Big Bend are to be found in the pages of the *Journal of Big Bend Studies*. In making our selection of articles for this volume, we attempt to provide portals into the full range of this varied and exciting history, thus demonstrating the regional and interregional potential of further multidisciplinary research. We begin our journey in *Big Bend's Ancient and Modern Past* with Part I, "Prehistory Meets History." In this section three articles discuss the prehistoric period of the Big Bend, and the fourth uses both prehistory and history to broaden understanding of life in the early Big Bend region.

The first article, Solveig A. Turpin's "Cradles, Cribs, and Mattresses: Prehistoric Sleeping Accommodations in the Chihuahuan Desert" (*JBBS* 9 [1997]: 1–18) explores the artifacts left by some of the earliest of Big Bend inhabitants. Turpin discovered two dry-rock shelters, one in northern Coahuila and one in southwestern Texas, which produced well-preserved examples of early bedding. Six radiocarbon dates indicate that the beds range in age from Middle Archaic to Late Prehistoric, but all are similar in design and use readily available fibrous material. Each consists of a base, in all cases overlapping prickly pear pads, a frame of sticks, rocks, or bent agave, and padding, either grass or shredded sotol leaves. The one infant nest was apparently also warmed by heated rocks placed beneath the sotol padding. As Turpin reported, the variability of the beds is in part attributable to differences in resource availability, but she also credits the women who were probably responsible for their construction. The beds' features, which apparently were designed to counteract the ubiquitous ashy dust and inclement weather, are but an early example of the expedient efficiency of the regional fiber industry.

The selections continue as Robert J. Mallouf offers "Comments on the Prehistory of Far Northeastern Chihuahua, the La Junta District, and the Cielo Complex" (*JBBS* 11 [1999]: 49–92). As Mallouf notes, examination of private artifact collections in northeastern Chihuahua helped scholars to recognize tentative patterns in the distribution of stone projectile points and to develop a preliminary regional chronology based upon projectile-point styles. Mallouf provides an overview of the Late Prehistoric Cielo complex, together with previously unpublished chronometric data on the Cielo complex and the La Junta phase. He explores interpretive issues centering on sociocultural relationships of the Cielo complex to contemporary La Junta, Toyah, and Infierno phases of northeastern Chihuahua and Texas. In contrast to past interpreters, Mallouf suggests that La Junta phase peoples may have origins separate and distinct from those of peoples usually associated with them—the Jornada Branch of the Mogollon.

William A. Cloud also gathered important information on native life in the Late Prehistoric period; his article, "The Rough Run Burial: A Semisubterranean Cairn Burial from Brewster County, Texas" (*JBBS* 14 [2002]: 33–84), uses an early burial site to provide significant information about burial practices. A disturbed prehistoric, semisubterranean cairn burial in the western portion of Big Bend National Park was initially discovered in 1987 during a power line survey along Rough Run. Subsequent testing in 1988 revealed the presence of a buried cairn containing a number of Perdiz arrow points interspersed among the stones. Excavation in 1990 uncovered an interment that had been carefully positioned beneath the cairn. Grave goods recovered consist of seventy-three associated arrow points and arrow-point fragments, all but one of which are of the Perdiz type, and three pieces of debitage. This scientifically excavated internment offered a glimpse of the mortuary customs practiced by the makers and users of the ubiquitous Perdiz arrow point.

Famed archaeologist J. Charles Kelley brings the discussion to the river routes of the Big Bend and, using both history and archaeology, moves the dialogue from prehistory to history in his formidable article, "The Río Conchos Drainage: History, Archaeology, Significance" (*JBBS* 2 [1990]: 29–41). The Río Conchos drainage is the main river system of Chihuahua. Its major tributaries originate in the Sierra Madre Occidental, one of them (the Río Florido) in the state of Durango. The Río Conchos joins the Rio Grande (Río Bravo) at La Junta de los Ríos, near Ojinaga, Chihuahua, and Presidio, Texas. At the river junction the Río Conchos is the master stream; reportedly, the Rio Grande above La Junta formerly went dry on occasion, and the average annual runoff was relatively very low. In the period 1900–1913, before Elephant Butte Reservoir was established on the Rio Grande above El Paso and several other reservoirs were constructed on the Río Conchos, the gauging station on the Rio Grande just above La Junta recorded an average runoff of 645,246 acre feet. In the same period the station just below the mouth of the Río Conchos recorded an average annual runoff of 2,045,769 acre feet, over three times the runoff above the junction.

In Part II, "History Meets Native Americans," the lives of the early inhabitants of the Big Bend are looked at from a historical perspective, that is, since the time when Europeans encountered the native inhabitants of North America. Following a construct similar to that of J. Charles Kelley, Enrique R. Madrid, in "Native American and Mestizo Farming at La Junta de los Ríos" (*JBBS* 8 [1996]: 15–31), used archaeological, historical, and ethnographic data to create a picture of nearly a millennium of Native American and mestizo agricultural practices at La Junta de los Ríos, the junction of the Río Conchos with the Rio Grande.

Stacy B. Schaefer, in his thoughtful and persuasive article "The Peyote Religion and Mescalero Apaches: An Ethnohistorical View from West Texas" (*JBBS* 12 [2000]: 51–70), notes that the border region of Texas and northern Mexico is a native habitat for a small, spineless cactus known as peyote (*Lophophora williamsii*). For centuries peyote has been used by indigenous peoples in religious rituals and has been revered for its mind-altering effects. Schaefer's article reviews the route of diffusion of peyote religion proposed by scholars who, like Weston La Barre, credit the Lipan Apaches with introducing peyote religion to tribes in the United States. James Mooney, on the other hand, believed that the Mescalero Apaches were the purveyors of peyote religion. Following Mooney's reasoning, Schaefer discusses the idea of "differential diffusion" suggested by La Barre and also gives a short history of Mescalero trading and raiding practices. He proposes an additional route by which the traditional Mexican peyote religion may have spread into the United States: that is, from Chihuahua, through West Texas, and into New Mexico, via the Mescalero Apaches. He compares similarities in Mescalero and Tarahumara peyote use and, based on his research and on conversations with anthropologist Claire R. Farrer, discusses the manner in which peyote continues to be used ritually by some Mescaleros today.

The Apaches and later the Comanches also figure prominently in the research and writings of Elizabeth A. H. John, whose *Storms Brewed in Other Men's Worlds: The Confrontation of Indians, Spanish, and French in the Southwest, 1540–1795,* opened up new ideas and vistas regarding Native American life for students of not only the Big Bend but also the entire Southwest. In her article "Spanish-Indian Relations in the Big Bend Region during the Eighteenth and Early Nineteenth Centuries" (*JBBS* 3 [1991]: 71–80), John argues that for most of the eighteenth century, the Big Bend was really Apache country. Apache warriors acquired the land of the Big Bend when they were newly empowered by horses and drawn toward the Spanish supply of those animals. However, by the 1770s, southward-moving Comanches threatened to make the Big Bend as dangerous for Apaches as Apaches had made it for others a few decades earlier. To add to the mix, the Spanish claimed and occupied the land, and Spanish-Indian relations thus evolved through a complex mix of hostilities and tentative friendships, of alternate—or sometimes even simultaneous—raiding and trading. The tenor of their relationships varied according to the circumstances and perceived self-interests of the various Big Bend inhabitants.

As with all history, myths intrude themselves into the supposed base of knowledge about Big Bend. Franklin W. Daugherty and Luis López Elizondo, in their article "New Light on Chisos Apache Indian Chief Alsate" (*JBBS* 8 [1996]: 33–49), find that although the history and folklore of the Texas Big Bend is replete with references to the legendary Alsate, few people are aware of the important part that Alsate's Spanish forebears played in the early exploration, colonization, and development of northern Mexico and Spanish Texas. In this readable study, Daugherty and Elizondo closely examine documents that raise a number of questions about the historical accuracy and completeness of past accounts of Alsate's life and death.

In Part III, "Settlers and Settlements," six authors consider the evolution of society and culture in Big Bend, and the mixture of peoples who lived there, in the years from 1759 to 1900. In his article "Settlements and Settlers at La Junta de los Ríos, 1759–1822" (*JBBS* 3 [1991]: 43–70), prominent historian Oakah L. Jones, noted for his *Los Paisanos: Spanish Settlers on the Northern Frontier of New Spain,* addresses about the same years and region that Elizabeth John addressed in her article, but whereas John examined Native Americans' relationships with each other and with the Spanish, Jones focuses especially on the Spanish settlers. He describes the region that Spanish officials referred to as "La Junta de los Ríos del Norte y Conchos," reviews the sporadic visits made by Spain and its attempts to establish the region of La Junta, and examines in some detail Spanish settlers there between the founding of the first presidio at the junction of the two rivers (1759–60) and the end of the Spanish period. Jones discovered that the Indians and Spanish settlers did not remain apart in this time and place, but practiced *mestizaje* (racial mixing) openly.

In his insightful article "Mexican American Traditional Foodways at La Junta de los Ríos" (*JBBS* 2 [1990]: 1–27), folklorist and astute observer and student of folk culture Joe S. Graham finds that "as in many other cultures, food among the Mexicanos of La Junta is important beyond its function of nurturing the physical body." Graham begins his investigation in prehistory, continues with Spanish contributions, and then considers more contemporary food usages. He describes dishes made of corn, beans, squash, and such meats as goat, pork, and beef, in the process telling us much about food, folklore, and history in the Big Bend.

Not all inhabitants of the Big Bend are of Native American, Spanish, or Mexican American descent. One small group, the Black Seminoles, stemmed from a Native American and African American background in a tortuous and intriguing history. In "Naming Practices among the Black Seminole of the Texas-Mexico Border Region" (*JBBS* 11 [1999]: 119–44), Mischa B. Adams takes an anthropological perspective to examine Black Seminole naming practices. Since Seminole family relationships, as represented by surnames recorded in genealogies, historical accounts, military and government census reports, and enlistment data, are so complex as to confound the specialists, Adams's contribution is seminal. Adams discovered that a number of factors contribute to the complexity: traditional Native American and African practices regarding family names, Seminoles' acquisition of Spanish names and language upon immigrating to Mexico, and the tendency of both historical and contemporary Seminole families to use different surnames depending upon whether they live on the Texas or Mexican side of the border.

African Americans came into the Big Bend region as soldiers of the US Army during the later nineteenth century. One of their commanders was then-Colonel William R. Shafter. Paul H. Carlson writes about this intrepid leader in his article "William Rufus Shafter with the Frontier Army in the Big Bend" (*JBBS* 1 [1989]: 71–82). Shafter, who in 1898 led the American expeditionary force to Cuba in the Spanish-American War, served for nearly seventeen years on the Texas frontier. As a lieutenant colonel of the black 24th Infantry, he was bulky, lumbering, and overweight, but he was considered the most energetic man of his rank on the Texas frontier. Although he was coarse and abrasive, Shafter's record in Texas, including the Big Bend country, reveals courage, zeal, and intelligence. His official explorations in the region produced some of the most thorough early reports on the Big Bend available to the army and to settlers entering the region.

Among those who attempted to profit from the Big Bend were an Englishman, John Humpris, and his partners. In 1892 the San Carlos Coal Company leased and purchased fifty-four thousand acres of land in northwest Presidio County with the intention of mining coal. Because of the remote location of the line, it was necessary to build a twenty-six-mile railroad from the Chispa siding on the Southern Pacific Railroad to San Carlos. John Humpris thought that the railroads and their crews presented great opportunities for businessmen and consequently opened a chain of general stores in the Big Bend. But, as Glenn Justice in "Englishmen, Railroads, and the San Carlos Coal Mine" notes, no one benefited very much in this land of few people and vast and treacherous distances. The coal proved to be of varying quality and insufficient quantity, and the Rio Grande Northern Railroad was used only once. Mining operations ceased and the abandoned railroad was sold for unpaid debts by the sheriff.

Many other settlers arrived in the Big Bend during the later nineteenth century. They became involved in mining, land and community development, agriculture, ranching, the telegraph, and the church. Scholars writing for the JBBS have addressed those activities and many others as well. In "Transient Clergy in the Trans-Pecos Area, 1848–1892" (*JBBS* 18 [2006]: 7–45), the twelfth article in *Big Bend's Ancient and Modern Past*, Robert E. Wright portrays the lives of Catholic clergy who worked with the inhabitants of the Big Bend from the middle to the last part of the nineteenth century. In the process he provides us with glimpses into the lives of others in the region as well. Wright's is a fascinating and informative account of Big Bend settlers and settlement. It also demonstrates the commitment of the clergy who arrived in the Big Bend, often bereft of information about the region's open and hostile environment.

The final article in *Big Bend's Ancient and Modern Past,* Earl H. Elam's "Acculturation on the Rio Grande Frontier: The Founding of San José del Polvo and the Family of Lucia Rede Madrid" (*JBBS* 5 [1993]: 79–95), investigates the experiences of Lucia Rede Madrid and her parents and grandparents on Texas' Rio Grande frontier. Their lives, Elam reports, were comparable in many respects to those of settlers in other frontier areas of the United States. But there also were significant differences, the most obvious ones stemming from the ethnic background of the pioneers; on the Rio Grande frontier Hispanic Americans were in the majority. They brought with them unique cultural institutions and folkways.

From prehistoric times down into the present, the stark and majestic grandeur of Big Bend has distinguished it and set it apart. The earliest nomadic hunters, like the Spanish explorers and the Mexican and Anglo settlers after them, must have found in Big Bend an awful and forbidding aspect. Only the most determined persisted there, working and struggling to survive in an enclave always set apart from the dominant society, an enclave characterized by a pluralism observable not only socially and culturally but also ethnically. This book tells the stories of the extraordinary people who settled in a place that so forcefully both attracted and resisted settlement—and that remains "El Despoblado."

Notes

1. Bibliographical information for the essays that compose this book is cited in the text of the introduction. The other works discussed in the introduction are cited in the suggested readings at the end of the volume.

I
PREHISTORY MEETS HISTORY

1 Cradles, Cribs, and Mattresses

Prehistoric Sleeping Accommodations in the Chihuahuan Desert

Solveig A. Turpin

Although people spend more time sleeping than they do eating or producing tools, archaeologists know considerably more about food preparation and flint knapping than they do about beds and mattresses. Two dry rock-shelters, one in southwestern Texas and one in northern Coahuila, have produced some well-preserved examples of early bedding that was apparently specifically designed to counteract inclement weather while inhibiting the ever-present ashy dust. Simple but efficient, these beds reflect the expedient use of desert vegetation and the ingenuity that typifies the fiber industry in this region.

Excavations at the Wroe Ranch site (41TE307) in Terrell County, Texas, and Cueva Encantada, in northern Coahuila, exhumed a variety of features that primarily used fiber in their construction (fig. 1.1). Both sites are in the Chihuahuan Desert, where fibrous plants were a mainstay of both diet and industry. Cueva Encantada overlooks a high mountain valley (Turpin and Carpenter 1994) while Wroe Ranch faces out over the narrow floodplain of a dry creek canyon (Turpin 1995). Neither is presently near a permanent source of potable water. Although both sites are small, Cueva Encantada, with an area of 70 square meters, is adjacent to a much larger rock-shelter that has been completely emptied by relic hunters and erosion, leaving only a few areas in the alcove untouched. Wroe Ranch was also badly vandalized before systematic excavations were undertaken, but it is, in its entirety, approximately 110 square meters in floor area. Cueva Encantada has pictographs and deep mortar holes, the same features that are found in sites very near to Wroe Ranch, such as 41TE308 and 41TE312, both less than 1 km away. Thus, although Encantada and Wroe Ranch are at least 225 straight-line kilometers apart, the physical and social demands placed upon their occupants and their responses to those stimuli were very similar.

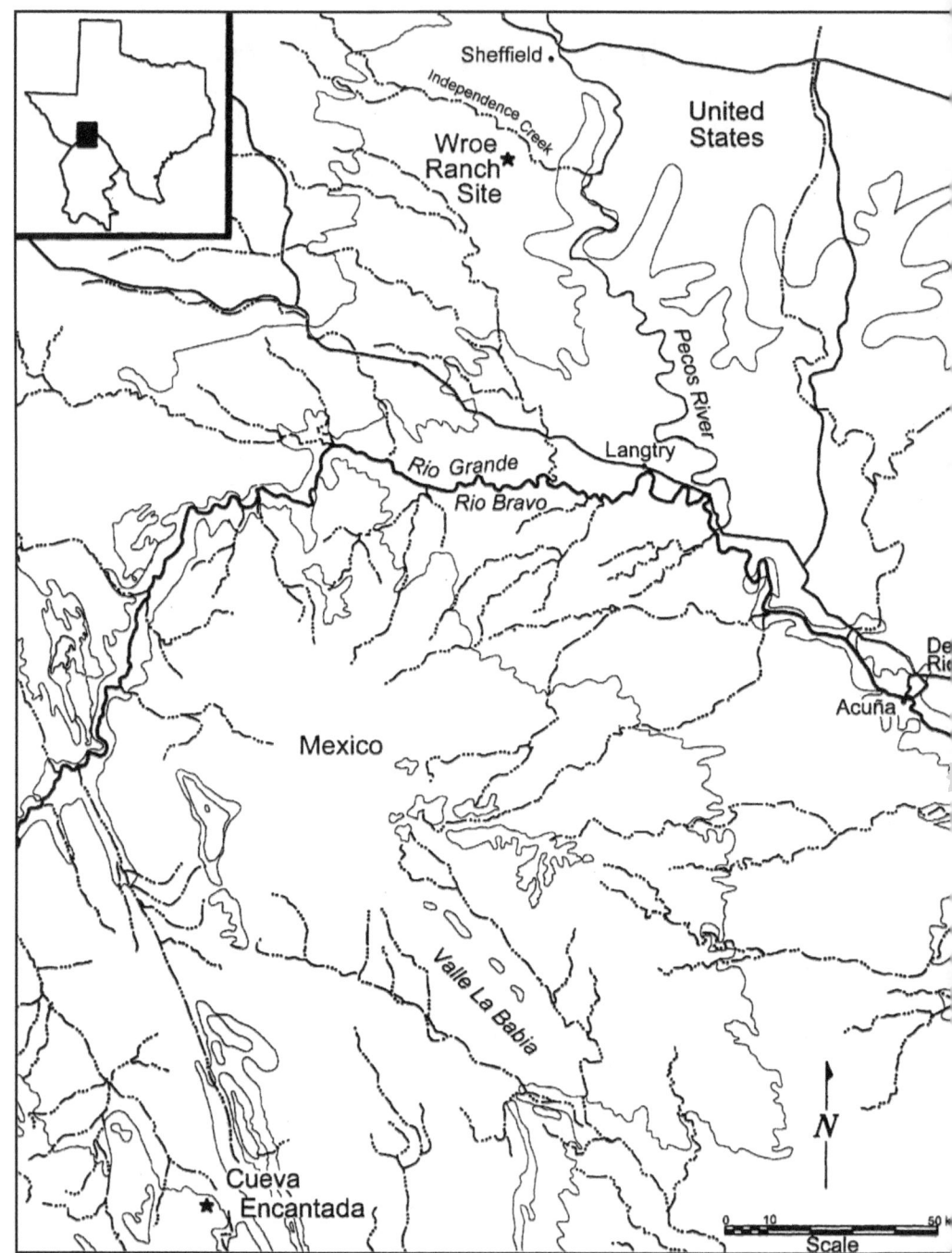

Figure 1.1. Map showing locations of Wroe Ranch in Texas and Cueva Encantada in Coahuila. Courtesy Center for Big Bend Studies.

TEMPORAL SEQUENCE OF OCCUPATION

The cultural chronology used here is borrowed from the Lower Pecos region, where many of the projectile point styles found in both shelters have been well dated. The Lower Pecos sequence is probably more appropriate to the Wroe Ranch materials, but to date, the only cultural context proposed for northern Coahuila (Taylor 1966) is not well fixed in time.

Nine radiocarbon dates place the occupation of Cueva Encantada between 660 and 4,520 years ago, or from 2570 BC to AD 1270, thus spanning the Middle and Late Archaic periods and extending into the Late Prehistoric period. The majority of the projectile points conform to Taylor's (1966) Jora or Bement's (1991) Arenosa dart point style, which is considered to be a Middle Archaic form, based on radiocarbon dates from Arenosa Shelter (Turpin 1991) on the Pecos River. The presence of the Pandale dart point style, although still Middle Archaic in age, indicates a somewhat earlier component, but the artifacts are not indisputably associated with extant features or radiocarbon samples.

Temporally diagnostic tools indicate that the occupation of Wroe Ranch began in the Early Archaic period and lasted through the Late Prehistoric period; ten radiocarbon dates obtained from stratigraphic excavations indicate that the extant features, with one exception, were laid down between 1,290 and 1,820 radiocarbon years ago, or between AD 100 and 660, during the latter half of the Late Archaic period, the Blue Hills subperiod (Turpin 1991). A well-preserved subadolescent burial wrested from the site by relic hunters a decade ago produced two radiocarbon dates attributable to the Late Prehistoric period, ca. AD 1060–1400, and an isolated ash pit extends the occupational period back to 3900 BC.

Six of the seven radiocarbon dates apply directly to the features described here as beds: three are from Wroe Ranch and three are from Cueva Encantada. Table 1.1 lists the radiocarbon date, its 13C-corrected range, and its calibrated age according to Stuiver and Reimer's (1993) Method A. The probability ranges calculated by Stuiver and Reimer's (1993) Method B are rounded to the nearest decade and are discussed in the text.

DESCRIPTION OF THE BEDS

Both of these rock-shelters were replete with intact features made of fiber; the majority were grass-lined, basin-shaped pits apparently intended as storage facilities or padding for various activities. The beds described here

Table 1.1. Periods in the chronology of the Lower Pecos River region

Period	Subperiod	Radiocarbon Dates BP (years before present)
Paleoindian		<12,000–
	Aurora	14,500–11,900
	Bonfire	10,700–9800
Late Paleoindian		9400–9000
	Oriente	9400–8800
Early Archaic		9000–6000
	Viejo	8900–5500
Middle Archaic		6000–3000
	Eagle Nest	5500–4100
	San Felipe	4100–3200
Late Archaic		3000–1000
	Cibola	3150–2300
	Flanders	2300–?
	Blue Hills	2300–1300
Late Prehistoric		1000–350
	Flecha	1320–450
	Infiermo	450–250
Historic		350–0

differ from these pits in size, shape, construction method, or, in the case of the presumed infant's nest, raw material. The Wroe Ranch burial pit, as described by the relic hunters who first unearthed it, is so similar to the adult bed found nearby that the dead child may literally have been laid to rest in its accustomed place.

The Cueva Encantada Beds

The Baby Nest

Grass-lined pits that have been interpreted as adult and infant "sleeping nests" (Shafer 1986, 99) are commonly found in dry rock-shelters. The baby nest (Feature 13, fig. 1.2) at Cueva Encantada, however, differs from the other grass-lined pits in several significant details, perhaps most importantly in its innovative design. First, as many as six broad

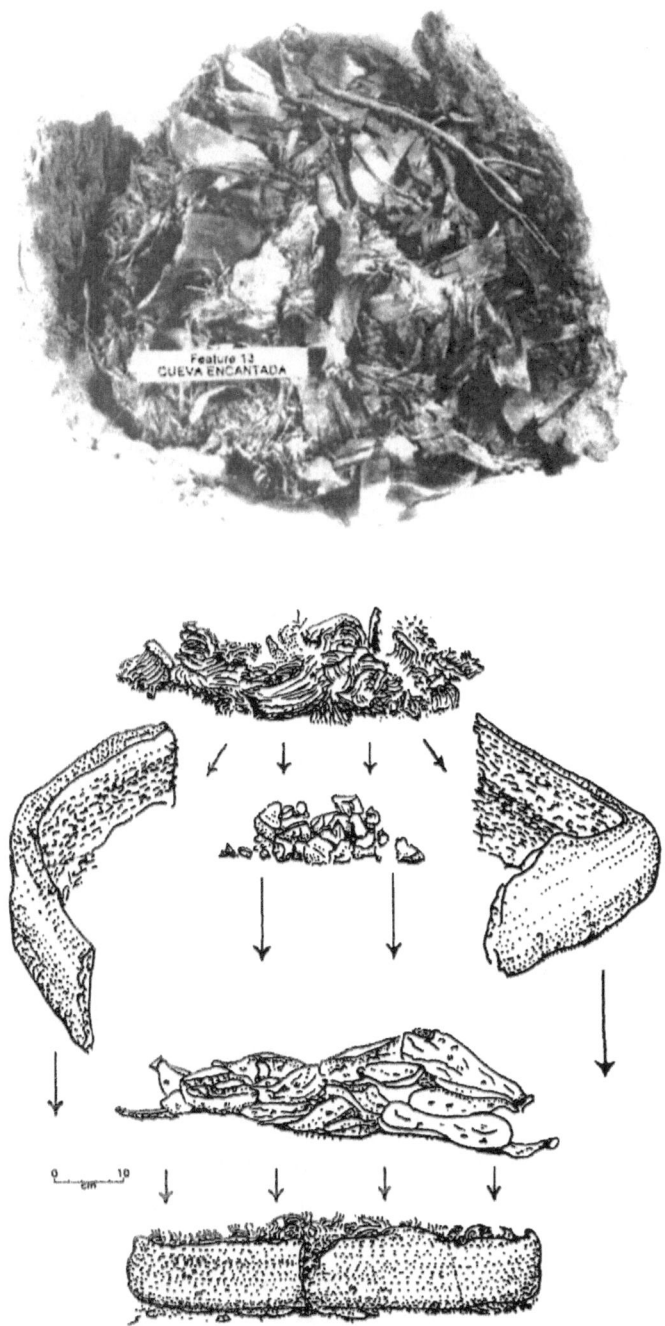

Figure 1.2. Infant nest (Feature 13) from Cueva Encantada; (top) photo of actual intact nest as removed from the site; (bottom) schematic drawing of construction sequence. Courtesy Center for Big Bend Studies.

prickly-pear pads were fanned out to line the bottom of the feature. Two sections of split maguey leaf, over 3 cm thick and as wide as 17 cm, were then forced into a circle 80 cm in diameter and set perpendicular to the pads to form the sides. A cluster of twelve to fifteen fist-sized and smaller burned rocks were laid atop the prickly pear inside the agave circle. Although the fill contains some charcoal, the absence of charring indicates that the rocks were placed inside the maguey walls after they had been heated. The interior was then stuffed with shredded sotol-leaf bases, a plant material that curls into a springy mass. Covered with matting or hide, the heated rocks radiated warmth into the contained area of the nest. This construction would have served admirably as a cold-weather infant bed. A sample of woody sotol heart from the padding produced a 13C-corrected radiocarbon age of 1,870±60 years ago (TX-8443). There is an 87 percent probability that the correct age of this assay is between AD 110 and 225, or 1840 and 1720 BP (Method B; Stuiver and Reimer 1993), during the Late Archaic Blue Hills subperiod in the Lower Pecos chronology.

Adult Beds

Under assorted discarded items and relic hunter backdirt in the rear of the cave, two temporally discrete activities had left their mark in the form of a latrine and an adult-sized bed. The sleeping area was delineated by an arc of rocks that curved around a rectangular mattress of shredded sotol leaves that was tucked up under the rear wall. The most intact end was still covered with a twined mat made of sedge, similar to one described by McGregor (1991) and dated to the Late Prehistoric period in the Lower Pecos region. The mat was folded under to raise one end, presumably the head, and sloped down to the hip area; the lower end, unfortunately, was under the latrine and had deteriorated. The sotol pad measured 115 cm long and 75 cm wide; the mat covered the upper 65 cm.

A second pad of shredded sotol, with a circular mass of lead-tree twigs and leaves at one end, extended under the baby nest. Although less well defined due to post-depositional disturbances, the remains of this pad were 75 cm long and 60 cm wide, roughly rectangular, and very similar to the better-preserved mattress of the adult-sized bed.

Sotol leaves from the adult-bed mattress produced a 13C-corrected date of 3,340±50 radiocarbon years ago (TX-8508). There is a 66 percent probability that the true age of this sample is between 1675 and 1595 BC, or 3545 and 3265 BP (Method B; Stuiver and Reimer 1993). The twined mat that covered the sotol pad assayed somewhat older: 3870±190 BP (TX-8442) with an 89 percent probability that the true age is between 2500 and 2030 BC, or 3980 and 4450 BP (Method B; Stuiver and Reimer 1993). Despite the four-hundred-year gap between the two, both fall in the Middle Archaic San Felipe period in the adjacent Lower Pecos chronology (Turpin 1991).

THE WROE RANCH BEDS

Tucked between a large block of roof fall and the right rear wall of the cave, Feature 19 (fig. 1.3) consisted of a series of grass bundles tied with coarse-knotted stems laid in rows atop a prickly-pear base, forming a cushion or mattress that was 80 cm wide and 120 cm long. The upper end was outlined with twigs and branches laid horizontally where they provided some purchase in the loose fill. At least five types of grass were included in the pad. The ripe seed heads still clinging to the stalks indicate that the grass was gathered in the spring or early summer. A radiocarbon assay of grass from this bed produced a 13C-corrected date of 1850±50 BP (TX-8603), which calibrates to the range between AD 120 to 240, or 1830 and 1710 BP (Method B; Stuiver and Reimer 1993). This date is corroborated by an assay of charcoal from a small hearth directly above the mattress that dated to 1,380 years ago, calibrated to 1290 BP, or AD 660 (TX-8595).

According to the relic hunters, the nearby burial pit was lined with bent sotol stalks driven vertically into the ground on three sides to form an enclosure (McGregor, n.d.) (fig.1.4). The flexed body was laid on a grass mat above a prickly-pear-pad base and covered with an antelope-skin robe and two mats. Another piece of antelope skin was placed under the head and torso. One of the sotol-stalk stakes produced a radiocarbon age of 570±60 BP (TX-5430), which was corrected for 13C to 700±135 BP. There is a 100 percent probability that the true age of this sample is between AD 1210 and 1410, or 740 and 540 BP (Method B; Stuiver and Reimer 1993). A prickly-pear pad from the base assayed 630±110 radiocarbon years ago, corrected to 760±160 BP, has a 69 percent probability of dating between AD 1160 and 1330, or 790 and 620 BP (TX-5431; Method B; Stuiver and Reimer 1993), thus confirming the Late Prehistoric age of this burial.

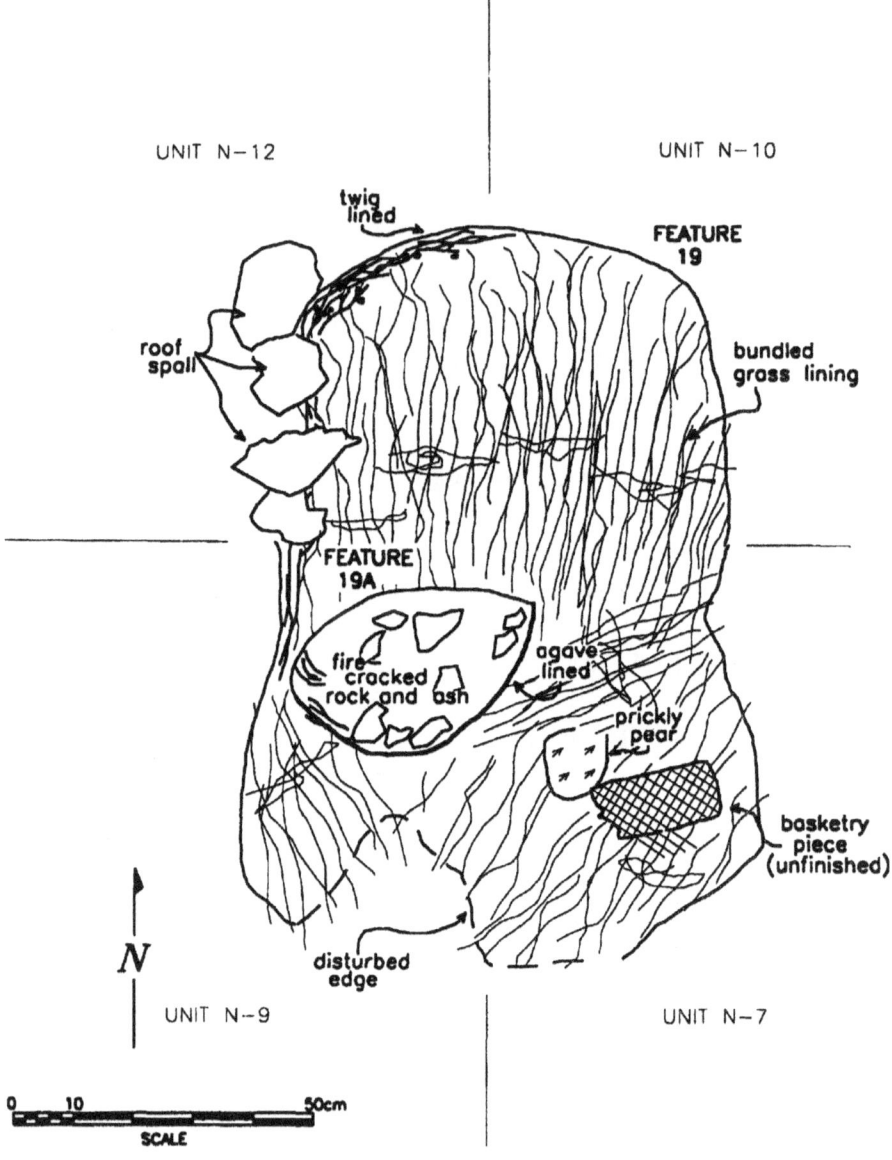

Figure 1.3. Plan drawing of Feature 19 showing the position of a warming hearth and discarded artifacts that lay atop the pad. Courtesy Center for Big Bend Studies.

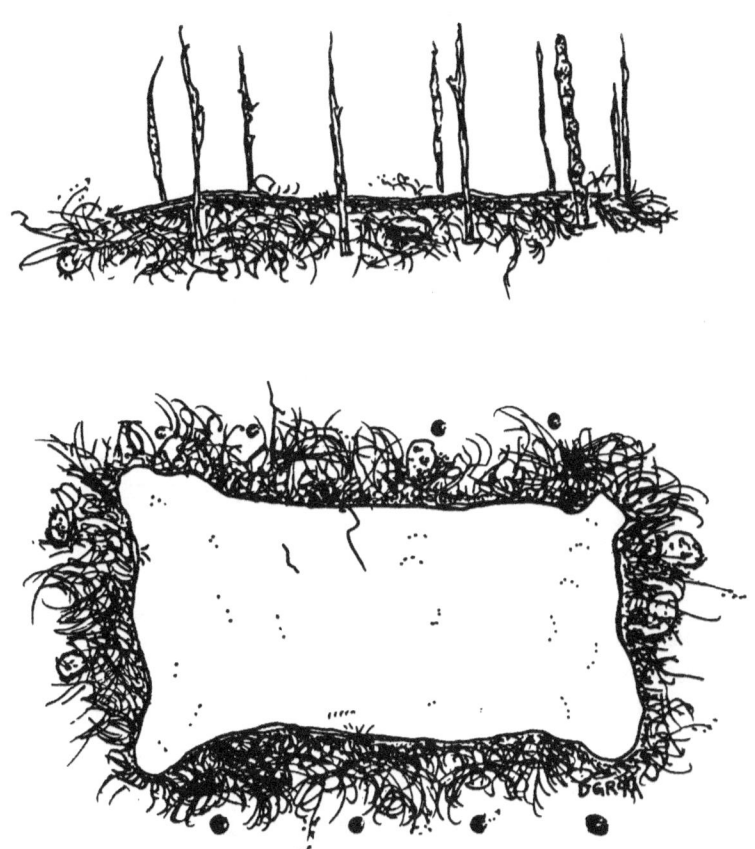

Figure 1.4. An artist's reconstruction of the staked pit, grass and prickly-pear padding, and antelope robe in the grave at the Wroe Ranch site. Based on descriptions provided by relic hunters. Courtesy Center for Big Bend Studies.

Discussion

Although differences in form appear to be related to the age and size of the sleeper, all of these beds were constructed according to the same basic template. Three shared components are the base (prickly pear); the frame (agave leaves, rocks, and sotol or wooden sticks); and the padding (grass or shredded sotol).

In addition, some form of cover was presumably laid over the mattress. In one instance, at Encantada, a twined mat was left in place directly atop the sotol padding, and antelope hides and two mats were interred with the burial at Wroe Ranch. Hinds Cave, near the Pecos River, apparently produced checker-weave sleeping mats (Shafer 1986, 99). However, labor-intensive, valuable, and portable items such as hides or mats were probably prized and curated.

The Base

Prickly-pear pads may seem an uncomfortable choice for mattress material, but invariably a layer of large overlapping *Opuntia* leaves formed the basal structure of the beds. Most of the fiber-lined pits that apparently served other functions were also lined with prickly-pear pads. These broad, thick pads are one of the few raw materials that can be used as a dust barrier to prevent the loose, ashy fill from permeating the grass layers that cushion the sleeper or protect the contents of storage pits.

The Frame

The purpose of the frame, keeping the padding from dispersing under the weight and movement of the sleeper, was achieved by a variety of materials. The Cueva Encantada sleeping area was outlined by an oval of rocks about the size of flattened cantaloupes. The purported baby bed was framed by split maguey leaves (agave) placed on edge, forming a crib. The loose grass used as padding material in the Wroe Ranch burial pit was held in place by sotol stalks driven vertically into the cave fill around the perimeter. The nearby adult bed was framed by twigs laid along the edges of the long axis but not fixed in place. This feature was, however, wedged behind a large block of roof fall that constrained one long side.

The Padding

At Wroe Ranch, both the adult bed and the lining of the burial pit were made of various grasses, pulled from the ground and tied together with coarse stems. Sotol leaves, both shredded and intact, were used for padding in two adult beds and an infant nest at Cueva Encantada. The differences in raw material selection between the two sites may be a function of seasonality, the relative abundance of each plant in the immediate vicinity of the site, broader environmental variation over time, or cultural preferences. Cueva Encantada contained a whole series of superimposed grass nests near the front of the cave, but Wroe Ranch produced only one feature with sotol leaves, and that was a bundle apparently brought in for processing.

INTERSITE POSITIONING

Obviously, the placement of the Wroe Ranch burial pit was influenced by factors other than sleeping comfort, but the abandoned grass bed was laid down between a large block of roof fall and the right rear lateral of the shelter wall, under the low ceiling. Tucked into the lee of the boulder, the bed was protected from the elements and from intruders, whether animal or human, friendly or threatening. The grass heads indicate a late spring or early summer harvest, so the placement was not predicated on expectations of extreme cold, but rain may well have been a factor.

The Cueva Encantada beds were also in the rear of the shelter, placed up against the back wall where the ceiling slopes down to meet the ashy deposits (see also Shafer 1986, 97). The infant nest and the other adult bed were nearby at a slightly higher elevation, keeping in mind that during the two-thousand-year period between the two radiocarbon-dated features, cave fill accumulated, burying the mattresses and raising the floor level to a point much higher on the sloping rear wall.

The configuration of Cueva Encantada suggests that the placement of the beds anticipated inclement weather. The large, high overhang that fronts the site is airy, bright, and breezy, while the cave itself is dark and poorly ventilated. The beds are at the rear of the alcove, an uncomfortable place in warm weather but well protected from wind and freezing temperatures, especially if fires were built nearer the entrance. Cold weather is also implied by the heated rocks placed in the infant nest.

OTHER EXAMPLES

Despite considerable differences in space and time, the presumed sleeping accommodations at Cueva Encantada and Wroe Ranch display similar methods of construction using the most readily available material at hand. The motivating forces behind such consistency are expediency and efficiency, so other methods could be employed if they were equally functional. An infant buried in a dry rock-shelter on the Pecos River may, like the one at the Wroe Ranch burial, have been laid to rest in its bed (fig. 1.5). According to the relic hunters who unearthed the burial, crossed sotol stalks and wooden stakes were driven into the ashy soil in an X-configuration (see Turpin and Bement 1988, 15, table 3). The upper bracket cradled a grass pad; the infant was swaddled in a rabbit-skin robe and covered with three mats. Fragments of matting produced an uncorrected, uncalibrated radiocarbon date of 2270±50 (table 1. 2), indicative of Late Archaic interment, ca. 400 BC (Turpin 1991, table 1.1; TX-6166). In this case, the crossed-stick cradle fulfilled the function of both base and frame components, holding the grass pad above the ash and dirt while constraining its sides.

Another variation may be expressed by a pit uncovered at the Perry Calk site (Collins 1969, 7) that has been reinterpreted as a crib or baby bed by Shafer (1986, 99). Described as 88.4 cm in diameter and 48.8 cm deep, the pit consisted of three distinct linings: from bottom to top, a base of seventeen small, thin, flat pieces of limestone underlay a thick padding of sotol and lechuguilla leaves intermixed with oak and croton branches, covered by a piece of tanned bison hide. Spring or summer construction was inferred from the green breaks on the branches that were bent to conform to the pit walls. Collins (1969, 7) attributed the feature to the most recent occupation of the site, in late prehistoric or early historic times. In this case, the rocks would have formed the base, the branches the frame, and the leaves the padding.

Figure 1.5. Artist's reconstruction of an infant burial on the Pecos River, with crossed sticks providing a frame for a grass pad beneath the bundled infant. Courtesy Center for Big Bend Studies.

Table 1.2. Radiocarbon assays of bedding fibers

Uncorrected Date (BP)	Corrected Date (BP)	Calibrated Date*	Site	Feature	Material	TX-
570±60	700±135	AD 1220–1400	Wroe Ranch	burial	sotol stalk	5430
630±110	760±160	AD 1060–1400	Wroe Ranch	burial	prickly pear	5431
1760±80	1850±50	AD 120–240	Wroe Ranch	adult bed	grass	8603
1860±60	1870±60	AD 80–240	Cueva Encantada	baby bed	sotol base	8443
2270±50	2400±125	770–370 BC	Pecos River	cradle	sotol mat	6166
3260±50	3340±50	1680–1520 BC	Cueva Encantada	adult bed	sotol leaves	8508
3870±190	3870±190	2580–2040 BC	Cueva Encantada	adult bed	sedge mat	8442

*Stuiver and Reimer 1993, Method A.

Conclusions

The basic template of base, frame, and padding was maintained for thousands of years because it efficiently counteracted the all-pervasive dust and ash, cushioned the sleeper, provided some protection from the elements, and used readily available, easily processed raw material. The differences between the examples given here may well be a reflection of the abundance of specific types of flora and fauna either locally or seasonally. For example, the adult grass bed at Wroe Ranch is roughly contemporaneous with the infant sotol nest at Cueva Encantada, but the former appears to be a spring-summer construct, while the latter was built to counteract cold weather. Antelope, the source of the hide coverings at Wroe Ranch, have long been gone from Terrell County, and the bison hide at the Perry Calk site is one of the rare indications of bison presence in the Lower Pecos late in prehistory or early in history.

However, not all of the variability is lodged in the materials used. Some credit for innovation must be given to the makers of the infant beds. In a traditional hunting and foraging economy, the task of keeping the children warm and dry undoubtedly fell to the mothers and their female kin. Both adults' and children's beds were built of materials usually gathered or processed by women—plant parts, mats, and tanned hides. The continuity between the resting places of the living and dead is consistent with such a gendered division of society and worldview.

Acknowledgments

Excavations at the Wroe Ranch site (41TE307) were funded by University Lands-West Texas Operations, under the direction of Steve Hartmann, who deserves credit for recognizing the merit of archaeological research on public lands. The project was authorized by Texas Antiquities Permit 1635. Mark Denton of the Texas Antiquities Committee has maintained an interest in site 41TE307 since he first recorded it in 1986. Duane Lindsey of Rankin, Texas, provided housing for the field crew during the excavations.

Cueva Encantada was excavated under the terms of a permit issued to Herbert H. Eling Jr. by the Instituto Nacional de Antropología e Historia (INAH) with the cooperation and assistance of INAH archaeologist Moisés Valadez Moreno. In Saltillo, Eduardo Enríquez and Arturo González of the INAH regional office for the state of Coahuila were of particular help in the analysis phase. Radiocarbon dates reported here were funded by a grant from the Texas Archeological Society Donor's Fund. Harry and Patrick Kelly of Eagle Pass first brought Cueva Encantada to our attention and provided logistical support for the excavations. Carlos Mondragón granted access to the site and allowed us to camp on his ranch.

Roberta McGregor of the Witte Museum contributed her analysis of the antelope-skin robe from the burial at 41TE307. Excavations at Wroe Ranch were conducted by Stephen M. Carpenter, Douglas Drake, Carole Medlar, Larry Riemenschneider, and the author. Carpenter and Medlar also worked at Cueva Encantada with Herbert H. Eling Jr. and Moisés Valadez Moreno. Carole Medlar prepared the photographic plates and generated the site maps, location map, and the plan of Feature 19 at Wroe Ranch. David G. Robinson drew the illustrations of the infant nest, cradle, and burial bed. Frank Garcia kindly read the shortened version of this paper for me at the Center for Big Bend Studies' third annual conference in Alpine in 1996.

References

Bement, Leland C. 1991. "The Statistical Analysis of Langtry Variants from Arenosa Shelter, Val Verde County, Texas." In *Papers on Lower Pecos Prehistory*, edited by Solveig A. Turpin, 51–64. Studies in Archeology 8. Austin: Texas Archeological Research Laboratory, University of Texas at Austin.

Collins, Michael B. 1969. *Test Excavations at Amistad International Reservoir, Fall, 1967.* Papers of the Texas Archeological Salvage Project 16. Austin: University of Texas at Austin.

McGregor, Roberta A. 1991. "Threaded and Twined Matting: A Late Introduction to the Lower Pecos." In *Papers on Lower Pecos Prehistory*, edited by Solveig A. Turpin, 141–48. Studies in Archeology 8. Austin: Texas Archeological Research Laboratory, University of Texas at Austin.

———. n.d. "An Antelope Hide Shroud from 41TE307, Wroe Ranch, Terrell County, Texas." Manuscript on file at the Witte Museum, San Antonio, and Borderlands Archeological Research Unit, University of Texas at Austin.

Shafer, Harry J. 1986. *Ancient Texans.* Austin: Texas Monthly Press.

Stuiver, M., and P. J. Reimer. 1993. *Radiocarbon Calibration Program 3.0.3.* Pullman: Quaternary Isotope Lab, University of Washington.

Taylor, Walter W. 1966. "Archaic Cultures Adjacent to the Northeastern Frontiers of Mesoamerica." In *Archaeological Frontiers and External Connections*, edited by Robert Wauchope, 59–94. Handbook of Middle American Indians 4. Austin: University of Texas Press.

Turpin, Solveig A. 1991. "Time Out of Mind: The Radiocarbon Chronology of the Lower Pecos River Region." In *Papers on Lower Pecos Prehistory*, edited by Solveig A. Turpin, 1–49. Studies in Archeology 8. Austin: Texas Archeological Research Laboratory, University of Texas at Austin.

———. 1995. *West of the Pecos: Archeological Reconnaissance on University Lands, Terrell County.* Cultural Resource Report 3. Austin: Borderlands Archeological Research Unit, University of Texas at Austin.

Turpin, Solveig A., and Leland C. Bement. 1988. "Seminole Sink: Excavation of a Vertical Shaft Tomb, Val Verde County, Texas." *Plains Anthropologist*, Memoir 22, 33 (November): 1–18.

Turpin, Solveig A., and Stephen M. Carpenter. 1994. "Prehistoric Sandals from the Sierra de la Encantada, Coahuila, Mexico." *La Tierra* 21 (2): 7–14.

2 Comments on the Prehistory of Far Northeastern Chihuahua, the La Junta District, and the Cielo Complex

Robert J. Mallouf

The far northeastern region of Chihuahua is defined arbitrarily as a rectangular area bound on the north by the Rio Grande (Río Bravo del Norte), on the west by the lower reaches of the Río Conchos, on the east by the Chihuahua-Coahuila border, and on the south by a line extending approximately from Cuchillo Parado on the lower Río Conchos to the Sierra Altares on the Chihuahua-Coahuila boundary (fig. 2.1). These roughly 12,000 square kilometers are located within the basin and range environment of the Chihuahuan Desert (Schmidt 1979). In addition to its rugged mountain ranges trending northwest-to-southeast, this arid land contains some of the lowest elevations (as low as about 800 m above mean sea level) to be found in the state of Chihuahua.

Included among the larger mountain ranges of the study area are the eastern portion of the Sierra Grande, the Sierra del Mulato, Sierra Matasaguas, Sierra Cuchillo Parado, Sierra Rica, Sierra Azul (Sierra de San Carlos), Sierra el Virulento, and Sierra Altares. These ranges comprise a mosaic of sedimentary (lower and upper Cretaceous) and igneous (Cenozoic) rock. The general vegetation zones found in the higher elevations are grassland and oak-juniper savannas; in the lower foothills, more diverse plant assemblages appear, including lechuguilla, sotol, yucca, ocotillo, and various cacti. Broad, arid basins between the mountains are dominated by creosote bush, tarbush, and mesquite (Lesueur 1945; Schmidt 1973). A good grasp of the actual complexities encountered in vegetational classifications of the Chihuahuan Desert, including the study area, can be gained by a perusal of Johnston (1977) and Henrickson and Johnston (1986). A wide variety of fauna, including white-tailed and mule deer, gray and kit fox, mountain lion, bobcat, black bear, badger, skunk, ringtail raccoon, black-tailed jackrabbit, audubon cottontail, mourning

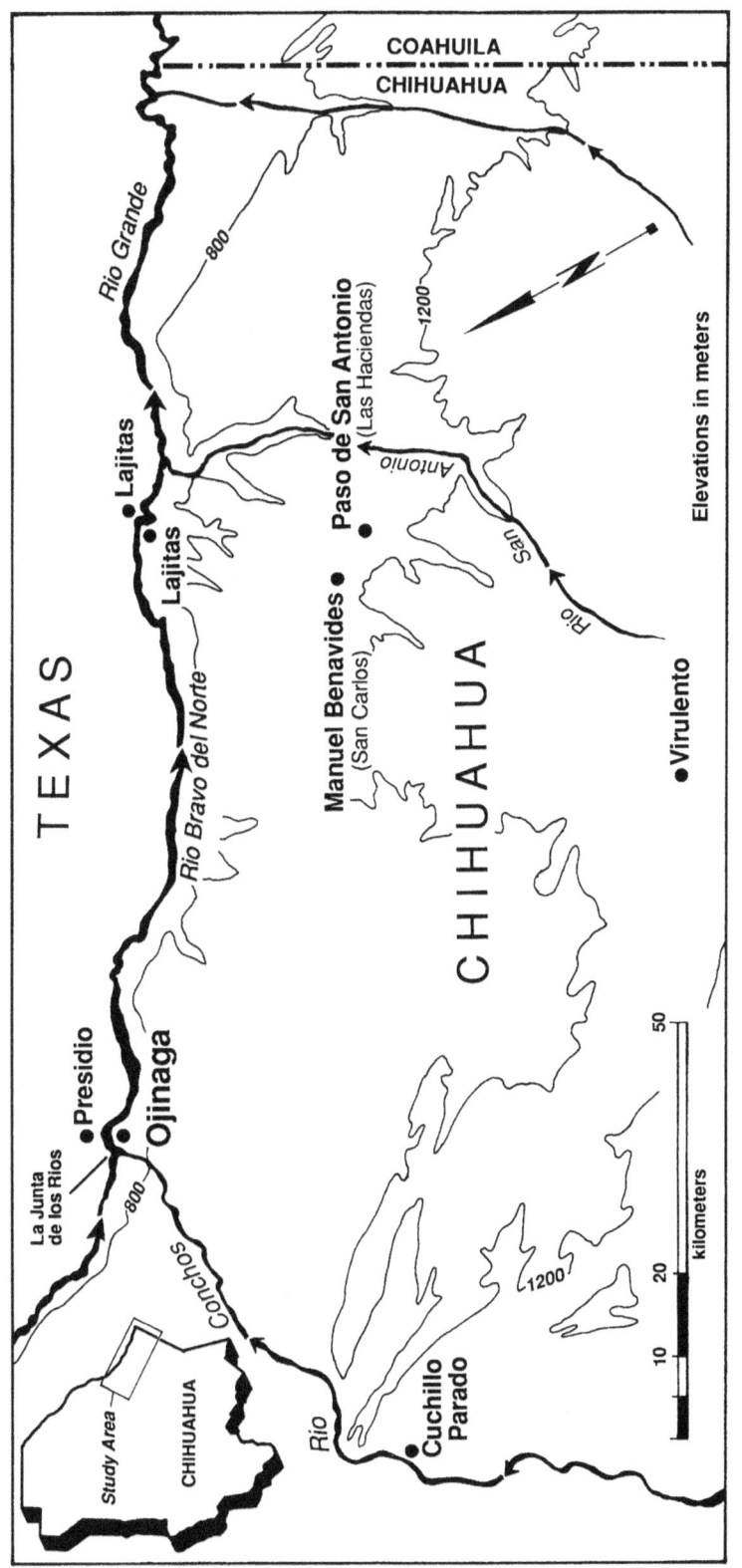

Figure 2.1. The study area in far northeastern Chihuahua. Courtesy Center for Big Bend Studies.

and white-wing dove, quail, buzzard, hawk, and turkey, occur in diverse habitats throughout the region.

The study area is drained on the west and north by the two largest perennial streams to be found in Chihuahua—the Río Conchos and the Rio Grande, respectively. The valleys of these rivers, in the vicinity of their confluence near Ojinaga, are known historically as La Junta de los Ríos and archaeologically as the La Junta district. While other significant water sources are scarce, there are numerous springs located along fault lines in the foothills of the mountains, one of the most notable being that of Ojo de San Carlos near Manuel Benavides (San Carlos). Much of the drainage is internal and provides important recharge to local groundwater aquifers. The broad basins are dissected by innumerable arroyos that are typically dry except during the monsoonal months of summer, when thunderstorms may cause abrupt and severe flooding along these drainage systems. This area of Chihuahua receives an average of only 250 mm of precipitation annually, and summer temperatures may rise as high as 118 degrees F (as of 1973, Cuchillo Parado held the state record high at 118.4 degrees F [48 degrees C]; Schmidt 1973).

A wide range of needed resources and raw materials was available to prehistoric populations of northeastern Chihuahua. These included potable water supplies, abundant sources of high-quality cryptocrystalline stone, diverse biotic communities, and appropriate habitation areas. Among the latter were well-elevated terraces and pediments, colluvial benches, and rock-shelters. Future work in this region can be expected to yield information that will strongly influence archaeological interpretations in surrounding areas, including Trans-Pecos Texas.

Past and Recent Research

With the exception of the La Junta district, past archaeological investigations in northeastern Chihuahua can best be described as intermittent and spasmodic. The little research that has been accomplished has typically been related but ancillary to larger-scale projects being conducted in adjoining regions or has come about as a reaction to site destruction from agricultural practices or looting.

Certainly, one of the more substantive projects to be undertaken in the region, and one of the earliest, was an archaeological reconnaissance and testing program initiated by J. Charles Kelley along the Río Conchos in 1949 (Kelley 1990) that resulted in the formal recording of about sixty sites. Kelley's work included the excavation of a roughly square pit house with an internal fire pit, an altar, and a possible roof entrance at the Loma Seca site, located several kilometers upstream from Ojinaga. On the basis of architectural style and associated ceramics, Kelley assigned this structure to his previously defined La Junta focus (Kelley et al. 1940; Kelley 1951). Through excavation of this house feature, Kelley conclusively demonstrated the presence of La Junta focus (now called La Junta phase) agricultural village sites on both sides of the Rio Grande and extending up the Río Conchos. As far as I am aware, this remains the only scientific excavation of a prehistoric site in far northeastern Chihuahua. A number of rather extensive excavations had previously been carried out by Kelley at related La Junta phase villages on the Texas side of the Rio Grande (Kelley et al. 1940; Kelley 1939, 1949, 1985, 1986). Excellent overviews of his findings, all of which are pertinent to the study area and address both prehistory and early history, appear in seven publications (Kelley et al. 1940; Kelley 1952a, 1952b, 1953, 1986, 1990; Foster and Kelley 1987).

Until recently, most other information concerning the northeastern Chihuahuan borderlands has been drawn from reconnaissances and surveys conducted on the northern periphery of the region, most notably by T. N. Campbell (1970) in Big Bend National Park. A very early reconnaissance by E. B. Sayles (1936) of various parts of Chihuahua barely touched on the study area.

From 1970 to 1995 the Office of the State Archeologist (OSA), Texas Historical Commission, at intervals conducted research at prehistoric and historic sites along the Rio Grande from Presidio, Texas, downstream through Big Bend National Park and the Lower Canyons. Much of this work consisted of noncollecting surveys. More recent investigations of the OSA have included work at the Cielo Bravo and Arroyo de las Burras sites of the Cielo complex, as well as the Polvo site in La Junta de los Ríos. During the course of the work at La Junta, we examined and photo-documented private collections from some areas of far northeastern Chihuahua. In another project important to archaeological interpretation on both sides of the Rio Grande, intensive documentation was carried out of a stone arrowpoint assemblage that had been looted from a Late Prehistoric cairn burial near Las Haciendas (Paso de San Antonio), Chihuahua, some 27 km south of the Rio Grande (Mallouf 1987). This undertaking represents the first intensive study conducted of a lithic assemblage from northeastern Chihuahua. In addition, during a boat survey through Colorado Canyon on the Rio Grande in 1977, we were fortunate to find a buried hearth eroding from a cutbank in a high, silt terrace system on the river. This feature, which had a dart point in direct association, has provided the first radiocarbon assay for the study area (discussed below).

In sum, the archaeology of the far northeastern corner of Chihuahua, with the notable exception of its northern periphery at La Junta, remains poorly known. Kelley's early work at La Junta provided a solid foundation of information concerning the lifeways of interacting Late Prehistoric and early Historic farming and nomadic peoples for subsequent researchers to build upon, but interested researchers have appeared on the scene only after a long hiatus of work in the area. As is the case for many places in northern Mexico and the southwestern United States, earlier prehistory in the study area, including the Paleoindian and Archaic periods, remains virtually unknown. In succeeding sections of this paper I will provide a preliminary summary of new information for the northeastern Chihuahua area that has been derived primarily from examining pertinent private collections, and I will conclude with some observations concerning the La Junta phase and the Cielo complex.

The private collections discussed below are from sites in the vicinity of four localities within the study area: the Mexican village of Paso Lajitas, on the south side of the Rio Grande a few kilometers upstream from the Chihuahua-Coahuila border; Manuel Benavides (San Carlos), about 20 km south of the Rio Grande at the base of the Sierra Azul; Paso de San Antonio (Las Haciendas), 16 km southeast of Manuel Benavides on the Río San Antonio; and the Sierra el Virulento, a small range along the arbitrary southern edge of the study area some 65 km south of the Rio Grande. Like their counterparts to the north of the Rio Grande, local collectors tend to focus their efforts on acquiring projectile points. The first half of this discussion, then, is largely dependent upon this class of artifact to extract meaningful data. The preliminary chronological periods discussed below are extrapolated from surrounding regions having similar projectile-point styles in better-known contexts. And they are, of course, subject to revision.

Paleoindian Period, 10,000–6500 BC

Surprisingly little evidence of Paleoindian tool forms has been forthcoming from examination of collections in northeastern Chihuahua. One

Plainview and a few Golondrina dart points, as well as two rather crude Angostura-like specimens, are noted in collections from sites near Paso Lajitas and from Manuel Benavides. While evidence currently is scarce, such finds do suggest the presence of nomadic Paleoindian bands in the study area at least during the latter part of the Paleoindian period, or roughly from 8000 to 6500 BC.

Supporting evidence for the presence of Plainview components in northeastern Chihuahua, and earlier Clovis and Folsom components as well, is forthcoming from northwest of the study area on both sides of the Rio Grande. To the northwest of the Ojinaga/Presidio area is a broad, north-south trending basin system that extends northward across Trans-Pecos Texas into southeastern New Mexico. In Texas this important natural feature is called Salt Basin in the vicinity of the Delaware and Guadalupe Mountains and is known as Lobo Valley from the vicinity of Van Horn, Texas, southward to the Sierra Vieja. During the terminal Pleistocene epoch, this broad valley contained a series of extensive, interconnected pluvial lakes that provided excellent habitat for biotic resources highly sought after by Paleoindian bands that camped along the lakeshores. The Chispa site, a large Folsom encampment south of Van Horn, occupies a position adjacent to one of these relict-basin lakebeds (Lindsay 1969; Joe Ben Wheat, personal communication 1987). A number of surface finds of Folsom and Plainview points also have been made in the general area (Hedrick 1968, 1975, 1988; Mallouf 1985). This long, uninterrupted basin system provided an attractive natural corridor between mountain ranges for the north-south movements of Paleoindian and later occupants of these regions. But even more importantly, there is good evidence to suggest that this basin system has, at intervals in the past, served as a physiographic and cultural demarcation between distinct cultural traditions to the east and west.

In northern Chihuahua just a few kilometers to the south and southwest of Ciudad Juárez lies the ancient pluvial lake system of the Samalayuca region. A number of finds of Clovis, Folsom, and Plainview points are known to have been made here in the general vicinity of the Laguna de Guzmán, and there are indications that relatively intact Paleoindian components may be present in the region (Alan Phelps, personal communication 1990; John A. Hedrick, personal communication 1989; George A. Agogino, personal communication 1989).

Ancient relict lake basins like those of Lobo Valley and Samalayuca are found in areas of far northeastern Chihuahua as well, particularly to the immediate south of our study area, where they have yet to be investigated by archaeologists. Knowledge of where Paleoindian encampments *should* be, however, does not necessarily mean they are easily located. There is good evidence from the north side of the Rio Grande to indicate that such ancient deposits may be very deeply buried within basin drainage systems and relict lakebeds. For instance, at the Adobe Walls Draw site (41BS751) near Terlingua, Texas, a radiocarbon assay obtained for a series of hearths buried 6.0 m below ground surface in an arroyo cut proved to be only Late Archaic in age (fig. 2.2). Even allowing for the fact that alluvium can accumulate quite rapidly—and admittedly having been fooled about the ages of such deposits before—I still was surprised at obtaining an assay of only AD 648 for this deeply buried component (TX-5861; one sigma correction based on Stuiver and Becker 1986, Method A). Other Big Bend examples of relatively recent cultural components in deeply buried contexts have been discussed by Kelley et al. (1940).

Suffice it to say that while we suspect the presence of Paleoindian components in the study area, it is likely that they will, in many cases, be deeply buried and virtually inaccessible—often requiring use of heavy machinery to facilitate both their discovery and their exploration. Our best chances for discovery during the normal course of archaeological reconnaissance and survey are in deep erosional cuts or blowouts adjacent to relict-basin lakebeds, and in the upper reaches and headwaters of arroyo systems that emanate from the foothills of the mountain ranges where the lateral migration of arroyo systems is relatively constricted.

Archaic Period, 6500 BC–AD 900

While evidence for the presence of Archaic components across the study area is quite strong, a dearth of both survey and excavation data severely limits our reconstruction of Archaic period lifeways. For this reason, it would seem premature to attempt an overview of Archaic lifeways that must draw exclusively upon information from better-studied adjoining regions. Instead, the intent here is to provide an initial set of empirical data that can be used as a springboard for subsequent studies. For summaries of what is known concerning the lifeways of Archaic hunter-gatherers in adjacent regions, the interested reader is referred to Kelley et al. (1940), Lehmer (1958), Taylor (1966), Campbell (1970), O'Laughlin (1980), Mallouf (1981, 1985, 1986), Gonzalez (1986a, 1986b), and Foster and Kelley (1987).

Figure 2.2. Stratified prehistoric components at Adobe Walls Draw site in southern Brewster County. Arrow indicates zone of buried hearths from which radiocarbon assay (TX-5861) was obtained. Courtesy Center for Big Bend Studies.

With the exception of the Las Haciendas assemblage, which is from a Late Prehistoric burial context, all examined private collections in northeastern Chihuahua are easily dominated by Archaic period projectile points. Examples of Early Archaic (ca. 6500–3000 BC) point types are, as might be expected, far less common than examples from the Middle and Late Archaic periods. In fact, only twelve out of several hundred specimens are positively identified as having Early Archaic affinities— and these are from the Manuel Benavides and Sierra Virulento areas. Six of these points are of the Baker-Bandy series (Turner and Hester 1985). The remaining specimens are classed as Bajada and Zorra points (fig. 2.3). Examples of what Taylor (1966) has termed Jora and Gobernadora points—from his Early and Middle Coahuila complex—also are present in the Manuel Benavides collections, but they appear on the basis of technological considerations to have stronger Middle Archaic than Early Archaic affinities. Because of our poor state of knowledge concerning the

Early Archaic period, it is quite conceivable that additional early forms of projectile points are present but remain unrecognized in these collections. For the time being, we can only assume that the study area is part of, or peripheral to, a geographically broad-based Early Archaic tradition extending, at least, to more northerly and easterly regions.

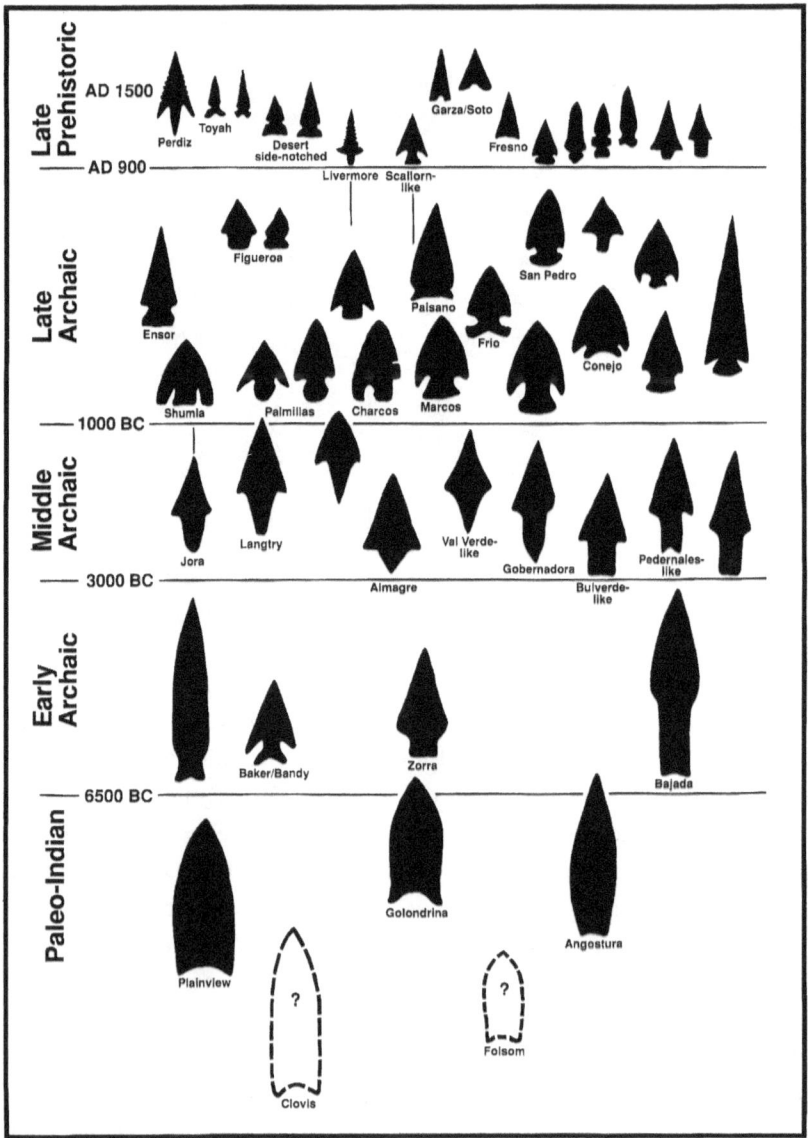

Figure 2.3. A preliminary projectile-point sequence for far northeastern Chihuahua. Courtesy Center for Big Bend Studies.

Like Paleoindian components, many Early Archaic components in far northeastern Chihuahua may prove to be deeply buried and difficult to detect. Middle Archaic (ca. 3000–1000 BC) dart points tend to be much more common in study-area collections. Distinguishable point types include Langtry (both classic and pointed-stern variants), Jora, Almagre, and Gobernadora, along with a few specimens having similarities to Val Verde, Pedernales, and Bulverde types. Jora points tend to be most common, while Gobernadora points are quite rare. Yet regrettably, we do not yet have Jora points from a well-dated context anywhere in northern Mexico, and their assignment here to the Middle Archaic is on the basis of style only. They may prove to be later than originally believed by Taylor (1966). Like those of adjoining regions to the north and east, Middle Archaic projectile points in far northeastern Chihuahua tend to have straight to contracting stems with convex, concave, straight, or pointed basal edges. A higher density of Middle than Early Archaic points in local collections can probably be attributed to more frequent exposure of these components along arroyo systems, differing settlement systems, or larger human populations than in preceding periods. However, tentative, current evidence would seem to indicate stronger affiliations during this period with cultures to the southeast, east, and northeast than with those west and north.

There is a striking dominance of Late Archaic (ca. 1000 BC–AD 900) projectile points in private collections of the study area. In the approximate order of their frequency of occurrence, the definable types include Shumla, Palmillas, Ensor, San Pedro, Figueroa, Frio, Marcos, Paisano, Conejo, and Charcos. There is also a multitude of variant styles, many of which seem to have resulted from the aboriginal refurbishing of broken points. And there are numerous unrecognized styles that probably represent distinctive types of points as well. Particularly noteworthy are the very late dart points (such as the highly variable Figueroa) that, because of their technology and diminutive size, seem to represent the transition from use of the atlatl to the bow and arrow. The sheer numbers of Late Archaic points present in the northeastern Chihuahuan collections recall collections one encounters in the adjoining Big Bend region of Texas. In the Big Bend, archaeological surveys have located Late Archaic components in virtually every available ecological niche, from the tops of mountain peaks to basin arroyo systems (e.g., see Mallouf and Wulfkuhle 1989). While greater erosional exposure of these components, with concomitant accessibility to artifact collectors, is one explanation, all evidence currently points to the fact that there were significant population increases during the Late Archaic period. These seem to correspond to a short-lived interval of more mesic environmental conditions (Mallouf 1985).

Several tentative patterns emerge from the Late Archaic point-type frequencies. As an example, there is an abrupt drop in frequency of Paisano points as one moves south from the Rio Grande, where they are fairly common, to Manuel Benavides, where they form only a tiny percentage of large collections, to the Sierra Virulent, where they are absent altogether from examined collections. While this may simply be a matter of sampling error, past experience has shown that local private collections tend to reflect the realities of local archaeological situations. This pattern may reflect a definable southern edge to the distribution of Paisano points within 30 to 50 km of the Rio Grande. Whether or not a cultural boundary is also indicated remains to be determined. While the Paisano point has in the past been characterized as indigenous to the Trans-Pecos (e.g., see Marmaduke 1978, 125–26), the possibility of more westerly origins should also be explored. Incidentally, the only radiocarbon assay for Paisano points west of the Lower Pecos River region comes from a buried, eroding hearth (Fiero site) in Colorado Canyon (Rio Grande) in the study area. The hearth, which had a Paisano point in direct association, yielded a date of AD 560±335 (TX-4638; Mallouf 1985), which roughly corresponds to Lower Pecos region estimates.

The Paisano point was thought by Kelley et al. (1940) to be a dominant type of the Chisos focus of the Texas Big Bend. As originally defined, the Chisos focus was considered to be indicative of hunter-gatherer bands that practiced an early form of rudimentary agriculture and were possibly ancestral to certain Historic groups in the region. At the time of its formulation, the Chisos focus was considered to be a tentative cultural construct in need of much additional work and clarification. In recent years the Chisos focus has generally been subsumed under the terms "Chisos Archaic" (Campbell 1970) and "Late Archaic" (Mallouf 1985), both of which reflect developmental stages—rather than a specific cultural entity—in regional prehistory. Use of the term "Late Archaic" seems most appropriate to the northeastern Chihuahua region, considering our present state of knowledge.

Late Prehistoric Period, ca. AD 900-1550

Although not as common as Late Archaic dart points, Late Prehistoric arrowpoints constitute a large percentage of projectile points in the private collections of far northeastern Chihuahua. Most of the common arrowpoint styles of the adjoining Big Bend and Coahuila regions are represented in local collections, including Toyah, Perdiz, Fresno, Garza/Soto, Scallorn, side-notched triangular (Desert Side-notched), and Livermore. Several of these styles, including Toyah, Fresno, Soto, and Desert Side-notched, also occur to the northwest at least as far as Casas Grandes. In addition, numerous distinctive untyped styles are present in the collections.

The Livermore point, a diagnostic type of the Livermore focus (ca. AD 900–1300) in the Texas Big Bend (Kelley et al. 1940; Kelley 1957), appears to have a restricted distribution in northeastern Chihuahua. Livermore points are present—but not common—in sites along both the Chihuahua and Texas sides of the Rio Grande, but they occur only rarely as far south as Manuel Benavides and Sierra Azul (fig. 2.4). As nearly as can be ascertained, their occurrence in Coahuila is also restricted to the northern periphery. A tentative southern boundary of Livermore point distribution, then, consists of a line roughly parallel to, and 30 to 40 km south of the Rio Grande from the vicinity of Cuchillo Parado on the west to Amistad Reservoir on the east. Interestingly, the western boundary of Livermore points in Trans-Pecos Texas seems to correspond roughly with the Sierra Vieja, Van Horn, and Sierra Diablo mountain ranges on the west side of Lobo Valley and Salt Basin (alluded to earlier as a possible cultural boundary at various times in the past). The densest known occurrences of Livermore points are in the Davis Mountains and Lobo Valley areas of the central Trans-Pecos, while more northerly occurrences are in the Guadalupe Mountains of Texas and New Mexico. Although by no means common, Livermore points are found occasionally in sites as far northeast as the Midland-Odessa and San Angelo areas in Texas.

Livermore points are characterized by an unusually high degree of stylistic variability—a fact that may account for the past reluctance of some researchers to recognize them as a formal type. These points are, however, quite distinctive both technologically and morphologically. Unfortunately, the archaeological components in which they are found remain poorly studied, and Kelley's original conceptualization of the Livermore focus as a Plains Indian migration into Trans-Pecos

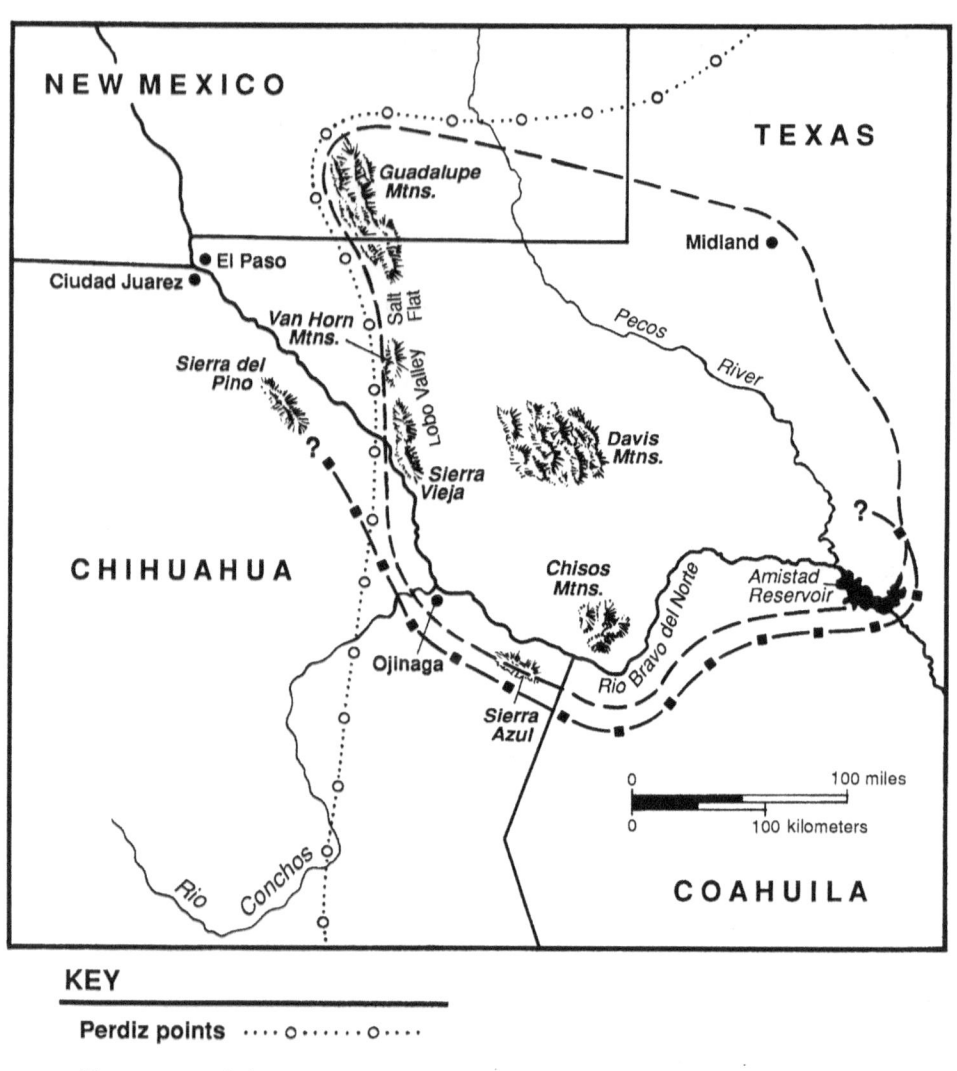

Figure 2.4. Distribution of Perdiz, Livermore, and Paisano projectile points in the study area and adjacent regions. Courtesy Center for Big Bend Studies.

Texas (Kelley et al. 1940) remains basically unexplored to this day. The possibility that Livermore focus populations were indigenous to the Trans-Pecos also is in need of serious investigation. For more meaningful exploration of the nature and origins of the Livermore phenomenon, it will be necessary to identify and excavate isolated or relatively pure components bearing Livermore points. Given the tendency for mixing of Late Prehistoric components in regional rock-shelters, we may want to look more closely at the possibility of locating such components in protected terrace systems on both the Chihuahua and Texas sides of the Rio Grande or along basin drainage systems of the Lobo Valley.

Perdiz points are one of the more common arrowpoint styles in eastern Chihuahua, as well as in much or all of Coahuila, the Texas Big Bend, and Central and South Texas. With the notable exception of a few areas (such as the northern Texas Panhandle), they are found throughout much of Texas. As is typically the case, Perdiz points in the study area come in a wide range of morphological varieties and stone types, as attested by the 180 Perdiz specimens in the Las Haciendas cairn burial at Paso de San Antonio (Mallouf 1987). Radiocarbon dating of Perdiz-bearing components at five sites in the Texas Big Bend indicates a range beginning as early as AD 1250 and possibly extending into the Protohistoric period for this point style. Like that of Livermore points, the westward distribution of Perdiz points essentially terminates along a physical—and postulated cultural—boundary created by the Sierra Vieja, Van Horn, and Sierra Diablo mountain ranges that form the west side of the Lobo Salt Flat basin system in Trans-Pecos Texas. Perdiz points are an important element of La Junta phase and Cielo complex lithic assemblages in the La Junta district and Texas Big Bend.

Also of considerable interest is the distribution of arrowpoints that are triangular, basal-notched, and basally indented—specifically the Garza, Soto, and Lott types. All three styles occur throughout the far northeastern Chihuahua study area, where they seem particularly abundant in Late Prehistoric and/or Contact period assemblages of the La Junta district. The Garza/Soto style occurs at least as far south as southwestern Coahuila and possibly as far west as Casas Grandes and beyond (e.g., see Phelps 1987). Basal-notched Garza points are found as far north as Lubbock and Post in the southern Texas Plains, where associated features have been radiocarbon dated to AD 1540–1665 (Johnson et al. 1977). The presence of basal-notched and basally indented styles in the La Junta area is of particular interest because of the possible linkage of these styles to Apachean occupation to the north in the Southern Plains (as in the case of Garza points; Johnson et al. 1977), and to possible Piman or Apachean occupation of the northwestern Chihuahua-southern Arizona regions (as in the case of Soto points; Fritz 1989). Like Perdiz points, these point styles also figure importantly in assemblages of both the agriculturalist villages of the La Junta phase and the base camps of the hunter-gatherer Cielo complex—a fact discussed at greater length below.

THE CIELO COMPLEX AND THE LA JUNTA PHASE

The findings from recent work on the Cielo complex (Mallouf, n.d.a) are expected to be directly relevant to future interpretations of La Junta district and northeastern Chihuahua archaeology. Therefore, a brief description of the Cielo complex, as currently understood, follows.

Two seasons of excavations have been conducted at the Cielo Bravo site (41PS52), one of two essentially pure Cielo complex type sites situated on high pediments overlooking the downstream end of the La Junta district near Colorado Canyon on the Texas side of the Rio Grande. Test excavations have also been conducted at two Cielo complex components—Equipaje Spring (41BS674) and Alamo Spring (41BS673)—in the Rosillos Mountains of Big Bend National Park. In addition, many sites believed to be attributable to the Cielo complex have been recorded and instrument-mapped by the author during surveys throughout much of the Big Bend.

In a broad sense, the Cielo complex is a Late Prehistoric to Contact period (ca. AD 1250–1680), aceramic manifestation that is found across most of the Texas Big Bend and for an undetermined distance southward into northeastern Chihuahua and northwestern Coahuila (Mallouf 1985, 1986). As currently defined, the complex consists of a range of individual site types that, taken as a whole, may be attributable to a single regional culture. From a functional standpoint, the complex includes base camps (short-lived residential sites) and specialized resource-procurement sites (such as hunting stations, observation posts, stone quarries, cache sites, and resource-collecting and -processing stations), as well as locales of ritual or other significance (rock art and mortuary sites, and possibly ritual cache sites). Among the archaeological features that are attributable to the Cielo complex are rather substantial stone-based dwellings (fig. 2.5b, e); a variety of temporary constructions (fig. 2.5a, c, d) related to special-function (e.g., shade ramadas) and special-purpose sites (e.g., hunting and collecting camp shelters); stacked-stone hunting blinds (both circular and linear); small circular and oval hearths (with and without stone linings; fig. 2.5h, i); small ash pits; simple middens and ring middens; stone cairns (fig. 2.5g) of varying size, configuration, and function (including burial and caching); linear stone alignments (fig. 2.5f); stone-lined cysts; stone storage platforms; and basin-shaped refuse and storage pits.

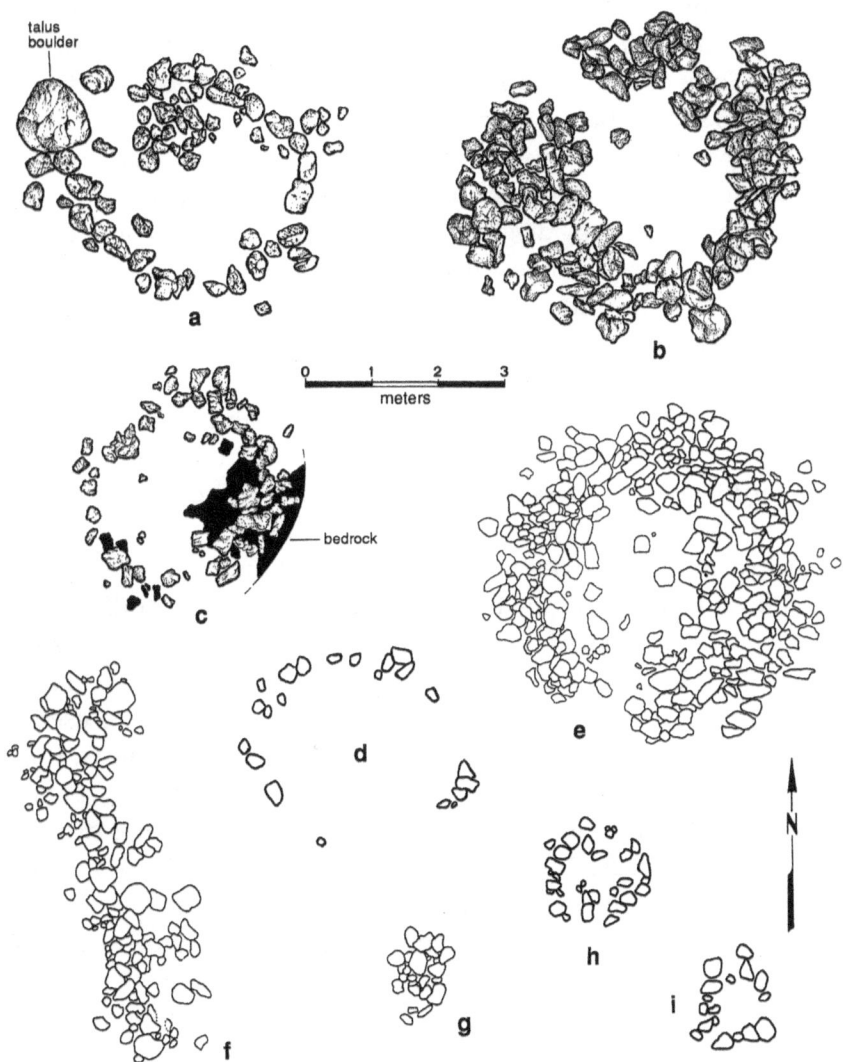

Figure 2.5. Examples of stone features from sites of the Cielo complex. Stone-based wickiups (a–c, e); temporary shade structure (d); linear alignment (f); cairn (g); hearths (h–i). Courtesy Center for Big Bend Studies.

Also believed to be related to the Cielo complex, but lacking the distinctive stone-based dwellings, are a wide variety of temporary encampments located at lower elevations along basin arroyos near foothills. These encampments often appear to be related to the hunting, collecting, and processing of specific kinds of plant and animal resources, such as sotol and deer. Such sites are characterized by the presence of multiple hearths, ring middens, and other subsistence-related features. While it is likely that some form of cursory shelter was also being used in these low-elevation camps, such features tend to be difficult to discern archaeologically.

Base camps of Cielo-complex peoples are characterized by distinctive, sometimes substantial, aboveground stone-based dwellings that are circular to oval in shape and have internal diameters of ca. 2.7 to 3.4 m. The construction of dwellings on sloping surfaces sometimes entailed the leveling of floors by digging out upslope areas of colluvium prior to placing the wall rock. House walls in base camps typically consist of from two to five tiers of variously sized cobbles and boulders that are uninterrupted except for narrow entranceway gaps (fig. 2.5b, e). Combinations of multiple-tier and single-tier structures may occur within individual sites. Superstructures probably consisted of beehivelike arrangements of large ocotillo stalks thatched with grasses and brush or covered with deer and/or bison skins—essentially forming circular to oval stone-based wickiups (Mallouf 1985).

Cielo complex sites with residential or special-function stone wickiups are almost invariably located on strategic, well-elevated landforms that provide panoramic views of desert basins and canyon drainage systems. On the Rio Grande at La Junta, Cielo complex sites occur on elevated pediments that overlook the river-basin terraces that were used for farming and habitation by coeval La Junta phase agriculturalists. Single, isolated dwellings are occasionally found in Cielo complex sites, but base camps typically contain from two to nine discreet wickiups dispersed across the landscape. The wickiups are usually spaced from 3 to 10 m apart and occur in irregular linear or loosely clustered layouts. Dwelling entranceways at individual sites tend to open to a common direction—often west, northwest, or south. Large village sites that overlook the Rio Grande may contain up to fifty or more wickiups, suggesting occasional (or seasonal) gathering of small bands. Not infrequently, two structures within a site may be contiguous, suggesting use by an extended family. On very rare occasions more than two houses may be tightly clustered together, as in the case of the Cielo Bravo type site near La Junta, where twelve dwellings coalesce to form a crescentic village pattern (an intrasite pattern thus far unique to this site).

The Cielo Bravo site is one of four type sites recognized for the Cielo complex (fig. 2.6). In addition to having a unique clustered patterning of wickiups, this site has been found to contain a substantial rectangular structure—probably a ramadalike affair—that was constructed inside a shallow pit. This pit feature bears similarities to some La Junta phase architectural remains found by Kelley (1985) at the Millington site a few kilometers upstream at Presidio. It was probably not unlike the freestanding, open-sided shade ramadas one sees adjacent to Mexican adobes in the area today. Significantly, both artifact assemblages and radiocarbon assays suggest rough contemporaneity of the ramada with the initial construction phase of aboveground circular house wickiups at the site, sometime between AD 1335 and 1375.

Excavations have yielded stratigraphic and radiometric data indicating at least four discreet occupations of the Cielo Bravo site during the period AD 1335–1690. Two of the occupations were rather substantial. These include an initial site occupation and wickiup-ramada construc-

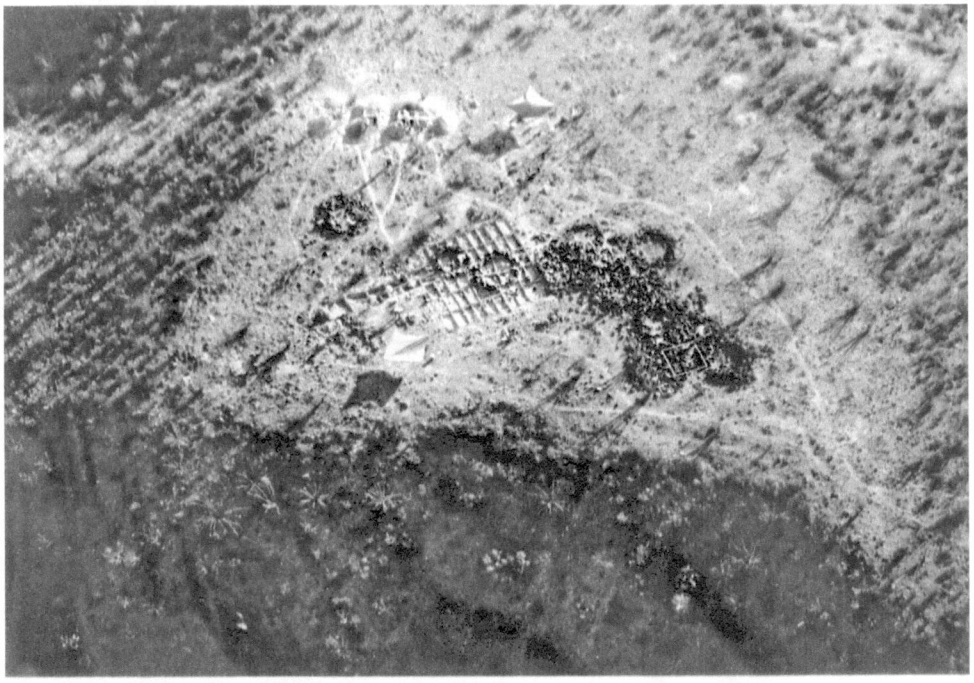

Figure 2.6. Aerial view of the Cielo Bravo site (41PS52) with clustered wickiup rings. Courtesy Center for Big Bend Studies.

tion phase between AD 1335 and 1375, and a final occupation sometime between AD 1650 and 1690. Two intermediate and less substantive occupations occurred at roughly AD 1440–1450, and somewhat later. Some minor reconstruction of dwellings, and possibly the addition of two to three new dwellings, occurred during these reoccupations. Other minor reoccupations are likely to have occurred as well, but are not yet distinguishable archaeologically.

The earlier occupations at Cielo Bravo appear, on the basis of common material assemblages, features, and intrasite patterning, to represent socially identical bands. Artifact assemblages are characterized by Perdiz arrowpoints (fig. 2.7) and preforms, flake drills, unifacial end scrapers and side scrapers, occasional fragments of beveled bifacial knives, a host of expediency tools fashioned on both flakes and blades, occasional oval pestles, a variety of manos, end-notched sinker stones, fragments of bone rasps, fragments of deer-ulna awls, small bone and stone beads, tiny turquoise beads, and a few *Olivella* shell beads. All in all, these early Cielo Bravo material assemblages are remarkably similar to those recovered from agriculturalist La Junta phase components explored by J. Charles Kelley from the 1930s through the 1950s at the Millington, San Juan Evangelista, and Polvo sites. Importantly, unlike the La Junta phase villages, the Cielo Bravo assemblages are entirely lacking in ceramics (Mallouf, n.d.b).

While the material assemblage of the fourth and final occupation at the Cielo Bravo site (between AD 1650 and 1690) is in many respects similar to earlier assemblages, there are some notable differences as well. One major and possibly significant difference is the addition of triangular, basal-notched Garza-like arrowpoints to the tool inventory. In addition, there seems to be a lower incidence of ground stone, a lack of end-notched sinker stones, and a higher incidence of triangular end scrapers and beveled knife fragments. Also present are several tiny trianguloid pendants, fashioned from small freshwater shells, that are virtually identical to one found in the Garza component of the Lott site in the Southern Plains (see Runkles and Dorchester 1986, 100). It is possible that these late changes appearing in the material culture at the Cielo Bravo site reflect an initial intrusion—or possibly a new wave—of Plains Apaches into the Big Bend and northeastern Chihuahua regions around AD 1650.

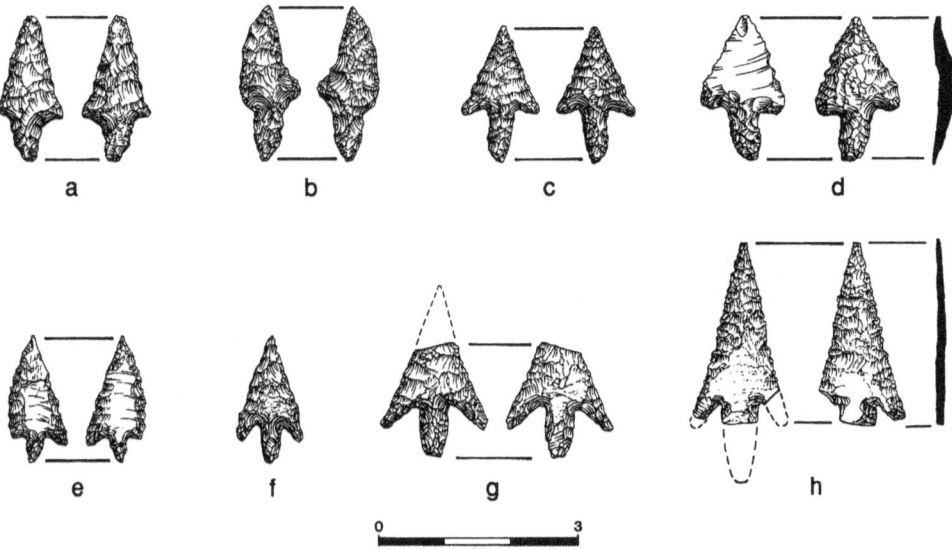

Figure 2.7. Examples of Perdiz points from the Cielo Bravo site (41PS52). Courtesy Center for Big Bend Studies.

Four Hypotheses concerning Cielo Complex–La Junta Phase Relationships

To those familiar with the archaeology of the Texas Big Bend and the La Junta district, the interpretive labyrinth posed by the Cielo complex is immediately apparent. For example, what is the cultural affiliation of hunting-gathering Cielo complex peoples, and what is their relationship, if any, to coeval agriculturalists of the La Junta phase as defined by Kelley et al. (1940)? What is the relationship of the Cielo complex to the Perdiz-bearing Toyah and Infierno phases in regions to the east, and to wickiup-using peoples of the Greater Southwest, northern Mexico, and the Great Plains? Patently obvious questions such as these are not easily answered. However, the development of a series of archaeologically testable hypotheses might prove useful in addressing them. Four such hypotheses are presented here.

Hypothesis 1
The strong similarities of Cielo complex material assemblages—particularly those from base camps overlooking the La Junta district—to contemporary assemblages of the La Junta agriculturalists indicate that the two assemblages have origins in the same ethnic and social group.

This hypothesis suggests that pit house–constructing agriculturalists of the La Junta phase and wickiup-constructing hunter-gatherers of the Cielo complex were ethnically and socially the same people, and that the differences in architecture and settlement systems simply reflect shifts in economic behavior at intervals. This would imply a highly flexible and rather loosely knit social fabric that allowed easy movement of individuals between related bands and between varying adaptations as the need arose. The need to modify adaptations could arise from crop failure, population pressures, or hostilities. Or, the Cielo complex sites might simply reflect seasonal activities by La Junta phase agriculturalists to directly procure wild foods to supplement their stores of cultigens. In this model, the distinctive dwellings of the Cielo complex, rather than indicating the presence of a different ethnic or social group, would instead reflect temporary or seasonal behavioral shifts to a hunting-gathering lifeway. Going a step further, one could suggest that the Cielo complex represents the remains of La Junta phase villagers who, upon the collapse of the Casas Grandes–Jornada Mogollon interaction sphere in the fifteenth century, shifted from semisedentarism to a full-blown hunting-gathering existence. However, chronometric data indicating contemporaneity of the La Junta phase (ca. AD 1200–1400) and the Cielo complex (ca. AD 1250–1700) currently seem to contradict this latter possibility.

Hypothesis 2
Peoples of the Cielo complex were ethnically and linguistically related to the La Junta agriculturalists but led a distinctive hunting-gathering, rather than agricultural-based, lifeway.

This "kissing cousin" model assumes that similarities in material assemblages are due to symbiotic interaction through time between socially distinct, but ethnically related, peoples. Possible ethnographic parallels can be drawn between the nomadic Chisos and the farming Conchos Indians, who are suspected by some researchers (e.g., Griffen 1969) to have had common linguistic and social roots. In this model, the pit ramada at the Cielo Bravo site is considered as possibly representing an initial occupation by La Junta agriculturalists that slightly predated occupation by wickiup-constructing hunter-gatherers. New radiocarbon data from the nearby Polvo site (41PS21) indicate that La Junta agriculturalists were constructing pit houses there at least as early as AD 1280–1320, predating the earliest dates from circular dwellings at the Cielo Bravo site by fifteen to twenty years. As a result, the hunter-gatherer occupation could be superimposed immediately over—or mixed with—that of the agriculturalists, and could represent either socially related or socially distinctive bands of hunter-gatherers.

Hypothesis 3
The hunter-gatherers of the Cielo complex were ethnically and socially distinct from the La Junta farmers, and similarities in material assemblages are attributable to a long-standing symbiotic relationship between the respective cultures.

This model draws heavily from early Spanish accounts that are interpreted by Kelley (1986) as indicating socially separate but symbiotically dependent cultural groups at La Junta—the Patarabueye (agriculturalists) and the Jumano (hunter-gatherers). Because of its strategic location relative to La Junta, and the presence there of both material and architectural similarities (e.g., a pit ramada), the Cielo Bravo site is seen as a possible interaction node of the two cultures. In this scenario, a well-documented Contact period trade of such items as deer and bison hides for cultigens is seen as having strong prehistoric antecedents. In addition, there exists a potential ancestral linkage of the Cielo complex to the Jumano, Cibolo, or Chisos Indians of sixteenth- and seventeenth-century Spanish accounts, as well as to a Jumano-Apache presence of the seventeenth and eighteenth centuries.

Hypothesis 4
The stone-based, circular forms that characterize some dwellings at archaeological sites in the Texas Big Bend and northeastern Chihuahua may not all be attributable to their builders' having shared a common social or ethnic group.

Stone-based dwellings both within and between sites sometimes reflect variability in construction techniques that, rather than reflecting functional differences as postulated earlier, may indicate occupations by contemporary but socially distinct bands of hunter-gatherers having similar material assemblages. This author's preference for continued use of the archaeologically flexible construct Cielo "complex," rather than Cielo "phase," is predicated on the foregoing possibility. Although it is not yet demonstrable archaeologically, some forms of dwellings could ultimately prove attributable to earlier peoples of the Late Prehistoric period, or even to Archaic period inhabitants of the region.

Discussion

Similar models have been developed that address the pressing problem of prehistoric relationships between the Cielo complex and hunting-gathering peoples of the Infiemo and Toyah phases of regions east and northeast. The Infiemo phase (Dibble 1978; Turpin 1982) of the Lower Pecos River region and, possibly, northern Coahuila, remains poorly known, but it has been characterized on the basis of surface evidence as having high-elevation enclosure-bearing sites with probable associations of ceramics, end scrapers, flake and blade industries, and a variety of arrowpoint styles including Perdiz. It has been hypothesized that the Infiemo phase represents an intrusion of Athapaskans or other Plains Indians into the Lower Pecos region very late in prehistory (Turpin 1982). Comparison of the Infiemo phase with the Cielo complex is presently rendered difficult in the absence of controlled excavations at Infiemo sites that might clarify artifact associations and temporal-cultural affiliations. However, significant differences in Infiemo enclosure-construction techniques, along with a presumed association of ceramics and very late arrival into the region, suggest that different social groups are indicated. The key to understanding the origins of the Infiemo phase may well depend upon determination of the origins of its associated ceramics.

The Toyah phase or "horizon" of Central and South Texas and portions of northeastern Mexico is, on the other hand, reasonably well defined (e.g., Jelks 1962; Prewitt 1983; Black 1986), and it bears some resemblance to the contemporaneous Cielo complex primarily in terms of the makeup of associated lithic assemblages, as well as in some characteristics of subsistence practices (deer and bison hunting) and postulated band sizes. Both Toyah phase and Cielo complex contain lithic assemblages characterized by Perdiz points, beveled knives, triangular end scrapers, flake perforators, core hammerstones, sequence-flake and blade-core reduction strategies, and conical cores—in other words, assemblages that seem indicative of a Plains bison-hunter technology and tool kit. On the other hand, the Toyah phase as currently defined lacks the distinctive stone-based wickiups and special-function enclosures, cache and burial cairns, ring middens, and other features attributable to the Cielo complex. Moreover, Cielo complex material assemblages north of the Rio Grande are lacking in ceramics, while Toyah phase assemblages are typified by various styles of ceramics. Other differences in material and feature assemblages exist as well. For example, alternately beveled knives and triangular end scrapers, although present, tend to be much less common in Cielo complex tool assemblages than in assemblages of the Toyah phase.

In sum, material similarities and temporal contemporaneity between the Cielo complex and the Toyah phase may be deemed strong enough to argue for a common Southern Plains, bison-hunter origin for both. If one adheres to this most obvious, and what will almost certainly prove most popular, interpretation, the next logical step is to explain apparent differences in settlement, subsistence, material assemblages, and social systems, primarily in terms of human adaptive responses to significantly disparate environmental circumstances and to diverse external cultural influences (e.g., the lack of ceramics in Cielo complex assemblages may be due to the difficulty of avoiding breakage in such rough, rocky terrain). Having thus compensated for differences in physical remains, and following the traditional logic among Texas archaeologists with respect to the creation of sociocultural units, the Cielo complex might then be conveniently pigeonholed as simply representing a western expression—a division or even a subphase—of a redefined Toyah phase.

In my opinion, such a categorization would be premature and possibly detrimental to our eventual understanding of the cultural dynamics involved. This is in part due to the fact that archaeological constructs such as phases, even when appropriately applied (e.g., see Johnson 1987), inexorably tie interpretative efforts into a rigid temporal framework based on similarities in artifact styles, while masking our understanding of the very cultural processes and causal factors that we hope to detect. This significant problem, which is much too involved to address properly in this paper, is most succinctly stated by Flannery (1986, 507): "We are therefore confronted with a paradox: the processes we wish to document proceed as a series of logistic curves, while our chronologies are composed of linear phases based on stylistic changes in artifacts that may have little or nothing to do with those processes."

Suffice it to say that, while there is artifactual and temporal evidence of a linkage between the Cielo complex and the Toyah phase, the nature of this linkage has yet to be determined. Some common denominators probably existed in the realms of language, subsistence patterns (e.g., bison hunting), and other factors. And while there is a very real likelihood of a common ancestry, we should exercise caution in attributing origins of both cultural constructs to the Southern Plains, the Piney Woods of Texas, or the upper coastal regions. Radiocarbon assays from Perdiz-bearing components of La Junta and the Big Bend (tables 2.1 and 2.2) are roughly comparable to the earliest accepted ages from other regions of Texas, and the origins of both the Toyah phase and Cielo complex might instead lie in the vast, archaeologically unexplored reaches of northern Mexico.

A hypothetical schematic showing two of the most likely source areas for origins of the La Junta and Toyah phases and the Cielo complex is offered in fig. 2.8. The Southern Plains hypothesis is predicated on cross-cutting similarities in material assemblages that reflect a Plains bison-hunting orientation and on archaeological and ethnographic analogies that suggest successive southward waves through time of Plains-oriented Indians into adjacent physiographic regions.

The north-central Mexico hypothesis bears resemblance to a much earlier Jumano model proposed by Kelley (1955). In this case, however, the hypothesis centers on anthropologically recognized tendencies of human groups to adapt their lifeways and technologies to take advantage of major shifts in resource availability. Similarities of tool assemblages, rather than indicating a single wide-ranging social group, may instead reflect common subsistence patterns among socially distinctive peoples, or a loose conglomeration of socially and linguistically affiliated bands (Mallouf 1987). The many distinctive bison-hunting cultures having similar material assemblages across the Great Plains of North America are a case in point. The reentry of large bison herds into the Southern Plains and adjacent areas in the thirteenth century, along with the development of new trade potential based in part upon bison products, would have provided an impetus for the diffusion of material traits.

Conclusions

Viewed collectively, the highly varied site types and features attributable to the Cielo complex reflect an intricate, dynamic, and flexible social system that was well adapted to the rugged desert-mountain environment of the Texas Big Bend and northeastern Chihuahua. Gaining real insight into the lifeways of Cielo complex peoples, however, will require long-term intensive studies that explore the full range of archaeological variability, including adaptational, behavioral, and site-abandonment processes, within the social system. Preliminary inferences such as those offered above can and must be tested archaeologically through extensive survey and large-scale, carefully controlled excavations that crosscut the full range of site variability.

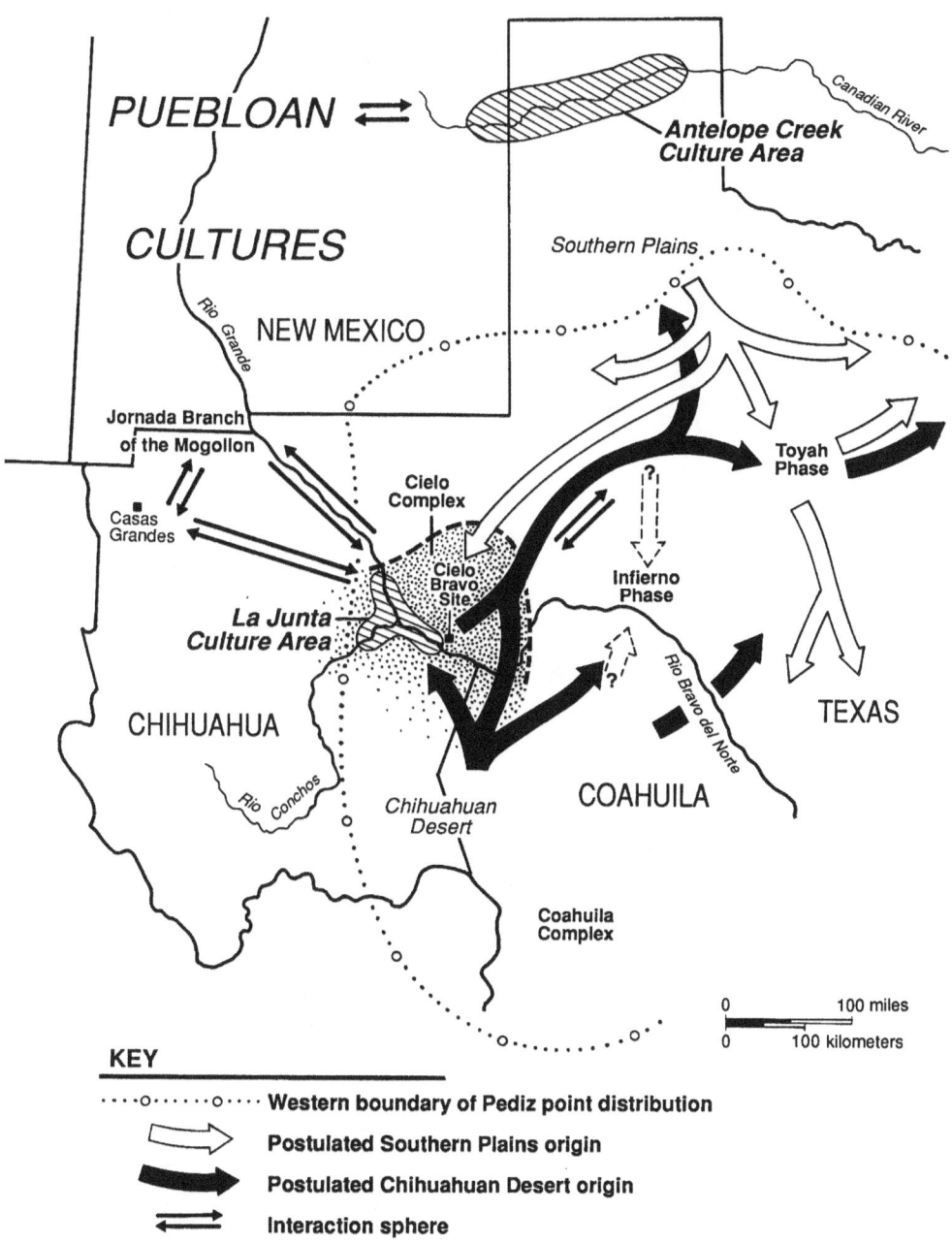

Figure 2.8. Postulated origins and interaction spheres of the La Junta phase and the Cielo complex. Courtesy Center for Big Bend Studies.

TABLE 2.1. RADIOCARBON ASSAYS FROM PERDIZ-BEARING COMPONENTS IN THE TEXAS BIG BEND

Site Name	Site Number	Cultural Affiliation	Sample No.	Sample Content	Kind of Sample	Uncorrected Age (BP)	C^{13} Adjusted Age (BP)	Calibrated Age Range	Highest Confidence Level (93%)	References
Polvo	41PS21	La Junta phase	Beta-29991	Charred beam from pithouse	Wood charcoal	680±60	*620±60	*AD 1282–1405	*AD 1315	Mallouf n.d.a, Kelley 1990
Polvo	41PS21	La Junta phase	Beta-29992	Charred beam from pithouse	Wood charcoal	750±70	*690±70	*AD 1262–1387	*AD 1281	Mallouf n.d.a, Kelley 1990
Cielo Bravo	41PS52	Cielo complex	Beta-21790	Wickiup living floor (E-10)	Wood charcoal	620±130	580±130	*AD 1280–1440	*AD 1330	Mallouf n.d.a
Cielo Bravo	41PS52	Cielo complex	Beta-21791	Posthole outside wickiup (E-11)	Wood charcoal	450±70	430±70	*AD 1421–1491	*AD 1441	Mallouf n.d.a
Cielo Bravo	41SS2	Cielo complex	Beta-21793	Posthole outside wickiup (E-11)	Wood charcoal	880±90	820±90	*AD 1068–1278	*AD 1219	Mallouf n.d.a
Cielo Bravo	41SS2	Cielo complex	Beta-21794	Living surface outside wickiup (E-10)	Wood charcoal	210±60	200±60	*AD 1647–1955	*AD 1665	Mallouf n.d.a
Cielo Bravo	41SS2	Cielo complex	Beta-21795 (AMS)	Pit ramada posthole	Wood charcoal		555±80	*AD 1301–1431	*AD 1335	Mallouf n.d.a
Cielo Bravo	41S25	Cielo complex	Beta-21796	Outside living surface (ash pit)	Bulk carbon	100±60	150±60	*AD 1662–1955	*AD 1681	Mallouf n.d.a
Cielo Bravo	41S25	Cielo complex	Beta-21797	Hearth inside wickiup (E-10)	Bulk carbon	350±80	410±80	*AD 1425–1623	*AD 1446	Mallouf n.d.a
Cielo Bravo	41PS52	Cielo complex	Beta-26707	Pit ramada posthole	Wood charcoal	520±40	480±40	*AD 1414–1440	*AD 1429	Mallouf n.d.a

Cielo Bravo	41PS53	Cielo complex	Beta-26709	Pit ramada posthole	Wood charcoal	310±40	260±40	*AD 1532–1659	*AD 1648	Mallouf n.d.a
Cielo Bravo	41PS53	Cielo complex	Beta-26711	Hearth outside wickiup (H-1)	Bulk carbon	100±50	150±50	*AD 1665–1955	*AD 1681	Mallouf n.d.a
Alamo Springs	41BS673	Cielo complex	TX-4383	Wickiup living surface	Wood charcoal	545±75		† AD1335–1480		Mallouf 1985, 1987
Persimmon Gap	41BS609	Cielo complex (?)	TX-2869	Burned rock feature	Wood charcoal	460±70		† AD 1385–1500		Baskin1978, Mallouf 1985, 1987
	41BS706-B	Cielo complex (?)	DIC-1	Hearth (F-1)	Wood charcoal	240±45		† AD1640–1950		Clifton 1986, Mallouf 1987
	41BS706-B	Cielo complex (?)	DIC-2	Hearth (F-9)	Wood charcoal	210±45		† AD 1515–1810		Clifton 1986, Mallouf 1987
	41BS706-B	Cielo complex (?)	DIC-3	Hearth (F-6a)	Wood charcoal	170±45		†AD 1500–1675		Clifton 1986, Mallouf 1987

*Age correction based on Stuiver and Becker (1986), Method A
†Age correction based on Klein et al. (1982)

TABLE 2.2: RADIOCARBON ASSAYS FROM PERDIZ-BEARING COMPONENTS IN THE TEXAS BIG BEND, INCLUDING THE CIELO COMPLEX AND THE LA JUNTA PHASE

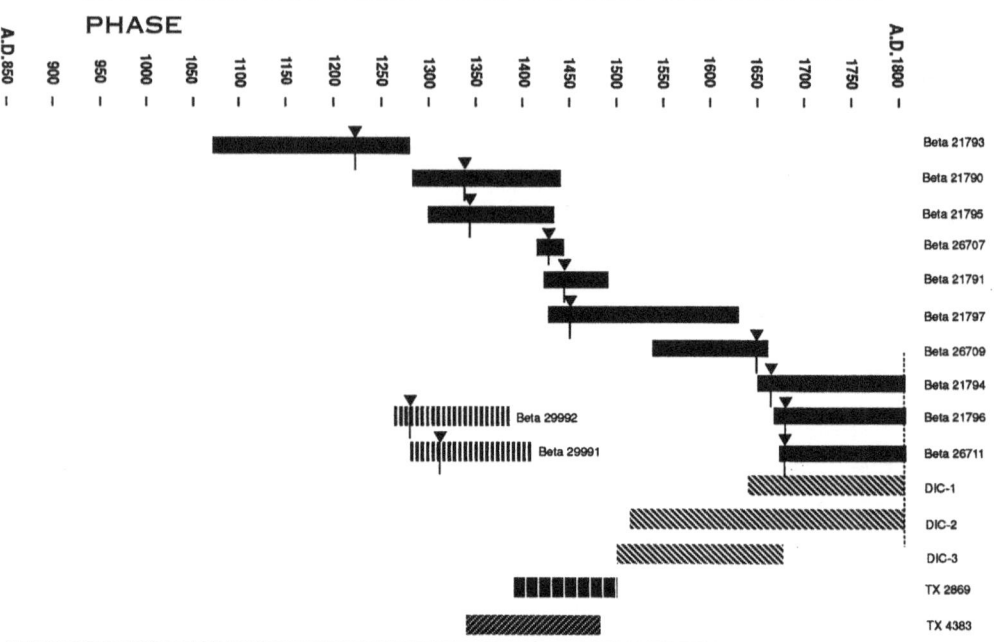

In conjunction with expanded study of the Cielo complex, I believe that we should reevaluate past interpretations of Kelley et al. (1940), Lehmer (1958), and Kelley (1986, 1990) that imply an ethnic and social linkage of La Junta phase agriculturalists to sedentary peoples of the Jornada Branch of the Mogollon. On the contrary, La Junta phase peoples may originally have been a hunting-gathering society indigenous to the Chihuahuan Desert region (or intrusive into the Trans-Pecos from the Southern Plains) that, through social interaction, merely adopted certain architectural, agricultural, and other traits of Jornada Mogollon peoples of the El Paso region. This interpretation would account for differences noted by Kelley in aspects of La Junta phase architecture, and for significant differences in material culture as well.

I see strong parallels to the La Junta culture area in the contemporary Antelope Creek phase of the Canadian River in the Texas Panhandle (fig. 2.8 p.59). Semisedentary peoples of the Antelope Creek phase were almost certainly indigenous to the Southern Plains and not of Puebloan origin, yet they adopted architectural, agricultural, and other aspects of Puebloan culture to the west. As was probably the case with La Junta, such influences were originally spawned among Antelope Creek hunter-gatherers as a result of their entry into symbiotic trade relationships, based in large part upon bison products, with sedentary Puebloan peoples. In the cases of both the Antelope Creek and La Junta cultures, differences in ethnic roots and socioeconomic systems are reflected archaeologically in their respective bastardizations of Puebloan architectural styles, and, even more significantly, in their retention of hunter-gatherer material assemblages. The use of ceramics by both cultures, rather than supporting ethnic affiliations with sedentary Puebloan cultures, in my opinion supports the argument for distinct ethnic roots. Although they obtained minor amounts of Puebloan wares through trade, Antelope Creek peoples relied heavily on a distinctive Plains style of utilitarian ware (Borger Cord-marked) that they themselves manufactured. La Junta phase peoples, on the other hand, rather than manufacturing their own pottery, obtained their wares almost exclusively through trade with sedentary peoples of the Río Conchos and Casas Grandes in northern Chihuahua and with the Jornada Mogollon of the El Paso region. In contrast to sedentary Puebloan cultures, La Junta and Antelope Creek phase peoples never fully made the transition to a sedentary, agriculture-based existence. Instead, their material assemblages reflect semisedentary lifeways with continued strong reliance on hunting and gathering as a means of supplementing their agricultural stores.

In closing, I must express a mixed reaction to Kelley's most recent (1990) reinterpretation of La Junta district archaeology. Like Kelley, I feel that our concept of the "Bravo Valley aspect" (including La Junta, Concepción, and Conchos phases), as originally defined (Kelley et al. 1940), should be subjected to careful revision. In light of new data from the region, it is unlikely that Kelley's original pivotal concept of a cultural continuum throughout the three phases will stand the test of time. It is to this exceptional scholar's credit that he was actively involved in the revision of his original, long-standing interpretations.

For reasons stated earlier, I do question Kelley's latest interpretation (1990) of the La Junta phase as being an ethnic satellite of Casas Grandes or the Jornada Mogollon and having the primary purpose of supplying raw materials to the parent redistribution center in northwestern Chihuahua. Instead, I propose that the relationship was based upon the symbiotic exchange of goods by semisedentary, non-Puebloan La Junta villagers with sedentary Puebloan groups to the west, as was the case with the Antelope Creek culture far to the north. Both cultural systems flourished as a result of the healthy flow of raw materials and products.

With the eventual collapse of the Casas Grandes interaction sphere around AD 1450 (Ravesloot 1988), the eastward flow of trade goods to La Junta dried up. Kelley (1990, 39) suggests that, as a result of the collapse of Casas Grandes, the Puebloan La Junta villagers subsequently abandoned the area, "leaving [it] occupied only by semi-sedentary hunters and gatherers living in simple structures. Around ca. 1550 cultural influences from the south, following the Río Conchos, may have combined with others introduced by the arrival of the Jumano (as early Apacheans?) at La Junta to form the protohistoric Concepción phase."

In contrast to Kelley's interpretation, I would offer—based upon examination of their material assemblages—that La Junta phase peoples were practicing a semisedentary, rather than sedentary, existence to begin with (as discussed earlier). Rather than abandoning the area upon the collapse of the Casas Grandes interaction sphere, they reverted to a largely hunting-gathering lifeway—a lifeway that is in part archaeologically manifested, both prior to and after the fall of Casas Grandes, in what I have termed the Cielo complex.

Contrary to Kelley's suggested arrival of the Jumano (as possible Apacheans) into the La Junta area around AD 1550, I would offer the possibility that both the La Junta phase and the Cielo complex are in fact ancestral manifestations of the sixteenth-century "Jumano" dating back to at least AD 1250 in the area, and that both have ethnic origins among non-Athapaskan hunter-gatherers of either the Southern Plains or the northwestern Chihuahuan Desert region. Based upon data from the Cielo Bravo site, a Jumano-Apache or Apachean presence is not materially manifested in the La Junta area until about AD 1650, but I would agree with Kelley that a somewhat earlier arrival date for the Apaches is a possibility. I also agree with Kelley (1990) that the protohistoric Concepción phase, if revised and retained, should reflect an Apachean presence, or at least a strong Apachean influence, at La Junta.

While space does not permit further discussion, there are other characteristics of La Junta phase villagers that suggest they were a people distinct from

Puebloan culture who, through influence and trade, merely adopted certain material aspects of Jornada Mogollon and Casas Grandes culture without ever really assuming full-blown sedentism. If this assessment is accurate, then the case for a common ethnic, linguistic, and socioeconomic linkage between the La Junta phase and the Cielo complex can be reasonably argued.

References

Baskin, Barbara J. 1978. *Test Excavations at a Prehistoric Stratified Campsite: Big Bend National Park, Brewster County, Texas.* Report submitted to the National Park Service, Southwest Region, Santa Fe, New Mexico. Austin: n.p.

Black, Stephen L. 1986. *The Clemente and Herminia Hinojosa Site, 41JW8: A Toyah Horizon Campsite in Southern Texas.* Special Report 18. [San Antonio]: Center for Archaeological Research, University of Texas at San Antonio.

Campbell, T. N. 1970. "Archeological Survey of the Big Bend National Park, 1966–1967." Unpublished report submitted to the National Park Service, US Department of the Interior.

Clifton, Don. 1986. *Archaeological Testing of Site 41BS706-B, Big Bend National Park, Texas.* Tularosa, New Mexico: Human Systems Research.

Dibble, David S. 1978. "The Infierno Phase: Evidence for a Late Occupation in the Lower Pecos River Region, Texas." Paper presented at the 43rd Annual Meeting of the Society for American Archaeology, Tucson, Arizona.

Flannery, Kent V. 1986. "Adaption, Evolution, and Archaeological Phases: Some Implications of Reynold's Simulation." In *Guila Naquitz: Archaic Foraging and Early Agriculture in Oaxaca, Mexico,* edited by Kent V. Flannery, 501–7. New York: Academic Press.

Foster, Michael S., and J. Charles Kelley. 1987. *Archaeological Investigations of Portions of Eight Sites within the Proposed Floodwater Diversion, Three Mile and Sulphur Draw Watershed, Culberson County, Texas.* El Paso: Jornada Anthropological Research Association.

Fritz, Gordon L. 1989. "The Ecological Significance of Early Piman Immigration to Southern Arizona." *Artifact* 27 (1): 51–109.

González, Leticia. 1986a. "Ejercicio de interpretación de actividades en un campamento de cazadorez-recolectores en el Bolsón de Mapimí." In *Unidades habitacionales mesoamericanas y sus áreas de actividad,* edited by Linda Manzanilla, 135–57. Mexico, DF: Universidad Nacional Autónoma de México.

———. 1986b. "Hunter-Gathers of the Chihuahuan Desert in Mexico." In *Invited Papers from the Second Symposium on Resources of the Chihuahuan Desert Region, United States and Mexico, 20–21 October 1983,* edited by Jon C. Barlow, A. Michael Powell, and Barbara N. Timmermann, 64–68. Alpine, Texas: Chihuahuan Desert Research Institute.

Griffen, William B. 1969. *Culture Change and Shifting Populations in Central Northern Mexico*. Anthropological Papers of the University of Arizona 13. Tucson: University of Arizona Press.

Hedrick, John A. 1968. "Plateau Station Area Survey (EPAS-68)." *Artifact* 6 (1): 1–16.

———. 1975. "Archaeology of the Plateau Site, Culberson County." *Artifact* 13 (4): 45–82.

———. 1988. "A Preliminary Report on Archeological Resources in Southern Culberson County in the Vicinity of Van Horn, Texas." *Bulletin of the Texas Archeological Society* 59:129–56.

Henrickson, James, and Marshall C. Johnston. 1986. "Vegetation and Community Types of the Chihuahuan Desert." In *Invited Papers from the Second Symposium on Resources of the Chihuahuan Desert Region: United States and Mexico, 20–21 October 1983*, edited by Jon C. Barlow, A. Michael Powell, and Barbara N. Timmermann, 20–39. Alpine, Texas: Chihuahuan Desert Research Institute.

Jelks, Edward B. 1962. *The Kyle Site: A Stratified Central Texas Aspect Site in Hill County, Texas*. Archaeology Series 5. Austin: Department of Anthropology, University of Texas.

Johnson, Eileen, Vance T. Holliday, Michael J. Kaczor, and Robert Stuckenrath. 1977. "The Garza Occupation at the Lubbock Lake Site." *Bulletin of the Texas Archeological Society* 48:83–109.

Johnson, LeRoy, Jr. 1987. "A Plague of Phases." *Bulletin of the Texas Archeological Society* 57:1–26.

Johnston, Marshall C. 1977. "Brief Resume of Botanical, including Vegetational, Features of the Chihuahuan Desert Region with Special Emphasis on Their Uniqueness." In *Transactions of the Symposium on the Biological Resources of the Chihuahuan Desert Region: United States and Mexico*. National Park Service Transactions and Proceedings Series 3:335–59. Washington, DC: US National Parks Service.

Kelley, J. Charles. 1939. "Archaeological Notes on the Excavation of a Pithouse near Presidio, Texas." *El Palacio* 46 (10): 221–34.

———. 1949. Archaeological Notes on Two Excavated House Structures in Western Texas. *Bulletin of the Texas Archaeological and Paleontological Society* 20:89–114.

———. 1951. "A Bravo Valley Aspect Component of the Lower Río Conchos Valley, Chihuahua, Mexico." *American Antiquity* 17 (2): 114–19.

———. 1952a. Factors Involved in the Abandonment of Certain Peripheral Southwestern Settlements. *American Anthropologist* 54 (3): 356–87.

———. 1952b. "The Historic Indian Pueblos of La Junta de los Ríos," pt.1. *New Mexico Historical Review* 27 (4): 257–95.

———. 1953. "The Historic Indian Pueblos of La Junta de los Ríos," pt. 2. *New Mexico Historical Review* 28 (1): 21–51.

———. 1955. "Juan Sabeata and Diffusion in Aboriginal Texas." *American Anthropologist* 57 (5): 981–95.
———. 1957. "The Livermore Focus: A Clarification." *El Palacio* 64 (1–2): 44–52.
———. 1985. "Review of the Architectural Sequence at La Junta de los Ríos." In *Proceedings of the Third Jornada Mogollon Conference*, edited by M. S. Foster and T. C. O'Laughlin. *Artifact* 23 (1–2): 149–59.
———. 1986. *Jumano and Patarabueye: Relations at La Junta de los Ríos.* Anthropological Papers 77. Ann Arbor: Museum of Anthropology, University of Michigan.
———. 1990. "The Río Conchos Drainage: History, Archaeology, Significance." *Journal of Big Bend Studies* 2:29–42.
Kelley, J. Charles, T. N. Campbell, and Donald Lehmer. 1940. *The Association of Archaeological Materials with Geological Deposits in the Big Bend Region of Texas.* Alpine, Texas: West Texas Historical and Scientific Society Publication 10, and Sul Ross State Teachers College Bulletin 21 (3).
Klein, Jeffrey, J. C. Lerman, P. E. Damon, and E. K. Ralph. 1982. "Calibration of Radiocarbon Dates: Tables Based on the Consensus Data of the Workshop on Calibrating the Radiocarbon Time Scale." *Radiocarbon* 24 (2): 103–150.
Lehmer, Donald J. 1958. "A Review of Trans-Pecos Texas Archeology." *Bulletin of the Texas Archeological Society* 29:109–144.
Lesueur, Harde. 1945. *The Ecology of the Vegetation of Chihuahua, Mexico, North of Parallel Twenty-Eight.* University of Texas Publication 4521. Austin: University of Texas.
Lindsay, Alexander J., Jr. 1969. "Current Research: Texas." *American Antiquity* 34 (1): 102–3.
Mallouf, Robert J. 1981. "Observations concerning Environmental and Cultural Interactions during the Terminal Pleistocene and Early Holocene in the Big Bend of Texas and Adjoining Regions." *Bulletin of the Texas Archeological Society* 52:121–46.
———. 1985. "A Synthesis of Eastern Trans-Pecos Prehistory." MA thesis, University of Texas at Austin.
———. 1986. "Prehistoric Cultures of the Northern Chihuahuan Desert." In *Invited Papers from the Second Symposium on Resources of the Chihuahuan Desert Region, United States and Mexico, 20–21 October 1983*, edited by Jon C. Barlow, A. Michael Powell, and Barbara N. Timmermann, 69–78. Alpine, Texas: Chihuahuan Desert Research Institute.
———. 1987. *Las Haciendas: A Cairn-Burial Assemblage from Northeastern Chihuahua, Mexico.* Office of the State Archeologist Report 35. Austin: Texas Historical Commission.
———. n.d.a. "The Cielo Complex: Late Prehistoric and Protohistoric Adaptations in the Big Bend of Texas." Manuscript in preparation, Center for Big Bend Studies, Sul Ross State University, Alpine, Texas.

———. n.d.b "The Cielo Bravo Site (41PS52)." Field notes on file, Center for Big Bend Studies, Sul Ross State University, Alpine, Texas.

Mallouf, Robert J., and Virginia A. Wulfkuhle. 1989. "An Archeological Reconnaissance in the Rosillos Mountains, Brewster County, Texas." *Journal of Big Bend Studies* 1:1–24.

Marmaduke, William S. 1978. *Prehistory at Bear Creek, Brewster County, Texas.* Office of the State Archeologist Survey Report 25. Austin: Texas Historical Commission.

O'Laughlin, Thomas C. 1980. *The Keystone Dam Site and Other Archaic and Formative Sites in Northwest El Paso, Texas.* Publications in Anthropology 8. El Paso: El Paso Centennial Museum, University of Texas at El Paso.

Phelps, Alan, L. 1987. "Soto: A Distinctive Projectile Point Type." *Artifact* 25 (4): 7–22.

Prewitt, Elton R. 1983. "From Circleville to Toyah: Comments on Central Texas Chronology." *Bulletin of the Texas Archaeological Society* 54:201–38.

Ravesloot, John C. 1988. *Mortuary Practices and Social Differentiation at Casas Grandes, Chihuahua, Mexico.* Anthropological Papers of the University of Arizona 49. Tucson: University of Arizona Press.

Runkles, Frank A., and E. D. Dorchester. 1986. "The Lott Site (41GR56): A Late Prehistoric Site in Garza County, Texas." *Bulletin of the Texas Archeological Society* 57:83–115.

Sayles, E. B. 1936. *An Archaeological Survey of Chihuahua, Mexico.* Medallion Papers 22. Globe, Arizona: Gila Pueblo.

Schmidt, Robert H., Jr. 1973. *A Geographical Survey of Chihuahua.* University of Texas at El Paso Monograph 37. El Paso: Texas Western Press.

———. 1979. "A Climatic Delineation of the 'Real' Chihuahuan Desert." *Journal of Arid Environments* 2:243–50.

Stuiver, Minze, and Bernd Becker. 1986. "High-Precision Decadal Calibration of the Radiocarbon Time Scale, AD 1950–2500 BC ." *Radiocarbon* 28 (2B): 863–910.

Taylor, Walter W. 1966. "Archaic Cultures Adjacent to the Northeastern Frontiers of Mesoamerica." In *Archaeological Frontiers and External Connections*, edited by Robert Wauchope, 59–94. Handbook of Middle American Indians, vol. 4. Austin: University of Texas Press.

Turner, Ellen Sue, and Thomas R. Hester. 1985. *A Field Guide to Stone Artifacts of Texas Indians.* Austin: Texas Monthly Press.

Turpin, Solveig A. 1982. *Seminole Canyon: The Art and the Archeology.* Research Report 83. Austin: Texas Archeological Survey, University of Texas at Austin.

3 *The Rough Run Burial*

A SEMISUBTERRANEAN CAIRN BURIAL FROM BREWSTER COUNTY, TEXAS

William A. Cloud

Prehistoric peoples traversed the rugged Trans-Pecos landscape for thousands of years focused on survival in this harsh and formidable environment. Over the course of time many Native Americans lived and died in the desert, with some remains ultimately interred or disposed of in accordance with various belief systems. Although numerous prehistoric burials are undoubtedly located in the region, few have been positively identified or scientifically excavated (Mallouf 1987). Early researchers in the area (Peabody 1909, 213; Fletcher 1931,10; Smith, n.d.) noted the presence of stacked stone cairns and suggested they were aboriginal burials; however, only a single feature of this type has been previously reported from the Big Bend (Mallouf 1987).

In 1987, an unusual stone feature located on a large open campsite (41BS844/Rough Run site) in Big Bend National Park (BBNP) was discovered during an in-house archaeological survey of an extant power-line route. The exposed portion of the feature was disturbed and contained two fragmentary Perdiz arrowpoints. Subsequent testing in 1988 and excavation in 1990 revealed the presence of a carefully constructed semisubterranean cairn containing an unusual burial. A total of seventy-three arrowpoints and arrowpoint fragments and three pieces of debitage were scattered throughout the feature. All but one of the arrowpoints fall within the Perdiz type (Suhm and Jelks 1962, 283–84; Turner and Hester 1985, 187).

While Perdiz points occur in Late Prehistoric and Protohistoric components throughout much of Texas and portions of the states of Coahuila and Chihuahua in Mexico, this is the first scientifically excavated Perdiz-bearing interment known to this author. The only other burial with associated Perdiz points was found and excavated by artifact collectors in northeastern Chihuahua, Mexico, on the outskirts of the small village of Las Haciendas (Paso de San Antonio). The grave goods from that cairn burial were subsequently analyzed and reported by Mallouf (1987), along with information from the excavators, offering an initial view of mortuary practices associated with Perdiz points. The Rough Run cairn burial differs in several respects from the Las Haciendas interment, very possibly as a result of differing statuses of the individuals.

Analyses of the Rough Run skeletal material, grave goods, and their juxtapositions within the interment have provided a wealth of data on the health of the individual and on mortuary practices and customs of the people responsible for the interment. Patterned behavior is evident throughout the assemblage and cairn, which, when compared with data from the Las Haciendas burial, allows a number of inferences to be made about the culture of these people.

Context of the Burial

Regional Cairns

Numerous cairns have been discovered in the northern Chihuahuan Desert region over the last hundred years. While many of these stacked-stone features are by-products of early and more recent surveying activities, or represent trail or other markers, others have been excavated revealing prehistoric or historic burials (Mallouf 1987). Early researchers in the area noted the presence of cairns and suggested that these rock mounds covered human burials (Peabody 1909; Fletcher 1931; Smith, n.d.); however, none of the early efforts produced any published evidence of cairn interments. The researchers usually stated as a matter of fact that the cairns covered "Indian burials"; however, no supporting documentation exists to confirm these findings.

In arid regions where soils are often shallow, stone cairns provide burials with a degree of protection from environmental forces and scavenging animals. Historic documentation of both Apache and Comanche burials indicates that stones were often used to cover interments. A 1797 account of Apache burial customs indicates that the cadaver was usually carried to a gully or handmade grave, tossed in, and then covered with stones (Cortes 1989, 77). An account of Comanche mortuary practices relates that "the body is . . . covered with sticks and earth, and sometimes stones are placed over the whole" (Yarrow 1988, 6–7).

Charles Peabody of Harvard University made the first, although brief, notation concerning cairn burials in the region. On a trip through the area he stopped at Bogel/San Esteban Rockshelter south of Marfa, Texas, and indicated that numerous human burials covered with stones and containing associated artifacts had been found on the ridge above the shelter (Peabody 1909, 213). Unfortunately, there were no other pertinent details concerning these features.

Victor J. Smith, an industrial arts professor from 1920 until 1951 at Sul Ross Normal College (now Sul Ross State University) in Alpine, Texas, was the next researcher to investigate regional cairns. Smith had an ardent interest in archaeology and spent much of his free time investigating rock-shelters and other sites in the area, eventually becoming curator of the museum at Sul Ross. On August 15, 1921, Smith visited a site north of Alpine where multiple cairns with burials in crouched positions had supposedly been found. Over two hundred mounds had been reported, but only about thirty were discovered during this trip. Smith's notes (n.d.) revealed that no skeletal or artifactual materials were present, indicating that at least one of the cairns was excavated.

Another early reference to cairn burials was made by Henry T. Fletcher in his overview of site types in the region. Fletcher (1931, 10) stated that "talus slope and open country burials are usually shallow and are indicated by low mounds of rather large stones placed with some care. The mounds are round or oval, the bodies often being buried in a flexed position."

The only cairn burial formally reported in the region is the Las Haciendas burial from northeastern Chihuahua (Mallouf 1987). That interment was located outside the small village of Las Haciendas (Paso de San Antonio)—about 27 km south of Lajitas, Texas—and was excavated by local residents in 1984. The cairn was positioned high (ca. 15 m above the basin floor) on an eroded bench along the gentle southwestern backslope of a cuesta. Mallouf (1987, 15), using information from the excavators, reported that the human remains were found within a shallow pit with a north-south orientation (head to the south). While the actual positioning of the body was not documented scientifically, the informants thought the corpse had been lying on its back in an extended posture. Almost all of the grave goods (194 arrowpoints, one small pendant, and one discoidal bead) were recovered below and on either side of skull fragments and teeth, suggesting that they had been originally encased in one or more perishable containers. The burial was subsequently covered with a low, oval mound of variously sized limestone fragments and topped in a tentlike fashion with two large, tabular rhyolite boulders; all stones were likely gathered from the immediate vicinity. The fragmented skeletal material from the interment was that of an adolescent of undetermined sex, but the six recovered teeth exhibited variable crown wear and coloration, suggesting the inclusion of two individuals beneath the cairn (Mallouf 1987, 15, 44). However, the cairn excavators were emphatic that they had found only one individual interred. The presence of numerous arrowpoints as grave goods was thought to be suggestive of a male interment (Mallouf 1987, 15).

Mallouf (1987) conducted a detailed analysis of the grave goods, with an emphasis on the 180 Perdiz arrowpoints within the assemblage. Based on inspectional sorting, he was able to separate these specimens into ten morphological groupings containing twenty-six varieties, as well as two miscellaneous groups. While this sorting indicated a high degree of morphological variability within the Perdiz assemblage, Mallouf (1987, 60) attempted to identify the parameters of the variability through a combined attribute analysis using simple two- and three-element (blade, barb, and stem-configuration) plottings. Based on these and other findings from the analysis, he suggested the likelihood of multiple knappers of the cairn arrowpoint assemblage, and the possibility that the points had been selectively curated with the intent of refurbishing damaged specimens. Using radiocarbon data for Perdiz points from West, South, and Central Texas, as well as postulated dating ranges for the non-Perdiz points within the assemblage, he suggests a temporal span from AD 1500–1750 was suggested for the burial (Mallouf 1987, 63).

Regional Burial Data

Data from thirty-four scientifically excavated burials in the region (western Coahuila, southern Nuevo León, and the Texas Big Bend) is succinctly summarized by Mallouf (1987, table 1). Several trends within this data set were noted: (1) Thirty-one of the thirty-four reported burials were primary interments containing single individuals; (2) nine of sixteen burials on the south side of the Rio Grande were in extended positions on the back, with the other seven in various semiflexed to flexed positions, while all of the burials on the north side of the river were flexed; and (3) burials on the south side of the river were usually oriented southeast-northwest or east-west, while those north of the river generally had southwest-northeast or north-south orientations (Mallouf 1987, 6). Mallouf pointed out that these trends were derived from a small data set and noted the need for additional burial data from the region for clearer patterning to emerge.

With the exception of the interment reported herein, only one other burial is known to this author to have been scientifically excavated in the Big Bend region since Mallouf's (1987) synthesis was published—Texas Archeological Research Laboratory personnel in the summer of 1988 conducted a salvage excavation at the Comanche Springs site just outside the small community of Lajitas, Texas. The burial consisted of a primary interment of an adult female, placed in a tightly flexed position with her head to the north. It was found eroding out of a collapsed rock-shelter along Comanche Creek and, through bracketed radiocarbon dates, is thought to be approximately two thousand years old. Three limestone slabs had been placed over the body, including a possible metate lying on top of the leg bones (Jeffrey Huebner, personal communication 1999).

Perdiz Arrowpoints and Cultural Considerations
Perdiz points are found throughout much of Texas and portions of northeastern Mexico and bridge the gap between the Late Prehistoric and Protohistoric periods (ca. AD 1200–1750) (Prewitt 1983; Black 1986; Mallouf 1987). They were originally discussed by Kelley et al. (1940) in their seminal work on Trans-Pecos archaeology. The distinctive type was later named Perdiz Pointed Stem by Kelley (1947), who encountered it in Central Texas. The name was shortened to Perdiz by Suhm et al. (1954) in the original edition of the *Introductory Handbook of Texas Archeology*. Perdiz points commonly occur in Late Prehistoric and Protohistoric components throughout much of Texas and portions of Coahuila and Chihuahua in northeastern Mexico. The type is missing from the northern portion of the Panhandle, the far western portion of the Trans-Pecos, and the Lower Rio Grande Valley. Taylor (1966) has called them Nopal points during his work in northeastern Mexico. The point style has been included in a number of cultural constructs over the years: the Bravo Valley aspect of the Texas Big Bend and northern Chihuahua region (Kelley et al. 1940); the Jora complex of Central Coahuila (Taylor 1966); the Toyah focus of Central Texas (Kelley 1947; Suhm et al. 1954; Jelks 1962); the Toyah phase of Central Texas (Prewitt 1981, 1983); the Toyah folk or the Toyah culture of Central Texas (Johnson 1994); the Toyah horizon of South Texas (Black 1986); and more recently the Cielo complex of the Texas Big Bend and adjacent areas of Chihuahua and Coahuila (Mallouf 1999).

Of the cultural constructs mentioned above, only the Bravo Valley aspect and the Cielo complex occur in the Texas Big Bend. The former relates to the agricultural village components of the La Junta district (La Junta, Concepción, and Conchos phases) dating roughly between AD 1200 and AD 1760 (Kelley et al. 1940; Shackelford 1951; Kelley 1986). On the other hand, the Cielo complex is a construct for hunter-gatherers in the region from approximately AD 1250 to 1680 who used circular to oval stacked-stone house foundations (Mallouf 1999, 65). While house construction differs greatly between the agricultural villages and the Cielo complex sites, the material remains from both groups are surprisingly similar, implying some type of trade or other interaction.

Mallouf (1999, 85) has offered a hypothesis for the cultural interactions at La Junta that potentially explains the similar tool kits found at both the agricultural villages (La Junta and Conceptión phase sites) and Cielo complex base camps: "Both the La Junta phase and the Cielo complex are in fact ancestral manifestations of the sixteenth-century 'Jumano' dating back to at least AD 1250 in the area, and . . . both have ethnic origins among non-Athapaskan hunter-gatherers of either the Southern Plains or the northwestern Chihuahuan Desert region. Based upon data from the Cielo Bravo site, a Jumano-Apache or Apachean presence is not materially manifested in the La Junta area until about AD 1650."

Kelley (1990, 39) had earlier suggested that Jumano Indians arrived in the La Junta area by AD 1550, possibly as early Apacheans, and Mallouf (1999, 85) agreed that "a somewhat earlier arrival date for the Apache" was a possibility. While it is tempting to affiliate Perdiz points from the Trans-Pecos with the Jumano based on historic accounts and suggestive archaeological data, firm evidence for such a link is still needed.

Environmental Setting

The Big Bend region is within the Chihuahuan biotic province, an area stretching northward from north-central Mexico to West Texas and southern New Mexico (Blair 1950, 105). The climate of the province has been classified as subtropical arid (Larkin and Bomar 1983) and is characterized by temperate winters and hot summers, with most of the annual rainfall occurring during the summer-to-early-fall monsoons. The Rough Run area has an average annual precipitation of about 11 inches and an average annual temperature of about 63 degrees F (Larkin and Bomar 1983, 18, 50).

The Rough Run site is located on the west side of BBNP in southern Brewster County, within the northeastern portion of the Chihuahuan

Desert (fig. 3.1). The site area encompasses several eroded benches above Rough Run, a major arroyo in this portion of the park. Rough Run drains a large section along the west-northwest boundary of the park before emptying into Terlingua Creek within the small community of Study Butte. The site covers an approximate area of 320 x 320 m or about 1.6 hectares along upper and lower benches above the arroyo (fig. 3.2). The center of the site is at an approximate elevation of 850 m above mean sea level.

The upper bench, which slopes slightly from northwest to southeast, encompasses approximately 90 percent of the site area. Its north end is relatively flat, free of large gravels or stone outcrops, and saw extensive use during prehistory. The burial reported here was placed within this area of the site.

The lower bench, which is very narrow in relation to the broad upper bench, is parallel to and immediately northwest of an intermittent tributary that forms the southeastern and eastern site boundaries. A seep spring located along this arroyo is notable, although it currently flows only during wet periods.

The site rests on eroded portions of the Javelina Formation (Maxwell 1968). This formation consists of bentonitic clay interbedded with poorly indurated, argillaceous sandstone layers. Dating to the Upper Cretaceous, the Javelina Formation can also contain dinosaur bones and silicified wood. Occasional exposures of sandstone occur at the site, which are partly responsible for topographic highs and lows between the upper and lower benches. Erosion has also contributed to the topography, as numerous gullies cut through portions of the site.

Vegetation at the site is relatively sparse, mirroring the typical Chihuahuan Desert flora found across much of the park at this elevation. Creosotebush (*Larrea tridentata*) dominates the vegetative community, with ocotillo (*Fouquieria splendens*), tasajillo (*Opuntia leptocaulis*), prickly pear (*Opuntia* sp.), whitethorn acacia (*Acacia constricta*), lechuguilla (*Agave lechuguilla*), dog cholla (*Opuntia schottii*), mesquite (*Prosopis* sp.), other cacti, and scattered clumps of various grasses also present.

Myriad animal tracks in the sand and mud along Rough Run testify to the faunal diversity found in this area of the park. Today, this broad drainage provides a convenient travel route for many animals, including bear, mountain lion, mule deer, coyote, raccoon, ring-tailed cat, bobcat, badger, fox, cottontail rabbit, black-tailed jackrabbit, skunk, porcupine, and quail.

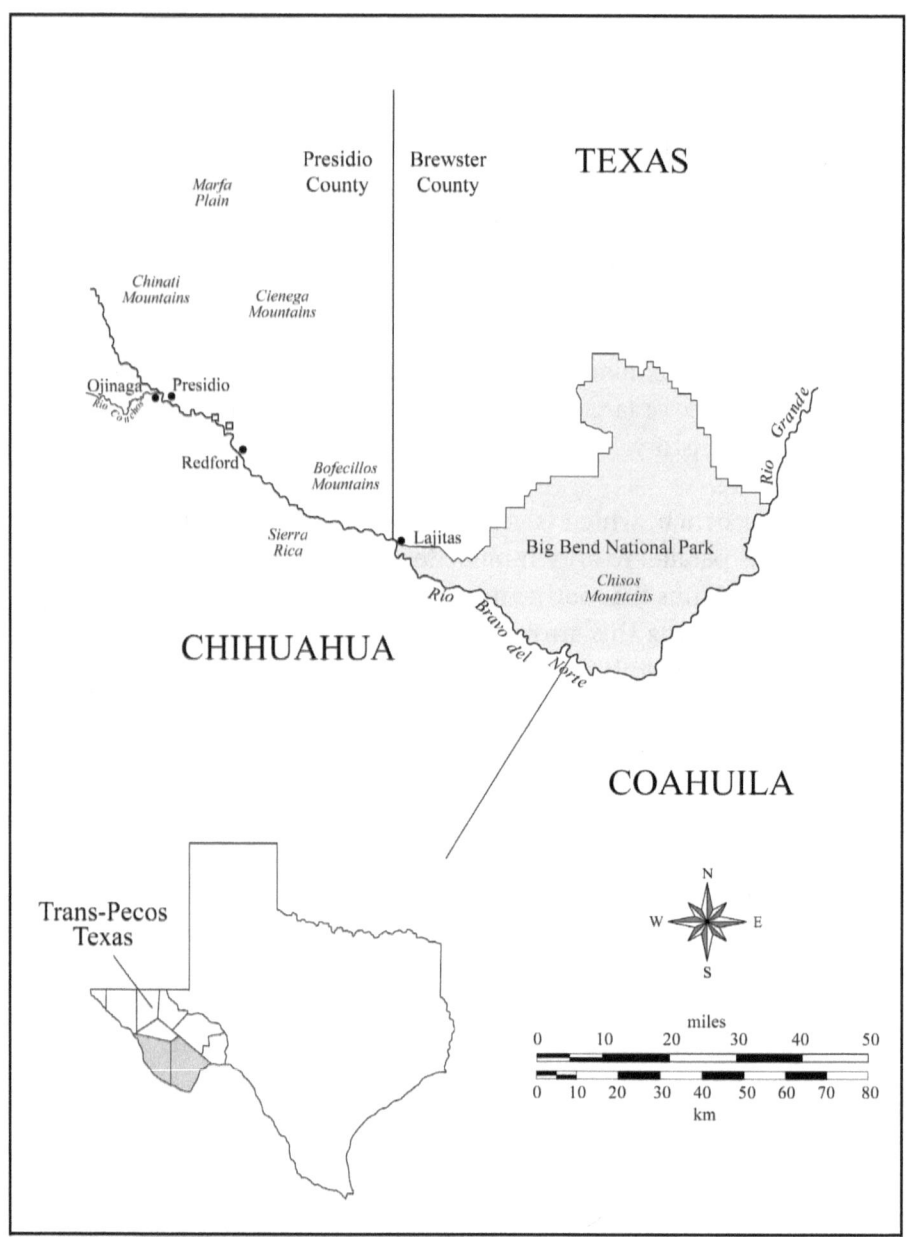

Figure 3.1. Map showing the location of Big Bend National Park in the Trans-Pecos. Courtesy Center for Big Bend Studies.

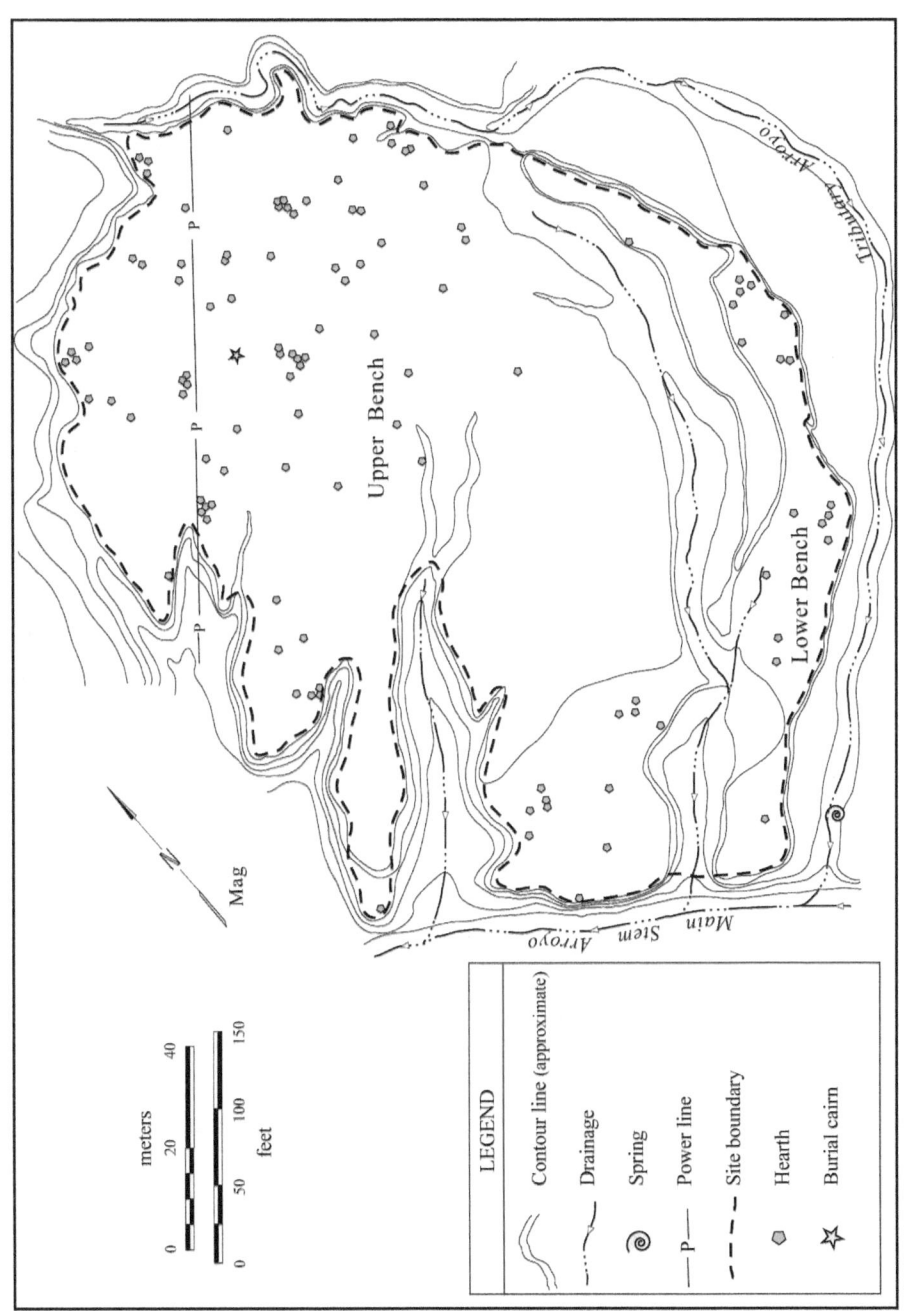

Figure 3.2. Plan view drawing of the Rough Run site. Courtesy Center for Big Bend Studies.

History of Investigations

The Rough Run site was initially discovered in 1983 by park archaeologist Thomas C. Alex while providing clearance for a spot-pole replacement along the power line that crosses the site. Alex assigned a temporary park number (BIBE-80) to the site and took notes on the cultural manifestations within the access route to the pole being replaced.

The site was formally recorded in March and April 1987 by the author during a BBNP in-house archaeological survey of access routes to power-line poles in this portion of the park. Most of the power lines in the park had been originally constructed in the mid- to late 1950s, before federal antiquity laws were in place. Thus, surveys to locate and identify significant archaeological resources along these routes were not conducted at that time.

Procedures during the project focused on recording descriptive and dimensional data for each feature, describing and drawing tools to scale, generating site maps with all features and tools plotted, and completing State of Texas archaeological site data forms. This methodology facilitated discovery of the burial reported here.

Upon casual inspection, the burial feature (F1) appeared to be one of over one hundred hearths exposed at the site. In plan view, it consisted of an intact, 1 x 1 m core surrounded by scattered stones. The stones were tabular and of a material type unique to the site, showing little or no signs of thermal alteration. In addition, two unburned Perdiz arrow-point fragments were discovered on the surface at the feature's edge. At this time the feature was recorded as a possible cairn or burial.

Testing was initiated over several days in February 1988 by Thomas C. Alex, Alan Van Valkenburg, and the author in order to determine the feature's function and integrity. This was deemed necessary because of its location along the edge of the power-line right-of-way and due to documented artifact-collecting at sites along Rough Run. Initially, a 3 x 3 m grid was established over the feature for mapping and collection purposes (fig. 3.3). Excavation was initiated at this time in the 1 x 1 m unit that bisected and included the entire western half of the feature. An arbitrary vertical datum of 100.00 m was established 5 cm above ground surface at the northwest corner of this unit. Excavation proceeded with trowels and paintbrushes, with all fill from the unit passed through nested 1/8" and 1/16" hardware cloth. Testing revealed the presence of an additional thirty-seven Perdiz arrowpoints and arrowpoint fragments interspersed in an intact, tightly constructed subterranean cairn. The cairn was within an excavated pit delineated by compacted soil and the feature stones. Due to time constraints testing was halted at a depth of 35 cm below the surface in the single test unit. The excavated area was then covered with black plastic and backfilled with feature stones and soil. At that time, only cairn stones, arrowpoints and arrowpoint fragments, and several small charcoal fragments had been uncovered. While the integrity of the feature had been established, its function remained in question.

It was not until late May 1990 that a team—then-Texas State Archeologist Robert J. Mallouf, Thomas C. Alex, and the author, with assistance from Betty L. Alex—was able to return and complete the excavation over a six-day period. The tested portion of the feature was uncovered before

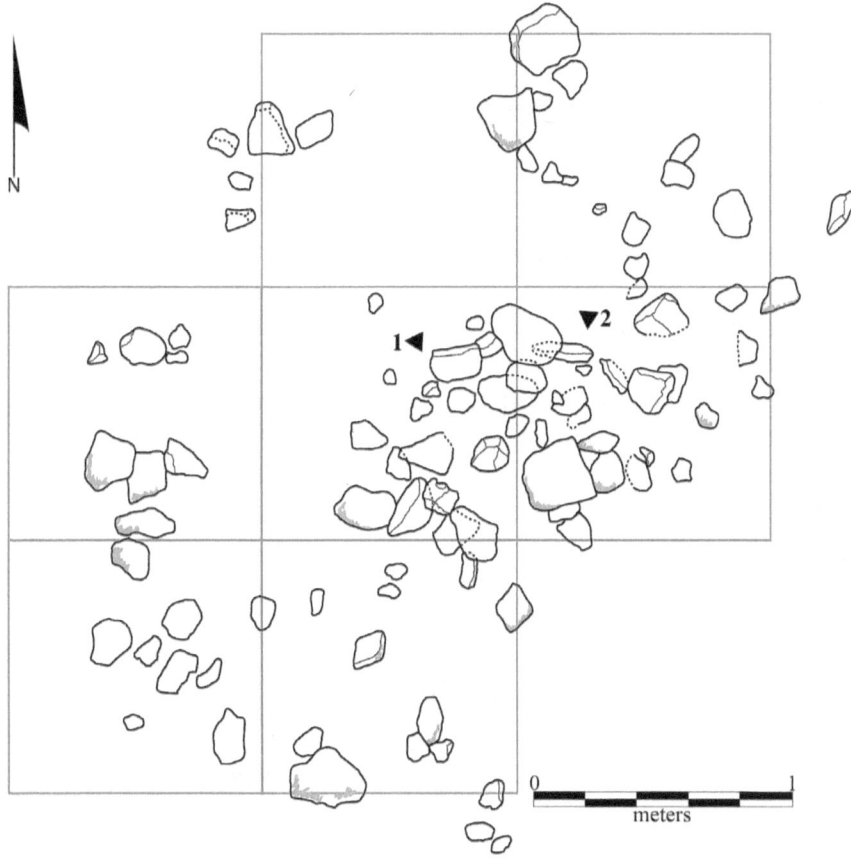

Figure 3.3. Plan view drawing of Feature 1 with superimposed grid prior to 1988 testing. Numbered triangles denote locations of surficial Perdiz arrowpoints (F1-1 and F1-2). Courtesy Center for Big Bend Studies.

excavation was initiated in the adjacent unit to the east (fig. 3.4). Once the eastern edge of the feature had been established, excavation proceeded by removing fill from the pit and plotting all artifacts and cairn stones. Nested 1/8" and 1/16" screens were again employed to search for minuscule items that might shed light on the function and/or use of the cairn. An additional thirty-three arrowpoint specimens (thirty-two Perdiz and one Harrell) were recovered from the fill between the stones composing the cairn. During this phase of the investigation, partially articulated human skeletal material was found beneath the cairn. Work on the feature ceased at this point until the National Park Service's regional office in Santa Fe was notified of the circumstances surrounding the excavation. Once the regional office granted its approval for removal of the burial, the interment was uncovered, mapped and recorded, and removed from the circular pit. A close examination of the surface in the vicinity of the burial resulted in the recovery of an additional five Perdiz arrowpoints and arrowpoint fragments. Although these specimens could not be positively related to the interment, their locations around and downslope of the feature suggest a possible association.

The author visited the site annually from 1990 to 1995, recovering an additional ten Perdiz arrowpoints from the surface immediately around and downslope of the feature. One of these was complete, the remainder fragmentary. Interestingly, one of these fragmentary specimens (F1–73) was found to fit onto two fragmentary specimens (F1–13 and F1–15) recovered from the cairn during the 1988 testing. Thus, a total of seventy-three individual arrowpoint specimens were directly associated with the interment, and an additional fourteen specimens from the surface around the feature were possibly related.

Description of the Burial

When first discovered, the feature appeared to have been dismantled to ground surface. The tabular stones that composed its top were scattered up to 2 m from the central core in loose groupings. Soil buildup around the dislodged stones suggested the disturbance was not recent. Approximately sixty stones had been removed from the top of the cairn, leaving an intact core measuring about 1 m in diameter. When intact, the feature was probably mounded 20–30 cm above ground surface.

The interment was placed within an oval to circular pit that measured 1.0 x 1.4 m in plan view on the surface and tapered down to about

Figure 3.4. View of upper portion of burial pit with 1988 test unit (foreground) and upper surface of adjacent unit (1990) exposed. Scale points north. Courtesy Center for Big Bend Studies.

50 x 50 cm at its base. At approximately 10–15 cm below the surface, the north, east, and west edges of the pit angle abruptly inward before tapering downward to the base of the pit at an elevation of 99.17 m or 83 cm below ground surface. The soil in this portion of the site is extremely compact and must have been very difficult to excavate with primitive tools—it is possible that water might have been placed in the pit to facilitate soil removal. There were no digging-stick or other discernible marks on the sides of the pit.

The human remains were placed in the pit before cairn stones were added. The skeletal material was incomplete. However, each limb was intact with almost all associated skeletal elements articulated (i.e., arm and hand bones and leg and foot bones were in anatomically correct positions). The mandible and skull were present, but separated. Torso elements in the interment consisted of both clavicles, the upper portion of the sternum (manubrium), the atlas vertebrae, and the right first rib (Colby and Steele 1995).

Skeletal material was recovered between the elevations of 99.23 m and 99.68 m. The arms were apparently placed in the pit first, flexed, lying roughly horizontal, and positioned together on the western side of the pit. Soil appears to have been placed on top of the arms before the flexed legs were placed on the east and west sides of the pit at vertical angles. The easternmost knee was pointing up and the western one down, so that one foot was located along the north wall well above the base of the pit and the other near the southern edge of the pit just above its base. The lower foot was covered by the only stream-worn stone found within the interment. This large cobble, measuring 13 x 20 x 27 cm, was completely rounded and unlike any of the stones in the above cairn. The skull was placed immediately above the northern edge of this cobble in the central portion of the pit, between the two angled legs (fig. 3.5). The facial portion of the skull was pointing upward at a slight angle, facing the north-northwest. The mandible was detached and positioned approximately 15 cm north-northeast of the skull near the northern edge of the pit. It rested on edge perpendicular to the skull.

Most of the cairn was placed above the skeletal material, between approximate elevations of 99.36 and 100.00 m, although the lowest stones were below the skull, mandible, and upper ends of the flexed legs, but above skeletal material in the southern portion of the pit. After the bones had been interred, it appears that soil was added to the pit to provide support for the cairn. Special attention had been focused on the

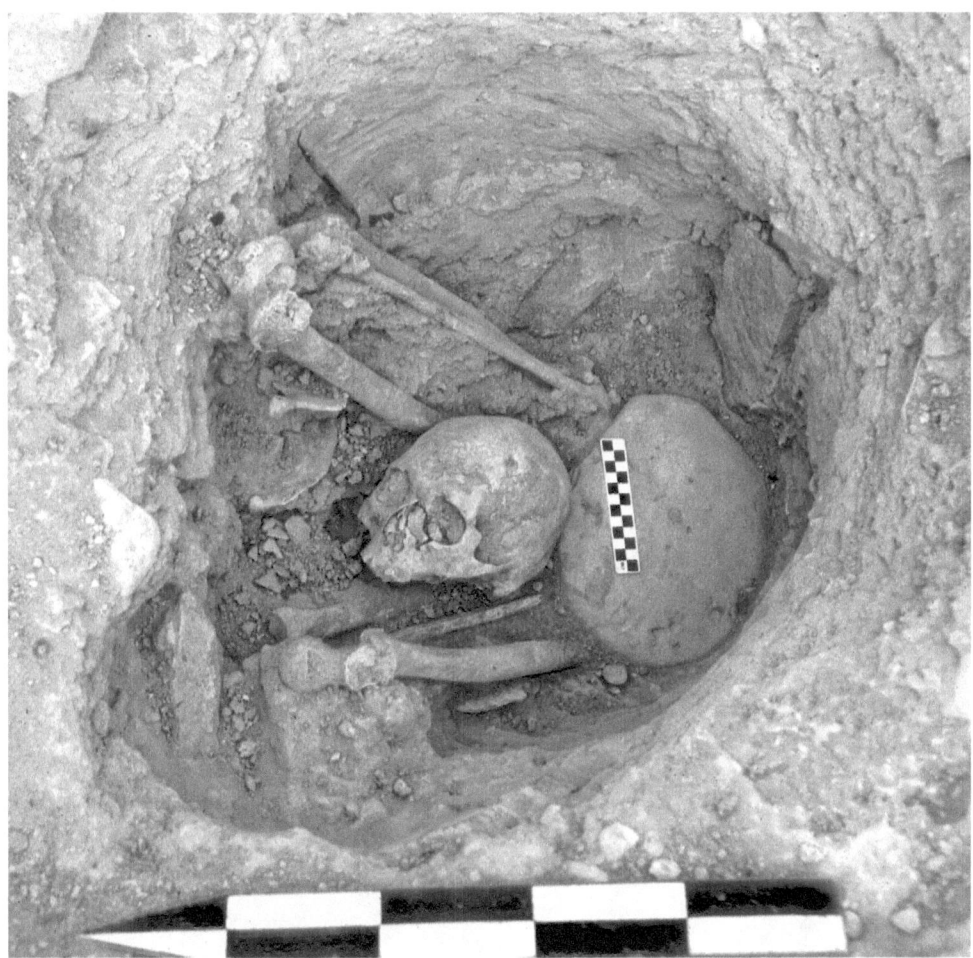

Figure 3.5. Photograph of the burial. Note position of the skull and mandible between the legs and immediately north of the large rounded cobble. Courtesy Center for Big Bend Studies.

skull, as four thin, tabular stones were angled over it, creating a boxlike cover, undoubtedly providing extra protection. Above these stones the cairn consisted of appreciably larger stones and smaller, chinklike stones. Most of the tabular stones had been procured at a nearby dike outcrop and appeared to be unaltered before placement in the cairn. Only a few of the cairn stones had been thermally altered (i.e., discolored and fractured from direct exposure to heat) before being placed in the pit. These stones were probably removed from nearby hearths, and were possibly added to the cairn to fill specific holes formed during its construction.

Over three hundred mostly tabular stones composed the tightly constructed cairn that dominated the upper 60 cm of the burial pit. The largest stones (n=12) measured 5 x 17 x 30 cm and were positioned within the middle to upper portion of the cairn. The majority of stones were medium-sized, roughly 5 x 15 x 20 cm. Numerous smaller stones were positioned among the larger stones, in some cases filling in gaps and in others lining the pit. Although the entire pit was not lined, a few portions had stones nestled snugly against the walls, suggestive of intentional placement. A single vertical slab, measuring approximately 4 x 20 x 20 cm, was positioned in the south-central portion of the cairn at an elevation between 99.70 and 99.90 m (fig. 3.6). This was the only large stone with a vertical orientation within the cairn and was most likely placed deliberately, perhaps with symbolism similar to that of the modern-day headstone. This author has observed one other prehistoric burial with a similar stone positioned above the interment, and this practice was apparently fairly widespread (Robert J. Mallouf, personal communication 1990).

Figure 3.6. View of cairn interior. Note vertical slab in south central portion of pit. Scale points north. Courtesy Center for Big Bend Studies.

Arrowpoints and arrowpoint fragments were placed within the cairn as it was being constructed. Thirty arrowpoint specimens were recovered in situ, with the remainder discovered dislodged from their original context within the pit, or in the screen. The lowest in situ specimen was found only 16 cm above the base of the pit at 99.33 m, just below the bulk of the cairn. However, about 66 percent of the points and point fragments were recovered from the upper 30 cm of the cairn (99.70–100.00 m), and 35 percent of the total, from the upper 10 cm (99.90–100.00 m). Surprisingly, no two of the in situ specimens were found adjacent to one another. They were instead scattered among the cairn stones above the skeletal material.

Almost all of the arrowpoints appear to have been cursorily or perhaps casually placed within the cairn. However, one finely chipped, extremely long, thin point (F1–58) was positioned in such a way as to suggest intentional placement by the executors of the burial. This delicate specimen, measuring 59 mm in length with a maximum thickness of 2.5 mm, was vertically oriented with the blade tip pointing straight downward. Interestingly, the specimen pointed to the south-central portion of the large stream-worn cobble that covered the right foot and served as a pedestal for the back of the skull. The top of this specimen was at an elevation of 99.66 m, whereas the top of the cobble was at 99.38 m.

Other cultural items recovered from the fill within the cairn were three pieces of debitage and seven small charcoal chunks. One of the debitage pieces was recovered from the surface of the feature, while the other two were found within the upper 5 cm. Like the arrowpoints, the charcoal samples were widely dispersed within the cairn from 99.38 to 99.80 m.

Description of the Assemblage

A total of 76 stone artifacts, 125 skeletal elements, and 7 small charcoal samples were recovered from the Rough Run burial. Analysis of the stone artifacts was completed by the author. Human bone from the burial was initially examined by Thomas C. Alex, then underwent a more detailed analysis at the Physical Anthropology Laboratory at Texas A&M University.

Arrowpoints (73 specimens)
Based on morphological attributes, the arrowpoints recovered from the Rough Run burial are separated into two categories, Perdiz and Harrell,

with the latter represented by a single specimen. Analytical data for these items are presented below.

Perdiz (72 specimens)

Perdiz arrowpoints are characterized by triangular blades with usually straight edges, well-barbed shoulders, and contracting stems (Suhm and Jelks 1962, 283–84). The seventy-two Perdiz specimens in the assemblage consist of complete as well as fragmentary arrowpoints. Complete or nearly complete specimens are classified as Perdiz based on morphological attributes commonly recognized for the point, such as contracting stems and barbed shoulders, while the more fragmentary specimens are classified as such based on other factors. Specimens classified as stems are placed within the Perdiz type due to their distinctive shape and workmanship, attributes that are readily apparent when these specimens are compared with the more complete Perdiz specimens in the assemblage. Similarly, the blade fragments are classified as Perdiz based on the presence of original flake-scar remnants on one face—a common Perdiz attribute, especially in the Big Bend region.

An attempt was made to refit fragmentary specimens from the assemblage. This effort resulted in connecting fifteen fragments to form seven individual arrowpoints, the majority of which are still incomplete (fig. 3.7). Three specimens were connected to form one fragmentary point, while the other fits consisted of two specimens for each arrowpoint.

After these fits were made, the assemblage consisted of sixty-four individual Perdiz points and point fragments (fig. 3.8), of which only three are complete, including one of the fitted specimens. An additional thirty-seven are relatively complete, just missing barbs or small portions of the blade tips, while the remainder are missing more significant portions. Ten specimens lack stems or large portions of their stems, with one of these also missing an appreciable portion of the blade. The remaining Perdiz specimens consist of eight stem fragments, four distal blade fragments, and two barb fragments. The fragments missing from the Perdiz assemblage may have been either carried off by whoever originally disturbed the cairn, or redeposited by sheetwash following that disturbance. However, it is possible that some of the missing pieces were never interred.

There are 116 fractures exhibited on the sixty-one broken Perdiz points. The fracture locations on these specimens are almost equally divided among the barbs, stems, and blades, with thirty-six having one or two barb breaks, twenty-nine having one or two stem breaks, and thirty-four

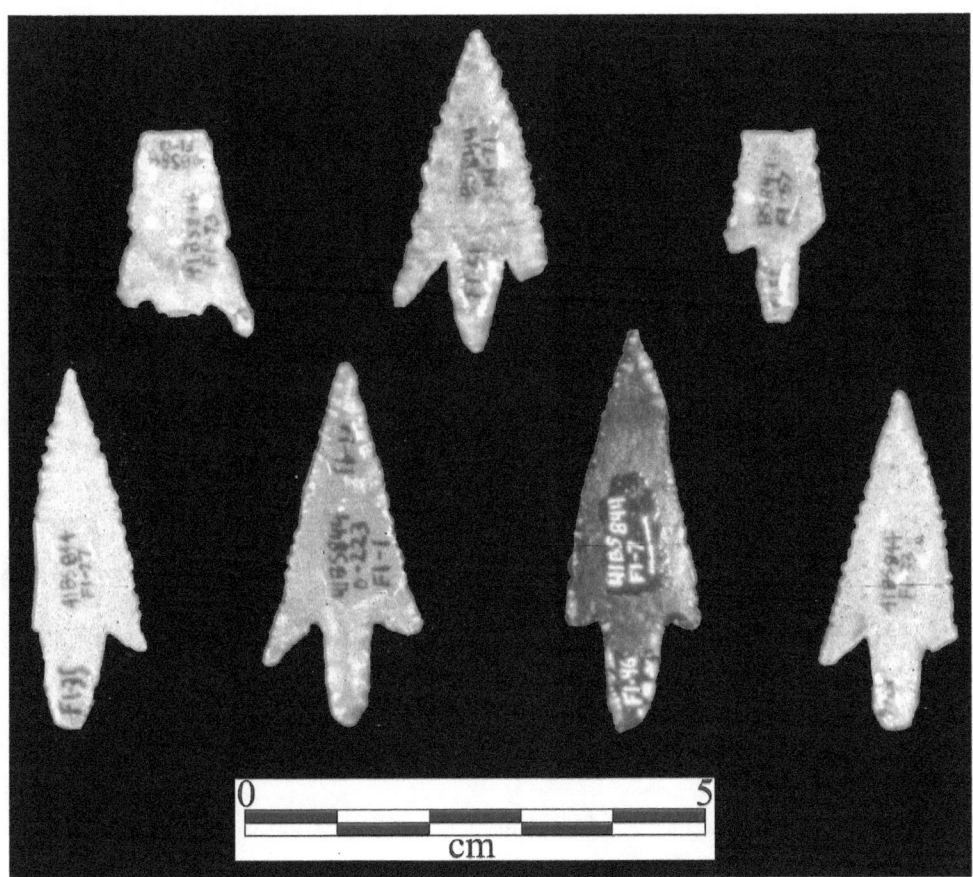

Figure 3.7. Refitted Perdiz specimens. Courtesy Center for Big Bend Studies.

having one or more blade breaks. Snap fractures account for two-thirds (67 percent) of the total. All broken surfaces that were fitted together appear to be snap fractures, which are characterized by relatively flat or slightly rolled breaking planes. Hinge fractures, which are characterized by obviously rolled breaking planes, account for the remaining 33 percent of the breaks. Interestingly, only a single specimen (F1–44) exhibits evidence of an impact fracture—a specific type of hinge fracture—which left only a slightly broken blade tip that allowed continued use of the specimen. The high incidence of snap fractures in the assemblage, in conjunction with the presence of snap fractures on all of the fitted surfaces, may indicate that some of the points were intentionally broken during the mortuary proceeding, possibly by hand. Since provenience of the fitted specimens does not appear to indicate post-burial fractures

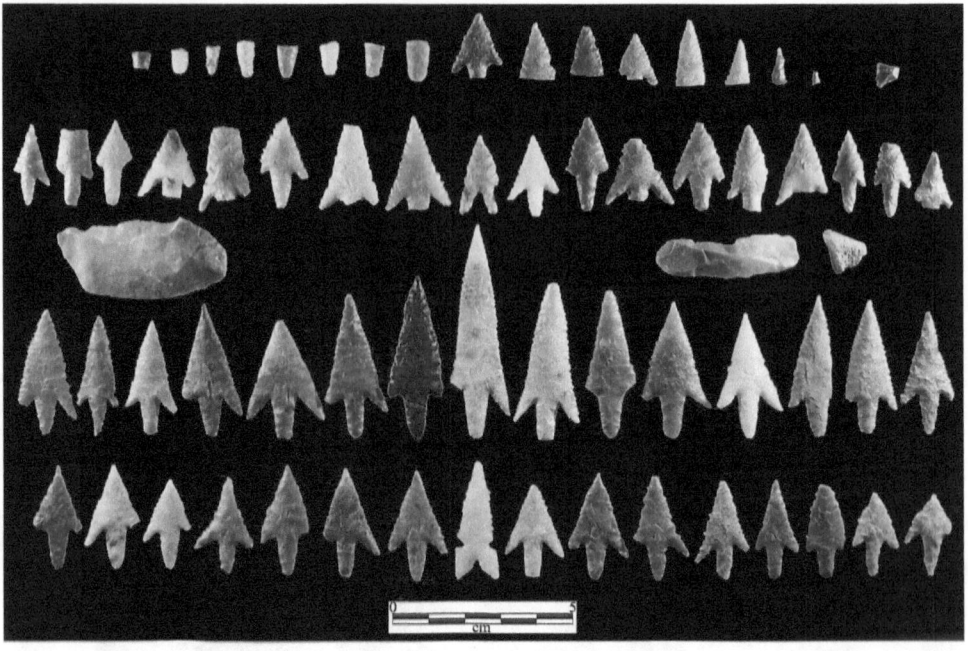

Figure 3.8. Burial assemblage consisting of sixty-four Perdiz arrowpoints and point fragments, one Harrell arrow point, and three pieces of debitage.

within the cairn, it seems reasonable to suggest ritual breakage prior to placement within the cairn.

The largest specimen in the assemblage (F1–58), as previously noted, may have been intentionally placed in the cairn to point down at a portion of the interment. No other points with a vertical orientation were uncovered within the cairn. The delicate workmanship on this specimen, especially its blade edges and distal tip, are particularly striking. The blade edges are finely serrated, which probably required a much narrower pressure flaker than was normally used. Serrations like these were not observed on any of the other specimens in the assemblage. Similarly, the distal tip is the only specimen within the assemblage that has alternate beveling and is extremely fragile. One barb is missing, which is probably a result of either a mishap during the manufacturing process or ritual breakage. The elongated and correspondingly thin nature of this point precludes its use as an everyday weapon. It seems probable that this specimen was never used and that it was a special offering intentionally placed within the cairn.

One of the specimens classified as Perdiz (F1–50) has been extensively reworked into a basally notched point. The point appears to have been refashioned after one of the barbs broke. The stem was "whittled" down to approximate the width and thickness of the intact barb, thus creating a usable arrowpoint from one that would not have functioned as well. A small protrusion along the lateral edge indicates the location of the broken barb. Further evidence supporting classification of this specimen as a Perdiz point is provided by a bifacial stem with a lenticular cross section and remnants of an original flake facet on one face of a plano-convex blade, attributes found on the majority of specimens in the Rough Run assemblage.

Another twenty of the Perdiz specimens show definite evidence of having been reworked, and an additional twenty-three were probably reworked. Some have blade edge angles that change abruptly, especially near the tip, while others have very long stems in relation to short blades. Still others have very short and/or asymmetrical barbs. Several exhibit more than one of these attributes, suggesting that a number of the specimens within the cairn were part of an active tool kit when buried.

The wide variety of stone material types and colors represented within the Perdiz assemblage is particularly striking when viewing the collection as a whole. Most of the material types are typically observed at sites within BBNP and, to a lesser extent, the Big Bend region. Various cherts, Burro Mesa "silicified tuff," jasperoid, silicified wood, agate, and chalcedony are all represented. There is a high occurrence of material from the Burro Mesa quarry within the assemblage, most probably a reflection of the relative proximity of the Rough Run site to the quarry area (ca. 6.0 km). This tuff outcrops within and adjacent to Apache Canyon, a small but steep-walled north-south trending canyon cut into the western midsection of Burro Mesa. The Burro Mesa quarry site is quite extensive, covering approximately 20 hectares, and materials from it are found at numerous sites in the park, especially those on the western side. The other stone materials represented in the Perdiz assemblage outcrop at a number of locations within and outside of the park. Of particular note is a single point (F1–59) made from a distinctive silicified wood exposed about 650 m west of the Rough Run site.

Unlike the Perdiz arrowpoints from the Las Haciendas burial, where Mallouf (1987, 25) was able to separate the 180 Perdiz specimens present into ten morphological groupings containing twenty-six varieties, the Perdiz artifacts in the Rough Run burial assemblage show a remarkable amount of continuity. This continuity suggests that a single, or perhaps only a few knappers were responsible for the manufacture of the points in the cairn. Similar attributes consist of cross section, stem shape, stem edge treatment, blade flaking, and maximum thickness. The majority of the arrowpoints (fifty-two of sixty-four) have stems with lenticular cross sections and blades with plano-convex cross sections. Four of the anomalous points have lenticular blades, seven have plano-convex stems, and a single specimen has a "twisted" cross section. Stem shape and treatment also are very uniform, as sixty of the sixty-four points have slightly contracting stems (two have straight to contracting stems and two have bulbous elongate to contracting stems) and fairly parallel stem edges. Stem margins have been uniformly smoothed on most of the specimens, with the "teeth" or small protrusions along these edges apparently removed through careful flaking. Blade flaking is still another attribute that is similar throughout the assemblage. The majority of blades have plano-convex cross sections as a result of extensive flaking on one face and minor trimming on the opposite face. The extensively flaked face typically has fine, parallel flake scars that are yet another "signature" suggestive of a single or small number of knappers. While the above attributes involve visual observations and some degree of subjectivity, the maximum thicknesses of the points is quantifiable. The mean maximum thickness of the fifty measurable specimens is 2.46 mm, with a range between 1.66 and 3.27 mm, a smaller mean and much tighter range than in the Las Haciendas Perdiz assemblage (mean of 2.86 mm and range between 1.6 and 4.2 mm) (Mallouf 1987, 49). Since these various data sets indicate striking continuity within the Perdiz points from the Rough Run burial, it seems plausible to suggest that a single or very few knappers were responsible for their production.

Harrell (1 specimen)

Harrell points were originally discussed and illustrated by Krieger (1946, 115–16) in his presentation of archaeological manifestations at the Harrell site located on the Osage Plains of North Texas. Although a formal name was not offered for any of the specimens at that time, Krieger (1946, 115) noted that 37 of the 192 points recovered from the site are triangular, with "side notches plus a notch in the base." The type name "Harrell" was first proposed by Suhm et al. (1954, 500) in their publication on archaeological types in Texas. They suggested an age between AD 1100 and AD 1500 for the type, but made no distinction between basal-notched points and those without this attribute. Bell (1958) was the first to propose separate type names for the basally notched and unnotched varieties, with Harrell applied to the specimens with the basal notch and Washita to those without it. In Texas, the Harrell point has been associated with the Antelope Creek, Henrietta, and Wylie foci, and in Oklahoma, with the Washita River, Custer, and Optima foci (Bell 1958). The point is common in the Panhandle, Rolling Plains, and Southern Plains regions of Texas, and occurs more sporadically in the Trans-Pecos (Turner and Hester 1985, 178; Prewitt 1995, 109). This point has a particularly wide distribution on the Great Plains "from northern Texas to Canada, east to the Mississippi Valley, and west to the Southwest, always associated with agriculture and pottery-making" (Suhm and Jelks 1962, 275). Harrell arrowpoints are characterized by a triangular shape, straight to slightly convex edges, small side notches from one-fourth to one-half the distance from the base to the tip, and a notch in the base (Bell 1958, 30).

The Harrell arrowpoint (F1–65) in the Rough Run burial assemblage is complete, with a length of 32.9 mm, a maximum width of 12.3 mm, and a maximum thickness of 2.7 mm. It is side and basally notched. Made of chalcedony, it has a lenticular cross section and blade edges that are slightly to moderately serrated. Unlike the Perdiz specimens in the assemblage, there are no flake-scar remnants on either face that can be assigned to an earlier stage in the manufacturing process. While the basic dimensions of this specimen and its general morphology fit well within the Harrell type, the shape of the basal area is somewhat unique. The basal edge on both sides of the notch angle upward, giving the basal "ears" a shape similar to those on a number of Toyah arrowpoints (Turner and Hester 1985, 193). Since the length of this specimen precludes placement within the Toyah type, it is classified as Harrell.

Debitage (3 specimens)
Three pieces of debitage were recovered from the upper 5 cm of the burial cairn. Two, F1–74 and F1–76, exhibit evidence of use as expediency tools, while the other specimen (F1–75) is undistinguished. All utilized edges on these specimens are strongly to slightly convex.

Skeletal Material (125 specimens)
Skeletal material recovered includes a detached skull and mandible, four articulated appendages, both clavicles, the manubrium, the atlas vertebrae, and the right first rib (Colby and Steele 1995). Since a number of skeletal elements were missing from the inventory, principally those of

the thoracic and pelvic regions, only tentative sex and age determinations can be suggested. Based on the robustness of the recovered elements the interred individual is thought to be male. Specifically, the relatively complete skull is classified as gracile, but contains more malelike features than female, including the eye orbit and its supraorbital margin, the supraorbital torus, parietal bossing, and the gonial angle of the mandible. The association of stone projectile points in the burial seems to support this conclusion (see Damas 1972, 43; Yarrow 1988, 4, 6). An age assessment of thirty-five years or older at the time of death was made using various analyses: post-cranial bone analysis, long bone and clavicular epiphysis analysis, dental analysis, and cranial suture fusion analysis (Colby and Steele 1995).

Stature estimation was determined by employing several different methods: one pioneered by Genoves (1967) using Mesoamerican males and another developed by Trotter (1970) comparing Mexican and Mongoloid males. Measurements from the femora, tibiae, and a combination of both bones, were used to suggest a stature for this individual between 164.7 cm and 173.24 cm (Colby and Steele 1995).

The Rough Run burial contained only nine teeth, the remainder apparently lost prior to death. The teeth recovered were extremely affected by wear, attrition, and alveolar resorption, with five also exhibiting caries or tooth decay. The state of the dentition may be related to a high carbohydrate diet, a high grit diet, and/or the use of the back teeth for shredding and holding fibrous plant material (Colby and Steele 1995).

The skeletal material revealed few signs of chronic health problems. However, degenerative joint disease and osteoporosis, age-related conditions, were noted by the researchers. The extent of degenerative joint disease is mild to moderate and was observed as minor lipping and osteophytic action of the periarticular surfaces on numerous bones from the burial. This condition probably manifested as an irritation rather than a severe limitation. The long bones had limited evidence of osteoporosis, which causes a decreased density of compact bone. Although there were no signs of significant injury, trauma, or medical disorders, the right patella (kneecap) is thought to have been damaged by a fall or hyperextension of the knee and the first left metatarsophalangeal (toe) joint displays the early stages of fusion (Colby and Steele 1995).

Although no ethnic affinity can be determined due to the paucity of material recovered, the skull and teeth exhibit attributes that have been observed on other skeletal material from the region. The skull is dolichocranic, that is, long and narrow. This trait has been associated with human skeletal material from West Texas for many years (Oetteking 1930, 342; Pearce 1937, 8; Woodbury 1937, 12; Neumann 1952, 16). The recovered dentition of the buried individual mirrors the dental condition commonly seen in Trans-Pecos skeletal remains (Goldstein 1948; Skinner et al. 1980, 5–6; Stodder 1989, 170). Stature estimation and robusticity are other aspects that conform well to data from Trans-Pecos populations. Therefore, while the individual interred at the Rough Run site cannot be placed within a specific ethnic group, the remains have several characteristics that are commonly observed in skeletal material from the Trans-Pecos (Colby and Steele 1995). Noting the unique bone assemblage and the presence of tiny cut marks on the heads of both femora (upper leg bones), Colby and Steele (1995) suggested that the Rough Run burial was a secondary interment. They hypothesized that the skull and appendages were selected for secondary burial, and that the presence of the clavicles, manubrium, and the right first rib may have been accidental, that these were possibly included as a result of strong ligamental attachments from the humerus across the front of the upper torso. Four cut marks were noted on the left femur perpendicular to the neck axis near the femoral head, while six or more similar marks were found on the right femur. These marks were probably a result of severing ligaments and muscular attachments while removing the legs from the torso (Colby and Steele 1995).

Radiocarbon Data
Seven charcoal samples were recovered from the cairn and burial pit during excavation. All were quite small, although several consisted of adjacent chunks. Two of the samples (C14 samples 6 and 7) were submitted to Beta Analytic, Inc., in Miami, Florida, for radiocarbon analysis by accelerator mass spectrometry (AMS). Sample 6, consisting of four separate charcoal fragments, was recovered about 15 cm south of the skull at an elevation of 99.38 m. This sample was beneath the bulk of the cairn, near the southern edge of the burial pit. Sample 7, consisting of three charcoal fragments, was recovered about 5 cm north of the skull at an elevation of 99.41 m. Radiocarbon data from these samples is provided in table 3.1.

Table 3.1. Results of Radiocarbon Dating of the Rough Run Cairn Burial

Lab. No.	Field Sample No.	Material Dated	$^{13}C/^{12}C$ Ratio	Conventional Radiocarbon Age	Calibrated Date AD (2-Sigma)*–Probability Distribution (.95)
Beta-063769	FS6	Charcoal	(-25)	400±60	Cal. AD 1420–1640
Beta-056189	FS7	Charcoal	(-25)	440±70	Cal. AD 1400–1640

Radiocarbon dating by Beta Analytic Inc., Miami, Florida
*Calibrations based on Talma and Vogel 1993 and Stuiver et al. 1998

Discussion

The Rough Run cairn burial is one of only two Perdiz-bearing interments reported from the Trans-Pecos and adjacent area of northern Mexico. Although single Perdiz-like specimens have been recovered from burials in the Lower Pecos (Turpin 1982) and Southeast Texas regions (Robert Rogers, personal communication 1999), this marks the first scientifically excavated interment containing abundant Perdiz points in the state. It has provided a wealth of mortuary and other data for a cultural group that used the Perdiz arrowpoint in the Big Bend region of Texas.

Morphological Similarities of Perdiz Points from the Cairn

The Perdiz points recovered from the cairn have a number of similarities that, when looked at as a whole and compared with other Perdiz assemblages, are suggestive of a single or perhaps only a few knappers. The cross section, stem shape, stem edge treatment, blade flaking, and maximum thickness of the Perdiz points have remarkable continuity. Comparing these and other attributes from the Rough Run and Las Haciendas Perdiz assemblages allows for a better understanding of the significance of this continuity.

While Mallouf (1987, 25) used inspectional sorting to separate the 180 Perdiz specimens from the Las Haciendas burial into ten morphological groupings containing twenty-six varieties, no such division was attempted with the Rough Run specimens, due to general homogeneity within the assemblage (except for portions obviously reworked). Metric data also support this apparent disparity in specimen shape between the two assemblages, as a tighter range is indicated by most of the categories examined (see table 3.2 for a comparison of these data). Of note is the maximum thickness category, which is perhaps the most significant indicator of the skill of a particular maker and, as such, a good attribute by which to distinguish individual knappers. It seems that thinning a small biface, or uniface for that matter, to a certain thickness may be part of an unconscious effort of the maker that corresponds to his capabilities. This aspect of the production process is extremely difficult, easily separating the craftsman from the less talented. Thus, this attribute may allow distinction between individual craftsmen.

Comprehensive metric analyses have been performed on Perdiz assemblages at the Hinojosa site in South Texas (Black 1986), the Las Haciendas site in northeastern Chihuahua (Mallouf 1987), and the Buckhollow site in West Central Texas (Johnson 1994). Comparison of these data with metric data from the Rough Run Perdiz points allows for a few observations (see table 3.3). The Rough Run points are generally shorter than those from Buckhollow or Las Haciendas, but are longer than the Hinojosa specimens. Since an appreciable number of the Rough Run specimens are reworked, they probably had lengths similar to those from Buckhollow and Las Haciendas when newly made, whereas the relatively short Hinojosa points are more than likely a result of the scarcity of resources on the lower Gulf Coastal Plain where the site is located. Since most of the lithics at that site had to be carried in, it is reasonable that conservation of this valuable material translated into smaller forms, or shorter lengths, widths, stem lengths, and stem widths. Except for the Hinojosa specimens, maximum widths are relatively similar, with the Las Haciendas specimens being the widest. The Hinojosa specimens have the greatest maximum thicknesses, while those from Rough Run are the thinnest by an appreciable margin. Buckhollow stems are the widest, while those from Las Haciendas are the longest. The stems from the Rough Run specimens are shorter than both the Las Haciendas and the Buckhollow stems, but appreciably longer than those from Hinojosa; however, the Rough Run stems are the narrowest from these four data sets. The mean weight of the Rough Run specimens is much less than the specimen weights from Buckhollow and Las Haciendas, and even less than the weights of the Hinojosa specimens. Since the lengths and widths of the Rough Run specimens are not vastly different from those of the Buckhollow and Las Haciendas specimens, it seems that the weight differences are primarily a reflection of the maximum thickness, or relative thinness of the points.

It should be noted that Perdiz points from the Buckhollow and Hinojosa sites were recovered during excavation of campsites and probably represent multiple occupations and numerous knappers. Conversely, the

TABLE 3.2. METRIC VARIABLES FOR PERDIZ POINTS FROM THE LAS HACIENDAS AND ROUGH RUN CAIRN BURIALS

Site	Length		Max. Width		Max. Thickness		Stem Length		Stem Width		Weight	
	Range	Mean	Range	Mean	Range	Mean	Range	Mean	Range	Mean	Range	Mean
Las Haciendas cairn burial (Mallouf 1987)	19–52	33.437	7–25	17.157	1.6–4.2	2.863	5.9–22.9	12.97	4.4–7.7	6.046	0.4–1.9	1.054
Rough Run cairn burial	22–59	31.613	10–22	15.214	1.7–3.3	2.456	6.4–12.6	10.215	3.7–7.0	5.466	0.4–1.3	0.785

Note: Weight is in g; all other measurements are in mm

TABLE 3.3. METRIC VARIABLES FOR PERDIZ POINTS FROM FOUR SITES: BUCK-HOLLOW OF WEST-CENTRAL TEXAS, LAS HACIENDAS OF EASTERN CHIHUAHUA, HINOJOSA OF SOUTH TEXAS, AND ROUGH RUN OF TRANS-PECOS TEXAS

Site	Length		Max. Width		Max. Thickness		Stem Length		Stem Width		Weight	
	No.	Mean	No.	Mean	No.	Mean	No.	Mean	No.	Mean	No.	Mean
Buckhollow (Johnson 1994)	22	34.846	42	16.369	65	2.683	44	10.234	63	6.665	17	1.321
Las Haciendas cairn burial (Mallouf 1987)	117	33.437	86	17.157	169	2.863	126	12.97	167	6.046	61	1.054
Hinojosa (Black 1986)	34	24.235	34	14.441	34	2.979	34	7.782	34	5.909	34	0.824
Rough Run cairn burial	34	31.613	16	15.214	50	2.456	38	10.215	49	5.466	21	0.785

Note: Weight is in g; all other measurements are in mm.

points from the Las Haciendas and Rough Run burials are from single events; thus it may be inappropriate to compare metric data from these points with data from points manufactured through time by numerous makers. Also of note in the assemblage from Las Haciendas, where an adolescent was buried, is the morphological variability of the points. This suggests a number of point manufacturers contributing to the grave goods. Since the Rough Run assemblage contains a high degree of continuity suggestive of a single or only a few knappers, comparison with the Las Haciendas points also may yield ambiguous results. However, at present the Las Haciendas material, because of its location and context, provides the most useful data for comparison with the Rough Run assemblage.

Temporal Affiliations of the Cairn

While evidence of fire within or adjacent to a Native American burial is not unusual or uncommon (Yarrow 1988; Cloud and Smith 1993), scattered charcoal within the Rough Run interment does raise a few questions. Of primary concern is whether or not the recovered charcoal is contemporaneous with the burial. Did it come from a mortuary fire adjacent to the interment, or could the charcoal have been accidentally placed within the burial pit as soil was added to protect the skeletal material? It is impossible to answer this question confidently without a bone collagen date; however, the overlapping ranges of the two dates (AD 1400–1640) do fall securely within AD 1200–1750—the period associated with Perdiz points in the state (Prewitt 1983; Black 1986; Mallouf 1987).

Radiocarbon dates for Perdiz-bearing components have been reported previously from five sites in the Big Bend region—the Polvo site (41PS21), the Cielo Bravo site (41PS52), the Alamo Springs site (41BS673), the Persimmon Gap site (41BS609), and site 41BS706-B. The La Junta phase is represented by the Polvo site dates, while the dates from the Cielo Bravo and Alamo Springs sites were taken from Cielo complex associations. The Persimmon Gap site and site 41BS706-B may have been affiliated with the Cielo complex, although neither site had the stacked-stone house foundations usually associated with that cultural manifestation. The highest confidence level (93 percent) for these dates (Stuiver and Becker 1986) indicates a time span between AD 1219 and AD 1681 (Mallouf 1999, 79). Thus, the two dates from the Rough Run site fall comfortably within the range established in the Big Bend for components associated with Perdiz points.

Cultural Affiliation of the Cairn
In the Texas Big Bend region, Perdiz arrowpoints are affiliated with the La Junta phase of the Bravo Valley aspect (Kelley et al. 1940) and the Cielo complex (Mallouf 1999). The La Junta phase is a cultural construct for the agricultural villages located along the confluence of the Rio Grande and Río Conchos, while the Cielo complex represents hunter-gatherers who, based on their tool kits, were most likely bison hunters (Mallouf 1999, 81). Cielo complex peoples built distinctive circular to oval structures on elevated landforms throughout the Big Bend, and it has been suggested that other open sites and rock-shelters (hunting-gathering locales) with Perdiz points may also be affiliated with activities of the complex (Mallouf 1999, 65–66).

The Cielo complex material culture is similar to that found in the agricultural villages of the La Junta phase, even though the presumed economies as well as the structures from these two cultural manifestations are completely different. While the similar tool kits are suggestive of a cultural link, the nature of the relationship is unknown at this time.

It is possible that Cielo complex peoples were the nomadic cultural group referred to as the Jumanos by the early Spanish explorers (Mallouf 1999, 85). This group apparently hunted bison on the Southern Plains and traded with numerous groups, including the La Junta agriculturalists (Kelley 1952, 277). Of note in this discussion is the fact that the Cielo complex has a lithic assemblage that is similar to assemblages from the Toyah phase of Central Texas and the Toyah horizon of South Texas. Both the Toyah cultures and the Cielo complex "contain lithic assemblages characterized by Perdiz points, beveled knives, triangular end scrapers, flake perforators, core hammerstones, sequence-flake and blade-core reduction strategies, and conical cores—in other words, assemblages that are indicative of a Plains bison-hunter technology and tool kit" (Mallouf 1999, 77).

The presence of the single Harrell arrowpoint within the assemblage also suggests contact with groups from the Southern Plains, as Harrell points typically are a more dominant type in that area (Prewitt 1995, 109). Although a firm connection between the Cielo complex and the Jumanos has not been made, both Spanish accounts and archaeological evidence suggest a relationship.

In light of the above discussion, it should be noted that surficial lithic artifacts recovered from the Rough Run site include Perdiz points, beveled knives, triangular end scrapers, and a single flake perforator. These were recovered from the general vicinity of the interment and may have been lost or discarded by the group responsible for the burial. The location of the Rough Run site is indicative of a hunter-gatherer economy, which would also suggest a link with the Cielo complex, rather than one with the Bravo Valley aspect. Thus, the Rough Run cairn burial would seem to have affiliations with the Cielo complex in some manner, and perhaps be representative of the Jumano as well.

Sociocultural Implications of the Cairn
Several observations concerning mortuary behavior and other sociocultural aspects of the Rough Run cairn burial are possible given the field and analytical data. Specific behavioral aspects of the mortuary ritual offer clues concerning the belief system of the culture responsible for the interment. Also, the status of the interred individual may be inferred from some of the behavior exhibited in the ritual.

Mortuary behavior manifested at the Rough Run burial is unique. The only other burial containing Perdiz points as grave goods within the areal distribution of the point is the one at Las Haciendas, Chihuahua, which was executed somewhat differently. Apparently the individual there was buried in an extended position within a shallow pit, covered with stones, then sealed with two large, thick tabular boulders. In contrast, the Rough Run burial contained the remains of a single individual interred in a relatively deep, circular pit and covered with a semisubterranean cairn containing scattered grave goods. This burial was missing numerous skeletal elements and appeared to be a secondary interment of an adult male. It is possible, and even probable, that the age and status of the persons interred were factors accounting for the different burial methods employed.

The Perdiz specimens from the assemblage that were connected or fit together provide additional data about the mortuary behavior manifested at the Rough Run burial. Several lines of reasoning can be used to argue that these specimens were ritually broken during the mortuary proceeding. The breaking or destroying of a deceased individual's possessions or of other items during a mortuary proceeding has been documented among a number of historic hunter-and-gatherer societies (Helm 1972; Yarrow 1988; Cortes 1989). This behavior was observed in the nineteenth century during a Comanche warrior burial where, with the body, "[were] deposited the bows and arrows; these, however, [were] first broken" (Yarrow 1988, 6). Similarly, an Apache burial in 1797 was reported to have involved cremation of the individual, as well as burning of his hut, "weapons, saddle, his wife's hair, skirts, and other skins that he wore" (Cortes 1989, 78). Among the Dogrib Indians of northwestern Canada, "personal eating utensils and certain similar possessions are often destroyed at the grave site" (Helm 1972, 85). The majority of Perdiz specimens in the Rough Run assemblage were broken and most of the breaks were snap fractures, which by itself would not necessarily be suggestive of ritual breakage. However, the occurrence of seven fitted specimens in tandem with their respective locations and elevations within the cairn (well separated from each other) is suggestive of such behavior. These specimens do not appear to have been broken by rocks being tossed into the pit or subsidence of the cairn (neither of which appears to have occurred), and it is unlikely that separate portions of individual points would have been curated following breakage during normal use or other means. Thus, ritual breakage appears to be the best explanation for this phenomenon. Given the examples of ritual breakage cited above, as well as the evidence for at least most of the Perdiz points' having been crafted by a single knapper, it is possible that the interred individual made most if not all of these points.

Within most prehistoric burials in the region and the greater Southwest, debitage is not a typical grave good. Thus, the inclusion of three pieces of debitage within the Rough Run cairn deserves some contemplation. All of these specimens were recovered from the upper 5 cm of the cairn and may have been fortuitous additions. As with the charcoal discussed above, the debitage may have been inadvertently added as soil was placed between and on top of the cairn stones—almost certainly the small corticate chip (Fl-75), because of its size and associated lack of utility, was an inadvertent addition to the cairn inventory. However, the two utilized pieces of debitage may have been intentionally placed in the cairn. These items were found at similar elevations, and it is possible that they were used to sever the limbs from the torso of the deceased, as suggested by the tiny cut marks on both femoral heads. If these cutting tools had been used for such a purpose, they were probably added to the interment as part of the customary mortuary behavior.

Like the debitage, the inclusion of fire-cracked rock and charcoal fragments within the cairn could have been accidental, or in the case of the fire-cracked rock, as suggested earlier, as "filler." However, these items may support the possibility of a mortuary fire's having been associated with the interment. By-products of mortuary fires (charcoal, ash, thermally altered stones, and charred food remains) and cremations have been documented both ethnographically in Native North American interments (Yarrow 1988) and archaeologically in Texas at a number of sites (Ray 1936; Morrow 1936; Jackson 1938; Jelks 1962; Stephenson 1970; Lynott 1978; Hall 1981; Cloud and Smith 1993). Yarrow (1988, 82) explained that the custom of building a fire in association with a Native American burial provided a certain purification of the soul, helping drive away demons or lighting the spirit land for the wandering soul. If such a fire had been made at the Rough Run site, perhaps part of the custom involved placing portions of the fire, like fire-cracked rock and charcoal, into the cairn that covered the body.

The majority of stones in the cairn were tabular and of a distinctive dark, intrusive igneous material. This black to dark gray rhyolitic stone outcrops near the site in the form of a dike feature, a striking geologic landform that cuts through the area. The stones were apparently gathered somewhere along this outcrop, then transported to the site for placement within the cairn. This material was chosen as the primary cairn stone despite the presence of a plethora of other, seemingly suitable stones much closer to the burial location. Undoubtedly, there was a strong cultural preference for this specific material in construction of the burial cairn. Whether this preference centered on the color or composition of the stone, its tabular nature, or some symbolic association with the dike is uncertain. A spring does occur along the dike at one location, and it is possible that the preference for the particular stone was somehow related to that resource. A definitive resolution to this question is unlikely, but it is apparent that a considerable amount of energy was expended in transporting the stones from the source to the burial location.

Several aspects of the interment indicate that the individual buried within the Rough Run site was of relatively high status. The burial pit was excavated with primitive tools to a depth of 83 cm through extremely hard-packed soil, an effort that must have taken a great deal of time and energy. Similarly, gathering the more than three hundred cairn stones from the dike outcrop and transporting them to the site also would have required an appreciable effort. The actual construction of the cairn was achieved through a well-conceived plan and attention to detail, all designed to provide maximum protection for the skeletal remains. There were many points of support within the cairn that helped accomplish this, as there were no signs of subsidence or collapse. The numerous carefully manufactured arrowpoints within the cairn, especially the largest and most delicate point in the assemblage (F1–58), may also attest to the individual's having been of high status. That particular arrowpoint, due to its size, thickness, and delicate blade tip, does not appear to have been manufactured for utilitarian use. Rather, it appears to have been made as a special or ceremonial item, perhaps even specifically as a mortuary offering.

Acknowledgments

I would like to thank several people who were instrumental in parts of this project. Heartfelt thanks are extended to Thomas C. Alex and Robert J. Mallouf for their assistance throughout the endeavor. They provided expertise and cheerful attitudes during the fieldwork, the bulk of which was accomplished in extremely hot weather (110+ degrees F). Thanks are also extended to Betty L. Alex and Alan Van Valkenburg, who assisted with various aspects of the fieldwork, including artifact and feature drawings. The late Ed Aiken assisted with the project by creating figure 3.3; David Hart of the Center for Big Bend Studies (CBBS) used his talents to draft figure 3.2. Field equipment and other supplies were shuttled to and from the site by Betty L. Alex, Don Corrick, Frank Garcia, and Karl Kibler, and all of the excavators were extremely grateful for this support. Gail Colby and Gentry Steele of Texas A&M University conducted the skeletal analysis with their usual attention to detail. Special thanks are extended to Kelly S. Garcia and Robert J. Mallouf of the CBBS for their direction and advice during preparation of the manuscript and their subsequent editorial expertise. The Office of the State Archeologist/Texas Historical Commission provided support for the fieldwork and much of the analysis. Finally, Big Bend National Park and the National Park Service are acknowledged for their patience with the author during the lengthy period of analysis and report preparation.

References

Bell, Robert E. 1958. *Guide to the Identification of Certain American Indian Projectile Points*. Special Bulletin 1. [Oklahoma City]: Oklahoma Anthropological Society.

Black, Stephen. 1986. *The Clemente and Herminia Hinojosa Site, 41JW8: A Toyah Horizon Campsite in Southern Texas*. Special Report 18. San Antonio: Center for Archaeological Research, University of Texas at San Antonio.

Blair, W. Frank. 1950. "The Biotic Provinces of Texas." *Texas Journal of Science* 2 (1): 93–117.

Cloud, William A., and James E. Smith II. 1993. "The Trinque Site (41ER27), Erath County, Texas." *Bulletin of the Texas Archeological Society* 64:269–327.

Colby, Gail R., and D. Gentry Steele. 1995. "Osteological Analysis of Feature 1, 41BS844: Human Skeletal Material Recovered from Big Bend National Park, Brewster County, Texas." Unpublished report submitted to Big Bend National Park by the Physical Anthropology Laboratory at Texas A&M University, College Station.

Cortes, José. 1989. *Views from the Apache Frontier: Report on the Northern Provinces of New Spain,* edited by Elizabeth A. H. John. Norman: University of Oklahoma Press.

Damas, David. 1972. "The Copper Eskimo." In *Hunters and Gatherers Today,* edited by M. G. Bicchieri, 3–50. New York: Holt, Rinehart, and Winston.

Fletcher, Henry T. 1931. "Some Types of Archeological Sites in Trans-Pecos, Texas." *Bulletin of the Texas Archaeological and Paleontological Society* 3:7–17.

Genoves, Santiago C. 1967. "Proportionality of Long Bones and Their Relation to Stature Among Mesoamericans." *American Journal of Physical Anthropology* 26:67–78.

Goldstein, Marcus J. 1948. "Dentition of Indian Crania from Texas." *American Journal of Physical Anthropology* 6:63–84.

Hall, Grant D. 1981. *Allens Creek: A Study in the Cultural Prehistory of the Lower Brazos River Valley, Texas.* Research Report 61. Austin: Texas Archeological Survey, University of Texas at Austin.

Helm, June. 1972. "The Dogrib Indians." In *Hunters and Gatherers Today,* edited by M. G. Bicchieri, 51–89. New York: Holt, Rinehart, and Winston.

Jackson, A. T. 1938. "Fire in East Texas Burial Rites." *Bulletin of the Texas Archaeological and Paleontological Society* 10:77–113.

Jelks, Edward B. 1962. *The Kyle Site: A Stratified Central Texas Aspect Site in Hill County, Texas.* Archeology Series 5. Austin: Department of Anthropology, University of Texas at Austin.

Johnson, LeRoy. 1994. *The Life and Times of Toyah-Culture Folk: The Buckhollow Encampment, Site 41KM16, Kimble County, Texas.* Office of the State Archeologist Report 38. Austin: Texas Department of Transportation and Texas Historical Commission.

Kelley, J. Charles. 1947. "The Lehmann Rock Shelter: A Stratified Site of the Toyah, Uvalde, and Round Rock Foci." *Bulletin of the Texas Archaeological and Paleontological Society* 18:115–28.

———. 1952. "The Historic Indian Pueblos of La Junta de los Ríos," pt. 1. *New Mexico Historical Review* 27 (4): 257–95.

———. 1986. *Jumano and Patarabueye: Relations at La Junta de los Ríos.* Anthropological Papers 77. Ann Arbor: Museum of Anthropology, University of Michigan.

———. 1990. "The Río Conchos Drainage: History, Archaeology, Significance." *Journal of Big Bend Studies* 2:29–41.

Kelley, J. Charles, T. N. Campbell, and Donald J. Lehmer. 1940. *The Association of Archeological Materials with Geological Deposits in the Big Bend Region of Texas.* Alpine, Texas: Sul Ross State Teachers College.

Krieger, Alex D. 1946. *Cultural Complexes and Chronology in Northern Texas.* Publication 4640. Austin: University of Texas.

Larkin, Thomas J., and George W. Bomar. 1983. *Climatic Atlas of Texas.* Austin: Texas Department of Water Resources.

Lynott, Mark J. 1978. *An Archeological Assessment of the Bear Creek Shelter, Lake Whitney, Texas.* Research Report 115. Dallas: Archaeology Research Program, Southern Methodist University.

Mallouf, Robert J. 1987. *Las Haciendas: A Cairn Burial Assemblage from Northeastern Chihuahua, Mexico.* Office of the State Archeologist Report 35. Austin: Texas Historical Commission.

———. 1999. "Comments on the Prehistory of Far Northeastern Chihuahua, the La Junta District, and the Cielo Complex." *Journal of Big Bend Studies* 11:49–92.

Maxwell, Ross A. 1968. *The Big Bend of the Rio Grande: A Guide to the Rocks, Landscape, Geologic History, and Settlers of the Area of Big Bend National Park.* Bureau of Economic Geology Guidebook 7. Austin: University of Texas at Austin.

Morrow, J. G. 1936. "A Prehistoric Cremated Burial of the Abilene Region." *Bulletin of the Texas Archaeological and Paleontological Society* 8:17–24.

Neumann, Georg K. 1952. "Archeology and Race in the American Indian." In *Archeology of the Eastern United States,* edited by J. B. Griffin, 13–34. Chicago: University of Chicago Press.

Oetteking, B. 1930. "Skeletal Remains from Texas." *Notes of the Museum of the American Indians, Heye Foundation* 7 (3): 336–47.

Peabody, Charles. 1909. "A Reconnaissance Trip in Western Texas." *American Anthropologist* 11:202–16.

Pearce, J. E. 1937. Editor's note. In G. Woodbury: *Notes on Some Skeletal Remains of Texas.* University of Texas Bulletin 3734:7–8. Austin: The University.

Prewitt, Elton R. 1981. "Cultural Chronology in Central Texas." *Bulletin of the Texas Archeological Society* 52:65–89.

———. 1983. "From Circleville to Toyah: Comments on Central Texas Chronology." *Bulletin of the Texas Archeological Society* 54:201–38.

———. 1995. "Distributions of Typed Projectile Points in Texas." *Bulletin of the Texas Archeological Society* 66:83–173.

Ray, Cyrus N. 1936. "Some Unusual Cremated Burials Found near Colorado, Texas." *Bulletin of the Texas Archaeological and Paleontological Society* 8:9–16.

Shackelford, William J. 1951. *Excavations at the Polvo Site in Western Texas.* MA thesis, Department of Anthropology, University of Texas at Austin.

Skinner, S. A., H. Haas, and S. L. Wilson. 1980. "The Elcor Burial Cave: An Example of Public Archaeology from West Texas." *Plains Anthropologist* 25:1–15.

Smith, Victor J. n.d. Field notes on file. Museum of the Big Bend, Sul Ross State University, Alpine, Texas.

Stephenson, Robert L. 1970. *Archeological Investigations in the Whitney Reservoir Area, Central Texas*. Bulletin of the Texas Archeological Society 41:37–277.

Stodder, A. L. W. 1989. "Bioarcheological Research in the Basin and Range Region." In *Human Adaptations and Cultural Change in the Greater Southwest*, by A. H. Simons, A. L. W. Stodder, D. D. Dykeman, and P. A. Hicks, 167–90. Research Series 32. Fayetteville: Arkansas Archeological Survey.

Stuiver, Minze, and Bernd Becker. 1986. "High-Precision Decadel Calibration of the Radiocarbon Time Scale, AD 1950–2500 BC." *Radiocarbon* 28 (2B): 863–910.

Stuiver, Minze, Paula J. Reimer, Edouard Bard, J. Warren Beck, G. S. Burr, Konrad A. Hughen, Bernd Kromer, Gerry McCormac, Johannes van der Plicht, and Mark Spurk. 1998. "INTCAL98 Radiocarbon Age Calibration, 24,000–0 cal BP." *Radiocarbon* 40 (3): 1041–83.

Suhm, Dee Ann, and Edward B. Jelks. 1962. *Handbook of Texas Archeology: Type Descriptions*. Austin: Texas Archeological Society Special Publication 1 and Texas Memorial Museum Bulletin 4.

Suhm, Dee Ann, Alex D. Krieger, and Edward B. Jelks. 1954. *An Introductory Handbook of Texas Archeology*. Bulletin of the Texas Archeological Society 25. Austin: Texas Archeological Society.

Talma, A. S., and J. C. Vogel. 1993. "A Simplified Approach to Calibrating 14C Dates." *Radiocarbon* 35 (2): 317–22.

Taylor, Walter W. 1966. "Archaic Cultures Adjacent to the Northeastern Frontiers of Mesoamerica." In *Handbook of Middle American Indians*, edited by Robert Wauchope, 59–94. Vol. 4 of *Archaeological Frontiers and External Connections*. Austin: University of Texas Press.

Trotter, Mildred. 1970. "Estimation of Stature from Intact Long Limb Bones." In *Personal Identification in Mass Disasters*, edited by T. D. Stewart, 71–83. Washington, DC: National Museum of Natural History, Smithsonian Institution.

Turner, Ellen Sue, and Thomas R. Hester. 1985. *A Field Guide to Stone Artifacts of Texas Indians*. Austin: Texas Monthly Press.

Turpin, Solveig A. 1982. *Seminole Canyon: The Art and the Archeology*. Texas Archeological Survey Research Report 83. Austin: University of Texas at Austin.

Woodbury, G. 1937. *Notes on Some Skeletal Remains of Texas*. University of Texas Bulletin 3738:9–16.

Yarrow, H. C. 1988. *North American Indian Burial Customs*, edited by V. L. Smith. Ogden, Utah: Eagle's View.

4 *The Río Conchos Drainage*

HISTORY, ARCHAEOLOGY, SIGNIFICANCE

J. Charles Kelley

The Río Conchos drainage is the major river system of Chihuahua. Its major tributaries originate in the Sierra Madre Occidental—one of them (the Río Florido), in the state of Durango. The Río Conchos joins the Rio Grande (Río Bravo) at La Junta de los Ríos, near Ojinaga, Chihuahua, and Presidio, Texas. At the river junction the Río Conchos is the master stream; reportedly, the Rio Grande above La Junta formerly went dry on occasion, and the average annual runoff was relatively very low. In the period 1900–1913, prior to the establishment of Elephant Butte Reservoir on the Rio Grande above El Paso and of several reservoirs on the Río Conchos, the gauging station on the Rio Grande just above La Junta recorded an average runoff of 645,246 acre feet. In the same period the station just below the mouth of the Río Conchos recorded an average annual runoff of 2,045,769 acre feet (Follansbe and Dean 1915), over three times the runoff above the junction.

HISTORY

In the early historic period the Río Conchos served as a major trail route for the early Spanish *entradas* designed to explore New Mexico; from La Junta these early expeditions followed the Rio Grande northward. By 1567, continuing Spanish exploration, following ancient Indian trails northward from Durango through Guatimape, Zape, and Inde, had reached the Parral area, and settlements (and rich mines) were established at Santa Bárbara (Santa Barbola) in the San Bartolomé (Allende) valley on one of the tributaries of the Río Florido. Santa Bárbara became the staging ground for the expeditions that followed the Río Conchos to La Junta and beyond (Hammond and Rey 1966, 4–6; Rocha 1938, 67–71). Shortly thereafter, slave-raiding parties followed the Río Florido to the Río Conchos and downstream at least as far as Cuchillo Parado. The classic entradas that followed were the Rodríguez-Chamuscado expedition of 1581–82 and the Espejo expedition of 1582–83 (Hammond and Rey 1966, 67–120, 153–231). Subsequently, the Spaniards heading for New Mexico discovered a shorter route leading through what is now Chihuahua City to Paso del Norte. However, Spanish expeditions continued to follow the Río Conchos to La Junta, which became a Spanish anchor point complete with Catholic missions and eventually a presidio (Kelley 1952a, 1953a). During the full historic period a drift of peoples (at first Indians, then Spaniards, and subsequently mestizos) and culture continued down the Río Conchos to La Junta, much of it originating in the Julimes area (Kelley 1952b, 257–95; 1953a, 21–51). Anglo-American occupation of the La Junta region did not begin until the middle nineteenth century; discussion of the Mexican and Anglo-American occupations is beyond the scope of this paper.

ETHNOLOGY

Most of the upper Río Conchos drainage from Santa Bárbara to the general region above Cuchillo Parado was inhabited in the Spanish contact period by Conchos Indians, a largely nonagricultural group, hypothetically Uto-Aztecan in speech (Sauer 1934, 59–64, 81). Although it is believed that Concho territory extended down the Río Conchos only to the area of Falomir, where the railroad crosses the river, various sources indicate that some if not all of the La Junta village groups were Concho in speech and on occasion may have been under Concho political control. Tarahumara occupation almost certainly extended into the upper tributaries of the Conchos on the northwest.

Beginning near Cuchillo Parado and continuing to La Junta and adjacent sections of the Rio Grande, the river valleys lying between mountain barriers were occupied by essentially sedentary groups whom the Spaniards nicknamed "Patarabueyes," who also may have been Uto-Aztecan in speech. These groups occupied individual village areas; they repeat in microcosm the same type of situation represented by the northern Rio Grande Pueblos—essentially independent villages united by a more or less common culture but differing in dialect or language (Riley 1987, 285–310). Some of the La Junta villages were occupied in the winter months, at least, by the nomadic Jumanos ("Jumanos y Cibolos"), who hunted buffalo and engaged in trade over much of aboriginal Texas (Kelley 1986). The Jumanos may represent the first Apachean groups to enter the area, or they may have been an earlier intrusive Plains group that later was absorbed by the Apaches. The mountain areas surrounding and partitioning the Río Conchos valley were occupied by various mobile groups, principally hunter-gatherers, identified by a bewildering variety of names, and whose culture and language are virtually unknown.

Archaeological Research in the Río Conchos Drainage and La Junta

To the best of my knowledge, archaeological reconnaissance and excavation in the Río Conchos drainage and at La Junta de los Ríos began in the latter area in the 1930s with minor reconnaissance by Victor J. Smith and E. B. Sayles (Sayles 1935). I carried out minor reconnaissance along both the Mexican and United States sides of the Rio Grande in the La Junta area in 1936 and 1938. Also, in 1936 I excavated a pit house (Kelley 1939) on the Texas side of the Rio Grande (less than three miles below La Junta itself) at the Millington site (the historic Indian pueblo of San Cristóbal [Kelley 1953a, 45–48]) located on the riverbank in the eastern part of Presidio, Texas. With Donald J. Lehmer, I carried out intensive excavations at this same site in 1938–39 (Kelley 1986, 71–85, figs. 2, 3, 4, 5), and in 1939 I also excavated at the Loma Alta site (the historic Indian pueblo of San Juan Evangelista [Kelley 1953, 25–29; Kelley 1986, 72–84]), located on the Texas side of the Rio Grande five miles upriver from Presidio, Texas. Excavations at these sites produced much valuable archaeological data, including identification of architectural types and development of a tentative sequence and chronology applicable to all of the La Junta sites then known.

Excavation of these La Junta sites was supported by Sul Ross State Teacher's College (now Sul Ross State University) and by small grants from the School of American Research in Santa Fe, New Mexico; labor was furnished by the Works Progress Administration. In 1948, I carried out an archaeological reconnaissance of the United States side of the Rio Grande from below Redford, Texas, to the vicinity of La Esperanza on the Rio Grande near old Fort Quitman. In the course of this reconnaissance, which was supported by the Latin American Institute and the Department of Anthropology of the University of Texas at Austin, I excavated two pit houses located at the La Junta Indian site of Tapalcolmes (Kelley 1953a, 40–42; Kelley 1949) in Redford (Polvo), Texas. The following year I supervised an archaeological field school at Redford for the University of Texas, during which time other pit houses were excavated (Shackelford 1955). Later the same summer I carried out an archaeological reconnaissance of the Río Conchos drainage between La Junta and the vicinity of Jiménez, located on the Río Florido tributary of the Río Conchos, exploring areas that could be accessed only by using a four-wheel drive vehicle. During this reconnaissance I excavated a pit house at the site of Loma Seca, located on a minor eastern tributary of the Río Conchos about 8 km above Ojinaga, Chihuahua. In 1951, I surveyed otherwise inaccessible mountainous sections of the Río Conchos between Julimes and Falomir, Chihuahua, on burro back, with financial support from the University Museum of the Southern Illinois University, Carbondale. In recent years numerous surveys have been carried out along the Rio Grande above and below La Junta, largely supported by archaeologists of the Texas State Historical Commission, including two seasons of excavations directed by State Archaeologist Robert Mallouf at the Cielo Bravo site, located down the Rio Grande from Redford, Texas; results of these recent researches, largely unpublished, are noted only incidentally in this chapter.

On the upper Río Conchos, as early as 1931, Robert M. Zingg excavated in caves located in the uppermost headwaters of the Río Fuerte (in Tarahumara country) just across the continental divide from the upper headwaters of the Río Conchos. His discoveries in this work are probably applicable to the archaeology of the upper tributaries of the Río Conchos as well (Zingg 1940). As previously noted, in the early 1930s E. B. Sayles carried out an archaeological survey of Chihuahua for the Gila Pueblo of Globe, Arizona (Sayles 1936); apparently his survey included at least the upper Río Conchos drainage, although in his published report Sayles does not specify the areas actually covered. In 1952, while directing an archaeological field school in Durango, Mexico, I surveyed areas of the upper Río Florido in the Durango-Chihuahua boundary area (Kelley 1953b, 172–76). Following the end of the 1952 field session, William J. Shackelford and his wife surveyed, on horseback, the Río Conchos drainage located above Camargo, Chihuahua, continuing through the valleys of Zaragosa and San Felipe de Jesús to the mouth of the Río San Juan tributary (Kelley 1953b, 175).

About 1955–56 Richard H. Brooks and his wife (Sheilagh) made an intensive archaeological survey of the eastern foothills of the Sierra

Madre Occidental in Chihuahua and northern Durango (Brooks 1971). In 1984 I made a tourist-type limited survey of the valleys of Zaragosa and San Felipe de Jesús on the upper Río Conchos. Other more limited surveys of the Río Conchos drainage may have been made, but, if so, I have no notes regarding them. I know of no other excavations made in the entire area. Much of the Río Conchos drainage remains archaeologically unknown.

Archaeology

On the upper Río Florido branch of the Río Conchos a few kilometers above Villa Ocampo on the Durango-Chihuahua boundary, I found in 1952 the type site of the Loma (or Cerro) San Gabriel culture, situated on a high ridge through which the Florido flows in a steep-walled canyon. The Loma San Gabriel culture is a sub-Mesoamerican semisedentary culture that extended along the upper eastern foothills and upland valleys of the Sierra Madre Occidental at least as far south as southern Durango and northern Jalisco (Kelley 1953b, 172–76; 1956, 132–33, in Willey 1956; Foster 1978; 1985, 327–51, in Foster and Weigand 1985). This culture may have extended as far north as the valley of San Felipe de Jesús on the main Río Conchos. In Durango the Loma San Gabriel culture was intimately associated with various phases of the Mesoamerican Chalchihuites culture and may have preceded the latter. It survived the disappearance of the Chalchihuites culture in about AD 1400–1500 and may represent the ancestral culture of the Tepehuán Indians and perhaps also of other groups of the high sierra. Its essentially lineal distribution in northern Durango delineates the route followed by early Indian traders and colonial "camino reales." In northern Durango this trade route was intersected by another major trade route connecting coastal Sinaloa with the highlands of Durango through the Topia gap in the Sierra Madre Occidental; this trade route was used by the bearers of the late Postclassic Aztatlan culture, which dominated the last phases of the Chalchihuites culture and may have extended into and influenced the great archaeological site of Casas Grandes, located in northwestern Chihuahua, and the American Southwest as well. (Kelley 1986, 81–104, in Mathien and McGuire 1986).

In 1952, on the upper Río Florido just below the Loma San Gabriel site, I found a small site on the low river terrace represented by a lithic scatter, disintegrating hearths, and rare plain brownware potsherds.

Among the lithic artifacts recovered were end-notched flat pebbles, a characteristic lithic artifact found all along the Río Conchos to La Junta de los Ríos and adjacent sections of the Rio Grande, where it represents one of the most common lithic artifacts. The settlement pattern of this Río Conchos culture, possibly the late prehistoric manifestation of the Conchos Indian occupation, is one of several small sites distributed at intervals along the river and on its lower terraces. The preferred location was an eroding low terrace remnant where a tributary stream or dry arroyo enters the river. In the mountainous middle reaches of the Río Conchos, steep-walled canyons alternate with small valleys. Sites of this occupance characteristically are to be found in the valley near the *boca* where the river emerges from the canyon above. One of the largest of these sites is located on the northern side of the Río Conchos below Julimes in the alluvial "delta" where the Río Chuviscar joins the Conchos. These sites consistently are found eroding from the near surficial alluvium of the river terraces; below them, buried deeply in alluvium, there are hearths and occasional lithic artifacts and debitage exposed in the riverbanks. These probably represent an Archaic occupation of the area, which also occurs in open sites in adjacent mountain areas.

Plain red and brown pottery in simple forms and sparse sherds of a similar ware with red-line decoration is characteristic of these Río Concho sites, as is a quite simple stone complex made up principally of chert or rhyolite chopping tools, knives, small arrowpoints, scrapers, and such pecked stone artifacts as hammer stones, milling stones, and end-notched pebbles. Nothing is known of the dwellings of this Conchoan culture (Kelley 1956, 132–33, in Willey 1956).

The extreme lower section of the Río Conchos and adjacent sections of the Rio Grande were a region of somewhat higher aboriginal culture. There, in the zone of La Junta de los Ríos, a sedentary culture formerly known as the Río Bravo Valley aspect first appeared about AD 1150–1250, and survived into historic times. The earliest period of this occupation, the La Junta phase, essentially represents an isolated colony of the El Paso phase of the Jornada branch of the Mogollon culture of New Mexico. Around a small linear El Paso-phase house group excavated at the Millington site, many small rectangular, and some oval or circular pit houses were constructed. Sites bearing Jornada branch and Casas Grandes ceramics, usually found in association with large areas of hearths and lithic scatters as well as numerous and large "mescal pits" (ring middens), are found along the Rio Grande from the Redford valley below La Junta to the El Paso area. The time period represented is ca. AD 1220 to 1400–1450; charred beams recovered from an eroding La Junta phase pit house at the Polvo (Tapalcolmes) site in Redford have been radiocarbon dated through the courtesy of State Archaeologist Robert Mallouf and the Texas Historical Commission; the dates are AD 1265–1405 (Beta 29991) and AD 1240–1350 (Beta 29992), supporting the dates earlier developed through cross-cultural comparisons. I now believe that all of these La Junta phase sites, including those on the lower Río Conchos and on the Rio Grande above the river junction, were procurement stations producing surplus local plant foods (especially mescal and mesquite beans), as well as bison skin and dried bison meat obtained from Plains groups trading at La Junta, and that the sites were extractive areas for minerals and stones. All these goods supplied the needs of the great redistribution center of Casas Grandes (Paquimé) located in northwestern Chihuahua (Di Peso 1974). The ceramics found in these La Junta phase components are almost all trade wares, derived either from Casas Grandes or from the Jornada branch sites of the El Paso area. Potential agricultural land and water for more than temporal farming are strictly limited in the Rio Grande areas above La Junta, suggesting some other reason for the occupance. The putative age of these sites, including the La Junta phase, parallels that of Casas Grandes (using the new unpublished dates of ca. AD 1250–1300 to 1450–1500); with the dissolution of the Casas Grandes interaction sphere and the abandonment of Paquimé, the "Central Place," these sites were also largely abandoned, even in the hearth area of the Jornada Branch near El Paso and in southeastern New Mexico.

Between about AD 1400–1450 and about AD 1550, the La Junta area along the lower Conchos and the adjacent Rio Grande drainage may have been almost entirely abandoned by pottery-making agriculturists, leaving it occupied only by semisedentary hunters and gatherers living in simple structures. Around 1550 cultural influences from the south, following the Río Conchos, may have combined with others introduced by the arrival of the Jumanos (as early Apacheans?) at La Junta to form the protohistoric Concepción phase. Shortly thereafter, in the early 1580s, the arrival of the Spaniards began the transformation of the La Junta cultures into those of the full mission-period Conchos phase.

This is a new hypothesis; formerly we had believed that there was continuity of basic features of the Bravo Valley aspect from the early Jornada branch–related La Junta phase into the historic Conchos phase. The research of Texas State Archaeologist Robert Mallouf in the Big Bend and La Junta regions has greatly influenced my thinking in this regard, as has our massive new database for Mesoamerican influences on northwest Mexico cultures, especially that of Casas Grandes. This new hypothesis may not survive the recovery of still more archaeological data in the La Junta area, but these new data should certainly produce other new explanatory hypotheses. All the new data that accumulate serve to demonstrate the importance of Chihuahua in our understanding of the archaeological history of northwestern Mexico and the American Southwest ("Greater Mesoamerica"). What is now urgently needed is the participation of Mexican archaeologists in exploring the archaeology of Chihuahua—and renewed attention by Texas archaeologists to archaeological research in the La Junta area.

References

Brooks, Pilchard H. 1971. "Lithic Traditions in Northwestern Mexico, Paleoindian to Chalchihuites." PhD diss., University of Colorado, Boulder.

Di Peso, Charles C. 1974. *Casas Grandes: A Fallen Trading Center of the Gran Chichimeca*. 3 vols. Dragoon, Arizona: Amerind Foundation.

Follansbee, Robert, and H. S. Dean. 1915. *Water Resources of the Rio Grande Basin, 1889–1913*. United States Geological Survey, Water Supply Paper 358. Washington, DC: GPO.

Foster, Michael S. 1978. "Loma San Gabriel: A Prehistoric Culture of Northwest Mexico." PhD diss., University of Colorado, Boulder.

———. 1985. "The Loma San Gabriel Occupation of Zacatecas and Durango, Mexico." In *The Archaeology of West and Northwest Mesoamerica*, edited by Michael S. Foster and Phil C. Weigand, 327–51. Boulder: Westview Press.

Galegos, Hernán. (1582) 1966. "Relation and Report of the Expedition Made by Francisco Sánchez Chamuscado and Eight Soldier Companions in the Exploration of New Mexico and New Lands, and Its Outcome." In *The Rediscovery of New Mexico, 1580–1594*, edited by George P. Hammond and Agapito Rey, 67–114. Albuquerque: University of New Mexico Press.

Hammond, George P., and Agapito Rey. 1966. *The Rediscovery of New Mexico, 1580–1594*. Albuquerque: University of New Mexico Press.

Kelley, J. Charles. 1939. "Archaeological Notes on the Excavation of a Pithouse near Presidio, Texas." *El Palacio* 46 (10): 221–34.

———. 1949. "Archaeological Notes on Two Excavated House Structures in Western Texas." *Bulletin of the Texas Archaeological and Paleontological Society* 20:89–114.

———. 1951. "A Bravo Valley Aspect Component of the Lower Río Conchos Valley, Chihuahua, Mexico." *American Antiquity* 17 (2): 114–19.

———. 1952a. "Factors Involved in the Abandonment of Certain Peripheral Southwestern Settlements." *American Anthropologist* 54 (3): 356–87.

———. 1952b. "The Historic Indian Pueblos of La Junta de los Ríos," pt. 1. *New Mexico Historical Review* 27 (4): 257–295.

———. 1953a. "The Historic Indian Pueblos of La Junta de los Ríos," pt. 2. *New Mexico Historical Review* 28 (1): 21–51.

———. 1953b. "Reconnaissance and Excavation in Durango and Southern Chihuahua, Mexico." *The American Philosophical Society Year Book* 1953: 172–76.

———. 1956. "Settlement Patterns in North-Central Mexico." In *Prehistoric Settlement Patterns in the New World,* edited by Gordon R. Willey, 128–39. Viking Fund Publications in Anthropology 23. New York: Wenner-Gren Foundation.

———. 1986a. *Jumano and Patarabueye: Relations at La Junta de los Ríos.* Anthropological Papers 77. Ann Arbor: Museum of Anthropology, University of Michigan.

———. 1986b. "The Mobile Merchants of Molina." *Ripples in the Chichimec Sea,* edited by Frances Joan Mathien and Randall H. McGuire, 90–104. Carbondale: Southern Illinois University Press.

Kelley, J. Charles, T. N. Campbell, and Donald J. Lehmer. 1940. *The Association of Archaeological Materials with Geological Deposits in the Big Bend Region of Texas.* Alpine, Texas: Sul Ross State College.

Pérez de Luxán, Diego. (1582) 1966. "Diego Pérez de Luxán's Account of the Antonio de Espejo Expedition into New Mexico, 1582." In *The Rediscovery of New Mexico, 1580–1594,* edited by George P. Hammond and Agapito Rey, 153–212. Albuquerque: University of New Mexico Press.

Riley, Carroll L. 1987. *The Frontier People.* Albuquerque: University of New Mexico Press.

Rocha, José G. (1938) 1958. "La Primera Española en Territorio Chihuahuense." *Boletín Sociedad Chihuahuense de Estudios Historicós,* July and September, 67–71, 152–58.

Sauer, Carl. 1934. "The Distribution of Aboriginal Tribes and Languages in Northwestern Mexico." *Ibero-Americana* 5. Berkeley: University of California Press.

Sayles, E. B. 1935. *An Archaeological Survey of Texas.* Medallion Papers 17. Globe, Arizona: Gila Pueblo.

———. 1936. *An Archaeological Survey of Chihuahua, Mexico.* Medallion Papers 22. Globe, Arizona: Gila Pueblo.

Shackelford, William J. 1955. "Excavations at the Polvo Site in Western Texas." *American Antiquity* 20:256–62.

Willey, Gordon R., ed. 1956. *Prehistoric Settlement Patterns in the New World.* Viking Fund Publications in Anthropology 23. New York: Wenner-Grenn Foundation for Anthropological Research.

Zingg, Robert M. 1940. *Report on Archaeology of Southern Chihuahua.* Denver: Center of Latin American Studies.

II

HISTORY MEETS NATIVE AMERICANS

5 Native American and Mestizo Farming at La Junta de los Ríos

Enrique R. Madrid

The lands of La Junta de los Ríos—the junction of the Río Conchos from Chihuahua and the Rio Grande or Río Bravo in the Texas Big Bend—have been home to farming peoples for many centuries. The origins of these farmers in the Late Prehistoric period may lie with migratory Puebloan groups—more properly Jornada Mogollon—who settled La Junta about AD 1200 (Kelley 1986) and who were linked economically to the great trading center of Casas Grandes in northern Mexico and culturally to their New Mexico homelands. Alternatively, La Junta peoples may have been hunter-gatherers from the northern Mexico desert or the American Southern Plains who settled there and adopted certain aspects of Jornada Mogollon lifeways (Mallouf 1990). In either case, the occupation of their lands by the Spanish in the Historic period created a mestizo people who have lived and farmed in the same river valleys up to the present day.

The La Junta landscape is dominated by eroded volcanic and limestone mountains that form the Presidio and Redford Bolsons. The bolsons are breached by the Río Conchos and Rio Grande, as well as by several important tributary streams (Groat 1972). The river floodplains, terraces, and nearby mountains were suitable for long-term occupation and were the site of fourteen historic Native American pueblos visited by Spanish explorers at various times (Applegate and Hanselka 1974). A Spanish expedition in 1582 estimated the population at La Junta to be ten thousand persons (Gómez 1990).

The climate has long been favorable for agriculturalists. Before modern-day damming, the Río Conchos-Rio Grande system most likely had at least two high-water periods during the year. Snowmelt from the Sierra Madre and Rocky Mountains typically reached La Junta in May or June (*New Encyclopaedia Britannica* 1986). A second peak tended to result from summer rains (Emory 1857). High summer temperatures still create convectional storms above the mountains—the Sierra Rica, the Bofecillos, the Chinati, and the Sierra Grande—and these storms sweep into the

La Junta valleys (Cordell 1984). The Mexican monsoon provides more than 70 percent of the annual precipitation to West Texas and the Mexican Plateau from May to October (Martin 1970).

The critical importance of summer rains to late prehistoric farming cultures is clear: where they were lacking—as in areas of California and Nevada—aboriginal corn-bean-squash economies failed to evolve (Martin 1970). Beginning in AD 1200–1500 and continuing until the 1880s, the climate at La Junta fell into the general precipitation pattern of light to heavy summer rains that predominates in the western United States (Martin 1970). Because their survival was tied so closely to annual floods, and because they possessed a "concept of the periodicity of flooding" (Applegate 1992) and saw life-giving rains form in the mountains, the La Junta natives must surely have been moved by powerful religious impulses (Jung 1963).

Farming—including floodplain agriculture—had spread over most of the southwestern United States by AD 900 (Martin 1970; Cordell 1984), but pending new archaeological evidence, what we know of prehistoric agricultural practices at La Junta is at most enlightened conjecture. Until a few years ago, archaeologists did not record agricultural features or collect paleobotanical data, so our knowledge is limited (Cordell 1984, 182–85). Despite certain interpretive risks, historical and ethnographic data—bolstered by archaeological findings—may have to be extrapolated into prehistory before we can arrive at verifiable hypotheses concerning human lifeways (Doolittle 1990; Cordell 1984; Binford 1983).

Constructed on or near arroyos, alluvial fans, and riverbanks, archaeological sites of prehistoric farms are likely to have hidden features such as channels, dikes, dams, weirs, furrows, and terraces. However, physical evidence of such ephemeral constructions is difficult to find because of the destruction wrought by erosion and the high rate of sedimentation in the river valley. Remote-sensing methods, aerial photo surveys, ground-scanning radar, pollen analyses, and soil cores from historic farms and from protected or buried sites may reveal farming techniques and the antiquity and variety of prehistoric cultigens (Lister and Lister 1984, 145–62). The same geological and hydrological constraints that preconditioned desert farming may help to pinpoint such locations. Currently, the Río Conchos and the Rio Grande are at their lowest levels in history, thereby opening up heretofore-ignored floodplain areas to scientific scrutiny (Kelley and Kelley 1990, 6).

Native American cultures of the Greater Southwest—including northern Mexico and West Texas—possessed a repertoire of arid-land farming methods that may have been known and used by the La Junta peoples. The Cochise culture planted at selected places and then left, to return later when the harvest was ready (Kopper 1986, 52). The Anasazis made use of underground water, planting crops in dunes near hills, or used earthworks or terraces on hill slopes to distribute floodwaters from small streams (Spencer 1977, 275). The modern Hopi and Zuñi Indians dry-farm their corn in washes using rain and groundwater (Spencer 1977, 172; Officer 1971, 50). Papagos use flash-flood farms on alluvial fans, and they store surplus water in natural waterholes using dirt embankments (Spencer 1977, 275). They use brush dams, dikes, and ditches to control rainfall and runoff (Cordell 1984, 198–99). The Tarahumaras practiced stream agriculture in the seventeenth century on river meanders. They also used springs for farming, building terraces on canyon slopes (Pennington 1963, 47–48). The Navajos still plant corn in shallow pits to concentrate rainwater and to collect arroyo runoff (Kopper 1986, 52–53). Shallow pits called *posas*, which serve a similar function, are still a common sight in modern La Junta home gardens. The Mimbres Mogollon people dry-farmed with subsurface water in their more arid southerly lands (Brody 1977, 35). Jornada Mogollon farmers along the Rio Grande in Hudspeth County, Texas, may have planted fields using water from arroyo channels and flood irrigation in the river's lowlands (Betancourt 1981, 37–47).

Spanish explorers of La Junta have left detailed records of aboriginal subsistence practices there. About 1535, when Alvar Núñez Cabeza de Vaca walked into the villages of La Junta, he was given beans, squashes, gourd vessels, and corn that the Indians had brought into the area (Di Peso 1974, 801; Hammond and Rey 1967, 62). The inhabitants were waiting for the end of a two-year drought before they could plant their own cornfields (Favata and Hernandez 1993, 101–102). The Indians cooked their pumpkins and other foods by a stone-boiling method; they reportedly had no pottery (Favata and Hernandez 1993, 102).

The Rodriguez-Chamuscado expedition reached La Junta in 1581 (Hickerson 1994, 33). The Amotomanco nation they found farmed only small amounts of corn, but many pumpkins and beans (Castañeda 1976, 160–61). The Espejo expedition of 1582 found the Otomoacos planting maize, beans, and calabashes along the Conchos (Hammond and Rey 1967, 56–58). The Abriache nation harvested maize, vegetables, calabashes, and gourds (Hammond and Rey 1967, 58–61). The Indians of the largest pueblo, Santiago, were all farmers; they had many "damp islands and bays" along the river on which to plant, moving from their pueblos to jacales in their fields at harvest time (Hammond and Rey 1967, 62).

Returning from New Mexico in August 1583, Espejo's men found the Río Conchos in full flood. They were fed ears of green corn, indicating a late summer harvest (Madrid 1994, 17). They also feasted on raw and roasted calabashes, beans, and fishes (Hammond and Rey 1967, 125–26).

A significant impact on farming lifeways was brought about by the Spanish missionaries. They returned to La Junta in 1629 and 1631 (Jordan 1975, 71) and again in 1660 and 1671 (Jones 1991, 4). In 1683, the López-Mendoza entrada reported corn and wheat in cultivation (Hickerson 1994, 133–34). The Chihuahua historian Francisco R. Almada, however, credits the introduction of wheat and cotton to Friar Andrés Ramírez between 1700 and 1715 (García, n.d., 1). By providing a winter crop, wheat essentially doubled the area's food supply (Bowden 1977, 74), and it would have stimulated the expansion of irrigation systems (Officer 1971, 50). Planting wheat in October after the late summer floods, the La Junta farmers would harvest it the following May (Madrid 1994, 17).

In addition to founding missions, the Trasviña y Retis expedition of 1715 left iron rings for making wheat-flour sifters, as well as garbanzos, lima beans, and seeds of fruit trees for the missionaries to plant (García, n.d., 7). With Catholicism came plows, iron tools, and Mexican and European cultigens such as chiles, watermelons, peas, peaches, onions, and fig and quince trees (Bowden 1977, 71; Officer 1971, 50).

Historic period farming is described in a report to the viceroy at Mexico City from Capt. Cmdr. Joseph de Ydoiaga after an expedition to La Junta in 1747–48 (Madrid 1992). His expedition was one of three that converged on La Junta that winter (Madrid 1994, 1). A farming technique that Ydoiaga described was temporal irrigation—*temporal* farming in Spanish—or collecting arroyo runoff in fields (Riley 1987, 298; Doolittle 1990, 91). But according to the Indians, such temporal farms in the desert arroyos were not as successful as the riverine farms (Madrid 1992, 60).

Farming along the riverbanks may be termed *humedad* farming. An *humedad* is a humid or moist place, a low basin on the floodplain with enough moisture left from receding floods or downward percolation of water through the soil to raise a crop. High water might drown a crop, while low water might wither it (Madrid 1994, 9). A sandbar would qualify as a *humedad* (Riley 1987, 298).

Humedad farming may be identified by several traits. It was carried out without artificial irrigation, instead using natural river overflows, and field preparation, such as clearing, was done prior to the flooding. Fire was used to clear the fields of brush, grass, and harvest stubble; it was a type of slash-and-burn farming. Field fertility, however, depended upon silting from annual floods. Planting was then done after floodwaters had receded from the riverbanks. In addition, the work was done without oxen or Spanish iron tools. This was precarious farming, subject to damage from river floods and fluctuations, and it failed to fulfill the food needs of the La Junta Indians; hunting and gathering remained essential (Madrid 1992, 82; 1994, 9–11).

Eight pueblos visited by Ydoiaga had humedad farms. Santa Cruz pueblo near La Junta had the most fertile and abundant fields, consisting of a half league of humedades, which was more than enough to feed 322 persons (Madrid 1994, 32). In spite of moderate flooding in 1747, corn, pumpkins, and vegetables were being planted in the pueblos. At San Christóbal a small corn crop would be supplemented with wheat. A very good crop would bring a year's supply of food plus a surplus for trading to the Apaches (Madrid 1992, 60).[1] Ten to twelve bushels of corn per acre probably met the needs of La Junta farmers (Officer 1971, 48).

The pueblos had spacious floodplains that might have been farmed if irrigation systems could have been constructed. But canal irrigation was impossible due to frequent and widespread flooding, the instability of the river channels, the sandy and loose soil of the banks, constant reworking of the floodplains, and the deposition of brush piles by the rivers. The canals and dams reported in 1715 (Doolittle 1990, 91; Applegate 1992, 57) lay in ruin by midcentury. Following Doolittle (1990, 45–46, 72, 74, fig. 3.16), early eighteenth-century diversion dams here may have been simple ones made of brush, stakes, rocks, and dirt, or built of piled rocks on the slower and shallower side channels or *brazos* rather than on the main channel of the river. The Indians, missionaries, and Spanish farmers had failed to secure them against the rivers' force. But as constructions they were much needed, or the inhabitants would not have worked so hard to build them (Madrid 1992, 92).

The floodplains and the land for three days' journey upstream on the Rio Grande were also choked with poor-quality grasses. These grasses may have resulted from the creation of a "fire ecology" by the Indians, as their repeated burnings suppressed mesquites and shrubs and favored grass growth (Madrid 1994, 10).

Oral histories collected from six area farmers and ranchers add to what we know from Ydoiaga about early Native American farming methods. With a few improvements, these methods are still in use almost 250 years later in La Junta.

Today, the Municipio of Ojinaga has 1500 hectares of temporal farms under cultivation. The majority are *temporales de arroyo*. *Temporales de bajío* or *charco* (i.e., in rain-catchment basins) are very rare. Humedad farming (technically, *siembra en tierra avenida* or flood-silt farming) is still practiced at the villages of Pilares, Barrancos de Guadalupe, and Fresnos on the Rio Grande (Gómez 1994). It was used near El Mulato downstream of La Junta until the Luis León Flood Control Dam was built on the Río Conchos in 1968 (Navarro Reynosa 1994; Porras Ruiz 1994).

Information has been provided by Jesús José Carrasco of Rancho San Nicolás, Chihuahua, and Pedro Minjares Sánchez of Santa Teresa, Chihuahua. Carrasco began farming in temporales with his grandfather over thirty years ago, when they used an iron planting stick called a *barra* to plant corn. Minjares is planting today in a temporal he has used for eight years.

Each man selected a flat field in an alluvial fan formed by an arroyo or near a large arroyo whose flow could be controlled. Both cleared the fan of brush and rocks, greasewood, and mesquites. Carrasco raised water spreaders or small check dams called *tapes*, *bordos*, or *estacados* in his field. Made of earth, brush, and rocks, and held in place by wooden stakes, their function is to slow, spread, and retain flash floodwaters to collect silt and to correspondingly level the field. The estacados are later raised into long, low embankments called *bunds* to hold water for irrigation. Outlets at the ends move water into the adjacent section. The bunds are 20 m (65.6 ft.) apart and are arranged perpendicular to the water flow. An *enramado* or low diversion dam built of loosely piled alternate courses of brush and rocks in an arroyo leads to a ditch entering the field. Should a flood become too violent, this brush dam is designed to collapse rather than to divert the waters into the field.

Instead, Minjares has built a *presita*, a small dam or estacado to extend the arroyo flow from behind a small ridge into the center of an alluvial fan where his field lies. He has plowed four radiating low-bordered ditches, each ca. 100 m (328 ft.) long, with a tractor and a border disc plow to catch the water and funnel it into the fenced 1.5 hectare temporal. He plans to plow and prepare the field, sow it with oats, and wait for rain in November. Carrasco waits until after a rain to plant corn, beans, pumpkins, and wheat.

Temporal farmers claim many advantages. The silt is rich, making it unnecessary to fertilize, while the soil is enriched with each rain. Insects and diseases are rare in the desert, and with rain, crop yields exceed those of river-bottom fields. Carrasco has harvested fifteen sacks of beans (one metric ton or three-fourths of an American ton) from a 3 hectare farm. Disadvantages include utter dependence on rain, and depredations by javelina, deer, and cattle. Only drought-resistant crops can be planted. Chiles, watermelons, and fruit trees must be watered from a spring. As a result, plant folk varieties or crop ecotypes (Nabhan 1989, 71) adapted to temporales are to be found—in particular a dwarf corn variety named "Maíz Venadito" which produces regular-sized ears, uses very little water, and is ready for harvesting within three months.

Humedad farming has been reported in the lower Rio Grande Valley in Texas from as early as 1828 until the late 1840s (Rubel 1966, 27–28), and in 1852 William H. Emory (1857, 89) reported it at La Junta, where the practice continues today, though it is not in widespread use. Mexican farmlands are now irrigated by the Toribio Onega Diversion Dam built in 1974 and its modern canal system. Humedad farming has become an emergency measure to ensure a small harvest when flooding ravages the river-bottom farms. It is also a form of "fortuitous farming" when floods open up extra land not normally irrigable by canals (Leyva Navarrete 1994).

Ordinarily only wheat and corn are planted on humedad farms, although one farmer reported planting rye grass and alfalfa for pasture. The plants the Indians were reported to be growing—beans, pumpkins, and lentils—are not considered suitable for humedad farming. Nor do the farmers prepare the fields, instead being content to look for small clearings after a flood. A half-hectare field is considered to be large.

As the banks begin to dry after a September flood, a mule and a small middlebuster plow may be used to prepare the soil and to cover the seed. If the soil is too muddy, the wheat is sown by throwing seed onto the drying ground, where it is then swept into the mud cracks with a broom of seepwillow branches. The moisture from a single flood is normally enough to produce a crop the following May. Corn can be planted by July with a pointed *barru* or *estaca*—with three or four kernels placed per hole and buried ca. 6.25 cm (2.4 in.) deep. When the stalks are 20 in. (51.3 cm) high, a 6 in. (15.4 cm) dirt mound is pushed up against each plant with a hoe to provide support and to retain water—a practice still in use by the Tarahumaras in their fields on the Upper Río Conchos (Fontana 1979, 71).

A singular achievement of the La Junta farmers involved solving the problem that had bedeviled them for centuries—successful damming of the rivers for purposes of irrigation (Doolittle 1990, 91). Around 1860, mestizo hydrologic technology in northern Mexico (Newcomb 1949, 23), knowledge of timber construction in Spanish mines, and simple natural observations of the activities of native beavers by La Junta farmers (Leyva Navarrete 1994) may have influenced creation of the first successful wood and rock structures to dam the rivers. One scholar of La Junta genealogies has noted a population boom in the 1870s (Pérez 1994). This influx of people was likely due to the opening up of thousands of acres of farmland by the construction of the new dams.

Called simply *presas* locally, the dams should technically be called *presas de burros y muertos,* or burro dams. This river-damming technique lasted almost a century, until the early 1950s, when burro dams evolved into simpler, more efficient, easier-to-repair, and sturdier rock-fill dams. Burro dams were built on the Río Conchos near Coyame, at El Mesquite, and at Ojinaga, as well as on the Rio Grande at El Polvo, El Mulato, San Antonio del Bravo, and Barrancos de Guadalupe (Velásquez 1994).

The author interviewed six farmers who had helped repair the dams and who knew the construction details. They didn't build the dams—their grandfathers and great-grandfathers did that—but the techniques and the materials they used were the same. Green cottonwood trees of proper size were cut and brought by wagon to the dam site. Depending on the height of the dam, tree trunks a meter thick and from 4 to 8 m (13 to 26 ft.) long, and even thicker forked trees of equal length were also cut down. The trunk was joined to a forked tree with a mortise and through-tenon joint, and these were firmly wedged together to form a tripod as high as 5 m (16.4 ft.). This timber tripod, looking like a donkey sitting on its haunches, was called a *burro*. It was assembled on the riverbank, erected, and maneuvered into the flowing river by ten to thirty men. Working underwater, they lifted the burros and set them in place—as many as it took to span the stream.

The burros were aligned by a rope stretched across the river. Once in place, they were tied together with two horizontal members or *vigas* called *gualdas*. Yucca fiber straps or ropes were used to tie the beams together. Vertical members called *palancas* were then attached to the gualdas. Flat, rectangular brush mats of seepwillow called *tapestes,* about 1.5 m by 4 m (4.9 ft. by 13 ft.), were then placed on top of the palancas until the whole front of the dam was covered. The final step involved covering the entire dam front with stone and seepwillow-branch bundles called *muertos,* weighing up to 35 kg (77 lbs.) each. After placement of thousands of muertos, the water would rise and flow into an irrigation canal to a depth of about 2 m (6.6 ft.).

Some muertos—made of dirt, mud, gravel, and wheat straw—were called *angelitos,* and they too weighed over 36 kg (80 lbs.). Each worker made about fifteen muertos a day, bringing them on donkeys or on four-man litters to the riverbank, where they were loaded into a *chalan,* or barge, ferried to the dam, and dumped into the water.

The dams were sturdy enough to divert the river's water, and a heavy flood could submerge them without harm, but they still needed frequent repairs. The legs or body of the burro might rot and break, or be chewed by beavers, or slump due to undermining by the current. Floods might break and carry off sections. Maintenance of the dam and the irrigation canal went on all year, even in winter. The work was organized by a *Sociedad de Agricultores,* that is, by the farmers themselves. The *Sociedad's* officers called the men to work when needed, and each farmer supplied labor in exchange for the water he used throughout the year. A twenty-four-hour period of irrigation meant six workdays of labor. The work was heavy and dangerous and women and children did not participate. Work groups for the different tasks were led by experienced men.

The farmers who were interviewed recalled long hours of working in the water with only beans, tortillas, and coffee for food and sotol liquor to keep them warm. They remembered the yelling and shouting as they scrambled over the dam and how as it accidentally gave way in the fast current, with an explosive crack it carried men and materials downriver. And they recalled having to start all over again, pulling the muertos, one by one, out of the river to be reused. These farmers attribute their arthritis and rheumatism in their old age to the hours of work in the freezing water. But they raised their dams and kept them up, and they irrigated their fields and fed their families at La Junta de los Ríos.

Notes

1. Recent archaeological findings suggest an Apache presence at La Junta by at least AD 1650 (Mallouf 1990, 21). By 1747, several Apache bands were living in the mountains nearby (Madrid 1992, 51–52), and they were trading with the farming Indians at La Junta for horses, corn, and beans. Although Apache groups hunted bison and deer for food, they

are also known to have practiced horticulture from prehistoric times, raising beans, corn, and pumpkins (Newcomb 1961, 113; Office of the State Archeologist 1984, 61–62), and they may have been planting small gardens at La Junta. But as Comanche pressure forced them into more arid regions of Texas and Mexico, the Apaches there may have virtually abandoned the growing of crops and have begun to rely more on wild foods (Newcomb 1961, 114). By the nineteenth century, some Apaches depended on hunting and gathering, with planting ranking third in importance as a means of subsistence (Driver 1970, 60).

The Spanish made several attempts to settle Apache bands on reservations at La Junta, providing them lands, seeds, and even farmers to help plant (Moorhead 1975, 244, 247–51, 259, 261). But while Apaches adopted certain aspects of La Junta culture (Myers 1971, 131), sedentism was not one of them. Spanish reservation experiments ended with the Apaches' refusal to build homes and to plant crops, and with their ultimate flight from the reservations around La Junta in the early nineteenth century.

References

Applegate, Howard G. 1992. "The Demography of La Junta de los Ríos del Norte y Conchos." *Journal of Big Bend Studies* 4:43–73.

Applegate. Howard G., and C. Wayne Hanselka. 1974. *La Junta de los Ríos Del Norte y Conchos.* Southwestern Studies Monograph 41. El Paso: Texas Western Press.

Betancourt, Julio. 1981. "Quitman Mountains of Southern Hudspeth County." In *Five Archeological Investigations in the Trans-Pecos Region of Texas,* edited by Julio Betancourt, 27–82. Texas Antiquities Committee Permit Series 6. Austin: Texas Antiquities Committee.

Binford, Lewis R. 1983. *In Pursuit of the Past: Decoding the Archeological Record.* New York: Thames and Hudson.

Bowden, Charles. 1977. *Killing the Hidden Waters.* Austin: University of Texas Press.

Brody, J. J. 1977. *Mimbres Painted Pottery.* Santa Fe: University of New Mexico Press.

Carrasco, Jesús José. 1994. Interview by author. September 22, Ojinaga, Chihuahua.

Castañeda, Carlos E. 1976. *Our Catholic Heritage in Texas.* Vols. 1 and 2. New York: Arno Press.

Cordell, Linda S. 1984. *Prehistory of the Southwest.* Orlando: Academic Press.

Di Peso, Charles C. 1974. *Casas Grandes: A Fallen Trading Center of the Gran Chichimeca*. Vol. 3, *The Tardi and Españoles Periods,* Amerind Foundation Series 9. Flagstaff: Northland Press.

Doolittle, William E. 1990. *Canal Irrigation in Prehistoric Mexico: The Sequence of Technological Change.* Austin: University of Texas Press.

Driver, Harold E. 1970. *Indians of North America.* Chicago: University of Chicago Press.

Emory, William H. 1857. "From Mouth of Devil's River to El Paso del Norte, 1853–1854." In *Report of the United States and Mexican Boundary Survey.* Vol.1, pt. 1. Washington: Cornelius Wendell.

Favata, Martin A., and José B. Hernández, trans. 1993. *The Account: Alvar Nuñez Cabeza de Vaca's "Relatión."* Houston: University of Houston / Arte Publico Press.

Fontana, Bernard L. 1979. *Tarahumara: Where Night Is the Day of the Moon.* Flagstaff: Northland Press.

García, Homero. n.d. "Información de Fco. R. Aimada: Dalos tornados par Homero García Gutiérrez de los archivos en la Escuela Secundaria Federal de Ciudad Ojinaga, Chihuahua, México." Typed transcript. Enrique R. Madrid, personal papers, Redford, Texas.

García Carrasco, Viviano. 1994. Conversation with author. September 26, Presidio, Texas.

Gómez, Arthur R. 1990. *A Most Singular Country: A History of Occupation in the Big Bend.* Charles Redd Monographs in Western History 18. Salt Lake City: Brigham Young University.

Gómez, Lerma. 1994. Conversation with author. October 7, Ojinaga, Chihuahua.

Groat, Charles G. 1972. *Presidio Bolson, Trans-Pecos Texas and Adjacent Mexico: Geology of a Desert Basin Aquifer System.* Report of Investigations 76. Austin: Bureau of Economic Geology, University of Texas Press.

Hammond, George Peter, and Agapito Rey, trans. 1967. *Expedition into New Mexico Made by Antonio Espejo, 1582–1583.* Vol.1. New York: Arno Press.

Hickerson, Nancy Parrott. 1994. *The Jumanos: Hunters and Traders of the South Plains.* Austin: University of Texas Press.

Jones, Oakah L. 1991. "Settlements and Settlers at La Junta de los Ríos, 1759–1822." *Journal of Big Bend Studies* 3:43–70.

Jordán, Fernando. 1978. *Crónica de un país bárbaro.* Chihuahua: Centra Librero de la Prensa.

Jung, Carl G. 1963. *Memories, Dreams, Reflections.* New York: Random House.

Kelley, J. Charles. 1986. *Jumano and Patarabueye: Relations at La Junta de los Ríos.* Anthropological Papers 77. Ann Arbor: University of Michigan.

Kelley, J. Charles, and Ellen Abbott Kelley. 1990. *Presidio, Texas (Presidio County) Water Improvement Project: An Archaeological and Archival Survey and Appraisal.* Ft. Davis, Texas: Blue Mountain Consultants.

Kopper, Phillip. 1986. *The Smithsonian Book of North American Indians before the Coming of the Europeans.* Washington, DC: Smithsonian Books.

Leyva Navarrete, Trinidad. 1994. Interview by author. September 24, El Divisadero, Chihuahua.

Licón Pando, Esteban. 1994. Interview by author. September 24, Presidio, Texas.

Lister, Robert H., and Florence C. Lister. 1984. *Chaco Canyon.* Albuquerque: University of New Mexico Press.

Madrid, Enrique R. 1992. *Expedition to La Junta de los Ríos, 1747–1748: Captain Commander Joseph de Ydoiaga's Report to the Viceroy of New Spain.* Office of the State Archeologist Special Report 33. Austin: Texas Historical Commission.

———1994. "The Expedition of Captain Joseph de Ydoiaga to La Junta de los Ríos, 1747–48." Paper presented at the 71st Annual Meeting of the West Texas Historical Association, Midland, Texas, April 8–9.

Mallouf. Robert J. 1990. "A Commentary on the Prehistory of Far Northeastern Chihuahua, the La Junta District, and the Cielo Complex." Paper presented at the Segunda Congreso Historia Regional Comparada, Universidad Autónoma de Ciudad Juárez, Mexico.

Martin, Paul S. 1970. *The Last 10,000 Years: A Fossil Pollen Record of the American Southwest.* Tucson: University of Arizona Press.

Minjares Sánchez, Pedro. 1994. Interview by author. September 27, Santa Teresa, Chihuahua.

Moorhead, Max L. 1975. *The Presidio: Bastion of the Spanish Borderlands.* Norman: University of Oklahoma Press.

Myers, Sandra L. 1971. *The Lipan Apaches.* Indian Tribes of Texas. Waco: Texian Press.

Nabhan, Gary Paul. 1989. *Enduring Seeds: Native American Agriculture and Wild Plant Conservation.* San Francisco: North Point Press.

Navarro Reynosa, Ing. Humberto. 1994. Conversation with author. October 7, Comisión Nacional del Agua Office, Ojinaga, Chihuahua.

Newcomb, W. W., Jr. 1949. "An Ethnographic Survey of Redford, Texas." Unpublished manuscript. Enrique R. Madrid, private papers, Redford, Texas.

———1961. *The Indians of Texas: From Prehistoric to Modern Times.* Austin: University of Texas Press.

Office of the State Archeologist. 1984. *The Years of Exploration.* Living with the Texas Past Series 3. Austin: Office of the State Archeologist, Texas Historical Commission.

Officer, James E. 1971. "Arid-lands Agriculture and the Indians of the American Southwest." In *Food, Fiber and the Arid Lands,* edited by William G. McGinnies, Bram J. Goldman, and Patricia Paylore, 47–77. Tucson: University of Arizona Press.

Pennington, Campbell W. 1963. *The Tarahumara of Mexico: Their Environment and Material Culture.* Salt Lake City: University of Utah Press.

Pérez, Elisa Luján. 1994. Telephone conversation with author. October 16.
Porras Ruiz, Alberto. 1994. Interview by author. October 5, Redford, Texas.
Riley, Carrol L. 1987. *The Frontier People*. Albuquerque: University of New Mexico Press.
Rubel, Arthur J. 1966. *Across the Tracks: Mexican-Americans in a Texas City*. Austin: University of Texas Press.
Spencer, Robert F. 1977. *The Native Americans: Ethnology and Backgrounds of the North American Indians*. 2nd ed. New York: Harper and Row.
Velásquez, Leonardo. 1994. Conversation with author. October 31, Presidio, Texas.

6 The Peyote Religion and Mescalero Apaches

An Ethnohistorical View from West Texas

Stacy B. Schaefer

Peyote, an unassuming, spineless cactus known for its mind-altering effects, has for centuries held a central place in the religious traditions of numerous indigenous groups in North America. Most of the contemporary border of the Rio Grande/Río Bravo between the northern Mexico states of Tamaulipas, Coahuila, Nuevo León, and Chihuahua and almost the entire southern border of Texas from as far east as Alamo and west as El Paso is included in the native habitat of peyote, as is the land farther south in the Mexican state of San Luis Potosi. From the early 1600s to late 1800s this border area was a common zone for trade, warfare, alliances, and cultural exchanges among diverse Indian peoples native to the region. Newcomers from elsewhere who fled to the region also became part of the greater diaspora brought on by the arrival of the Spanish.

In the early twentieth century a number of anthropologists and scholars viewed the peyote religion as a fascinating study in persistence and change and documented its diffusion and acceptance among Native Americans in the United States. This chapter will review the route of diffusion proposed by anthropologists Omer Stewart, Weston La Barre, and Morris Opler, who all credit the Lipan Apaches as the tribe responsible for bringing peyote religion from Mexico and introducing it to the Native Americans settled in reservations in Oklahoma, from which it spread to tribes in other states.

Following this summary, I will discuss the possibility that there may have been more than one route of diffusion and will turn to the work of James Mooney, who claimed that the Mescalero Apaches were the purveyors of peyote religion to Native Americans. A brief review of Mescalero history and their migrations south through the Davis Mountains, across the Rio Grande, and into Chihuahua will provide information about an alternate route, through Chihuahua and West Texas, by which peyote religion could have been brought in to the United States via the Mescalero. Another perspective regarding the origin and spread of peyote religion is one that La Barre (1960) refers to as "differential diffusion"—peyote religion took different forms as it spread to the United States. The Lipan Apaches, who had contact with Spanish missions, most likely incorporated the beginnings of syncretized Christian elements into the peyote ceremony, whereas the Mescalero Apaches retained many more elements of the "old peyote complex" practiced by Mexican Indians. In conclusion I will focus on a few specific aspects of peyote religion practiced by the Tarahumara and Huichol Indians, and their correspondence to Mescalero peyotism. But first, a brief description of peyote and the history of peyote religion to set the background.

Peyote Religion and its Diffusion from Mexico to the United States

Peyote religion revolves around a desert-dwelling plant known as peyotl to the Aztecs, hikuri to the Huichois and Tarahumaras, "medicine" to members of the Native American Church, and *Lophophora williamsii* to botanists. This sacred plant is revered by many for its psychotropic and medicinal qualities. Peyote contains over sixty alkaloids, of which mescaline is the major vision-producing agent. Having long been appreciated for its ability to assuage hunger and thirst and to promote wakefulness and energy for hours on end, peyote has also been demonstrated by scientific investigation to be a medicinal plant containing antibiotic agents (McCleary et al. 1960). Furthermore, experts have testified to its safety and benign qualities even for those who consume it extensively (Schultes 1938, 1940; Bittle 1960; Blum et al. 1977). Since the end of the nineteenth century, followers of peyote religion in North America have grown exponentially, particularly in the United States and Canada. The 1994 amendment to the Native American Religious Freedom Act of 1978 ensures legal guarantees for peyote's sacramental use in religious ceremonies.

Native religious traditions involving peyote have their antecedents in prehistoric times with indigenous groups living in or around the region where it grows. Judging from the remains in ancient rock-shelters inhabited by peoples from northeastern Mexico to the Texas borderlands, peyote was highly valued and revered as a sacred plant. In archeological sites from Coahuila to Texas, necklaces of peyotes strung like beads on fiber cord have been found in shelters and cave burials that date from AD 800 (Adovasio and Fry 1976; Bruhn et al. 1978) to as far back as 5000 BC (Furst 1989). In these shelters, peyote sometimes occurs in association with the toxic seeds of what has commonly been called the "mescal bean" (*Sophora secundiflora*). Experiments with peyote consumption and experiences derived from its psychoactive properties may have had profound influences on these early desert hunter-gatherers, as it continues to have on indigenous peoples in both Mexico and the United States. Some of the rock art in rock-shelters along the Rio Grande north of Eagle Pass, Texas, may have included intentional renderings of powerful peyote-related experiences and beliefs (Boyd and Dering 1996). Later on, peyote could very well have been a trade item which, like other precious goods, such as salt and obsidian, was exchanged along established networks during pre-Columbian times (Weigand 1981, 1985).

At the time of European contact, peyote was used by numerous indigenous cultures in what became the Spanish colony of New Spain. There it was commonly referred to by Spanish clergymen and chroniclers as "the diabolical root" (Cárdenas 1945). The following groups were reported to use peyote for religious, ceremonial, and medicinal purposes: Chichimecs, Aztecs, Tlaxcaltecas, Tarascans, Otomis, Zacatecos, Huichols, Coras, Tepecanos, Tamaulipecans, Coahuiltecans, Tarahumaras, Pimas, Opotas, Papagos, Caxcanes, Acaxees, and Carrizos (Arlegui 1737; Hernández 1790; Ortega 1887; Prieto 1873; Santoscoy 1899; Sahagún 1982; Stewart 1987). Spanish encroachment into the peyote lands and farther north disrupted peyote traditions and trading activities, which, in the wake of the chaos that ensued, transformed the border region along the present-day Texas-Mexico border into a refuge for fragmented indigenous groups. Some of the newly arrived were already familiar with peyote and its curative and religious powers. The establishment of colonial presidios (forts), missions, and settlements further impacted the border region on both sides of the Rio Grande. Spanish chronicles describe Indians located along the peyote lands of Texas and the Mexican states of Tamaulipas, Coahuila, Nuevo León, and Chihuahua. From these written reports and other firsthand accounts, anthropologists James Mooney (1896, 1897, 1898), Omer Stewart (1987), Morris Opler (1938), and Weston La Barre (1938) reconstructed the following scenario: the Mescalero Apaches occupied the peyote lands west of the Pecos River, including the Big Bend area; Lipan Apaches, who were firmly established in the region by 1800, made their territory east of the Pecos River, including lands near Carrizo Springs and Eagle Pass; and the Carrizo Indians, part of the general Coahuiltecan Indian cultural group, were situated on territory from Laredo west along the Rio Grande.

According to Stewart and Opler, the Lipan Apaches introduced peyote religion to Indian groups in the United States. Their reasoning is that between 1770 and the early 1800s, the Lipans had migrated one hundred miles north of the peyote gardens between Eagle Pass and Carrizo Springs. During that time they had contact with the Carrizo Indians, who had been roaming the peyote area of South Texas for centuries and carrying out their own rituals with this sacred plant. In 1830 the Lipans were reportedly seen with the Carrizo Indians in Laredo (Stewart 1987, 46). Additionally, in 1935, Lipan consultants living on the Mescalero reservation reported to Opler (1938, 273) that they had learned the use of peyote from the Carrizo Indians "before they had any experience with white people or Mexicans." Other studies that had bearing on Stewart's contention that the Lipan Apaches were the ones who introduced peyote religion to tribes in the United States were from botanical field collections. The most wide-ranging field documentation of peyote is credited to botanist Edward Anderson (1980). Although Anderson was not able to make field collections from all the peyote habitats in the border region, his research indicated that peyote was more abundant in South Texas than in the drier borderlands west of Laredo to El Paso. Stewart reasons that since the Lipan Indians were closer to the South Texas zone where peyote was abundant, they had greater access to the plant than other North American Indians. The Lipans subsequently shared their peyote religion with Indian groups sent to reservations in Oklahoma, such as the Kiowas, Kiowa Apaches, Comanches, and Mescaleros (Stewart 1987, 50). From these core tribes in Oklahoma, the religion diffused out to other tribes in the vicinity and across the nation.

While Lipan involvement with peyote may very well have spread the seeds of peyote religion that became the Native American Church, peyote ceremonialism was most likely diffused in various ways to other tribes. The Mescalero Apaches were considered by James Mooney (1896, 1897) to be responsible for bringing peyote religion from Mexico to the United States. From the Mescaleros, the ceremony spread to the Indian tribes in Oklahoma, where it was further diffused. Mooney, who worked among the Kiowas, was one of the first anthropologists to document the religious use of peyote in the United States. Recognizing the importance of this religion for Native Americans, he was highly influential in assisting Native American leaders at the turn of the twentieth century to establish the Native American Church as a bona fide religion recognized by the federal government. Mooney's belief that the Mescalero Apaches brought peyote ceremonialism to the United States is very plausible.

Cultural History of the Chihuahua-West Texas Region and the Mescalero Apaches

In Chihuahua, north of the western Sierra Madre of the Tarahumaras, lies an intermediate zone that leads to the confluence of the Río Conchos and the Rio Grande. This area was an important trading center known as the La Junta district. Some of the various hunting-and-gathering groups as well as the small-scale agriculturalists in this region included Abriaches, Otomoacos, Caguates, Tanpachas, Tompiros, Julimes, and Jumanos. The name Jumano was a common term used to refer to all the native peoples scattered throughout the river valley between La Junta and El Paso del Norte (Parrot 1994, 65–66). Indeed, archeological remains in the La Junta district include La Junta phase agricultural villages and nearby hunter-gatherer encampments such as the Cielo Bravo site, a type site of the Cielo complex found in the Big Bend and northeastern Chihuahua (Mallouf 1985, 1999). Both have yielded circular house floors and similar material remains indicating possible cultural affiliations (Kelley 1986). Interpreting these archeological findings, Mallouf (1990, 6 [in Parrot 1994, 227]) proposes that hunting-and-gathering groups coexisted with semisedentary peoples during the La Junta phase (AD 1200–1400) in the Big Bend area and "occasionally came together for purposes of exchange and other activities." This general region is also home to peyote populations. The collection and exchange of peyote may have been included in the long-distance trade operated out of La Junta.

The Jumano Indians, as the Spanish indicated in their writings from 1500–1700, inhabited more than the La Junta region; their territory reached from the northern part of Chihuahua into Texas, and into the southern Plains of the Llano Estacado in present-day Texas and New Mexico (Parrot 1994, 66–67). They were not the only indigenous group on the Llano Estacado; explorer Francisco Vázquez de Coronado on his 1540–42 journey through the area described small bands of buffalo hunters who Farrer (1991) and Habicht-Mauche (1992) are convinced were Apaches. It was not until the 1700s, however, that the Spanish began to distinguish between eastern and western Apache groups and the Mescalero Apaches were first mentioned as a distinct indigenous group (Farrer 1991, 217). The Apaches, experiencing displacement from their territorial lands in the diaspora created by Spanish expansion, aggressively dominated the lands farther south on the Llano Estacado, pushing groups of Jumanos southward as well. The expeditions of Alonso de Posada from 1632–54 indicate that the Jumanos were driven from the Río de las Nueces to the junction of the Rio Grande and Río Conchos. Franciscan missions established at El Paso in 1680 and La Junta de los Ríos in 1683 were populated by groups of Jumanos who had lost access to their lands (Parrot 1994, 152–53). By 1750 the Jumanos were an extinct cultural group, having succumbed to either assimilation or death from diseases contracted from the Spaniards, or by being incorporated into Apache bands (Griffen 1988, 1–2; Parrot 1994, 208).

Migrating Apaches in the late 1600s, particularly Mescalero Apaches, claimed Jumano territory as their own and, with the Comanches who arrived in the 1700s, made inroads into Chihuahua, Durango, Zacatecas, and San Luis Potosi (Griffen 1988, 2). It is not unreasonable to assume that in these regions, Mescaleros came into contact with Indian peyotists, particularly in the peyote lands of the Tarahumaras and Huichols (Stewart 1987, 46). The Mescaleros shared their raiding territory with the Comanches; both were powerful forces to contend with as they raided and traded their way throughout the region (Griffen 1988, 2–4). One major trade route the Mescaleros monopolized from the late 1600s to mid-1700s extended from around Chihuahua City to Taos, New Mexico. The Spanish furiously retaliated against these Indian forces, and near the end of the 1700s, bands of Mescaleros sought refuge in the Davis Mountains of West Texas and the mountains of southeastern New Mexico (Claire R. Farrer, personal communication 2000). Shortly thereafter, until Mexican independence from Spain in 1824, the Spaniards responded to Mescalero Apaches with a new tactic. Those who continued to roam the Chihuahua area were enticed by the colonial government to settle in "peace establishments" (*establecimientos de paz*) set up in the Spanish presidios. Food, supplies, and sometimes healthcare were provided to the Apache residents. This was an unusual arrangement in Indian-Spanish relations; unlike in the mission establishments, religion and religious conversion played little part in the colonial operation—the underlying goal was to engage the Apaches in peaceful settlement and to control their movement. Spanish authorities demanded that Apache residents obtain written permission from the fort commander when traveling distances from the presidio (Griffen 1988, 12–17). Despite the military's attempt to manage their lives, fort Apaches maintained communication with their free-roaming Apache kin in the hinterlands, and food and goods found their way to Apache brethren in the mountains.

Ten years after Mexico's independence from Spain in 1824, the Mexican government decided that the peace establishments were too costly a welfare program and discontinued them. This in turn sparked another epoch of tumultuous raids and brutal warfare among Mexicans and Apaches and Comanches. Apaches, most likely Mescaleros, infiltrated Tarahumara country, where the Tarahumaras were reported to have helped them. Other reports disclose that Tarahumaras who had aligned themselves with the Spanish and then the Mexicans were considered by the Apaches to be friends of the enemy and were attacked as well. The explosive relationship between Apaches and Mexicans was inherited by the United States along with the southwestern states acquired under US treaties of 1848 and 1853 (Farrer 1991, 219). Crossing back and forth across the Rio Grande, Apaches continued to carry out raids during the Civil War. The US Army and the Texas Rangers roamed the border region and began rounding up Mescaleros during the years 1862–64. Some remnant groups of Mescaleros fled for the Llano Estacado or hid in the Sacramento Mountains, while others disappeared across the Rio Grande into Mexico. They were at home traversing the riverways and rugged mountain terrain, far from the clutches of the government roundup parties. Eventually, in 1873, the Mescalero reservation was established in New Mexico, where the Mescaleros were joined by their Apache cousins, the Lipans, who arrived in wagonloads in 1904–05. Later, in 1911 and 1912, 468 Chiricahua Apaches were relocated to the Mescalero reservation; the remainder stayed in their last prisoner-of-war camp at Fort Sill, Oklahoma (Farrer 1991, 225–27). Near the end of the nineteenth century, anthropologist James Mooney began his research on peyote religion. A Mexican man who had been captured by the Mescaleros as a youth in the 1860s, informed Mooney that in their tepee gatherings they did indeed carry out peyote ceremonies (Methvin 1899, 37 [in Stewart 1987, 48]).

The Mescalero Apaches and the Diffusion of Peyote Religion from Mexico through West Texas to New Mexico

The history of Mescalero Apache migrations discussed above points to this Apache group as taking over the Jumano territory around La Junta before the end of the seventeenth century. The Mescaleros expanded their domain, controlled the trade route from Chihuahua City to Taos until the mid-eighteenth century, and roamed the region until the latter part of the nineteenth century. Certain portions of this area were native habitat for peyote; on the north side of the border in West Texas, peyote populations have been documented around Langtry, Shatter, and Big Bend National Park (Stewart 1987, 11, 13). South of the Rio Grande, peyote has been found in various areas of Chihuahua known to the Tarahumara Indians (Lumholtz 1902; Bennett and Zingg 1935; Pennington 1963; Bye 1979). It is possible that during this time peyote was one of many special items that were moved, sometimes clandestinely, along the trade route from Mexico, through West Texas, and into New Mexico. As with all trading activities, past and present, the exchange of goods also involves the exchange of ideas, including religious beliefs and practices. Along with the trade of peyote came the diffusion of peyote religion.

At the end of the nineteenth century the Norwegian explorer Carl Lumholtz passed through this region, spending time with the Tarahumaras, Huichols, and numerous other indigenous Mexican groups. Lumholtz wrote about the Tarahumaras and their peyote traditions, as well as about the Huichols. Later, in the 1930s, anthropologists Wendell Bennett and Robert Zingg (1935) also traveled to the Tarahumaras and documented their cultural traditions, including the ritual use of peyote. Botanist Campbell Pennington studied the plants used by the Tarahumaras, including peyote. The areas where the Tarahumaras collected peyote included land around the mouth of the Río Conchos. Lumholtz (1902, 362) described the areas where the Tarahumaras traveled to collect peyote as the foothills of the Sierra Almoloy near the railroad station of Jiménez, and the Sierra de Margoso farther past Santa Rosalia de Camargo and across the tracks of the Mexican Central Railroad. Bennett and Zingg (1935, 136) wrote that the Tarahumaras also secured peyote not far from Presidio, Texas. Pennington (1963, 166) discovered that the Tarahumaras collected peyote upon the "ridges adjacent to the road leading south from Ojinaga,

Chihuahua to La Mula"—the area that once bordered their lands in the late sixteenth to early seventeenth centuries.

Over the two-hundred-year period that the Mescaleros roamed the West Texas-Chihuahua border area, they came in contact with Tarahumara Indians. One account from 1838 tells of a Tarahumara who helped spy for Apaches south of Namiquipa along the Sierra Madre near the Río Santa María (Griffen 1988, 156). However, not all Tarahumaras formed alliances with the Mescaleros; another report from 1845 describes a Mescalero assault on three Tarahumara Indians in a Spanish settlement (Griffen 1988, 107–8). Even at the end of the 1800s, Lumholtz (1902, 36) was told by Tarahumara consultants that they were wary of Apaches and believed that peyote, being their powerful protector, would prevent the Apaches from firing on them with guns. Since Mescalero Apaches, along with allied Comanches, were known to have carried out trading and raiding activities in Coahuila, they likely came in contact with Carrizo Indians. The Mescaleros were known to have ranged as far south as the state of San Luis Potosí, the area where Huichol Indians collect peyote. There they may have crossed paths with groups of Huichol Indians making the pilgrimage to these lands to gather the sacred plant (Stewart 1987, 46). Thus, encounters between Mescalero Apaches and other Mexican Indian peyotists, such as Huichol, Tarahumara, and Carrizo groups, could have been the means by which peyote and its religious use were introduced to the Mescaleros. Interestingly, the Apaches were not the only ones who were introduced to peyote. Lumholtz (1902, 358) learned that during the Civil War, Texas Rangers, "taken prisoners and deprived of all other stimulating drinks, used mescal buttons (peyote buttons), or 'white mule,' as they called them. They soaked the plants in water and became intoxicated with the liquid."

There is no evidence that the Texas Rangers used peyote within a religious context as did the Apaches.

The peyote religion of the Indians of Mexico, referred to as "old peyote cult complex" by some anthropologists studying the diffusion of the peyote religion, must have included ritual elements meaningful to Mescalero traditional values and concepts (La Barre 1938, 1960; Stewart 1987). Unlike the form of peyote religion modified by the addition of syncretized Christian symbols and beliefs that the Lipan Apaches presumably introduced to the Indian groups in Oklahoma, Mescalero peyote traditions documented by Opler in the 1930s were purely aboriginal, with no trace of Christian elements. Opler (1936, 144) viewed Mescalero adoption and practice of peyote religion as an intensification of their traditional indigenous beliefs, values, and identity. Although Opler's consultants said peyote religion was introduced among Mescaleros around 1870, it is important to point out that Opler was not allowed to stay overnight on the Mescalero reservation, hence hindering his ability to personally observe a peyote ceremony. Most of his consultants were not Mescalero but Chiricahua Apaches, among whom Geronimo was an important leader (Claire R. Farrer, personal communication 2000). The territory that the Chiricahuas once roamed was farther west, especially around the border region of Arizona and Sonora. They, like the Lipan Apaches, were sent to the Mescalero reservation at the beginning of the twentieth century, thirty years after the Mescalero Apaches had settled there. Opler in his treatise on peyote religion refers to all Indians on the reservation as Mescalero Apaches.

Taking this fact and other historical information regarding the Mescalero Apaches into consideration, an alternate theory is that the Mescaleros learned independently about peyote religion during the two-hundred-year period they inhabited the West Texas-Chihuahua borderlands. They molded elements of the religion to meet their cultural worldview, needs, and concerns. The concept of differential diffusion coined by La Barre in his call for future studies on peyote religion is important here. Further consideration should be given to the possibility that peyote religion reached the United States through various routes of diffusion. In addition to the Lipan, one must look to the Mescaleros and perhaps to other tribes as well. Another issue to be addressed with the concept of differential diffusion is the varied form and content of Peyote-related rituals among the Mexican Indians who practiced the "old peyote cult complex." The earliest descriptions of peyote use by Spanish chroniclers, and more recent Mexican, American, and European accounts, indicate that indigenous groups such as the Carrizos, Huichols, and Tarahumaras had their own specific, culturally bound ways of worshipping with this mind-altering plant. In turn, Native Americans who were introduced to the ritual use of peyote accepted and began to practice this new tradition only if it resonated within their own cultural beliefs and values. Even then, some changes and modifications were made by peyotists in order to better fit this new religion into their lives in a meaningful way. La Barre suggests that since the Mescalero peyote ceremony did not contain Christian elements, it may reflect the transitional phase between "the old peyote cult complex" and the newer version of peyote religion of the Native American Church.

Opler's study of Mescalero peyote rituals continues to be a valuable piece of work for various reasons. It is the earliest and most comprehensive study of peyote use on the Mescalero Indian reservation. Just as importantly, in it Opler examines the manner in which Mescalero peyotism was practiced, directing special attention to the importance of shamans in traditional Mescalero Apache culture and their integration into peyote ceremonialism. He writes, "It may be said, then, that the Mescalero Apache were a tribe of shamans, active or potentially active. . . . Mescalero were considered candidates for supernatural experiences with peyote and Mescalero who had gained their peyote ceremony through transmission from another might have that knowledge and power enhanced by a personal supernatural encounter of the traditional Mescalero type" (Opler 1936, 146, 148).

The overall intent of the Mescaleros' peyote meetings was to cure individuals who had fallen ill. According to their shamanic beliefs, illness could be cured only with help from the supernatural, and "it was acceptable to the Mescalero mind, therefore, to think of peyote as an agency through which other powers could be approached and utilized" (Opler 1936, 152).

The integration by the Mescaleros of their shamanic world and curing practices with the peyote ceremony is reminiscent of peyote rituals reported among the Tarahumaras. Bennett and Zingg wrote that in the region of Nararachic, peyote was used primarily by shamans. The peyote shamans in this Tarahumara area were considered the most powerful of all shamans—their specialty was their ability to cure with the help of peyote. The manner in which they used peyote was described as resembling "an elaborate curing ceremony rather than a cult" (Bennett and Zingg 1935, 294). Huichols training to become shamans formed an alliance with the peyote and learned important lessons imparted to them by their gods through their peyote visions (Furst 1972; Eger 1978; Schaefer 1996). Additionally, Huichols under the direction of the shaman may have gone on pilgrimages to the peyote desert of San Luis Potosí for the purpose of being healed.

The religious use of peyote among the Mescalero Apaches appears to have quickly declined in the twentieth century. Opler believed that one of several reasons for this was the difficulty in procuring peyote, especially at the end of the nineteenth century when no Indians were officially allowed to live in or travel through Texas. Because of the violent history of white and Indian encounters in South and West Texas, it was an extremely hostile environment for Indians (Stewart 1987, 57). It is interesting to note that despite the general intolerance of Texans toward Indians at the time, in 1884 a Comanche chief named Quanah Parker traveled freely through West Texas and was reported to have stayed at Fort Davis. He had recently been introduced to peyote religion, possibly influenced by Mescalero Apaches, since he was traveling through land once claimed by the Mescaleros in the Davis Mountains and its surrounding hinterlands. Parker stayed at Fort Davis and was reported to have been on his way to Mitre Peak in search of the sacred peyote (Scobee 1951). Unlike most Apaches or Comanches, Quanah Parker had a special relationship with Texas ranchers, based on his leasing of tribal grasslands to cattlemen (Jackson and Jackson 1963). Later on, when he became a charismatic leader of peyote religion, his general good standing with the Texas ranching community and local authorities enabled him to send a representative to Mexico to bring back peyote—as many as eight thousand peyote buttons at a time (Stewart 1987, 76). The Mescaleros were not looked upon as favorably as Quanah Parker and lacked the means by which to procure the needed peyote for their ritual use.

Opler suggests another crucial reason why Mescalero peyote ceremonialism lost momentum may have been that the evolving peyote ceremony was not in keeping with traditional shamanic curing ceremonies. These involved one shaman who, through his link with the supernatural, worked alone to heal the patient. Instead, Opler saw a conflict in the traditional power structure of authority and autonomy among shamans when they gathered together for the peyote ceremonies. The peyote religion that emerged in the form of the Native American Church, which from written descriptions and from my own observations has Christian overtones and elements of a church gathering, was less familiar to traditional Mescalero ways. Seeing that the Mescaleros had minimal Christian influence, the Spanish established military peace settlements rather than missions to resettle them. Because the Mescaleros continued to maintain a shamanic hunting and gathering ideology, the new form of peyote religion that was spreading throughout Indian country in the United States had little relevance for them.

In closing, although a traditionally aboriginal form of peyote religion may have been brought to the United States by Mescaleros and introduced to other Native Americans, the group social structure of peyote ceremonialism lost favor among the Mescaleros. It did not gain momentum or followers as did the peyote practices of the budding Native American

Church. Instead, some Mescalero medicine men who continued to use peyote did so in a context that was more in line with their shamanic traditions and their search for greater powers to communicate with the supernatural. According to anthropologist Claire R. Farrer (personal communication 2000), who has spent over thirty years working among the Mescalero Apaches, contemporary Mescaleros claim they introduced peyote to their allies because through the ingestion of peyote, they can reach their vision quest much more quickly. But, as she learned from the wise, respected medicine man Bernard Second, the Mescaleros see peyote as only a tool. After the shaman has mastered the teachings, he does not need to achieve further visions because he can now open the doorway to the supernatural world. As for Mescalero relationships with the Tarahumaras, Farrer (1991, 226, and personal communication 2000) recounts that Mescaleros think highly of the Tarahumaras and their continuing traditions and that even today Mescaleros refer to the Tarahumaras as their "cousins" in Mexico.

References

Adovasio, J. M., and G. F. Fry. 1976. "Prehistoric Psychotropic Drug Use in Northeastern Mexico and Trans-Pecos Texas." *Economic Botany* 30:94–96.

Anderson, Edward F. 1980. *Peyote: The Divine Cactus.* Tuscon: University of Arizona Press.

Arlegui, José de. (1737) 1851. *Crónica de la provincia de San Francisco de Zacatecas.* Hogel, Mexico.

Bennett, Wendell, and Robert Zingg. 1935. *The Tarahumara: An Indian Tribe of Northern Mexico.* Chicago: University of Chicago Press.

Bittle, William. 1960. "The Curative Aspects of Peyotism." *Bios* 3 (1):140–48.

Blum, Kenneth, S. L. Futterman, and P. Pascarosa. 1977. "Peyote, A Potential Ethnopharmacologic Agent for Alcoholism and Other Drug Dependencies: Possible Biochemical Rationale." *Clinical Toxicology* 11:459–72.

Boyd, Carolyn E., and J. Philip Dering. 1996. "Medicinal and Hallucinogenic Plants Identified in the Sediments and Pictographs of the Lower Pecos, Texas Archaic." *Antiquity* 70 (268):256–75.

Bruhn, J. G., J. E. Lindgren, B. Holstedt, and J. M. Adovasio. 1978. "Peyote Alkaloids: Identification in a Prehistoric Specimen of *Lophophora* from Coahuila, Mexico." *Science* 199 (4336):1437–38.

Bye, Robert A. 1979. "Hallucinogenic Plants of the Tarahumara." *Journal of Ethnopharmacology* 1:23–48.

Cárdenas, Juan de. (1591) 1945. *Primera parte de los problemas y secretos mara-*

villosos de las Indias. Edited facsimile edition. Madrid: Ediciones Cultural Hispánica.

Eger, Susan. 1978. "Huichol Women's Art." In *Art of the Huichol Indians,* edited by Kathleen Berrin, 35–53. [San Francisco]: Fine Arts Museums of San Francisco.

Farrer, Claire R. 1991. *Living Life's Circles: Mescalero Apache Cosmovision.* Albuquerque: University of New Mexico Press.

Furst, Peter T. 1972. "To Find Our Life: Peyote among the Huichol Indians of Mexico." In *Flesh of the Gods: The Ritual Use of Hallucinogens,* edited by Peter T. Furst, 184–236. New York: Praeger.

———. 1989. Review of *Peyote Religion: A History,* by Omer Stewart. *American Ethnologist* 16:386–87.

Griffen, William B. 1988. *Utmost Good Faith: Patterns of Apache-Mexican Hostilities in Northern Chihuahua Border Warfare, 1821–1848.* Albuquerque: University of New Mexico Press.

Habicht-Mauche, Judith A. 1992. "Coronado's Querechos and Teyas in the Archaeological Record of the Texas Panhandle." *Plains Anthropologist* 37:247–59.

Hernández, F. 1790. *De historia plantarum novae Hispaniae opera cum editatum inedita, ad autographi fidem et inintegratem expressa.* Madrid: Ibarra Heredum.

Hickerson, Nancy Parrot. 1994. *The Jumanos, Hunters and Traders of the South Plains.* Austin: University of Texas Press.

Jackson, C. L, and G. Jackson. 1963. *Quanah Parker: Last Chief of the Comanches.* New York: Exposition Press.

Kelley, J. Charles. 1986. *Jumano and Patarabueye: Relations at La Junta de los Ríos.* Anthropological Papers 77. Ann Arbor: Museum of Anthropology, University of Michigan.

La Barre, Weston. 1938. *The Peyote Cult.* Norman: University of Oklahoma Press.

———. 1960. "Peyote Studies, 1941–1960." *Current Anthropoloqy* 1(1):45–60.

Lumholtz, Carl. 1902. *Unknown Mexico.* 2 vols. New York: Scribner's and Sons.

Mallouf, Robert J. 1985. "A Synthesis of Eastern Trans-Pecos Prehistory." MA thesis, University of Texas at Austin.

———. 1990. "The Cielo Complex: Archaeological Evidence of the Jumano and Jumano Apache in the Texas Big Bend." Paper presented at Chiricahua and Mescalero Apache Conference. Truth-or-Consequences, New Mexico, Nov. 9.

———. 1999. "Comments on the Prehistory of Far Northeastern Chihuahua, the La Junta District, and the Cielo Complex." *Journal of Big Bend Studies* 11:49–92.

McCleary, J. A., P. S. Sypherd, and D. L. Walkington. 1960. "Antibiotic Activity of an Extract of Peyote (*Lophophora williamsii* [Lemaire] Coulter)." *Economic Botany* 14 (3):247–49.

Methvin, J. J. 1899. *Andele, or the Mexican-Kiowa Captive.* Louisville: Pentecostal Herald Press.

Mooney, James. 1896. "The Mescal Plant and Ceremony." *Therapeutic Gazette* 12 (11):7–11.

———. 1897. "Mescalero and Lipan Apache Notes." Manuscript 425. Washington, DC: US Bureau of American Ethnology.

———. 1898. "The Mescal Plant and Ceremony." *Bureau of American Ethnology Annual Report 7, 1895–1896.* Washington, DC: GPO.

Opler, Morris E. 1936. "The Influence of Aboriginal Pattern and White Contact on a Recently Introduced Ceremony, the Mescalero Peyote Rite." *Journal of American Folklore* 49:142–66.

———. 1938. "The Use of Peyote by the Carrizo and Lipan Apache Tribes." *American Anthropologist* 40 (2):271–85.

Ortega, José de. (1754) 1887. *Historia de Nayarit, Sonora y ambas Californias.* Mexico: E. Abadiano.

Pennington, Campbell W. 1963. *The Tarahumara of Mexico, Their Environment and Material Culture.* Salt Lake City: University of Utah Press.

Prieto, A. 1873. *Historia, geografía, y estadística del estado de Tamaulipas.* Mexico: Tip. Escalerillas.

Sahagún, Bernardino de. (1545–1590) 1982. *Historia de las cosas de Nueva España.* Mexico: Porrúa.

Santoscoy, Alberto. 1899. *Nayarit.* Gualajara, Mexico: Yguiniz.

Schaefer, Stacy B. 1996. "The Crossing of the Souls: Peyote, Perception and Meaning among the Huichol Indians." In *People of the Peyote: Huichol Indian History, Culture and Survival,* edited by Stacy B. Schaefer and Peter T. Furst, 138–68. Albuquerque: University of New Mexico Press.

Schultes, Richard Evans. 1938. "The Appeal of Peyote (*Lophophora williamsii*) as a Medicine." *American Anthropologist* 40:698–715.

———. 1940. "The Aboriginal Therapeutic Uses of *Lophophora williamsii.*" *Cactus and Succulent Journal* (US) 12:177–81.

Scobee, Barry. 1951. *Alpine Avalanche.* Historical Booklet.

Stewart, Omer C. 1987. *Peyote Religion.* Norman: University of Oklahoma Press.

Weigand, Phil. 1981. "Differential Acculturation among the Huichol Indians." In *Themes of Indigenous Acculturation in Northwest Mexico,* edited by Thomas Hinton and Phil Weigand, 9–21. Anthropological Papers No. 38. Tucson: University of Arizona Press.

———. 1985. "Considerations on the Archaeology and Ethnohistory of Mexicaneros, Tequales, Coras, Huicholes and the Caxcanes of Nayarit, Jalisco and Zacatecas." In *Contributions to the Archaeology and Ethnohistory of Greater Mesoamerica,* edited by William J. Folan, 126–87. Carbondale: Southern Illinois University Press.

7 Spanish-Indian Relations in the Big Bend Region during the Eighteenth and Early Nineteenth Centuries

Elizabeth A. H. John

For most of the eighteenth century, the Big Bend was really Apache country. Apache warriors had grabbed this land when they were newly empowered by the horse and irresistibly drawn toward the Spanish frontier source of that animal. In taking the region, Apaches ousted, destroyed, or absorbed countless little groups of indigenous peoples, who vanished into the mists of history.

But Apache dominance in the Big Bend was secure for little more than half a century. By the 1770s, southward-moving Comanches threatened to make the Big Bend as dangerous for Apaches as Apaches had made it for others a few decades earlier.

How did Spaniards figure on these volatile Indian frontiers? From the early 1600s onward, Spanish relations with Apaches evolved through a complex mix of hostilities and tentative friendships, of alternate—or sometimes even simultaneous—raiding and trading. There was not the incessant, all-encompassing warfare that is often imagined. The tenor varied according to the circumstances, and perceived self-interest, not only of the Apaches and the Spaniards involved in any given situation, but also of peoples linked with the Spaniards, particularly the Pueblo peoples of New Mexico.

Certainly the pattern varied among Apache tribes: for instance, from the 1720s onward, the Jicarillas lived peacefully on the northern frontier of New Mexico, near the pueblos of Taos and Picuris. Moreover, Lipanes maintained relatively peaceful treaty relations in Texas and Coahuila after the 1740s. In both cases, Comanche pressure drove those eastern Apaches to seek sanctuary on the Spanish frontier.

The vast Big Bend country—in many respects ideal Apache habitat—sheltered four Apache tribes. Westernmost were the Faraones, who inhabited mountain ranges between the Rio Grande and the Pecos

River. They maintained close relations with the neighboring Mescaleros, who generally inhabited the mountains nearer the Pecos, extending southward toward the Bolsón de Mapimí, and northward toward the Comancheria. East of the Mescaleros were the Llaneros, a very numerous people, subdivided into Natages, Lipiyanes, and Llaneros proper. They ranged the plains and deserts lying between the Pecos and Colorado rivers and down to the Rio Grande. It was the Llaneros, often leagued with the Mescaleros, who most frequently skirmished northward with the Comanches, particularly during the winter's buffalo-hunting season. Llaneros, Mescaleros, and Faraones all preyed sporadically on the Spanish frontier, sometimes in loose concert. Easternmost, ranging the Texas and Coahuila frontiers, were the Lipanes, who were loosely connected to the Mescaleros and Llaneros by ties of kinship and tradition and their mutual hatred of the Comanches.

Spaniards had little occasion to venture far into the Big Bend except in pursuit of Apaches. Those punitive expeditions were generally long on hardship and short on results, but one had memorable repercussions. In the autumn of 1770, Capt. Bernardo de Gálvez, the new young military commandant of Nueva Vizcaya and Sonora, led about 135 frontier soldiers and Indian allies from Chihuahua to the Pecos River, where he surprised a big Apache camp. At the cost of only one casualty—a wounded Spaniard—the Gálvez's force killed twenty-eight Apaches and captured thirty-six. The booty included 204 horses and mules, which Gálvez distributed among the Indian allies, and two thousand pesos' worth of buffalo and antelope hides.

Most important for the long run were the results that Gálvez obtained by generous treatment of those thirty-six Apache captives. Within six months, some of those were accompanying Spanish troops as guides and auxiliaries. Other Apaches heard of the kindness those captives experienced from Gálvez, and some proposed a general cessation of hostilities. That "general peace" of 1771 proved as short-lived, if not indeed illusory, as skeptics predicted. But Gálvez never forgot his success in conciliating Apaches, and he never ceased to admire their fortitude and skill.

When duty called Gálvez back to Spain at the end of 1771, fourteen of his Apache captives from the Big Bend rode with him to Mexico City, where he enrolled them in the College of San Gregorio. And when he sailed home with his uncle, the Visitador José de Gálvez, now returning to Spain to become minister of the Indies, Bernardo de Gálvez found that his views concerning Apaches won some interest in high places.

Unfortunately, the successor to Gálvez on this frontier was the grim hardliner Hugo O'Conor, who believed that harsh punishment was the only effective way to deal with the Apaches, or indeed most indigens of the northern frontier. There would be no further experimentation with "kinder and gentler" techniques without a firm directive from the Crown. But even that would be futile unless its implementation could be entrusted to officers with enough imagination and skill and nerve to try it.

Surprisingly enough, those conditions did materialize, as part of a great burst of reform in the 1770s. The Big Bend was the first arena of the experiment.

The Royal Order of 1779 specifically endorsed the principle of peace by persuasion rather than by military persecution. It authorized the congregation around the presidios, more or less permanently, of bands seeking peace, on virtually any terms requested by the Indians who volunteered. Forcible internment at presidios was out; gentle encouragement to settle in or near Spanish communities and to adopt Hispanic lifeways was in.

Mescaleros were the first to seize the opportunity. In midsummer 1779, some of their leaders asked for help in forming villages under the protection of the presidio of La Junta (also known as El Norte). Accordingly, in October 1779, Lt. Col. Manuel Muñoz met with the chiefs at Presidio del Norte and helped them define—just a musket shot away from the presidio—the site for their new pueblo: Nuestra Señora de la Buena Esperanza. The first concern of the chiefs was to have Spanish soldiers protect their people against Comanches during their northward migration for the winter buffalo hunt, and ten soldiers were indeed assigned to that escort duty. Given such concrete proof of the value of the Spanish connection, at least four bands of Mescaleros came to live at Buena Esperanza, which soon burgeoned to 113 houses, guarded by two protective bastions.

But twin disasters struck the new pueblo in August 1780: first an epidemic of smallpox, and then a flood that wiped out the cornfields. All the Apaches fled the pueblo, but many took refuge at the presidio. Some eventually returned to Buena Esperanza; others remained at the Presidio del Norte; but by March 1783 all the Mescaleros were gone, and this first experiment in settling peaceful Apaches had ended.

What was the score? The effort had not been cheap: the Mescaleros had helped very little in construction or planting, and their rations had been costly. On the credit side, those Mescaleros had been at peace for more than a year, and they had given significant help to Spanish campaigns against Gila Apaches and also against some hostile Mescaleros. It warranted another try, but the experience would dictate more specific ground rules in future.

And what an opportunity arose! In 1785, Bernardo de Gálvez—still very much the boy wonder and now famous as the victor of Pensacola—returned in triumph to New Spain as viceroy, with an ambitious agenda. As the first viceroy with any personal knowledge of the northern frontier provinces, he was sure he knew how to end the Indian wars that had so long stunted development in the region. Of course, that would require solving the "Apache problem." But on the basis of his experience in Big Bend country fifteen years before, Gálvez remained passionately convinced of the peaceful potential of the Apaches. As viceroy, he would be both sympathetic and tough-minded: Apaches would be given every opportunity and incentive to settle peacefully in the vicinity of designated presidios near their homelands; relentless, systematic war would be waged against those who clung to the predatory lifestyle.

In his certainty that he, and only he, could solidify control of the northern frontier, Viceroy Gálvez persuaded the Crown to give him direct authority over the Commandancy-General of the Interior Provinces—which, since its creation in 1776, had reported directly to Spain. Soon, Gálvez engineered the appointment of a highly skilled new commandant general, Jacobo Ugarte y Loyola, who fully sympathized with the viceroy's objectives. Before taking command, Ugarte conferred at length with Gálvez in Mexico City, so the two men understood each other well. And thanks to their discussions, Ugarte's experience and more current knowledge of the frontier situation figured in the landmark Instruction on Indian policy that Gálvez issued a few months later, in August 1786.

The principles of the Gálvez Instruction agreed so well with Ugarte's own convictions concerning Indian policy that Ugarte followed them from the moment he took command in April 1786, months ahead of the public announcement of the Instruction. Better still, by the end of 1786 Ugarte had in place at the presidio of Janos, in Nueva Vizcaya, an exceptionally able new commandant, Capt. Antonio Cordero, who knew Apaches well and would make Janos a model of Apache peace establishments—i.e., *establecimientos de paz*, whose participants were called *apaches de paz*.

What a promising situation at all levels: knowledgeable, strongly committed viceroy, commandant general, and presidial commandant working in harmony on a well-formulated program. But before the Gálvez Instruction could even reach Spain, the young viceroy died of the epidemic fever that swept Mexico City in the fall of 1786. His Instruction outlived him: in February 1787, the king gave it the force of a royal ordinance. But Commandant General Ugarte's ability to make it work would hinge upon the attitude of the next viceroy.

Again, the Big Bend was a key arena for the experiment in pacification of Apaches, because Mescaleros were especially receptive to the proposition. In 1787, Commandant General Ugarte set strict conditions for acceptance of a large body of Mescaleros at the Presidio del Norte, where he stipulated that they must form a permanent settlement. They would be assigned plots of bottomland on the Rio Grande, where Spaniards would assist them in planting crops. These apaches de paz would be expected to sustain their families by farming and raising livestock rather than relying on rations issued by the Spanish authorities. (However, Ugarte later authorized weekly rations of corn, wheat, sugar, and tobacco until they could support themselves by farming, and it wasn't long before general rations were a standard feature of the peace program.) Their traditional foods remained important to them, and the apaches de paz could leave their pueblos to hunt game and gather wild fruits, *if* they obtained prior permission from the commandant of the presidio.

To forestall disputes of ownership, the apaches de paz were required to present their horses and mules for branding. (Wouldn't it be interesting to find the presidio's brand book?) They could choose either to adopt the Catholic faith or to accept the authority of the principal chief—whom they required to select among themselves, subject to approval by the Spanish authorities.

By the end of March 1787, eight Mescalero chiefs brought their bands to the Presidio del Norte: a total of about four hundred warriors with three hundred families. Two other bands also came—not Mescaleros, but closely related Natages and Lipiyanes. They were all very hungry, so the designated peace commissioner at the presidio, Capt. Domingo Díaz, issued rations at once. It was soon obvious that the presidio's provisions were insufficient for so many families, so Captain Díaz let these apaches de paz move their encampments to specified sites up in the mountains, where they could support themselves on game and wild fruit.

Then tragedy struck. From their newly assigned campsites, some of those Mescaleros strayed into terrain patrolled by Spanish troops from Coahuila. Their commandant, Col. Juan de Ugalde, was ignorant of the truce granted the Mescaleros at El Norte and totally unsympathetic to such policies. So, in March, before Ugalde learned of the truce, he attacked a Mescalero camp in the Chisos Mountains; then, in April, after he was informed, he attacked two more. Ugalde stubbornly refused to honor the cessation of hostilities or to release his Mescalero captives, and he deliberately attacked the mountain campsites of four of eight Mescalero bands involved in the peace agreements at Presidio del Norte.

Why couldn't Commandant General Ugarte bring Colonel Ugalde under control? Because Viceroy de Gálvez, in his zeal for personal control of the northern frontier, had divided the military command of the Interior Provinces into three sectors, authorizing the commandant of each to report directly to the viceroy and giving each of them wide discretion with regard to peace or war with the Indians in his sector. Thus Ugarte, who was assigned the westernmost sector, Sonora and the Californias, did not have the military command of the Big Bend region. That lay with the other two commands: the midsector—Nueva Vizcaya and New Mexico, under Commandant Inspector Rengel at El Paso, and the eastern sector—Coahuila, Texas, Nuevo León, and Nuevo Santander, commanded by the fractious Ugalde. Although normally subordinate to the commandant general, the other two commandants could flout his orders unless the viceroy objected.

Commandant Inspector Rengel tried to repair Ugalde's mischief by relocating the Mescalero pacification project westward, near his headquarters at El Paso. He argued that there was not enough good farmland at El Norte to support a large number of Indians, and also that El Norte was too isolated to foster the development of Apache trade with Spanish communities that was an objective of the peace program. Rengel also considered El Norte too dangerously close to the Comanche range. But the Mescaleros much preferred El Norte, where they felt safer from their enemies. They also preferred to support themselves by hunting and gathering rather than farming, and they wanted to live in separate camps—as Apaches always had—instead of congregating under the control of a principal chief as the Spaniards expected.

Captain Díaz came to understand that the Mescaleros dearly loved their liberty and traditional lifeways, and that they really wanted to live in the mountains where they had been born and reared, in the region of Presidio del Norte. But he believed that they would honor their commitments if fairly treated, just as the late Viceroy de Gálvez had also believed. So Díaz did his utmost to foster the pacification program. At the end of

August 1787, ten Apache bands were in residence near El Norte, but they were on the verge of a general revolt because Ugalde was still refusing to return his Mescalero captives to their families as the peace agreement had stipulated.

In October 1787, the pacification program in this sector was effectively destroyed by the new viceroy—Manuel Antonio Flores. He ordered Commandant General Ugarte to yield all of his powers of war and peace with the Mescaleros to Ugalde in Coahuila, and to force the bands at El Norte to move to the presidio of Santa Rosa, where Ugalde was trying to form a peace establishment under his own harsh terms. Ugarte resisted until the spring of 1788, but was then forced to expel the Mescaleros from El Norte. Those who tried to work with Ugalde at Santa Rosa came to grief: three Mescalero chiefs and at least seventy-five of their followers starved to death in Ugalde's jail, after he treacherously seized them during peace negotiations, killing two warriors who tried to resist.

Meanwhile, at a safe distance westward from Ugalde's reach, Ugarte continued to promote the peace process with considerable success at the other presidios. But the grim impasse in the Big Bend prevailed until 1789, when the enlightened Conde de Revillagigedo replaced Viceroy Flores. Revillagigedo promptly removed Ugalde, restored Ugarte to full authority over all eight of the Interior Provinces, and authorized renewal of peace negotiations with Apaches in Nueva Vizcaya. So it was back to the Big Bend to try again. In December 1790, just before his term as commandant general expired, Ugarte rode to El Norte to conclude a formal peace with eight Mescalero bands, which then established themselves near the presidio. He also won back to peace the Lipanes in Coahuila whom Ugalde had alienated, and welcomed significant numbers of Chiracahuas, Mimbreños, and Faraones into peace establishments at various presidios in Nueva Vizcaya and Sonora.

Happily for all concerned, the next commandant general, Pedro de Nava, was just as able as Ugarte and just as committed to the peace program. Better still, Nava served for twelve years, which gave the peace program some badly needed continuity, and his successor, also committed to the peace program, served for ten years. Despite many ups and downs, the peace establishments persisted well into the Mexican period at several presidios, including that of El Norte.

El Norte was one of the more troubled peace establishments. From the time of its third beginning in 1790, the Mescaleros refused to build permanent settlements or to engage seriously in farming. But they did provide warriors to serve with the troops of Nueva Vizcaya as auxiliaries, scouts, and emissaries. After nearly five years of relative stability, several bands revolted and fled in July 1795. But even then, about a third of those Mescalero apaches de paz remained faithful to their peace pacts. In keeping with established policy, the Spaniards declared war on the deserters, and that was still raging in 1799. Yet El Norte remained—on and off—a hub for peaceful interaction with many Mescaleros and kindred bands.

Why did the Mescaleros—and other Apaches—persist in such a difficult undertaking, which in many respects ran counter to their own cherished lifeways? Largely for protection against the Comanches, who had shattered the eastern Apacheria early in the eighteenth century and had made life miserable for many Apaches ever since. After 1786, when the Comanches became active allies instead of enemies of the Spaniards in New Mexico and Texas, the Spaniards could concentrate on solving their Apache problem, with Comanche help. Comanches could now count upon Spanish encouragement and assistance in pursuit of the common enemy. So Apaches from the Rio Grande eastward would know no security except that offered apaches de paz in the shadow of Spanish presidios.

Consider, then, the choices confronting the Apaches of the Big Bend: they could settle at one of the presidios in Nueva Vizcaya or in Coahuila, or they could take their chances with Comanches and other tribes pressing from the north and with Spanish troops—assisted by Apache auxiliaries and scouts—campaigning into their territory from south and west.

No wonder so many tried the peace path. Although the pacification never embraced all Apaches, enough settled peacefully at the designated presidios to validate the concept. Think what might have happened if all those striving Apaches and Spaniards had been permitted the time necessary for this well-intended process to mature. Instead, with the demise of New Spain, time ran out.

For those who wish to know a bit more, a short reading list is appended: just three articles and five books to lead you on. If you are particularly curious about the way Apaches operated in terrain such as the Big Bend, the first four publications on the list will be the most rewarding—as well as much the shortest. They are reports that Spanish officials wrote about Apaches between c.1786 and c.1804, and their information meshes very interestingly with modern anthropological perceptions of historic Apache lifeways.

Whether or not you choose to read more, the next time you're up in the Chisos Mountains or over at Presidio, do think about all those Apaches and Spaniards who were there before you. And do remember what Spaniards learned two centuries ago: it's unsound to generalize about Apaches. By the latter eighteenth century Spaniards knew Apaches in many contradictory roles on this frontier: as vengeful foes and rapacious raiders; as allies, indispensable scouts, guides, and couriers; as residents—though often erratic—of presidial communities and occasionally missions; as peaceful traders and sometimes poachers. Those contradictions posed a grave dilemma for Apaches and Spaniards then; they pose a tremendous challenge to our historical understanding now.

Further Reading on Spanish-Indian Relations in the Big Bend Region

A series of Spanish reports that show evolving comprehension of Apaches and neighboring tribes appears in the four following publications.

1. For informal reflections on Apaches and presidial soldiers, written c.1786 by Bernardo de Gálvez, see Elizabeth A. H. John, "A Cautionary Exercise in Apache Historiography," and "Bernardo de Gálvez on Apaches: A Cautionary Note for Gringo Historians," in *Journal of Arizona History* 25 (Autumn 1984):301–15, and 29 (Winter 1988):427–30, respectively.

2. Daniel S. Matson and Albert H. Schroeder, eds., "Cordero's Description of the Apaches—1796," in *New Mexico Historical Review* 32 (1958):335–56.

3. Elizabeth A. H. John, ed., and John Wheat, trans., *Views from the Apache Frontier: Report on the Northern Provinces of New Spain by José Cortes, Lieutenant in the Royal Corps of Engineers, 1799* (Norman: University of Oklahoma Press, 1989).

4. Elizabeth A. H. John, ed. and John Wheat, trans., "Views from a Desk in Chihuahua: Manuel Merino's Report on Apaches and Neighboring Nations, c.1804," *Southwestern Historical Quarterly* 95 (October 1991) 139–76.

Detailed information on the development of the apaches de paz program appears in two books by Max L. Moorhead: *The Apache Frontier: Jacobo Ugarte and Spanish-Indian Relations in Northern New Spain, 1769–1791*

(Norman: University of Oklahoma Press, 1968) and *The Presidio: Bastion of the Spanish Borderlands* (Norman: University of Oklahoma Press, 1975). In the latter, see especially chapter 10.

The most detailed information yet available on long-term operations of the apaches de paz program is presented in William B. Griffon, *Apaches at War and Peace: The Janos Presidio, 1750–1858* (Albuquerque: University of New Mexico Press, 1988).

To examine the Apache situation in a broader, intertribal context, see Elizabeth A. H. John, *Storms Brewed in Other Men's Worlds: The Confrontation of Indians, Spanish, and French in the Southwest, 1540–1795* (College Station: Texas A&M University Press, 1975).

8   *New Light on Chisos Apache Indian Chief Alsate*

Franklin W. Daugherty and Luis López Elizondo

Behind every place name in the Big Bend region of Texas there is a story, and some of these stories are fascinating. Many names are descriptive of a feature or a locality, and their origins are obvious. As examples, Mitre Peak near the Brewster-Jeff Davis county line was first known as Bishop's Mitre for its shape, and Tornillo Creek in southern Brewster County was named for the Mexican screwbean or tornillo plant, which abounds along its course. Other names may commemorate a person or event associated with a locality, such as Johnson's Farm in Big Bend National Park. The origins of some place names are less evident, requiring considerable historical research, and all too many cannot be established at all. Finally, the origins of some names must be considered in the realm of folklore and are not verifiable by any reasonable evidence or theory.

One of the most interesting names that has been applied in the Big Bend area is Alsate, which forms part of six names: Charco de Alsate, Alsate Creek, Alsate Formation, Alsate's Face, Cueva de Alsate, and Alsate Spirit Lights. Those familiar with the history and folklore of the area can identity Alsate as the chief of a band of Apaches sometimes referred to as the Chisos Apaches because their homeland encompassed the Chisos Mountains (Raht 1963, 273). Alsate and his people were, according to many accounts, the scourge of the Big Bend and neighboring Mexico from about the late 1840s until around 1882.

An earlier name for Kokernot Springs, the location of Sul Ross State University's Kokernot Lodge in Alpine, was Charco de Alsate (Williams 1968, 258). *Charco* signifies a standing pool or pond of water in the Spanish language, but Charco de Alsate is not a standing pool of water today. Prior to the drought of the 1950s it was a lagoon about one hundred feet long, and it was a favorite swimming hole for area youths before there was a swimming pool in Alpine. The name originated because Alsate and his band of Apaches roamed the area when wagon trains of freight rolled along the Chihuahua Trail, beginning in the late 1840s. Only a few immigrants traveling to California passed by this spring, however, for the vast majority traveled from Ojo de Comanche (Comanche Springs), site of present-day Fort Stockton, through Fort Davis and El Paso on the Overland Trail.

Some allege that the earliest known name for Kokernot Springs was San Lorenzo, given by Juan Domínguez de Mendoza, who traveled through the area in January 1684, but there is some uncertainty as to the actual route taken by his expedition.[1] Charco de Alsate was also known as Burgess Springs, and this name was derived from the fact that it was a favorite stopping place of John D. Burgess, a pioneer freighter who operated between San Antonio and Presidio del Norte, present-day Ojinaga, Chihuahua (Raht 1963, 164–65).

As for the other names, Alsate Creek is located a few miles south of Marathon; Alsate Formation was named for rocks exposed along Alsate Creek (King, n.d., 148); Alsate's Face is a ridge along Green Gulch in Big Bend National Park whose profile resembles a man's face looking skyward (Maxwell 1968, 69); and Cueva de Alsate is a cave in the Chisos Mountains of Big Bend National Park overlooking Mexico, where legend says that Alsate's mummified body was found (Maxwell 1968, 70). Recently the name Alsate Spirit Lights has appeared in print as an alternate name for the so-called Marfa Lights (Brueske 1989, 33). This was probably inevitable and likely resulted from tales by shepherds and vaqueros who have long claimed to see mysterious lights at night in the Chisos and Chinati mountains in Texas and the Sierra del Carmen in Mexico.

The name Alsate is mentioned in several books that treat of the history of this area, but were it not for the scholarly works of O. W. Williams of Fort Stockton, it would be virtually unknown. The name first appeared in print in a brief, privately printed pamphlet entitled *Alsate—The Last of the Chisos* (Williams, n.d.a).[2] This story and others are also included in a book written by Williams (1968). Some of Williams's Alsate stories were included by Carlysle Graham Raht in *The Romance of Davis Mountains and Big Bend Country* (published in 1919 and reprinted with minor changes and additions in 1963). Practically all references to Alsate in other books published after 1919 derive in large part from Williams's book and pamphlet, or Raht's book.

Williams, a civil engineer, was a Harvard graduate who surveyed Blocks G-4 and G-12 in southern Brewster County in 1901 and 1902. One of his assistants on this project was Natividad Luján, an elderly Mexican from the village of San Carlos in Chihuahua, a few miles across the Rio

Grande from Lajitas (Williams, n.d.b).[3] Luján had an intimate knowledge of a large area on both sides of the border, the events that had taken place there during his lifetime, and the folklore of other times and happenings. During the evenings around a campfire, Luján would regale his audience with his stories, and Williams, an inveterate writer with a keen memory, would write them down. Luján knew and played with Alsate as a boy when Alsate and his father lived near San Carlos, and the Apaches were on friendly terms with the people of that village. At other times they lived in various Apache rancherías[4] in Mexico and the Big Bend but returned from time to time to trade at San Carlos.

Luján's stories about Alsate as told to Williams make fascinating reading. The essentials of Luján's Alsate stories are that Alsate was the son of a Mexican, Miguel Múzquiz, who had been captured as a child by Mescalero Apaches from the vicinity of the town of Santa Rosa, present-day Múzquiz, Coahuila (Williams 1968, 258). The full name of that town, founded around a presidio in 1739, was Santa Rosa María del Sacramento (Santos Landois 1993, 13). Miguel Múzquiz was adopted into the tribe and reared as an Indian; he fathered Alsate by an Indian wife. After reaching manhood and demonstrating his bravery and audacity in war, Alsate became the chief of a band of these Apaches (Williams 1968, 257).

The locations of the rancherías of these Indians depended upon the seasons, need for shelter, availability of game and native plants used for food, and safety from enemies. A ranchería of Alsate's band might be on Limpia Creek in the Davis Mountains, in the rugged Chisos Mountains, or on the highest elevations of the Sierra del Carmen and Santa Rosa Mountains in Mexico (Williams 1968, 257).

In the early days these Indians were mostly hunters and gatherers who moved their rancherías with the seasons, but as time passed their energies became increasingly devoted to raids upon isolated settlements, ranches, and unwary travelers. An increasing demand for livestock by border Indian traders, cattle barons in the Big Bend, and comancheros (traders with the Indians from New Mexico) was a strong inducement for Indian raids on isolated cattle ranches and villages in Mexico and, to a lesser extent, in Texas. These raids were conducted far from safe havens near the border where the Indians were free to sell or trade their booty with impunity. The largest and best organized raids were made mostly by the Comanches, some of whom came from afar to raid deep into Mexico, but the Apaches, who were closer at hand, were not far behind in these ventures.

One of the most prominent establishments trading with the Indians in the Big Bend borderlands belonged to Ben Leaton, an American. It was located on the Texas side of the Rio Grande five miles downstream from present-day Presidio. Leaton arrived in the area about 1848 and purchased farmland bordering the Rio Grande. Ruins of extensive ancient adobe structures, known locally as El Fortin, were present on the terrace above the floodplain of the river, and Leaton soon put them to use. He restored and added to the old buildings, creating a hacienda-style building with forty rooms. The courtyard of this complex was surrounded by high, thick adobe walls to make a fortress that came to be known as Fort Leaton. Ample room was provided within the walls for protection of livestock, which could be driven through a single entryway with wide swinging doors constructed of heavy timbers, capable of being quickly opened and securely closed. Lookout towers at each corner were provided with loopholes to protect defenders firing on attackers. Defensive weapons, according to folklore, included a cannon kept in readiness to be fired through the gateway in the event of attack (Thompson 1985, 50). The use to which Ben Leaton put his fortress soon became notorious on both sides of the border. A letter, dated October 10, 1849, from Chihuahua governor Angel Trías to Col. Emilio Langberg, inspector of military colonies for the Mexican federal government, accused Leaton of "committing a thousand abuses, and of so hurtful a nature that he keeps an open treaty with the Apache Indians, in opposition to what he has been expressly advised not to do." Langberg forwarded this letter to Major Jefferson Van Horn, commander of American troops at Paso del Norte, present-day El Paso, writing: "In return for plunder which this person takes from the Indians, he furnishes them with arms, powder, lead and other articles of ammunition." (Thompson 1985, 54).

As time passed, the growth in traffic of immigrants and freight over the Chihuahua and Overland Trails attracted the interest of various Indian tribes that ranged the borderlands of the Big Bend. The resulting increase in attacks by the Indians led to the establishment of Fort Davis and Fort Stockton in 1854 as bases for army operations in campaigns against the marauding Apaches and Comanches. Abandonment of these forts during the Civil War led to an increased Indian menace, which was not materially diminished until at least ten years after the war ended.

The name Charco de Alsate arose from a confrontation in 1867 between Alsate's band and some freighters. John D. Burgess's wagon train, loaded with salt from the saline lakes in present-day Crane County and bound for Presidio del Norte, was surrounded at the Charco by these Indians. Burgess's party was heavily armed and prepared for any eventuality. Finally, a conference between the two sides, assisted by gifts from Burgess to Alsate, resulted in a truce. One gift was Burgess's fine long overcoat, which Alsate admired and coveted. Well after Alsate's band left for unknown parts, Burgess's heavily laden wagons resumed rolling toward Presidio del Norte, where his Mexican wife and family awaited him. Alsate's band arrived in Presidio del Norte a few days before the Burgess wagon train. When Alsate, wearing John Burgess's easily recognizable overcoat, showed up in town, he was jailed and placed on trial for his life. Alsate's protests that Burgess had given him the overcoat were to no avail, but fortunately Burgess arrived in time for Alsate's life to be spared (Raht 1963, 169–70).

At that time the military authorities and merchants of both Presidio del Norte and San Carlos had a tacit "live and let live" understanding with Alsate's Apaches and other Indians. Peaceful relations existed because of their obvious commercial advantages for both Mexicans and Indians. Alsate's people sold or traded to the merchants of both towns the livestock, other plunder, and captives that they had obtained by robbery and murder in both the United States and Mexico. In exchange they received liquor, arms, ammunition, tobacco, clothing, trinkets, and other goods. The Mexicans, for their part, enjoyed not only a lucrative business but also immunity from warfare with their clients (Williams 1968, 257). Furthermore, for a time the official policy of the state government of Chihuahua was to issue rations to presumably peaceful Indians, who took full advantage of this largesse, being careful to conduct their depredations in distant areas in intervals between distributions of rations, or in the neighboring state of Coahuila, which had no policy at the time for provisioning Indians (Griffen 1988, 55, 191–94).

Finally, in 1878, complaints and pleas from the Mexican people and the governors of the states of Chihuahua and Coahuila for relief from these Indians led Pres. Porfirio Díaz of Mexico to order the capture and imprisonment of Alsate's band. Orders were sent to Col. José Garza Galán of Santa Rosa to take a force of one hundred soldiers to San Carlos to meet troops led by a Colonel Ortiz to capture Alsate's band. This was easy to accomplish because, at that time, Alsate's ranchería was located not far from San Carlos (Guajardo, n.d.). The unsuspecting Alsate and his band were seized, shackled, and taken to Santa Rosa where they waited a few days for wagons to transport them to the Casa de la Acordada (Raht

1963, 277), a grim prison in Mexico City which had been used for more than a century to confine incorrigible Apaches who had been deported from the northern frontier.

One member of the band was Alsate's father, Miguel Múzquiz, who was now old and blind (Raht 1963, 276). Since the founding of Santa Rosa in 1739, one of the most prominent families living in the area had been the Múzquiz family, and in 1850 the name of the town was changed to Melchor Múzquiz in honor of a native son who had a distinguished military career and served as provisional president of Mexico for a brief period (Santos Landois 1993, 16).

A prominent citizen in Santa Rosa at the time the captive Apaches arrived was Manuel Múzquiz, the man for whom Muzqúiz Creek and Canyon near Fort Davis were named. Múzquiz was a political refugee from Mexico in 1854 when he established his homestead near Fort Davis. The family returned to Mexico about 1861 because of depredations by the Apaches and a changed political climate in Mexico (Williams 1968, 293n).

While the Indians were being held at Santa Rosa, Alsate's father, Miguel, sent for Manuel Múzquiz. Upon Manuel's arrival, Miguel asked for his help, telling him that they were brothers. As proof of their kinship he told Manuel the name of their mother and his own name in Spanish. Manuel suspected that Alsate's father might be an imposter who learned these details from someone else, and to test his veracity, asked Miguel to remove the moccasin from his right foot. As improbable as it might seem, some members of the Múzquiz family have a sixth rudimentary toe on the right foot, and Manuel knew that his kidnapped brother was one with this genetic defect. When the blind man removed his moccasin, an extra toe was not to be seen, but a scar testified that it had been there at one time. This rudimentary toe had been amputated because it was painful to travel in the mountains with a toe that supplied no support to the foot (Williams 1968, 258).

Manuel Múzquiz secured his brother's release because he had been a captive of the Indians since childhood, but he was unable to do likewise for his nephew, Alsate, an Indian by birth and, moreover, chief of a band of Apaches who had long been responsible for raids on many Mexican ranches and settlements. This unmistakable evidence of their kinship led Manuel Múzquiz to seek to help Alsate and his people. Although there was no way that transport of these people to prison in Mexico City could be avoided, Manuel knew an influential person there, General Blanco, a member of Pres. Porfirio Díaz's *ayuntamiento* or governing council.

Manuel Múzquiz wrote a letter to General Blanco and gave it to Alsate with instructions to present it to the general upon arriving in Mexico City. From Santa Rosa the Indians were transported in wagons to Mexico City, where they were imprisoned. When brought before General Blanco, Alsate produced the letter written by his uncle and made an impassioned plea for release. The Indians were returned to prison, but, according to Williams, were soon loaded into wagons to be returned to their ranchería near San Carlos. The implication is that their release was somehow related to Manuel Múzquiz's letter to General Blanco.

Williams wrote that when the Indians arrived in familiar territory they jumped from the wagons and took to the hills (Williams 1968, 259–60). Soon the younger braves, with Alsate as their war chief, resumed their old ways of depredation and murder. Numerous complaints once again went to the Mexican government, and a decision was made to put an end to this band of troublesome Apaches. Accordingly, orders were sent to state troops in Presidio del Norte to capture Alsate and all his band. The commander of the troops was Colonel Ortiz, who knew this would be an arduous task fraught with danger. Lives could be lost and scarce resources expended with no assurance of success, so he determined to resort to guile. Word was sent to the Apaches, by means of a renegade who had taken part in some of their raids, that the Mexicans wished to celebrate a peace treaty with them in San Carlos. After agreement on a treaty, lavish gifts would be given the Indians. Thenceforth, they would be given rations each month, as the United States government did with the Indians who remained at peace.

In due time, the Indians went to San Carlos to ratify the peace treaty. A barbecue was provided and liquor flowed freely. Promises were made as to the gifts that would be forthcoming the following day. The rest of the day was spent feasting, drinking, and dancing. By nightfall nearly all the Indians were intoxicated, and they soon fell into sleep; by daybreak they were surrounded by Mexican soldiers. Many had been bound with ropes in their sleep, but a few died fighting. That day the captives, consisting of 63 warriors and about 150 women and children, were taken to Presidio del Norte, where Alsate was executed. The remaining Indians were sent to southern Mexico to be dispersed and sold into slavery (Williams 1968, 259–63).

An interesting question to be considered is the historical accuracy and completeness of what has been printed concerning Alsate's life. This fascinating story is far from being entirely filled out, and several questions immediately arise:

Was "Alsate" an Indian or a Spanish name?

The evidence is that it was a Spanish name or, more likely, a variant of a Spanish name. Raht stated that Alsate was named after Mexican army lieutenant Francisco Alsate (he meant "Arzate"), who was stationed at Presidio del Norte. Although Alsate (spelled with either an "s" or a "z") can be a Spanish name, it appears to be uncommon. O. W. Williams gave no origin for the name, but S. D. Myres, who edited and annotated Williams's book, believed Alsate to be a misnomer for Arzate. He cited Joe Cordero of Fort Stockton, grandson of Capt. Francisco Arzate, who stated that when the Indian chief was first imprisoned at Presidio del Norte, the officers wanted to know his name. Upon seeing Captain Arzate pass by, the Indian inquired his name, then said he would take it as his own (Williams 1968, 292n). Recent inquiry of a native of San Carlos revealed that no one in that village has the surname Alsate, but at least one family bears the name Arzate (Subia 1994).

Further suggestion that the name Alsate is a corruption of the name Arzate is confirmed by the residential telephone listings in the 1994–95 Southwestern Bell combined telephone directory of El Paso, Texas, and her sister city, Ciudad Juárez, Chihuahua. A total of fifty-three telephones were listed in the name of Arzate, but none in the name of Alsate or Alzate.

What was Alsate's name in the Apache tongue?

The answer is unknown and may be unknowable. Apache Indians were loath to reveal their Indian names when dealing with non-Indians. Captain John C. Cremony, who had close contact with Apaches in the southwest and northern Mexico for a dozen or more years in the 1850s and 1860s, and was fluent in their language, wrote that "it is not unusual for them to refuse giving their Apache names when interrogated," and they "will endeavor to give some Mexican appellative in its place" (Cremony 1868, 243).

Was the presence of an extra toe on one foot a distinctive characteristic of some members of the Múzquiz family?

All evidence indicates that it was. Dr. W. E. Lockhart, longtime Alpine physician, wrote Dr. Clifford B. Casey in 1965 telling him that a Mexican boy with the surname Múzquiz, from the village of Santa Elena, across from Castolon in Big Bend National Park, came to him for amputation of an extra toe on his right foot (Lockhart 1965).

Further confirmation of this genetic defect in the Múzquiz family was obtained when the senior author of this paper and his wife visited friends on their ranch north of Múzquiz. Visiting there also was Alberto Múzquiz, a member of a prominent ranching family in northern Coahuila. Múzquiz affirmed that the Manuel Múzquiz who from about 1854 until about 1861 had the homestead near Fort Davis, was indeed a member of that extensive family, but he was unsure of the exact relationship. When asked to remove his right boot so that his toes could be counted, he replied, "I have only five toes, but an uncle of mine has six" (Múzquiz 1994).

If Alsate's Spanish surname was Múzquiz, what would have been his given name in Spanish, if he had one?

Alsate's given name in Spanish was Pedro, and it must have been given to him by his father. Proof of this name is given in Circular Number 12, dated March 4, 1880, from the Secretaría del Gobierno de Coahuila, which was sent to various municipalities in the state reporting the escape of some Mescalero Indians from Mexico City during the night of December 21, 1879. The name of their chief was given as Pedro Múzquiz, alias Alsate (Estado de Coahuila 1880). The circular warned citizens to take all precautions to prevent loss of life and property to these Indians because their presence would be announced only by the victims that they sacrificed and the robberies and depredations of all kinds that they were committing in their northward journey.

A Mexican historian, General Luis Alberto Guajardo, offered a somewhat different story of the "escape" of Alsate and his people from the prison in Mexico City. He stated that after a time in prison the Indians were provided with new clothing and released to the freedom of the city streets. They disappeared one night; the next morning Alsate turned up mounted and armed, and he and his people headed northward to their old homeland. In their flight they kept to the mountainous areas to avoid detection, and stole horses and arms as they went (Guajardo, n.d.). This version is entirely possible, because well into the twentieth century it was not uncommon in Mexican cities to see wives and children of imprisoned men on the sidewalks begging for money to provide food for the incarcerated males. Many families of prisoners shared a cell with the prisoner and were allowed great latitude in their movement in and out of the facilities. It requires no great stretch of the imagination to believe that escapes of prisoners were not unusual under such circumstances.

It is evident that Manuel Múzquiz's letter and Alsate's plea to General Blanco for release from prison in Mexico City were to no avail, inasmuch as the official warning concerning the flight of Alsate's band northward announced their escape from prison in Mexico City. Thus Williams's statement that Alsate and his people were loaded into wagons for transport to their homeland is in error.

Was there a relationship between General Blanco and Manuel Múzquiz that would lead Múzquiz to believe that a letter to the general would result in Alsate's release?

Baptismal records in the parish church of Múzquiz reveal that General Blanco was more than a friend to Manuel Múzquiz. These records show that the full name of the child who later became General Blanco was José Miguel Blanco Múzquiz. He was born September 12, 1814, in Santa Rosa and christened three days later. His mother was María Josefa Múzquiz González and his father was Victor Blanco, who later twice became governor of the combined Mexican states of Coahuila and Texas (Libro de Bautismos 5:79). General Blanco's mother, María Josefa, was an elder sister to the brothers Manuel and Miguel Múzquiz, and thus her son, the general, was a nephew to both Manuel and Miguel Múzquiz and first cousin of Pedro Múzquiz, known as Chief Alsate.

What is known about the ancestry of Miguel Múzquiz, Alsate's father?

Baptismal records in Múzquiz show the full name of Alsate's father to be José Miguel María del Refugio Sabas Múzquiz González. He was born

December 3, 1800, and baptized eight days later in Santa Rosa (Libro de Bautismos 3:35). José Miguel's father and mother, grandparents of Alsate, were Miguel Francisco de Eca y Múzquiz,[5] born in 1745, and María Catarina González de Paredes, born in 1760. They were married August 20, 1785, in Santa Rosa (Libro de Matrimonies, Folio 109). The father was at that time an *alférez* (ensign) in the Spanish army stationed at the Presidio de San Antonio Bucareli de la Babia. Later he served as a lieutenant at Nacogdoches, Texas, and retired with the rank of captain. The father died in 1826 (Libro de Defunciones, Folio 133), and the mother in 1855 (Archives de Ciudad Melchor Múzquiz, n.d.).

At the time of José Miguel's birth his father was a lieutenant in command of the garrison at Nacogdoches. In the summer of 1800 he had been warned to be alert for the expected arrival in Texas of Philip Nolan, mustanger and Indian trader, suspected of being an agent of the American government. In October of that same year Nolan, accompanied by twenty-eight armed men, set forth for Spanish Texas. News of the arrival of this force in Texas created more than a little anxiety, and scouting parties were sent out seeking the whereabouts of this suspected band of filibusters. In March 1801, Lieutenant Múzquiz learned from Indian scouts that Nolan and his men had a camp on the Brazos River near present-day Waco. Múzquiz assembled a force of seventy soldiers and fifty militiamen to search for their camp, and on March 21 the Indian scouts led the expedition to Nolan's "fort." After a brief parley, gunfire broke out and Nolan and several of his men were killed. The remaining men surrendered and were sent to prison in Mexico City (Bannon 1970, 209).

The great-grandparents of Alsate were Joseph Joachín de Eca y Múzquiz and Mariana de la Garza Falcón (Libro de Bautismos 1:31). Mariana was born in 1719, the daughter of Gen. Bias de la Garza Falcón (governor of Coahuila and Texas, 1723–29 and 1733–35) and Beatriz de Villarreal. Mariana's brother was Capt. Miguel de la Garza Falcón, founder of the Presidio de Santa Rosa in 1739. After Captain de la Garza Falcón left Santa Rosa in 1744 or 1745, Lieutenant Joseph Joachín de Eca y Múzquiz was appointed commander of the presidio.

In 1750 Joseph Joachín was delegated to investigate sites for a permanent presidio to protect three missions on the San Xavier River (the present-day San Gabriel River) near Rockdale, Texas (Weddle 1968, 240). In 1757 Joseph Joachín was serving under Col. Diego Ortiz Parrilla at the newly established Presidio de San Luis de las Amarillas on the San Saba River near present-day Menard, Texas. In March of that same year an estimated two thousand Comanches and their allies, equipped with firearms, attacked the nearby mission at Santa Cruz de San Saba and murdered its two priests and many of its Indian neophytes (Weddle 1968, 240, 260).

Plans were made for a punitive expedition to the homelands of the Indians responsible for the massacre, but it was not until August of 1759 that Lt. Joseph Joachín de Eca y Múzquiz and a large force of soldiers, militia, and Indian allies, from presidios and towns of Coahuila, Nuevo León, and Texas ventured forth under the command of Colonel Parrilla. A surprise attack on a Tonkawa Indian village somewhere beyond the Clear Fork of the Brazos River killed 55 and captured 149 Indians. A second battle with many Comanches, Wichitas, and allied tribes at a fortified village on the Red River, north of Nocona, Texas (near present-day Spanish Fort), resulted in a draw, and casualties were high on both sides (Weddle 1968, 263–64).

The father of Joseph Joachín de Eca y Múzquiz, Alsate's great-great-grandfather, was Joseph Antonio de Eca y Múzquiz, a Creole Spaniard who served as interim governor of Coahuila in 1717. His exact date of birth is presently unknown but must have been about 1665; his signature begins to appear on official documents in 1688 (Weddle 1968, 137, 168n). In March 1707, Captain Joseph Antonio de Eca y Múquiz, in command of seven soldiers and citizens from the Villa de Santiago de Monclova, accompanied Capt. Diego Ramón on a twenty-six-day-long *entrada* or expedition into Texas. The purpose of the expedition was twofold: to punish Indians of the ladino nations who had been inciting mission Indians in Nuevo León to rebel, and to entice them to accept mission life in order to replace Indians who had died during an epidemic of smallpox. In 1724 he assumed command of the Presidio de San Juan de Bautista del Río Grande upon the death of Capt. Diego Ramón, and in 1737 he presided at the ceremony that founded the Mission San Francisco Vizarrón (Weddle 1968, 73–76, 168, 217–18).

Capt. Joseph Antonio de Eca y Múzquiz died in 1738 at the Presidio de San Juan Bautista del Río Grande. His life and career were summed up by the eminent historian Robert S. Weddle, who wrote, "He had served almost half a century on the northern frontier of New Spain, during the period when the most stirring history was being made; and . . . he left descendants who would carry his name deep into the story of Texas" (1968, 218).

Was Alsate a Mescalero or Lipan Apache?

All references to Alsate published in English and some in Spanish identify him as a Mescalero, but General Guajardo referred to Alsate as a Lipan. In either case, the differences between the two groups of Apaches are more apparent than real, because they were bonded by the same language, customs, and hatred of their common enemy, the Comanche. The distinction between the two tribes of Apaches has been based on minor linguistic and cultural differences, but no evidence has been found to date which would allow one to make a judgment about which group of Apaches Alsate's band belonged to. This judgment perhaps could be made if a description of Alsate's appearance were available. Some Lipan warriors cut their hair short above the left ear but allowed the hair on the right side to grow so long, almost to the ground, that it was folded and wrapped with string or ribbons to shoulder level. Moreover, both ears were customarily pierced: the right ear with one or more holes and the left, with six to eight holes. On ceremonial occasions, an earring was worn in each perforation (Newcomb 1961, 110).

Is there a description of Alsate that would give us some idea of his appearance and his abilities as a warrior and chief of his band of Indians?

There are two descriptions of Alsate. A physical description dates from 1850 when a truce was declared between Coahuila state troops and local forces commanded by Col. Francisco Castañeda and a large host of Comanches, Mescaleros, and Lipans who had united on a rare occasion for an attack on Santa Rosa. The attack was planned for the night of Christmas Eve in 1849, when practically everyone in the town would be attending religious services at the church. Fortunately, the Mexicans had advance notice of the impending attack from a captive of the Indians who had escaped to deliver the warning, and preparations were made to battle the Indians well before they reached the town. After several battles in which the Indians suffered large casualties, the opposing forces agreed to a peace conference. Alsate, war chief of one band of the Apaches, took an active role in the talks. He was described as "a tall youth, thin, muscular, with a nose slightly aquiline an eagle eye and a calm mien"

(Guajardo, n.d.). From all accounts he spoke Spanish well, and in 1850 he might have been about thirty years of age.

The other description of Alsate relates to his abilities as a leader of his band and was given in January 1878 by Lt. John L. Bullis before the Committee on Military Affairs of the House of Representatives (Texas Border Troubles, House Miscellaneous Document no. 64, 195, 43rd Congress, 2nd session). Bullis testified that in November of the preceding year he and his Seminole scouts had crossed the Rio Grande following a twenty-three-day-old trail of Indians who had raided into Texas. After six days on the trail, Bullis's force surprised and attacked the Indians in their camp in the Sierra Carmel (Sierra del Carmen). Two Indians were killed and three wounded. The camp was destroyed and about thirty horses and mules captured.

Bullis testified:

> This party of Indians was that of Alsate, a Mescalero Apache.... He is called the most cunning Indian on all the frontier of Texas and Mexico, and that was the first time he had ever been hit. He is about sixty years of age, and is as cunning as a fox. He always camps on the highest peaks, even if they are a mile or more in height. The reason he was so careless at that time was that the weather was extremely cold, so much that the water in our canteens was frozen, and the canteens burst asunder.

How, when, and where did Alsate die, and what disposition was made of his body?

The answer is unknown for certain. General Guajardo (n.d.) postulated that Alsate was among those Indians who were forcibly removed to a reservation in New Mexico or Arizona. This seems unlikely because Alsate's notoriety was such that mention of his name would have been made in some of the many books that relate to the placement of Mescaleros and other Apaches on reservations.

Kevin Mulroy in *Freedom on the Border* states that Bullis and his Black Seminole Scouts surprised Alsate and his Indians in their village in the Sierra del Carmen and "killed two of the Mescaleros, including the band leader, Alsate" (1993, 128). This account is in error. Bullis's testimony was: "We killed two Indians, wounded three, captured about thirty head of horses and mules, and destroyed the village" (US House 1878, 195). If

Alsate had been killed in this action, that would have been sufficiently noteworthy to be included in Bullis's testimony.

O. W. Williams said that Alsate was executed and buried at Presidio del Norte. This apparently was derived from information supplied to Williams by his informant, Natividad Luján, who knew Alsate in San Carlos (Williams 1968, 263). Furthermore, Cecelia Thompson wrote that "Ruperta Góngora was married to Anastacio Luján in Shafter in 1887. Born in Ojinaga in 1850, Ruperta remembered when the Mescalero Apache Indian Chief Alsarte [sic] was captured. She expressed grief for him and believed him to have been executed by Mexican soldiers" (1985, 268).

Almost certainly Alsate was indeed executed about 1882 at Presidio del Norte after his band had been lured into a trap by Colonel Ortiz with promises of a peace treaty and gifts. This act would have represented the Mexican government's "final solution" to the multitude of problems created by Alsate and his band.

Was the line of descent from Miguel Múzquiz extinguished with the death of his son, Pedro Múzquiz, better known as Chief Alsate?

Miguel and Alsate's line was not extinguished with the death of Alsate. Glenn Burgess, news reporter and longtime manager of the Alpine Chamber of Commerce in the 1950s and 1960s, interviewed Alsate's grandson, who told him that Alsate was executed by a firing squad in San Carlos (Miles 1976, 45). Furthermore, logic indicates that there are more than a few direct lineal descendants of Miguel and Alsate to be found on both sides of the Rio Grande in the borderlands of the Big Bend.

There are several reasons to support this conclusion. First, Apaches were polygamous and females outnumbered males because of losses in warfare (Cremony 1868, 249). This consideration alone makes it unlikely that Alsate was the sole progeny of Manuel Múzquiz; there must have been other children by more than one wife. Inasmuch as Miguel lived to be at least eighty years of age, it seems probable that at the time of his death there would have been at least three generations of his descendants. Furthermore, since his son, Alsate, lived to the age of about sixty and apparently was in vigorous good health up to the time of his death, he also could have left two or more generations of descendants.

The memory of Alsate has been perpetuated in print, but few, if any, who have heard or read the folklore about that Chief of the Chisos

Apaches, have any knowledge of the important roles that Alsate's Spanish forebears played in the early exploration, colonization, and development of northern Mexico and Spanish Texas.

Notes

1. A bronze plaque on a boulder on the grounds of Kokernot Lodge reads: "LORENZO—ROUTE OF JUAN DE DOMINGUEZ MENDOZA, January Fifth, 1684, CHIHUAHUA TRAIL," but J. W. Williams in *Old Texas Trails* (Burnet, Texas: Eakin, 1979), identifies "San Lorenzo" as present-day Barrilla Spring in Jeff Davis County (188).

2. Eight-page pamphlet, n.d., but written before 1914 and printed after 1919.

3. Twenty-eight-page pamphlet, n.d., but written before 1919.

4. Temporary camps or small villages, usually seasonal.

5. According to Miguel Múzquiz, an authority on the Múzquiz family, the *Eca* was used by the Múzquiz family until the latter part of the nineteenth century, when it was dropped from use altogether (conversation with the junior author, 1996).

References

Bannon, John Francis. 1970. *The Spanish Borderlands Frontier, 1513–1821*. New York: Holt, Rinehart,, and Winston.

Brueske, Judith. 1989. *The Marfa Lights*. Alpine, Texas: Ocotillo.

Cremony, John C. 1868. *Life Among the Apaches*. San Francisco: A. Roman.

Estado de Coahuila de Zaragoza. 1880. Secretaría del Gobierno Circular 12, March 4.

Griffen, William B. 1988. *Utmost Good Faith: Patterns of Apache-Mexican Hostilities in Northern Chihuahua Border Warfare, 1821–1848*. Albuquerque: University of New Mexico Press.

Guajardo, General Luis Alberto. n.d. *Guajardo Notes*. Microfilm reel 4. Beinecke Rare Book and Manuscript Library, Yale University, New Haven.

King, Phillip B. 1937. *Geology of the Marathon Region, Texas*. US Geological Survey Professional Paper 187. Washington, DC: GPO.

Libro de Bautismos. Parroquia de Santa Rosa. Box 1, Folio 31; Box 3, Folio 35; Box 5, Folio 79.

Libro de Defunciones. 1826. Parroquia de Santa Rosa. Years 1805–1830, Folio 133.

Libro de Matrimonios. 1855. Parroquia de Santa Rosa. Years 1756–1804, Folio 109.

Lockhart, W. E. 1965. Letter to Casey. Accession No. 1990.2, Box 9, Alsate Folder, September. Archives of the Big Bend, Bryan Wildenthal Memorial Library, Sul Ross State University, Alpine, Texas.

Maxwell, Ross A. 1968. *The Big Bend of the Rio Grande: A Guide to the Rocks, Landscape, Geologic History, and Settlers of the Area of Big Bend National Park.* Guidebook 7, Bureau of Economic Geology, University of Texas at Austin.

Miles, Elton. 1976. *Tales of the Big Bend.* College Station: Texas A&M University Press.

Mulroy, Kevin. 1993. *Freedom on the Border: The Seminole Maroons in Florida, the Indian Territory, Coahuila, and Texas.* Lubbock: Texas Tech Press.

Múzquiz, Alberto. 1994. Conversation with the senior author, November.

Múzquiz, Miguel. 1996. Conversation with the junior author, February.

Múzquiz, Ciudad Melchor. Family archives. Múzquiz family tree. Coahuila, Mexico.

Neighbours, Kenneth F., ed. 1979. *Old Texas Trails: 1716–1886.* Burnet, Texas: Eakin Press.

Newcomb, W. W., Jr. 1961. *The Indians of Texas: From Prehistoric to Modern Times.* Austin: University of Texas Press.

Raht, Carlysle Graham. 1963. *The Romance of Davis Mountains and Big Bend Country.* Odessa, Texas: Rahtbooks.

Santos Landois, Jesús. 1993. *El Ojo Parado: El Saqueo del Valle de Santa Rosa.* Ciudad Melchor Múzquiz: Coahuila, Mexico.

Subia, Erasmo. 1994. Conversation with the senior author, June.

Thompson, Cecelia. 1985. *History of Marfa and Presidio County, 1553–1946.* Austin: Nortex.

Weddle, Robert S. 1968. *San Juan Bautista: Gateway to Spanish Texas.* Austin: University of Texas Press.

Williams, Oscar W. 1968. *Pioneer Surveyor, Frontier Lawyer: The Personal Narrative of O. W. Williams, 1877–1902.* Edited with annotations by S. D. Myres. El Paso: Texas Western Press.

———n.d.a. *Alsate, the Last of the Chisos Apaches.* Fort Stockton, Texas: n.p.

———n.d.b. *By the Campfire in the Southwest.* Fort Stockton, Texas: n.p.

III

SETTLERS & SETTLEMENTS

9 *Settlements and Settlers at La Junta de los Ríos, 1759–1822*

Oakah L. Jones

"La Junta de los Ríos del Norte y Conchos," as Spanish officials frequently called the region, was indeed an appropriate title for it. Located where the Río Conchos empties into the Rio Grande in the vicinity of today's Ojinaga, Chihuahua, and Presidio, Texas, it has been the center of human habitation along the Rio Grande in the borderlands between Del Rio and El Paso for thousands of years, from the pre-Columbian era to the present-day. However, the descriptive term "La Junta de los Ríos," used by the Spaniards from the late seventeenth century until the separation from Mexico in 1821, did not refer solely to the point where the two rivers met. Instead it embraced a region of hundreds of square miles, roughly extending along both banks of the Río Conchos from Cuchillo Parado to present day Ojinaga, and along both the eastern and western banks of the Rio Grande, approximately from today's Lajitas, Texas, to the village of Pilares in Chihuahua.

The purpose of this study is to review the sporadic attempts made by Spain to establish the region of La Junta, and to examine in some detail Spanish settlers there in the period from the foundation of the first presidio at the junction of the two rivers (1759–60) to the end of the Spanish period, or a total of approximately sixty years—the two generations in which there was continuous close contact between Spanish soldiers and *vecinos*[1] on the one hand with Amerindians living in villages on the other. It is evident that the two groups did not remain apart in this period and region, but practiced *mestizaje* (racial mixing) openly and frequently. Using the La Junta church records from El Templo de Nuestro Padre Jesús Nazareno in Ojinaga, photographic copies of which are in the Archives of the Big Bend at Sul Ross State University,[2] one can determine from marriage and baptismal records the presence of soldiers and officers (both on active duty and retired), their marriages to local residents, and their offspring. Since "Indians" are occasionally mentioned in these baptismal and marriage records, perhaps their apparent assimilation into the prevailing society may explain the disappearance upon Spanish contact of the Amerindians from the villages they inhabited.

Fortunately, to supplement these records, there are occasional references to the size of the La Junta garrison and other presidios established in the region. However, no detailed numbers or family listings in Spanish census returns for the period 1760–1821 have been found to date. More importantly, for background on the area there are some published studies available. One of these, Col. Russell J. Gardinier's "The Physical Geography of a Significant Border Region, La Junta de los Ríos,"[3] describes the mountains, river basins, climate, soils, flora, and fauna of this region in the Chihuahuan Desert. With an elevation of about 2,500 feet, a terrain of gravel, bolson deposits, and alluvium soil, annual rainfall of just over eight inches, and sustained high summer temperatures ten to fifteen degrees above 100° F,[4] La Junta seems unfit for human occupancy. As Colonel Gardinier observes: "Too hot, too dry, too remote, too poor, too wild, too far from God, too close to the Devil, ignored by governments and forgotten by history, the land in the area of Presidio, Texas and Ojinaga, Chihuahua, bears with stoic resignation its unheralded role in the development of several human cultures in a harsh physical environment of northern Mexico and the American Southwest."[5]

It is these human cultures to which archaeologists, anthropologists, and ethnohistorians have addressed themselves, one, J. Charles Kelley, for the past sixty years. Kelley's extensive archaeological investigations began in the 1930s, resulting in a doctoral dissertation at Harvard University in 1947, publication of numerous articles in professional journals, and finally, in 1986, the publication of his *Jumano and Patarabueye: Relations at La Junta de los Ríos.*[6] Kelley's meticulous research in archaeological and historical primary sources enabled him to differentiate between nomadic Jumanos on the plains north of the Rio Grande and the village-dwelling agricultural Patarabueyes (a term used in the Luxán journal of the Espejo expedition of 1582–83) in the region of La Junta de los Ríos, where the two Amerindian cultures came into contact, and also to identify the archaeological sites of Patarabueyes people in the La Junta district.

Two other ethnohistorians/archaeologists have also enriched our knowledge of La Junta. Carroll L. Riley's revised edition of *The Frontier People: The Greater Southwest in the Protohistoric Period* included a special chapter, "The La Junta Province," which provided descriptions of the physical geography, the sequence of occupations through the early Spanish mission period, and the customs of the Amerindians at La Junta.[7]

William B. Griffen has also provided insights about the Franciscan missions at La Junta and the process of cultural contact between the Spaniards and the Amerindians as a portion of his work relating to Chihuahua, principally in the eighteenth century.[8]

All of these important works tend to concentrate upon the Amerindians before Spanish contact and the period of early missionary activity. Little attention has been paid to the last half of the eighteenth century and the first two decades of the nineteenth, when Spanish soldiers and civil settlers lived at La Junta and came into close contact with the village-dwelling Amerindians who were already there and who had been subjected to Franciscan missionary activity sporadically from the 1680s to the 1750s. Only Rex E. Gerald's *Spanish Presidios of the Late Eighteenth Century in Northern New Spain,* Max Moorhead's *The Presidio: Bastion of the Spanish Borderlands,* and Oakah L. Jones's *Nueva Vizcaya: Heartland of the Spanish Frontier* examine limited topics pertaining to La Junta's military presence.[9] Even these works do not address assimilation and development of the region after 1760, except for the Apache conciliation policy. Perhaps one reason for this neglect is the scarcity of primary sources, especially in the last thirty years or so of Spanish settlement at La Junta, and the lack of detailed censuses for the region when those of other frontier communities were being so carefully compiled from the late 1770s to the early 1790s.

While the Spanish presence at La Junta and contact with the Amerindians there can be traced to the visits of Alvar Núñez Cabeza de Vaca with his three companions in 1535, and to the expeditionary forces of Francisco Sánchez Chamuscado and Fray Agustín Rodríguez in 1581–82 and of Antonio de Espejo in 1582,[10] missionary efforts on a temporary or sustained basis did not take place until the mid-1680s, after the Pueblo revolt in New Mexico drove Spaniards southward into the vicinity of El Paso del Norte (present Ciudad Juárez, Chihuahua). Although there have been references to missions being established at La Junta as early as 1660 and to missionary visits there by 1671,[11] it is apparent that no ecclesiastical presence survived in the region when Juan Sabeata, a Christianized Jumano, appeared at El Paso in October 1683, requesting missionaries be sent and missions be established for his people. He said that he had lived at La Junta with many of his people and with Julimes Indians.[12] Fray Nicolás López at San José del Parral responded to Sabeata's request. With official sanction, he and two other priests accompanied Jumanos in late 1683 from Parral to La Junta, where they found that the

Amerindians were already Christians and had a "large church of grass." Settled in villages, the La Junta peoples (Julimes, Jumanos, Rayados, and Patarabueyes principally) raised corn, wheat, beans, calabashes, watermelons, cantaloupes, and tobacco. Father López reported that he said mass and baptized more than five hundred Amerindians during his stay at La Junta.[13] When Juan Domínguez de Mendoza arrived from El Paso in December with a party of soldiers, Fathers López and Juan Zavaleta accompanied them and Juan Sabeata's Jumanos on an expedition northeastward beyond the Rio Grande to the vicinity of the Pecos River ("Río Salado") and the Middle Conchos River ("Río Nueces," but not the present river) near today's San Angelo, Texas. After more than six weeks' absence and an attack by Apaches, the force returned to La Junta (without Juan Sabeata, who was in disfavor with Domínguez de Mendoza). When the expedition subsequently returned to El Paso, Father López accompanied it, but Father Antonio Acevedo remained at La Junta to carry on the missionary work there.[14]

Not for long. In the spring and early summer of 1684, four years after the Pueblo revolt had caused the migration of settlers and friendly Pueblos from New Mexico to the environs of El Paso del Norte, almost all the native nations in northern Chihuahua—Mansos, Sumas, Janos, Apaches, Julimes, and Conchos—arose in rebellion. The Christian Amerindians at La Junta, however, remained faithful, warned the priests, and conducted them and the sacred ornaments and vessels from the churches safely to San José del Parral.[15]

Soon after, the presence of the French party commanded by Robert Cavelier, Sieur de La Salle, in southern Texas was reported to the Spanish authorities by "Don Nicolás," a Jumano Amerindian of La Junta who was well versed in the Spanish language. This report resulted in renewed missionary activity and a military reconnoitering expedition in the late 1680s. Fray Agustín de Colina, president of the La Junta missions, testified in 1688 regarding reports of the French in Texas, indicating that the La Junta nations were once again friendly to the Spaniards. Capt. Juan Fernández de Retana, presidial commander at San Francisco de los Conchos, arrived at La Junta in 1689 with an expedition, charged with investigating the rumors of French activity and finding the French camp beyond the Rio Grande. Met by Juan Sabeata at the Pecos River, Captain de Retana heard about the destruction of La Salle's Fort Saint Louis and the death of the venture's leader. The Spanish force returned with Sabeata and Don Nicolás (the interpreter) to Parral, where its commander rendered a full report to the governor of Nueva Vizcaya. Their presentation was accompanied by two sheets of paper torn from a French book, a parchment with a painting of a ship, and a lace neckcloth.[16]

Successful missionization of the La Junta nations resumed in 1715 and continued sporadically until midcentury. Don Juan Antonio de Trasviña Retis, sergeant-major of the presidio of San Francisco de los Conchos, with permission from the viceroy of New Spain, the Duque de Linares, led an expedition to complete a survey and census of the Amerindians at La Junta and reestablish missions there. With four Franciscan missionaries, an escort of twenty soldiers, and a friendly Amerindian named El Coyame, Trasviña peacefully obtained the loyalty of eleven pueblos of Amerindians at La Junta and established six missions in the region, for a total of 1,652 persons.[17] He observed that the natives were polite and good-natured, and that both men and women were well dressed, some with Cordoba shoes and Brussels silk stockings. On arrival, the Spaniards found churches already existing, irrigated fields, and eighty La Juntans absent, working on the farms at Valle de San Bartolomé (probably descendants of those who had fled from La Junta in 1684).[18] Trasviña recommended that permanent missions be established at La Junta and that Spanish settlers not be allowed to reside in the region. Responding to these suggestions, the viceroy dispatched six priests in 1716. They founded the five missions of Nuestro Señor la Redonda de Collamé, Nuestro Señor Padre San Francisco, San Pedro del Cuchillo Parado, San Juan, and San Cristóbal. Spanish officials supplied the Amerindians with cattle, sheep, and tools to cultivate their lands. Francisco, the Amerindian governor, carefully supervised both the churches and the cattle.[19] By March 1717, a sixth mission had been established at Nuestra Señora de Santa Ana y San Francisco de Xavier, with 141 Conchos and Chinarras in all (thirty-one married men, thirty-one married women, twenty-eight widowed and single, twenty-seven boys, twenty-three girls, and "Bernardina, wife of Don Esteban [all] governed by Don Santiago Xavier.")[20] For their subsistence Trasviña issued them meat, corn, tools, clothing, and forty-seven head of cattle (fifteen people with two each, seventeen people with one each) amounting in all to a value of 840 pesos. In addition, he supplied weekly rations of beef, wheat, and corn.[21]

Although these three missions began auspiciously, the missionaries and their charges (including Francisco) were forced to flee a few years later when non-Christian Amerindians conspired to kill the priests, who escaped first to Coyame and then to San Felipe el Real de Chihuahua.

There they initiated a request for a presidio to protect the missions, but Viceroy Marqués de Valero refused. Subsequently missionaries returned to La Junta, but again were forced to flee when another revolt occurred in the mid-1720s. Once again reestablished in 1732–33, the missions at La Junta were still functioning in 1746 when Fray Juan Miguel Menchero repeated the earlier request for a presidio to protect them. The Spanish expeditions of Capt. Joseph de Ydoiaga (or Idoiaga) in 1747 and Gov. Pedro Rábago y Terán of Coahuila both visited La Junta de los Ríos or the region south of the junction. Captain Ydoiaga, ordered by the viceroy to reconnoiter the region for locating possible sites for a presidio, conducted his expedition of soldiers and Amerindian auxiliaries to Cuchillo Parado and finally to the junction of the two rivers itself. There in the latter part of November and early December 1747, he compiled a list of Amerindians residing at each pueblo, specifying persons by name, marital status, and number of children, and commenting on the land, villages, and economic pursuits of the Amerindians.[22] By 1750 there were still two to four religious at La Junta, and the missions of San Francisco, San Cristóbal, and San Pedro still functioned in the mid-1750s. Six missions and five resident missionaries occupied the region when the first presidio was established in 1759–60.[23]

The foundation of Real Presidio de Nuestra Señora de Bethlen y Santiago de las Amarillas de la Junta de los Ríos Conchos y del Norte (its original name, but later understandably known as Presidio de la Junta de los Ríos or Presidio del Norte) opened an entirely new era in the region. Contact between Spanish soldiers and vecinos with the La Junta Amerindians thereafter led to great socioeconomic and demographic changes in the structure of society, along with an increased secularism and a corresponding decline and gradual abandonment of missions. Although recommendations by missionaries, as well as military and civil officials, for the establishment of a presidio in the region had been made for more than thirty years,[24] the actual foundation of a presidio there did not occur until late December 1759. To counter the frequent "invasions and hostilities . . . which the *indios barbaros*" perpetrated on northern Chihuahua, Viceroy Marqués de las Amarillas convoked *a junta de guerra* (war council) in Mexico City on July 31, 1757. Testimony of military officials there recommended the establishment of two new presidios, one at Carrizal (between El Paso del Norte and today's city of Chihuahua) and the other at La Junta de los Ríos. Both were to be assigned to the jurisdiction of the kingdom or province of Nueva Vizcaya and were to be financed by the royal treasury. The viceroy accepted these recommendations and issued a *cedula* (decree) on August 12, 1757, for their foundation.[25]

Two unsuccessful efforts to establish the new presidios at La Junta were made in 1759. The first occurred when Capt. Alonso Rubin de Celis of El Paso del Norte dispatched a squadron of fifteen soldiers, accompanied by two missionaries, to determine an appropriate site for the garrison. Enthusiastically received by the Amerindians at La Junta and visiting bands of Natage and Salinero Apaches, the commander of this squadron encountered opposition from Father Joseph Páez, the custodian of the Franciscan missions, who objected strongly to having a presidio and soldiers in his jurisdiction. He urged on July 1 that the squadron leave the area, and Capt. Rubin de Celis so ordered after he received notification of the missionary's opposition. Father Páez then visited Gov. Matheo Antonio de Mendoza at the *villa* of San Felipe el Real de Chihuahua. Unable to convince the governor of Nueva Vizcaya to counter the viceroy's decree, Father Páez returned to La Junta, and Mendoza issued a new order on September 27, 1759, to Capt. Rubin de Celis to establish a presidio at the junction of the two rivers or whatever other place he found suitable, but not to encroach upon existing Amerindian towns or lands. This time, on October 5 Celis himself led an expedition of forty-nine soldiers and 351 horses, financed by six thousand pesos from the royal treasury. Although he was met by Father Páez and reconnoitered various sites, he encountered opposition from the Amerindians of the district (perhaps influenced by the Franciscan custodian). Rubin de Celis failed to establish the presidio, so Governor Mendoza suspended him as presidial captain, ordered him to move to his mother-in-law's hacienda, and turned over the remaining finances to an interim commander for the proposed La Junta presidio, Capt. Manuel Muñoz.[26]

With six officers, forty-three soldiers, and 305 horses, Captain Muñoz carried out the governor's orders to establish the new presidio, arriving in the La Junta region on December 20, 1759. Completed the following year and according to its plan, the presidio's construction was supervised by Don Joseph Sagardia, and it was supplied with 145 wagonloads (*cargas*) of clothes, provisions, powder, balls, shotguns, pistols, swords, and tools for its erection. During this construction Captain Muñoz visited each of the missions, where he received Amerindian pledges to recognize the king's authority, to remain peaceful, and to be loyal. He also compiled a list of the seven towns of the Amerindians and the names of the persons residing in each one or its environs.[27]

Thus began the military presence that would continue, with a temporary absence from 1766 to 1773, until the end of the Spanish period in 1821. The presidio of La Junta de los Ríos remained at the junction of the two rivers (probably on the south bank of the Río Conchos opposite the Amerindian village and mission of San Francisco) until 1766, when it was moved upriver to Julimes. The Marqués de Rubí and Nicolás de LaFora did not visit it during their inspection of the northern presidios from 1766 to 1768, because it was in the process of being moved. However, Rubí thought that the presidio should be relocated to its former site at the confluence of the two rivers, and the Reglamento de 1772 so ordered.[28] Lt. Col. Hugo O'Conor, the newly appointed *comandante inspector* of the Provincias Internas del Norte, carried out the provisions of the royal regulation by reestablishing the garrison at La Junta with a fifty-man force between October 1 and November 1, 1773. At the same time he established another presidio near the spring of San Carlos (about eleven miles southwest of present-day Lajitas, Texas), and later (between January 9 and March 27, 1774) founded a third presidio named El Principe at the campsite of Los Pilares (about one-quarter of a mile south of Pilares, Chihuahua, between La Junta and El Paso del Norte).[29] Thus by 1774 three presidios had been established in the general vicinity of La Junta de los Ríos and along the upper and lower sections of the Rio Grande. While those at Pilares and San Carlos were subsequently abandoned and then reoccupied between the 1780s and 1815,[30] Presidio del Norte continued uninterruptedly to the end of the Spanish era.

Fifty soldiers and a captain constituted the original complement of Presidio La Junta de los Ríos.[31] By 1765 Bishop Pedro de Tamarón y Romeral noted that there were 52 families totaling 138 persons at La Junta.[32] Two years later Nicolás de LaFora reported a garrison of 50 soldiers at Julimes,[33] but by 1783 Presidio del Norte had 106 men, according to Commandant-General Felipe de Neve's official report.[34] This same figure was reported in the census of 1788 for Nueva Vizcaya, and again in a military list of 1790–92, with 144 men at the presidios of El Principe and San Carlos.[35] In 1817 there were 87 soldiers plus 25 retired ones (*invalidos*) at Presidio del Norte and 119 at San Carlos, all cavalry.[36] In 1820 one report reflected 1,235 persons residing at "Norte" (evidently La Junta de los Ríos) under the heading of "*compañías presidiales y voluntarios*" (presidial companies and volunteers).[37]

With this complement of active duty and retired soldiers, families, and some vecinos congregated in the La Junta region over a continuous period of forty-eight years, it is apparent that they had considerable impact upon the dwindling number of Amerindians at the Franciscan missions (still six of them in 1794).[38] The process of intermixing and racial assimilation of natives into the prevailing Spanish society intensified during this period, although evidence of Amerindian acculturation—for example, speaking Castilian, adopting Spanish tools and crops, and accepting Christianity—began before 1759–60. While no detailed censuses of the population have been found to date, the marriage and baptismal records of the church of Nuestro Padre Jesús Nazareno in Ojinaga reveal unions of soldiers and local women (including Amerindians), children born of such parents, and witnesses of ceremonies who were soldiers, vecinos, and Amerindians. These records tend to support the contention of Edward H. Spicer "that there was probably a good deal of intermixture of the unattached soldiers with Indian women and some consequent marriages" and that after the expulsion of the Jesuits in 1767, the increased secular program of the Spanish authorities—civil and military—resulted in the disintegration of mission communities.[39]

Marriages and baptisms at La Junta from 1775, two years after the presidio returned there from Julimes, until the end of the Spanish period reveal some information concerning soldiers, vecinos, and Amerindians of the region.[40] Petitions of soldiers and vecinos to marry local women are exemplified by those of Manual Caro (a soldier of Presidio El Principe) and Cristomo Caraval (a *vecino* of that presidio). In a letter addressed to the presidial captain, Caro requested permission to marry Roberta Zamora (a vecina of Presidio del Norte or La Junta de los Ríos). A note on the margin of the petition indicated that permission was granted.[41] Caraval, a vecino of the presidio at La Junta, requested that the presidial chaplain grant him permission to marry Manuela Villa, also a vecina, and the daughter of Ygnacio and Francisca de la Cruz, "*Yndios Nortenos*" of this garrison.[42]

Yet these petitions are not the only indications of marriages, since the more extensive baptismal records show the names and status—soldiers, vecinos, and Amerindians—of a child's parents and godparents. Chap. Fernando de Ysaguirre of the Presidio de la Junta de los Ríos Norte y Conchos performed most of these baptisms (one was conducted by Fray Raphael Blanco, the chaplain of the presidio of Pilares) in the period 1775–80, and they evidently occurred at the presidio itself. Father Ysaguirre on February 19, 1775, baptized an infant son of Mariano Enriques, a native of the Valle de San Bartolomé, and Rita de Acosta, a native of

Julimes. Neither of these parents appears to be Amerindian. In March of the same year, Father Ysaguirre baptized a "mulatto son" of Diego de Villa, soldier, and María Sánchez; a *mulata* daughter of Miguel Eredia, "soldier of this company," and María Luján; and an *"español* son" of Guadalupe Ramírez, "soldier of this company," and Victoria de Herrera. On May 5, 1776, he baptized an infant son of Juan Joaquín, "Yndio," and María Montoya, "Yndio," noting in the margin that they were auxiliaries of the presidial company. On August 23, 1776, he baptized and named María Petra, noting that "she is a *collota* (*coyote* or mixture of Spaniard and Indian) and the daughter of Joseph Andriaga, *español*, and Dolores Luján, Yndio."[43] From 1775 to 1779 Father Ysaguirre baptized sixty-three children in all—thirty-nine those of soldiers (twenty-two boys and seventeen girls), twenty-three those of vecinos (ten girls, thirteen boys), and one the son of Amerindian auxiliaries.[44] That this process continued is evident in the baptismal records of 1780 (one daughter of Vicente Becerro, an Indian soldier of the presidio of Pilares, and María Phelipa de la Cruz, an "Yadia chola") and those of other priests in the district, especially Father Vicente Lechon of the chapel of Nuestra Señora del Pilar de Coyame from 1807 to 1822 and beyond.[45]

Thus it can be seen that acculturation and intermixing of Amerindians, soldiers, and vecinos residing in the proximity of the presidios of El Norte, El Principe, and San Carlos began soon after the troops returned from Julimes to La Junta, and continued for the remainder of the Spanish period. From the early 1790s onward, however, there is another illustration of Amerindian acculturation at La Junta—the baptisms of numerous Apache children.

These Apaches, largely Mescaleros, were bands that had accepted offers of a truce from Commandant-General Teodoro de Croix in 1779, and other offers from Jacobo de Ugarte y Loyola and Pedro de Nava during the 1780s. In compliance with the king's order of February 20, 1779, to congregate peace-seeking bands of Apaches and others at the presidios of the northern frontier, Croix sent Lt. Col. Manuel Muñoz to conclude a formal agreement with a group of Mescaleros who sought protection at La Junta and offered to serve as auxiliaries. Muñoz arrived there on October 25, 1779, and negotiated with the Mescalero chiefs (six of them), one of whom, named Alonso, was allowed to select a site to the northeast, and only a musket-shot from the presidio. There a pueblo of adobe bricks and timber, named Nuestra Señora de la Buena Esperanza, was constructed for Alonso's band of forty-five Apaches. Another pueblo for other Mescaleros (eighty of them) was established at the abandoned mission of San Francisco (across the Río Conchos from the presidio), but the Apaches refused to live in it and departed on a buffalo hunt. When they returned in January 1780, they asked Muñoz to establish a single pueblo for all the Mescaleros. Muñoz extended the boundaries of Buena Esperanza to 120 *varas* (about 334 feet) on each side, and by June 1780, at least four bands resided there. Two months later they abandoned it because of an epidemic of smallpox, and flooding of both rivers that destroyed the corn crop. They returned in November, camping near the presidio instead of the abandoned 113 houses and two bastions at La Esperanza. For the construction of a new pueblo, Muñoz hired sixteen Spanish laborers at three *reales* per day, because the Mescaleros would not "lift a single adobe brick." He also sent troops into the mountains to cut necessary lumber. In all Muñoz said that the total bill for constructing the new pueblo, planting crops, and issuing rations to the Apaches (eight bushels of corn and three of beans every week) amounted to 4,120 pesos. Yet the cost was worth it. The Apaches remained at peace and served as auxiliaries on campaigns against hostile Gila Apaches.[46]

However, Croix, suspecting that some Mescaleros were still raiding Spanish settlements, in July 1781 sent Muñoz new instructions. Hereafter no further food, clothing, ammunition, or other supplies were to be issued to any Mescalero until he settled securely at La Esperanza or some other pueblo or until he served faithfully as an auxiliary. Weekly rations of food and necessities would be issued to those families who settled at one of the pueblos, but no Mescalero could leave them without the permission of the presidial captain, and then only for a specified time. Spanish day laborers would be provided to plant and care for fields for one year, but Mescaleros were to assist them. Those who settled in a pueblo and served as auxiliaries would be exempt from all construction and agricultural labor, and they were to be paid three *reales* or the equivalent in supplies per day for their military service. Those who did not settle but did serve as auxiliaries were to receive the supplies they needed for military campaigns, but nothing else. Finally, those who neither settled nor served as auxiliaries were considered enemies and were not to be admitted to the presidios or towns of the frontier. Three Mescalero chiefs—Alonso, Domingo Alegre, and Patule—accepted these new terms in September 1781, returning to La Esperanza by October. However, by March 1783, most of them had once again fled.[47]

After February 1787, Ugarte repeated the experiment with the Mescaleros. Captains Juan Díaz and Juan Bautista Elguézabal completed new arrangements with the Apaches, whereby they must stop raiding, surrender all their captive Spaniards, adopt Christianity, and form a permanent settlement near Presidio del Norte. There they would be assigned plots of bottomland along the Rio Grande and assisted by the Spaniards in planting crops and raising livestock, but they were not to receive rations. They were permitted to leave their pueblo to hunt game and to gather wild fruits. By the end of March 1787, eight Mescalero chiefs and their bands arrived at Presidio del Norte. Captain Díaz estimated that there were about four hundred warriors and three hundred families of Apaches at La Junta, suffering greatly from acute hunger, so Díaz issued them rations, thereby violating his original instructions. Four Apache bands left the pueblo, but by August had returned, and all ten bands resided near the presidio. At the request of Governor-Intendant Felipe Díaz de Ortega from Durango, the superintendent of the royal treasury in August approved the payment of three thousand pesos charged against the Chihuahua funds for the subsistence of the "Apaches at peace in the Presidio del Norte," and the king approved the expenditures the following February.[48]

Yet in the interim, on October 8, 1787, the new viceroy, Manuel Antonio Flores, alarmed by continued reports of Apache hostilities on the frontier, ordered that all the bands assembled at El Norte remove to Santa Rosa in Coahuila and that war be declared on those who refused to move. Commandant-General Ugarte ordered their removal on May 7, 1788, thus ending the second effort to establish peaceful Apaches at La Junta.[49]

After unsuccessful efforts had been made to settle Apaches in Coahuila, in 1790 Viceroy Conde de Revillagigedo authorized the resumption of peace negotiations with the Mescaleros. Once again Captain Díaz met with eight Apache bands and concluded a formal peace with them before the end of the year. They settled near Presidio del Norte, and some 230–250 warriors (perhaps eight to nine hundred persons in all) were still there three years later. The Apaches would still not farm, but they did serve as auxiliaries. When they revolted in 1795, about one-third of them remained loyal to the Spaniards and stayed in the La Junta region.[50]

Thus the Apaches had been present at La Junta in temporary peaceful settlements from 1779 to 1795, and some remained as settlers thereafter until the end of the Spanish period. Some accepted Christianity and became a part of the racially mixed population of the region. Baptismal records after 1792, extending to 1822, reveal Apaches as Christians and as

"*Indios Infieles.*" Fray Manuel Acevedo, the parish priest of the presidio at El Principe, on November 9, 1792, baptized twins, one named Juan José Miguel Teodoro, an "Apachito" (Apache boy) of about two years of age, and another, an "Apachita" (Apache girl), both orphans in the home of the presidial captain.[51] Father Pedro Antonio Camargo in January 1793 baptized a boy about three years old, the son of a "Christian apostate and a *gentil* of the Mescalero Apache nation whose parents sought peace in this royal presidio." Father Vicente Lechon of the chapel of Nuestro Señora del Pilar de Coyame baptized numerous Apache children between 1807 and 1814. Some he called "*criatura,*" others "*criaturas coatas*" and "*infantas coatas,*" indicating that these "creatures" were Apaches and their parents "*infieles*" or non-Christian.[52]

La Junta de los Ríos del Norte y Conchos has had thousands of years of human occupancy—Amerindian, Spanish, and Mexican. Its isolated location, extreme climate, sparse rainfall, and rocky soil may seem at first glance to inhibit such occupancy. But the archaeological and historical records indicate that such has not been the case. La Junta's low humidity, long summer season, and mild winters have attracted settlers to the region. As elsewhere in the southwestern United States and northern Mexico, water is the key to survival in such an environment. That resource is one of La Junta's great attractions—the Río Grande del Norte and especially the Río Conchos, which exceeds the flow of the Rio Grande at La Junta by more than two to one.

Important strides have been made in the past fifty or sixty years to improve our knowledge of this district that has been so significant for settlement, trade, and human development. J. Charles Kelley, William Griffen, and Carroll Riley have given us scholarly, soundly researched studies of the archaeology and ethnohistory of La Junta through the missionary era. As John Speth stated in the introduction to Kelley's *Jumano and Patarabueye,* "La Junta de los Ríos contains one of the most important and exciting archaeological records in western North America, one that desperately deserves conservation and further research."[53]

But what of La Junta's history and heritage after the establishment of its presidio and the arrival of soldiers, families, and civil settlers in the last sixty years of Spanish presence? What became of the Amerindians at the junction of the rivers? Riley notes that twentieth-century Mexicans and Americans have lost and "no longer know their history."[54] Aside from the useful presidial studies of Max Moorhead and Rex Gerald, little has been done to examine the records of Spanish settlement, trade, Amerindian contacts, and acculturation, and the growth of an integrated population at La Junta from 1760 to 1821.

It is to be hoped that through preliminary study and future research in church and civil records, including those of parishes such as the one at Ojinaga, and censuses (if any exist), additional information can be uncovered concerning the people of this region. Kelley notes that La Junta Amerindians disappeared after 1800, and he speculates that "it is probable that most of the La Junta peoples, who had become increasingly acculturated by Spanish contact, were slowly absorbed into the rising tide of Spanish settlement."[55] Griffen also notes the decline of the Amerindian population at the Franciscan missions over the last fifty years of the Spanish colonial period, concluding that these missions, because they were practically "devoid of people," disappeared not long after 1765, "probably within the next 20 years."[56]

Marriage and baptismal records of the church at Nuestro Padre Jesús Nazareno in Ojinaga and their photostats at the Archives of the Big Bend may not show us all we need to know. Yet they do reveal the continued presence of La Junta Amerindians and their intermingling with Spanish soldiers and vecinos. Also, civil records and those at the La Junta church show the presence of Mescalero Apaches and their temporary peaceful settlement in the region between 1779 and 1815. Thus it appears that documentary evidence exists to suggest that La Juntans acculturated and were indeed assimilated into the Spanish population through their acceptance of Christianity, employment of new farming methods, trade with the Spaniards, acquisition of the Spanish language, service as auxiliaries on campaigns, and intermarriages with the Spaniards. While the evidence is still not full and complete, it is possible, based on existing sources, to conclude tentatively that La Junta Amerindians did indeed become part of the polyglot population in this important and neglected region of the Spanish borderlands.

The acculturation of La Junta Amerindians took place in three stages: first, through contact with Spanish explorers; second, through extended missionary activity from the 1680s to the 1790s; and finally, through continued close contact with presidial soldiers and civil settlers, who had families of their own or married locals, including Amerindians. What began with Columbus's explorations in the Caribbean, bringing Amerindians and the Spanish into initial contact, culminated three centuries later at La Junta de los Ríos on the Spanish frontier with the establishment of a mixed population that is the basis of La Junta's people today.

Notes

I am indebted to Melleta Bell, archivist of the Archives of the Big Bend; Kenneth Perry, Director of the Museum of the Big Bend; and especially Earl Elam, PhD, director of the Center for Big Bend Studies, and his wife, Eleanor, all of Sul Ross State University, for their help and hospitality during my research for this study.

1. The term *"vecinos"* defies exact translation. It means the principal residents or family heads in Spanish frontier communities, not the total number of inhabitants. They might be male or female, married or single, and were specifically recognized by officials and listed in the Spanish census returns.

2. La Junta Church Records, 1775–1857, Collection 48, Archives of the Big Bend, Sul Ross State University, Alpine, Texas. These are photostats of the records of El Templo de Nuestro Padre Jesús Nazareno, Ojinaga, Chihuahua, obtained with the permission of the priest in charge of the church by Col. Russell Gardinier in 1973 and given to Director Earl Elam, who placed them in the Archives of the Big Bend in 1981. Note that the record begins two years after the final relocation and reestablishment of the presidio at La Junta in 1773.

3. Russell J. Gardinier, "The Physical Geography of a Significant Border Region, La Junta de los Ríos," *Journal of Big Bend Studies* 1 (January 1989): 25–50.

4. Ibid., 25, 29, 37, 39.

5. Ibid., 25.

6. J. Charles Kelley, *Jumano and Patarabueye: Relations at La Junta de los* Ríos (Ann Arbor: Anthropological Papers 77, Museum of Anthropology, University of Michigan, 1986). This is the publication of Kelley's 1947 PhD dissertation at Harvard University, with a foreword added by John D. Speth, director of the Museum of Anthropology at the University of Michigan. See also Kelley's two-part article "The Historical Indian Pueblos at La Junta de los Ríos," in *New Mexico Historical Review* 27 (October 1952): 257–95 and 28 (January 1953): 21–51.

7. Caroll L. Riley, *The Frontier People: The Greater Southwest in the Protohistoric Period*, rev. ed. (Albuquerque: University of New Mexico Press, 1987). Chapter 10 treats the Amerindians of La Junta.

8. William B. Griffen, *Culture Changes and the Shifting Populations in Central Northern Mexico* (Tucson: Anthropological Papers of the University of Arizona 13, University of Arizona Press, 1969), and *Indian Assimilation of the Franciscan Area of Nueva Vizcaya* (Tucson: Anthropological Papers of the University of Arizona 33, University of Arizona Press, 1979).

9. Rex E. Gerald, *Spanish Presidios of the Late Eighteenth Century in Northern New Spain* (Santa Fe: Museum of New Mexico Press, 1968); Max Moorhead, *The Presidio: Bastion of the Spanish Borderlands* (Norman: University of Oklahoma Press, 1975); Oakah L. Jones Jr., *Nueva Vizcaya: Heartland of the Spanish Frontier* (Albuquerque: University of New Mexico Press, 1988). An overview of La Junta de los Ríos from pre-Columbian times to the 1960s is provided in a brief monograph of sixty-four pages, based upon published sources, in Howard G. Applegate and C. Wayne Hanselka, *La Junta de los Ríos del Norte y Conchos* (El Paso, Texas: Southwestern Studies Monograph 41, 1974).

10. Kelley, *Jumano and Patarabueye*, 47–48, 50–51, 52–53; Riley, *Frontier People*, 292–93.

11. Pedro Alonso O'Crouley, *A Description of the Kingdom of New Spain,* trans. and ed. Sean Galvin ([San Francisco]: John Howell, 1962), 62, notes that two missionaries founded the first missions at La Junta de los Ríos in 1660, but after two years of activity there a bloody civil war broke out between those Amerindians who wanted to accept Christianity and those who did not. The latter group apparently succeeded, stripped the missionaries of their robes, and drove them out of the region to refuge at San José del Parral, while the Christian Amerindians of La Junta moved to nearby Valle de San Bartolomé, where they continued to reside until the missions were reestablished at La Junta in 1715. Kelley *(Jumano and Patarabueye,* 57) notes that Fray García de San Francisco visited La Junta from El Paso and said Mass "before 1691," and Fray Juan de Sumestra visited the region shortly thereafter. Instead of missions, these early instances of Franciscan missionary activity seem to be more *visitas* from other ecclesiastical centers, such as the one at El Paso del Norte.

12. Kelley, *Jumano and Patarabueye,* 23.

13. Ibid., 24, 58.

14. Ibid., 24–26. During the expedition Sabeata revealed that his real reason for requesting Spanish missionaries was not a religious one, but to obtain military assistance against his enemies, the Apaches.

15. Ibid., 58.

16. Ibid., 28–30.

17. Manuel San Juan de Santa Cruz to His Majesty, Parral, December 21, 1717, Archivo General de Indias (hereafter AGI), Sevilla, Spain, Guadalajara, 109. Kelley, *Jumano and Patarabueye,* 61–62, states the names of three missionaries in the expedition, says there were thirty soldiers, and notes that a total of 1,405 Amerindians were counted in the pueblos. See also Francisco R. Almada, *Resumen de historia del estado de Chihuahua* (Mexico: Libros Mexicanos, 1955), 93, for the date of June 2, 1715, as the foundation of the mission San Francisco de la Junta de los Ríos.

18. Kelley, *Jumano and Patarabueye*, 62.

19. Ibid., 63.

20. Padre Visitador Antonio Arias de la Compañía de Jesús, List of Indians, Parral, March 10, 1717, AGI, Guadalajara, 109.

21. Juan Antonio de Trasviña, Relación, Pueblo of La Señora Santa Ana y San Francisco Xavier, December 24, 1716, AGI, Guadalajara, 109.

22. Joseph de Ydoiaga, Cuaderno . . . , Real Presidio del Valle de San Bartolomé, October 6–December 27, 1747, Carta y testimonio sobre la visita a los presidios del Norte y Conchos (1746–51), AGI, Mexico, 1347, microcopy. I am indebted to Earl Elam for making this document available to me.

23. Kelley, *Jumano and Patarabueye*, 63–65.

24. Franciscan missionary suggestions for the establishment of a presidio at La Junta began in the 1720s (see above) and were reiterated by Fray Juan Miguel Menchero in 1746. Although he did not actually visit La Junta de los Ríos in his general inspection of presidios from 1724 to 1728, Brig. Pedro de Rivera reported an uprising of Amerindians and their allies there in which two missionaries and two servants had been slain. He included in his report a recommendation for the establishment of a presidio at La Junta. See Pedro de Rivera, *Diario y derrotero de lo caminado, visto, y observado en el discurso de la visita general del Precidios . . .* , Guillermo Porras Muñoz, ed. (Mexico, DF: Costa Amic, 1945), 61; and Thomas H. Naylor and Charles W. Polzer, *Pedro de Rivera and the Military Regulations for Northern New Spain, 1724–1729* (Tucson: University of Arizona Press, 1988), 83n56, 146–7. Governor Juan Bautistade Belaunzarán of Nueva Vizcaya in May 1744 also concurred in Rivera's recommendation, suggesting that a presidio be established at La Junta with fifty soldiers (including a captain, lieutenant, and *alférez* or junior lieutenant) drawn from other presidios of Nueva Vizcaya. The new presidio's purpose was to prevent invading "*indios barbaros*" from raiding the province and Coahuila. See Belaunzarán to Viceroy, Mexico, May 25, 1744, AGI, Guadalajara, 186.

25. Testimonio de el primo. Quaderno de Autos que se formararon en el ano . . . en razon de la Poblazon de el Parage nombrado Carrizal, fundación y construcción de un Nuebo RI. Presidio en la junta de los Ríos del Norte y Conchos . . . , AGI, Guadalajara, 327; Jones, *Nueva Vizcaya*, 152.

26. Testimonio, AGI, Guadalajara, 327; Jones, *Nueva Vizcaya*, 155–57.

27. Testimonio, AGI, Guadalajara, 327; Jones, *Nueva Vizcaya*, 57. Muñoz on one list indicated the pueblos of San Francisco (with seventeen Amerindians, including its governor, *cacique* or chief, war captain, and three tailors); San Juan (with thirty-one, including the governor, cacique, three former governors, a *fiscal*, an *alguacil*, a corporal, and one *alférez*); the pueblo of Los Conejos (with ten, including a governor and a cacique); the pueblo of Mesquites (with eight,

including its governor, one former governor, and former *alcalde* or chief magistrate); and the pueblo of Guadalupe (with three, including a *mulato* named Pedro who had been governor and now was *"cacique general,"* one corporal, and a carpenter). On his second list, dated December 22,1759, Muñoz indicated the pueblos of San Francisco (with eleven Amerindians); San Juan (with ten); Los Conejos (with four); Los Mesquites (with four); Guadalupe (with twenty-eight); San Cristóbal (with two); and Los Puliques (with one). Thus there were seven pueblos containing a total of 129 Amerindians—twenty-eight at San Francisco, forty-one at San Juan, fourteen at Los Conejos, twelve at Mesquites, thirty-one at Guadalupe, two at San Cristóbal, and one at Puliques.

28. Moorhead, *The Presidio,* 57n26, 65; Sidney B. Brinckerhoff and Odie B. Faulk, *Lancers for the King: A Study of the Frontier Military System of Northern New Spain, with a Translation of the Royal Regulations of 1772* (Phoenix: Arizona Historical Foundation, 1965), 55, 57; Lawrence Kinnaird, *The Frontiers of New Spain: Nicolás de LaFora's Description* (Berkeley: Quivira Society, 1958), 12.

29. Moorhead, *The Presidio,* 69–70; Gerald, *Spanish Presidios,* 27–28, 37–39.

30. Although Gerald (*Spanish Presidios,* 38) states that San Carlos was an "abandoned locality" by April 1787, census reports of 1788 and 1790 still reflected garrisons at El Principe and San Carlos. A later report of 1817 also indicated that there were still 119 soldiers at San Carlos.

31. Estado de al Compañia de Presidiales, December 13, 1759, in Testimonio, AGI, Guadalajara, 327. In this general inspection of the troops turned over to Captain Manuel Muñoz there were six officers (one lieutenant, one alférez, one sergeant, and three corporals) and forty-three soldiers, plus 305 horses.

32. Pedro Tamarón y Romeral, *Demostración del Vastísimo Obispado de la Nueva Vizcaya–1765,* ed. Vito Alessio Robles (México: Antigua Libreria de José Porrua e Hijos, 1937), 155–57. Bishop Tamarón noted that there were fifty families of soldiers with a total of 133 persons, and two of vecinos with five persons.

33. Kinnaird, *Frontiers of New Spain,* 72–73.

34. Phelipe de Neve to Joseph de Gálvez, Arispe, December 1, 1783, Relación concisa y exacta del estado en que ha encontrado las Provincias Internas, AGI, Guadalajara, 268.

35. Almada, *Resumen,* 144; Francisco Josef de Urrutia, "Estado Militar de la Provincia de Nueva Vizcaya en los anos 1790–1792," Archive General de la Nación (hereafter AGN), Historia, 522. There were seventy-one soldiers in the company of the presidio of El Principe and seventy-three at San Carlos.

36. Lista de Revista de las once compañías de dicha, Provincia, Nueva Vizcaya, January-April, 1817, AGN, Provincias Internas, 206.

37. "Lista o noticia de los jurisdicciones o partidos de a comprención de la Provincia de Nueva Vizcaya . . . ," Biblioteca Nacional de México, Mexico City, Archive Franciscano, 18:387.

38. Kelley, *Jumano and Patarabueye,* 64.

39. Edward H. Spicer, *Cycles of Conquest: The Impact of Spain, Mexico, and the United States on the Indians of the Southwest, 1533–1960* (Tucson: University of Arizona Press, 1962), 302, 307.

40. See note 2 for full citation of these records.

41. Manuel Caro, soldier of the cavalry company that garrisons the Presidio of El Principe, to presidial captain, August 16, 1789, La Junta Church Records, 1775–1857, photostat, Archives of the Big Bend, Collection 48, box 1, folder 2. Hereafter citations to La Junta Church Records are cited as box and folder numbers.

42. Cristomo Caraval, "vecino of this presidio," to Father Juan Marañón, September 16, 1790, La Junta Church Records, box 1, folder 2.

43. Chaplain Fernando de Ysaguirre, baptism of María Petra, August 23, 1776, La Junta Church Records, box 1, folder 1.

44. Compilation of baptismal records of Father Fernando de Ysaguirre, 1775–79, La Junta Church Records, box 1, folder 1.

45. Chaplain Fernando de Ysaguirre, baptism of María Paula, June 11, 1780, La Junta Church Records, box 1, folder 1; Father Lechon of the Chapel of N. S. del Pilar de Coyame, La Junta Church Records, box 2, folders 11–13.

46. Moorhead, *The Presidio,* 85, 245–48.

47. Ibid., 249–50.

48. Fernando Josef Mangino to Exmo. Sor. Marqués de Sonora, Mexico, August 12, 1787, AGI, Guadalajara, 511, file 24, photostat; and Antonio Valdés to Viceroy, El Pardo, February 11, 1788, AGI, Guadalajara, 497, file 24, photostat, both in La Junta Presidio Collection, Archives of the Big Bend, Collection 47, Sul Ross State University, Alpine, Texas.

49. Moorhead, *The Presidio,* 109, 250–57.

50. Ibid., 258–61.

51. Friar Manuel Acevedo, baptisms of Juan José Miguel Teodoro and María de la S.S. Trinidad Gertrudiz Teodora, La Junta Church Records, box 1, folder 5.

52. Vicente Lechon, Chapel of N.S. del Pilar de Coyame, baptisms, December 13, 1807–October 16, 1814, La Junta Church Records, box 2, folder 11.

53. John D. Speth, introduction to Kelley, *Jumano and Patarabueye,* xvi.

54. Riley, *Frontier People,* 310.

55. Kelley, *Jumano and Patarabueye,* 6.

56. Griffen, *Indian Assimilation,* 103.

10   Mexican American Traditional Foodways at La Junta de los Ríos

Joe S. Graham

As in many other cultures, food among the Mexicanos of La Junta[1] is important beyond its function of nurturing the physical body. It is at the center of many important social events, from family meals to larger fiestas, including more private rites of passage such as weddings and *fiestas de las quinceañeras* (puberty rites celebrating girls' fifteenth birthdays) and such public rites of intensification as *el día de los muertos* (the Day of the Dead). And even among the poor, food is symbolic of their willingness and desire to share what they have, even with strangers like me.

Perhaps more than any other single aspect of Mexican culture, its foodways have been accepted in Anglo culture, and they have influenced the way Anglos eat. Many Anglos have become aficionados of Mexican food. To have something as fundamental as food be not only accepted but liked, sometimes passionately, is to have one's culture validated. It is a small but important victory over Anglo culture, which is often quite hostile to other aspects of Mexican American culture. To reject the foodways of a culture is to profoundly deprecate it. As hosts like to have family and guests appreciate their culinary arts, so a whole culture is validated when both members and outsiders show appreciation for its foodways.

Thus foodways, because they are so central to our lives, are a significant source of information about us, about the way we see ourselves, about our historical and cultural ties with others, and about our worldview. Although little has been written about the foodways of the La Junta area, in 1979–80 I spent nine months conducting intensive fieldwork on both sides of the Rio Grande, documenting the foodways of Hispanics in the area (cf. Graham 1983, 1984). In addition to collecting many hours of taped interviews and thousands of photographs, I was able to distribute and collect (through the schools on both sides of the border) over three hundred eighteen-page questionnaires on foodways. In this paper, I shall attempt to describe in as much detail as space permits the foodways of the Mexicanos of La Junta and to provide a historical context for those foodways, which truly reflect a confluence of cultures.

Pre-Hispanic Foods at La Junta

While there is insufficient information available to describe in detail the foodways of the prehistoric inhabitants of La Junta, they shared some of the basic foods of the present-day cultures, including corn, beans, tomatoes, potatoes, squash, pumpkins, sunflower seeds, and peppers (chiles). These cultivated foods were supplemented by wild plants and animals, as well as the domesticated turkey. Diego Pérez de Luxán, who accompanied Antonio de Espejo in the 1582 entrada to La Junta, gave a few details about the foodways of the inhabitants of the area. He wrote that up the Río Conchos from La Junta, the Conchos Indians "live in peace and support themselves on fish, mesquite, and mescal (a food made of agave)" (Luxán [1582] 1966, 155–56). Espejo's own account is more detailed, noting that the Conchos "live on rabbits, hares, and deer, which they hunt and which are abundant, and on some crops of maize, gourds, Castilian melons, and watermelons, like winter melons, which they plant and cultivate, and on fish, *mascales,* which are the leaves of *lechuguilla,* a plant half a vara in height, the stalks of which have green leaves. They cook the stocks of this plant and make a preserve like quince jam. It is very sweet, and they call it *mascale*" (Bolton 1916, 170).

The Spaniards found this pattern of diet shared pretty much by Indians all along the Río Conchos, down to La Junta, where Espejo records that the Jumanos had "maize, gourds, beans, game of foot and wing, and fish of many kinds from two rivers that carry much water" (Bolton 1916, 172).

Corn was the earliest of the major cultivated foods of the Americas and the only cereal cultivated in the Southwest before the introduction of wheat and other grains by the Spaniards. Even after the appearance of the other important cultivated foods, corn remained the most important single staple in the diet. As we shall see, it continues to play a significant, though diminished, role in the lives of the descendants of the early La Junta inhabitants.

Pre-Hispanic La Juntans processed corn in much the same way as their ancestors to the northwest and their cousins throughout Mexico. In earlier phases of civilization, they relied on the mortar and pestle to grind the hard corn. Later they used the metate and mano to process the corn into various dishes, grinding it raw and kneading it with hot water to make a paste for tortillas, tamales, or cornbread, or grinding roasted corn into *pinole* (fr. Nahuatl), often eaten dry or mixed with water. *Atole* (fr. Nahuatl), a thin gruel made of finely ground corn, was also common in the area. And, of course, in its roasting-ear state, corn would have been either cooked in the shuck over coals or boiled and eaten.

Cultivated squash, beans, and pumpkin supplemented the corn diet (Smith 1871, 158–62). The beans were either the kidney bean (*Phaseolus vulgaris*) or the tepary (*acutifolias*) or both (Lantz et al. 1953, 6; Holden and Lamb 1962, 219). The squash was likely the *Curcurbita moschata* (the cushaw, or winter squash type), which could be eaten in its tender stage or allowed to mature as a pumpkin to be stored for winter, although *C. pepo* (a pumpkin, or summer squash) may also have been raised (Holden and Lamb 1962, 219–20). Setzler (1935) found that squash was known in the Big Bend as early as the cave dwellers.

In addition to these cultivated crops, the Indians of La Junta relied on wild plants, animals, and fish to supplement their diet. They ate the nopal (prickly pear) and its fruit, the *tuna. Pitahaya, a* very sweet cactus fruit, grows profusely in the region. Throughout the area one can find middens around pits used to bake the heads of the sotol plant, which made a sweet and nutritious food. Several types of agave, including the century plant and the smaller lechuguilla, were very important to the Indians of the region, who used the crowns, stalks, and hearts of the maguey and the root sections of the lechuguilla. One maguey plant could provide as much as seventy pounds of food (Winkler 1962, 45), but it had to be cooked in pits before it could be eaten.

Perhaps one of the most important wild plant foods in the area was the mesquite bean, which could be eaten either in its green stage or dried and stored. The beans and pods, which are quite sweet, can be pounded into a flour and then used as pinole, or mixed with water to make a paste that can be baked or dried for later use (Felger 1977, 156–58). Mesquite beans are plentiful in the La Junta region, even in the driest years.

There are many other wild plants in the area that may have been used by the early Indian farmers of the La Junta area, and these plants have been discussed most competently by Winkler (1982) in her study of wild plant food sources used by nomadic groups in the desert Southwest.

Foods of the Spanish and Post-Spanish Eras

The first actual *pobladores,* some fifty to sixty families of pioneer settlers (nonclerics and nonsoldiers), arrived in La Junta in 1759, forming the nucleus of the developing civilization that would persist to the present. There is little specific information about these early pioneers. We know that they came from the area that was then the province of Nueva Vizcaya, later to become the state of Chihuahua. The large majority of these settlers on the Spanish frontier were "real settlers, established in formal communities, and absolutely dependent upon tilling the soil and raising livestock for their livelihood" (Jones 1979, 4–5).

Unlike Anglo settlers who attempted to displace the Indians from coveted lands, early Spanish settlers mixed with, and accepted into their communities, indigenous populations both peaceful and hostile. Thus in the veins of present-day La Junta inhabitants flows some of the blood of such peaceful Indians as the Patarabueyes, Julimes, and other smaller tribes, as well as that of the hostile Apaches and Comanches.

When the Spaniards entered the La Junta valley, they brought with them a number of new food sources and the technology for enhancing the production of cultivated native foods. Irrigation dams and canals, fairly crude, but effective, permitted the watering of many acres of land along both sides of the Conchos and Rio Grande. By the time the first Anglo travelers and settlers arrived in the La Junta region in the middle of the nineteenth century, Spanish and Mexican influence was pervasive. During the mid-nineteenth-century boundary survey, W. H. Emory discovered at Vado de Piedra (about twenty-five miles above Presidio) "large cultivated fields, which were watered by acequias, and yield abundant crops of wheat and corn" (1857, 89). And the wooden plow pulled by a brace of oxen had replaced the Indian planting stick (Bieber 1938, 314–15).

Among the more important food sources introduced by the Spaniards were wheat and various domesticated animals—pigs, goats, cattle and sheep, as well as a number of fruits and vegetables to supplement the basic foodstuffs cultivated by the Indians. They also brought new modes of preparing the foods and a variety of new dishes.

Wheat was introduced at a relatively early stage in the Spanish conquest. As early as 1684 Mendoza reported that the Indians at La Junta, whom he called Julimes, spoke the Mexican (Nahuatl or Aztec) language and that "all sow maize and wheat" (Bolton 1916, 325).

There is no record of how wheat was used by these early Indians, but one would assume that the soldiers and especially the missionaries used it to prepare breads and pastries in the style of the Spaniards, and later the Mexicans. The Indians, particularly those closely involved with the missions, would have learned to appreciate and use wheat and flour in their diets. The first mills probably came in with the settlers in 1759, though there may have been earlier ones.

While we have no records of specifically how the various meats were prepared during the Spanish and Mexican periods, we can assume that the typical Spanish and Mexican methods of baking, barbecuing, frying, and stewing were common. Five dishes, which we will examine in more detail later, were probably brought in along with the European animals: *morcilla,* a dish made of pork blood boiled inside a pig's cleaned stomach and fried with chile, garlic, and spices; *cabrito en su sangre,* or *sangríta,* a kid cooked in its own blood in a large pot or cauldron on top of a stove or on coals; *cabrito* (barbecued in a pit); *chicharrones,* which we now think of as pork rinds or crackling, which also included the edible internal parts and the ears, tail, and feet of a freshly butchered swine; *burruñate,* made of the edible internal parts of a freshly butchered goat, cooked in an oven; and *menudo,* or tripe stew, a Spanish dish in which corn has been substituted for the chickpeas of the original dish.

Likewise, we have no record about when certain other fruits and vegetables were brought into the area. Watermelons had been introduced to South Texas as early as 1690 (Bolton 1916, 415), and when Emory and his party arrived in Presidio del Norte on July 8, 1852, they found watermelons ripe and corn in tassel (Emory 1857, 85). Three years earlier (1849), Whiting, also working with the Boundary Commission, had arrived in La Junta. He accompanied Ben Leaton and two other Anglos into Ojinaga and met with the commandant of the Mexican soldiers stationed there. He describes what must have been a sumptuous meal to a man so long on the trail: "stewed chicken flavored hotly with *chile Colorado;* tortillas; a roast turkey exceedingly well cooked; and finally frijoles and coffee. We ate to repletion" (Bieber 1938, 286). It is unclear where the meal was eaten—in a restaurant, military quarters, or a private residence.

Further information about the diet of the period is found in John W. Spencer's "Day Book," or diary. In it he kept records of transactions, especially credit sales from his general store and ranching operations. Between 1858 and 1862 he recorded the purchase and sale of a number of food items: coffee, green tea, sugar, salt, lard, molasses, cheese, corn, beans, goats, wheat, *piloncillo,* rice, pumpkin, dried snaps, and *asadosos* (in parenthesis next to the word was written "chitlings"). He also sold milk, dried pumpkins, figs, and garden seeds. It is interesting that there is no entry for flour, even though he and Milton Faver had put in a mill in Presidio sometime shortly after 1854 (unpublished manuscript accompanying Spencer's diary).

Another early record of Mexican foodways in the region was left by C. A. Hawley, business manager for the Chisos Mining Company in Terlingua during the 1890's. Manager of the company store, he was remarkably unprejudiced toward Mexicanos and their customs, unlike many Anglos of the time. He described in some detail the diet of those who mined for quicksilver, noting that white corn and California pink beans were its main staples. Using a metate or mill ("Montezuma Tortilla Mills," available in the company store for ten dollars), they ground the corn for tortillas or tamales. He noted that tamales were more or less a luxury among the poor, probably because of the expense of the meat. Tortillas and enchiladas were more common among the workers because they were less expensive. Hawley claimed the he had "never tasted food of any kind" that he preferred to tamales, noting also that enchiladas, when prepared without too much chile, were "as appetizing and nourishing a food" as he had eaten (1964, 37). These miners and their families had a passion for chili and sweets in any form, and they drank a lot of Arbuckle coffee. Goats also played an important role in their diets, providing meat for chile con carne and tamales and milk for drinking (Hawley 1964, 39). He noted their fondness for cheese, but did not record their making *asadero* from goat's milk, a common practice in the area still today.

Don Cosme Alvarado, who grew up at Luz del Desierto (about five miles downriver from Redford), remembered a number of foodstuffs that could be bought in local stores shortly after the turn of the century. One could buy such staples as beans, corn, rice, chile of various types, sugar, molasses, coffee (*café crudo,* which had to be roasted and ground), tea, lard (no shortening), and cheese (both yellow Wisconsin and asadero made locally). One could also buy a number of canned items: corned beef, wieners, lunch tongue, sardines, tuna, green peas, green beans, peaches, pears, and pineapple. Also available were such dried fruits as raisins and prunes, and such luxuries as soda pop, saltine crackers, lemon snap cookies, and graham crackers. While there were no fresh vegetables, one could buy *elotes* (roasting ears) in season. According to Don Cosme, most people raised their own chile, frijoles, corn, pepinos, and fresh vegetables, and many raised a few animals for food, such as pigs, goats, and cattle.

Present-Day Foodways

Many present-day foods are derived from the staples cultivated by pre-Hispanic Indians of the area: corn, beans, squash, melons, and pumpkins. It should be noted that because of their complementary nature, corn, beans, and squash, when eaten together, provide all the amino acids (thus proteins) necessary for survival (Winkler 1982, 50, 72). Other foods provide supplementary nourishment, vitamins, and minerals.

Dishes Made of Corn

Corn is raised for home consumption by many (perhaps most) of the rural folk in the region—anyone who has a bit of land and access to water for irrigation. Those who do not may buy corn in its various forms from neighbors or from stores. In its different stages, it provides a source of food throughout the year.

In its tender stage, corn is eaten as *elote* (fr. Nahuatl), boiled fresh on the cob and often sprinkled with ground red chile. During season, it is commonly eaten at home and remains popular at fiestas and with street vendors. Also made from corn in the roasting-ear stage are *chacales* (fr. Nahuatl), which form the base of a number of dishes and can be used throughout the year. Chacales are made by boiling fresh, tender corn and drying it, either on or off the cob. Stored in cans or simply hung up in a dry, protected area, they will last through the year or longer, to be used in various dishes. One of the most popular Lenten dishes in the area, *comida de cuaresma*, is made of chacales cooked with fresh chopped onions and a touch of salt and garlic. Chacales are also popular in soups of various kinds.

One of the early methods of processing the hard, dry kernels of corn was to parch and grind them. Pinole, used by Indians and adopted by Spaniards, Mexicans, and Anglos, has been an important staple in the diet of many Mexicanos in this region. Toasted kernels of corn are ground on the metate or in the small hand mill and mixed with cinnamon or other flavoring and sweetened with sugar or *piloncillo* (a crude, or raw, sugar usually formed into a solid cone).

Although atole may be made from wheat, rice, and even mesquite-bean flour, its oldest form in the area is corn, parched and ground, mixed with water or milk, flavoring and sweetener, and cooked into a thin gruel that may be eaten or drunk. It is a common breakfast food in the region and can now be purchased readymade in the local food stores.

Another common way of preparing dry kernels of corn for consumption is to heat them in water containing lime to break down the hard outer shell. Very much like hominy, they may be eaten whole or ground and fashioned into a number of foods. *Pozole* (fr. Nahuatl) is made of corn processed thus and cooked into a soup-like dish containing pieces of pork (usually internal parts) spiced with onion, garlic, chile, and salt. While it may be eaten at any meal, it is a popular breakfast dish.

Corn processed with lime is the basis of some of the most common foods in the culture. One of them is the *tamal* (fr. Nahuatl, Anglicized to *tamale*), which is made of corn kernels processed in lime water and ground to a coarse paste on a metate or in a small hand mill. Mixed with lard, salt, and meat broth, this *nixtamal* is spread on a moist corn shuck, filled with a mixture of meat and red chile, wrapped in the shuck, and steamed. While any meat will do, the most popular is pork; perhaps because of limited alternative uses, the pig's head is most often made into tamales. Something of a luxury among the poorer folk because of the meat, tamales are usually eaten only when an animal is butchered. During the Christmas and New Year's season, many in the area make sweet tamales, which contain sugar and various fruits instead of the meat and chile mixture.

Masa made from cooked ground corn is often formed into a patty one-half to three-quarters of an inch thick and cooked on a *comal* or stovetop. It becomes a *gordita* (fr. Spanish) when sliced and filled with meat (ground or shredded), chopped lettuce and tomatoes, and grated cheese.

Perhaps the most common food made of corn is the *tortilla* (fr. Spanish), a food that has existed since long before Spanish influence in the area. The term is Spanish, but the food is Indian. The corn tortilla is the basis for a number of dishes of considerable antiquity, some of whose origins are rather obscure. *Enchiladas* and *tacos* are of pre-Hispanic origin, as are a number of *caldillos*, *adobos* and *salsas* based on chile (Farga 1980, 85). Various meats, part of the Spanish contribution to the diet, resulted in a better variety and quality of native dishes, as well as some new additions still eaten in the La Junta region: meat enchiladas, tacos, *chilaquiles, chalupas, quesadillas, tostadas,* and *gorditas* (Farga 1980, 88). Enchiladas in the region are prepared flat (preparing them in this fashion does not require an oven). Many Anglos have the impression that Mexicanos eat these with great frequency, but the survey I conducted in 1979–80 indicates that about 75 percent of the families in Presidio eat enchiladas no more than once every two weeks or even less often.

Other dishes based on the corn tortilla include *tostadas,* the crisp fried quartered corn tortilla, used as a spoon to eat *guacamole, pica de gallo* (a mixture of finely chopped onion, chile, tomato, garlic, cilantro, and salt—all fresh, not cooked) or *chile macho* (similar to pica de gallo except that the chile and sometimes other ingredients are cooked). Tacos, soft as well as crisp, differ little from those prepared elsewhere. The soft taco is more popular in this region. *Chilaquiles* are corn tortillas fried crisp in grease and covered with chile, much like an enchilada, usually served with grated cheese. *Nachos* are *tostadas* covered with melted cheese and sliced jalapenos. *Botanas* are refried beans on crisply fried tortillas, topped with grated cheese. *Flautas* are chopped, grated, or ground meat or chicken rolled tightly in a corn tortilla and fried crisp, usually served with a fresh lettuce, tomato, cucumber, and avocado salad and sour cream. *Quesadillas* are hot corn tortillas folded with melted asadero (the homemade cheese common to the area) inside—a sort of asadero soft taco. *Chalupas* are crisply fried corn tortillas with the edges turned up slightly, covered with a layer of refried beans, some type of prepared meat (optional), shredded lettuce, grated cheese, and sometimes sour cream and black olives. There are a number of variations of this dish, depending on one's taste, but it is basically a crisp salad on a crisp tortilla. Apparently a local dish, the *loca* is a thick bean and *chile con carne* mixture put into crisp, fairly thick cup-shaped corn tortillas, covered with cheese and put into a hot oven before serving.

Pan de matz, or cornbread cooked in the oven or on top of the stove, is a fairly common food in the region, although it is not eaten nearly as often as tortillas. This food, dating to pre-Hispanic times, is now made from cornmeal, not the masa of tortillas or the nixtamal of tamales.

The flour tortilla has replaced the corn tortilla as the daily bread in the La Junta region. According to old timers in the area, this change began in the 1930s, when flour became more readily available and affordable to working-class Mexicanos. The principal reason for the change appears to be convenience and ease of preparation. Mixing up the flour for tortillas is much easier and requires far less time than processing and grinding corn masa—which often takes three to four hours.

Dishes Made from Beans

While the beans used by the Indians were probably the common kidney bean or the tepary, the bean of choice in the La Junta area is overwhelmingly the *fryol mantequilla,* or pinto. The black beans so popular in southern Mexico are almost unknown in the area. The pinto bean is ubiquitous, served by rich and poor alike, and makes up at least part of almost every meal except for light breakfasts, though I have visited in homes where beans are eaten for breakfast as well. As they are cooked, beans go through a number of phases, each new phase constituting a new dish. They are cooked in *ollas* (purists say the ollas must be of clay, though these are seen very seldom on the Texas side of the border), often spiced with onion, garlic, and/or jalapenos, and sometimes meat chunks. In this form, beans are called *frijoles enteros, frijoles de la olla,* or *frijoles graniados* (granados). These may be reheated once or twice. As they are reheated, they tend to become soupy, and in this phase are called *frijoles familiares.* Next, the whole beans may be fried in a bit of lard, and are called *frijoles fritos* (fried beans). Finally, they are mashed and refried in lard with green chile and onions or garlic, the well-known dish found in burritos and served as side dishes with most Mexican foods in restaurants—refried beans, *or frijoles refritos.* Most Anglos fry the beans only once and thus fail to understand the term "refried beans."

Other dishes are created when beans are combined with other foods: *frijoles con queso* (grated cheese on frijoles enteros or frijoles familiares); *frijoles con chorizo* (beans with Mexican sausage); *frijoles con quelites* (beans with pigweed, an edible plant growing wild in the area). As noted above, beans are also used in botanas and other dishes.

Dishes Made from Squash

The third of the primary Indian foods, squash, is also prepared a number of ways in a number of dishes. It is eaten fresh in season or dried (called *rueditas*) for later use. Boiled or steamed and served with butter, it is called *calabaza* (or *calabaza cocida*). With fresh asaderos added, it is known as *asaderos con calabaza*. Perhaps the favorite squash dish is *calabacita,* or squash boiled, chopped, and fried with onions, tomatoes, and cheese (preferably asadero). When cooked with meat to make a sort of stew, it is called *calabacita con carne.*

Pumpkins, also known to the Indians, are used in *empanadas* (much like turnovers) or eaten baked, or are boiled and sugared. As noted above, the watermelon was reported early in the area, but there is some question as to what other melons were cultivated. Don Cosme Alvarado indicated that the *melón costilludo* (a ribbed melon) was common when he was a child, but that it was replaced a few years ago by the *melon chino,* or cantaloupe, which has become a popular cash crop for farmers in the area. In the last decade, the honeydew melon has also become quite popular as a cash crop.

Dishes Made from Other Foods of Indian Origin

Other foods inherited from the Indians and still eaten in the area include turkeys, *nopales,* and *tunas* from the prickly pear, fish (mostly catfish), *pitahayas,* and such wild greens as *verdolaga* (purslane) or *quelite* (pigweed). The antiquity of these foods is indicated by the fact that the terms *guajalote* (turkey, called by the Spaniards *gallina de la tierra*), *nopal, pitahaya,* and *mesquite* are all derived from Nahuatl, the Aztec language.

One of the more popular Thanksgiving and Christmas dishes is *guajalote relleno* (baked turkey stuffed with cornbread). Most Anglos think this is a dish taken over from Anglo culture, but the day of celebration, not the dish, was borrowed. From Aztec times, stuffed turkey has been a popular dish throughout Mexico (Novo 1973, 49; Bancroft 1886, 362–63). Turkey meat is also used in stews, tacos, *picadillo* (hash), and in sandwiches. Chicken is prepared in much the same way turkey is, but it is eaten more often and in a much broader variety of ways: *pollo en mole* (chicken in *mole* sauce), *barbacoa a la parrilla* (barbecued over a grill), *pollo frito* (fried), *caldo de gallina* (chicken soup), *guisado* (chicken stew), *pollo relleno* (stuffed and baked chicken), *arroz con pollo* (chicken with rice), *gallina con tortillas* (Mexican-style rolled dumplings), and *gallina con chile Colorado* (chicken with red chile). Chicken is also eaten in tacos, flautas, tamales, and enchiladas. At least three well-known dishes are made from chicken eggs: *chorizo con huevos* (Mexican-sausage scrambled eggs—also excellent in burritos); *huevos rancheros* (perhaps one of the best known of Mexican breakfasts); and *huevos con chile verde* (eggs scrambled with green chiles, onions, and other spices).

As to foods found in nature, pitahayas are still sought after in season, especially by rural folk. *Nopalitos* (the tender pads of the prickly pear with thorns removed), once eaten by most families, have recently become less popular (over 60 percent of the respondents in the Presidio survey reported never having eaten them at all), perhaps because of the influx of many other green vegetables and because of the inconvenience of collecting and preparing them. When used, they are cooked with eggs and sometimes put in casseroles and salads. The tuna, or red fruit of the prickly pear, is eaten raw, dried, or made into a firm, dark, sweet food called *queso de tuna* (literally, cheese of prickly pear fruit). Like the nopalito, however, its use is much rarer than in earlier days, when the tuna provided one of the rare sweets available.

Fish, especially catfish, used by inhabitants of the region since long before the Spaniards arrived, is eaten by almost everyone surveyed. Fish is most commonly eaten fried (*frito*), or as *caldo de pescado* (fish soup), also called *caldo do oso* (bear soup) for no reasons apparent to me or my informants. *Seviche*, eaten by almost half of those surveyed, is raw fish preserved in tomato sauce, lemon juice, and spices.

Dishes Derived from Foods Brought from Spain

The Spanish contributions to the foodways of the La Junta region are significant in many ways. The Indian foods still constitute much of the staple diet, but the Spanish contribution is responsible for the great variety found in present foodways. And the contribution was a matter not only of substance, but also of form.

Wheat (the substance) and the ways of preparing it (the form) have changed the diet in many ways. *Pan blanco* (small loaves of white bread, also called *bolillos* in the area), although not as common as the flour tortillas (the substance Spanish and the form Indian), has assumed an important role in the diet of many Mexicanos on both sides of the Río Bravo. Also, an incredible variety of pastries of wheat flour are made in the homes and bakeries of the region. A number of ritual foods, such as those eaten on *el día de los muertos*, are made of wheat—*pan de muerto*, for example. Finally, wheat flour is used in a variety of dishes as a thickening agent, and atole made from wheat flour is almost as common as that made from corn.

The introduction of domesticated animals has also had a profound impact on how and what La Juntans eat. Although the different dishes discussed below are clearly important, their impact goes beyond them. For example, the lard rendered from butchered hogs has an incalculable impact on almost every popular dish in the area. With very few exceptions, Mexicanos cook with lard, and the aesthetics of taste and smell will keep lard popular in spite of the health factors associated with it. Vegetable shortening is used by a minority of people in the area. Too, the lard once provided another means of preserving food, an important consideration in an era before refrigerators, freezers, and handy local supermarkets. Cooked or uncooked meat immersed in hot lard and allowed to cool, would remain edible for long periods of time, since air and bacteria could not get in it.

The products made from cow and goat milk have also added to the variety and wholesomeness of the diet. Mexicanos tend to drink little milk, but they use it in a variety of ways in cooking. Cheeses have long been popular in the area, and many dishes would not be complete without cheese, either the fresh-milk asadero or the aged cheddar bought from stores. The most common drink in the area is *café con leche* (coffee with milk) drunk in typical Mexican style. *Leche quemada* (literally, "burned milk") is one of the most popular Mexican homemade candies. *Cajeta,* often made of goats' milk, is also quite popular.

Dishes Made from Goat Meat

In the past, prior to the availability of meats in local stores, goats were the most accessible meat source. They were inexpensive and could be raised fairly easily because of their foraging habits—they eat almost anything.

While adult goats are sometimes eaten by the Mexicanos of the region, the overwhelming favorite is kid, varying in dressed weight from eighteen to twenty-five pounds. The young goat's size often determines how it will be cooked, while the method of butchering goats is quite consistent throughout the area. The goat is held flat on the ground on its side, with its neck stretched out and its chin extended. A sharp-pointed knife is quickly inserted into the throat just behind the jawbone, and a cut is made to the outer part of the neck, severing the throat, the windpipe, and the various arteries and veins in the neck, permitting effective bleeding of the animal. For some dishes, the blood is caught in a pan to be used in cooking. When the animal is dressed and skinned, all edible internal parts are kept: the heart, liver, kidneys, stomach, small and large intestines, and even the *tela,* the layer of fatty tissue which surrounds the viscera.

The most common way of preparing goat is barbecuing it in a pit, or *en el pozo,* a primitive version of the pressure cooker. Borrowed from the

Aztecs (Farga 1980, 21), this method of barbecuing is especially important at fiestas. The dish, called *cabrito,* is commonly served in Mexican restaurants. However, what is called cabrito in many eating establishments should more properly be called cabrito *al homo,* since it is baked in an oven rather than cooked on a pit. Though relatively unappreciated by Anglos, barbecued goat head is popular among older folks and those who think of themselves as "real Mexicans."

There are two other goat dishes with similar social values attached: sangríta or cabrito en su sangre (kid in its blood), and *burruñate (buriñate* or *buroñate;* in New Mexico spelled *burrañate;* in South Texas called *machitos*)—a dish made of the internal parts of the goat, parts frequently thought of as not fit to eat by Anglos and some Mexican Americans. Sangríta is made by taking the freshly killed goat, cutting it into pieces, putting it into a large pot on top of the stove, along with the heart, liver, stomach, tripe, and blood. Garlic, onion, and chili are added. Burruñate is made by taking the internal parts of a freshly killed goat—the heart, kidneys, small intestine, and stomach (well cleaned)—chopping them into small pieces, then adding onion, chile, spices (comino, oregano), garlic, salt, and black pepper, and sometimes chopped potatoes. It is mixed well and then wrapped tightly in the tela (visceral lining). The large intestine, well cleaned, is wrapped around and around it tightly, and then the burruñate is put into an oven or on a grill and cooked until the outside is brown and crisp.

Goat meat is also prepared commonly as *asado* (roasted in the oven, also call *cabrito al homo*) or *guisado* (a stew). Goat meat makes good tacos and burritos as well. When no other kind of meat was available or affordable, the poorer folk used goat meat in chile con carne and in tamales.

Dishes Made from Pork

Those who do not have enough pasture for cattle or goats often raise hogs, which require far less space and can be used as a disposal of sorts for table scraps and whatever surplus corn one can grow in the field. A number and variety of dishes are prepared from pork and pork by-products (considered fit to eat by rural folk, but not by many of their city cousins), and rural Mexicanos eat just about everything but the squeal, including many parts not eaten from the goat or beef.

As in earlier days, many rural Mexicanos on both side of the Rio Grande butchered hogs once or twice a year, depending on the family's finances.

November and December, when the weather is cool and the major holiday season is in swing, are popular months for hog butchering. The animal may be killed in much the same way as the goat, especially if the blood is to be saved. If not, hogs are commonly shot in the head with a rifle, a process that renders at least some of the meat inedible. Since *morcilla* (blood sausage or blood pudding) is still quite common in the area, and since the undamaged head is popular for making tamales, most people prefer simply to cut the animal's throat, collecting the blood in a pan to make morcilla. Once dead, the animal is laid out on boards or hung in a tree, scalded generously with boiling water from a tub or caldron, and scraped to remove most of the coarser hair. When the animal is dressed, the butcher is careful to save the heart, liver, kidneys, stomach, and intestines for processing. The carcass is carefully washed inside and out with clean water, and the cutting-up process begins.

One of the dishes considered to be very "Mexican" in the area (but depreciated by both Anglos and acculturated Mexican Americans) is *morcilla,* a dish still prepared in rural areas of Spain, where it is called *morcilla negro* when prepared with blood. Morcilla is made by boiling the pig's blood inside its cleaned stomach, then frying it with chile, chopped onion, chopped tomatoes, garlic, and oregano. An older tradition calls for adding raisins and nuts to make it a bit sweet. Morcilla is a pleasant, rich, tasty dish once one gets beyond the idea of eating blood.

Most of the meat will be eaten fresh, and since few have freezers, it cannot be stored long and must be disposed of quickly. If the animal is large, much of the meat will be shared with others, a gift that will be reciprocated when other families butcher. This sharing insures fresh meat from time to time for several nuclear families.

Commonly, when a pig is butchered, a large cast-iron caldron is placed nearby over a low flame. As the butchering process continues, the heavy layers of fat (including the skin) are cut into small pieces and dropped into the caldron to be rendered for cooking lard. Into this caldron are thrown other parts such as the ears, the tail, and sometimes the feet and certain of the edible internal parts. The contents of the cauldron are stirred with a wooden stick from time to time, and when the rendering is complete, the lard is removed and placed into containers for future use. What is left behind is called *chicharrones,* a very popular dish with families raising hogs. Both the dish and its name are preserved from the Spanish (Pugay Parga 1972, 246). Hog lard is more common than beef suet, simply because beef in the area do not get as fat as pigs.

While ham, bacon, and sausage have become more common than they were a generation ago, they are bought at stores and are used in much the same ways Anglos use them. Curing bacon and ham was never part of the Mexicano food-preservation techniques of the region. The two principal ways of preserving pork are to make either *chorizo* (more recently called *chorizo mexicano,* Mexican sausage, to distinguish it from other sausage available in the store) or *carne adobada,* a fairly popular dish made by preserving pork (ribs, chops, and other cuts) in red chile and other spices (called adobo) and drying it.

Chorizo is made of ground, shredded, or finely chopped fresh lean pork and pork fat, combined with vinegar, red chile, garlic, cilantro, salt, pepper, and other spices thoroughly mixed together and stuffed into the carefully washed small intestine to make links, which may be eaten by themselves or in various dishes with other ingredients. Chorizo may be dried and stored for use at a later date. *Papas con chorizo* (potatoes chopped and fried with chorizo) and *huevos con chorizo* (chorizo and eggs scrambled together in a skillet) are two common dishes made from this sausage. Either of these dishes may become the main ingredient in burritos.

While pork chops (*chuletas,* prepared more in the Anglo tradition), have become quite popular, the most common ways of preparing pork are as *asado* (a stew made of pork, garlic, oregano, red chile, salt, etc.) cooked outside in a Dutch oven or inside on the stove top, or as *picadillo* (also, *guisada*), chopped pork meat fried in lard with garlic, tomato, onion, and sometimes chile and other spices. Both of these dishes are of unknown antiquity in the area, though one would suspect them to be of Spanish origin. Two other dishes common in this region are *carne de puerco con chile verde* (pork with green chile) and *carne de puerco con chile Colorado* (pork with red chile). Pork is also a favorite meat for empanadas, or turnovers. Another popular dish made of pork is *carnitas,* which are thin slices of pork rolled in flour and fried crisp in lard.

Of the informants surveyed at Presidio, almost half either raised and butchered their own hogs or bought hogs for butcher from someone else in the community. There is, of course, a high correlation between those who butcher pigs and those who make and eat chicharrones, morcilla, carne adobada, and homemade chorizo. The latter two dishes, although still fairly common on the Mexican side of the Rio Grande, are less common in Texas because they are less necessary. One can buy fresh pork from the store in portions that do not require preservation, and one who butchers a pig no longer has to rely on older techniques of preserving the meat.

Dishes Made of Beef

Even before becoming available first in meat markets and later in supermarkets, goat meat and pork were affordable to even the less affluent. Beef, however, was principally available to the well off, those with enough land to raise some cattle to butcher. While chile con carne is normally thought to be a dish made from beef, Hawley noted that the Mexican miners at Terlingua made it with goat meat (1964, 37). And not even the affluent kept fresh beef on hand all the time. Strips of beef were dried for preservation. There were occasions, however, when beef was a social necessity, even in the lives of the more humble folks, especially in fiestas associated with weddings, quinceañeras, and special holidays. In more recent times, thanks to supermarkets, beef became more generally available to working-class people because they could buy as little as they needed or as much as they could afford. Consequently, it is difficult to know for sure which dishes were common at any given time except the present. It is clear that *barbacoa,* perhaps the most common food at fiestas of all kinds, has its roots in antiquity.

Informants claim that the "real" *barbacoa* is done in *el pozo,* in a process dating to pre-Hispanic Aztecs (Farga 1980, 21). And the process is almost identical, except that new technologies and materials have produced some minor changes. The procedure is simple, and not unlike baking *sotol* or *mescal.* One digs a pit large enough to accommodate the animal (or piece thereof) to be barbecued and a yard or so deep, then lines it with rocks which absorb the heat well, then builds a good fire in the pit and lets it burn out, leaving the rocks very hot. A preparer from the poorer working class will wrap the meat in *costales de mania* (sacks made of cotton cloth), place this inside *costales de cotense* (coarse gunny sacks) to keep the dirt out, then cover it with a metal lid. Finally, the whole affair is covered with dirt and left several hours until it is time to eat. Folks who can afford buckets cook their meat in the pit inside these containers (galvanized trash cans are fairly common), covered with a thick layer of dirt. The meat comes out very tender—the product of a prehistoric pressure cooker. One of the most popular ways of cooking beef and goat heads is to prepare *barbacoa de cabeza,* a delicacy popular throughout the region and in South Texas. *Barbacoa a la mexicana* requires no barbecue sauce.

Another dish that can be traced to antiquity, but that has its roots in Spain, is *menudo,* or beef tripe stew. While the focal ingredient is beef tripe, another main ingredient is corn prepared into a sort of hominy by heating it in lime water. In Spain, menudo is made with chickpeas instead, since the Spaniards did not have corn until after the conquest. Spiced with chile of varying heat, it is a well-known treatment for *la cruda,* or hangover.

Other popular dishes include *caldo de res*—ribs, meat, and bones boiled with vegetables and seasoned with *azafrán* (saffron), *ajo* (garlic), and other herbs and spices. *Caldillo* is a sort of poor man's stew made of chopped beef and potatoes cooked on top of the stove in a skillet and seasoned with chile and other spices. *Picadillo,* a hash often used in burritos or tacos, is finely chopped beef and potatoes fried with chile and other spices. *Carne guisado is* beef cut into fairly small pieces and fried fairly crisp in very hot lard. Onion, tomatoes and red chile are commonly cooked with the meat, spiced with ajo, comino, and oregano. Chile con carne, almost the national dish of Texas and the focus of many cookoffs, is made of ground or chopped beef cooked in a savory red chile sauce and flavored with various other spices, garlic, etc. *Chile verde con carne* is usually made of onions, potatoes, tomato, and either jalapeno or the milder *chilaca* (also used for making *chiles rellenos*). *Carne asado* is roast, pot roast, or ribs baked in an oven.

Large families who have little meat can stretch what they have by preparing dishes such as *fideo con carne* (vermicelli with meat) and *calabacita con carne* (squash with meat). The emphasis is on the fideo and calabacita, for each contains chopped beef in whatever quantities are available. Meat can also be stretched by cooking it with potatoes.

A number of dishes reflect the growing Anglo influence: steak (*bistec*) is broiled over coals, while hamburger meat is made into hamburgers, meat loaf, and meatballs (*albóndigas*), or used in tacos. Chicken-fried steak has also found its way into the diet of Mexican Americans, as well as that of their cousins across the river. One finds that spam, lunch meats such as bologna, and various other meats become more common as they become more affordable and as people become more affluent.

OTHER IMPORTANT DISHES

Perhaps one indication of the importance of given foods in a culture is the elaboration of their uses. Wheat flour and potatoes are excellent examples of this principle. Brought into the area by the Spaniards, wheat, processed into flour, plays a major role in the diets of the people living in the La Junta region. Beginning in the 1920s and 1930s, the flour tortilla slowly replaced the corn tortilla as the daily bread of choice. The same masa used to make tortillas is also used to make *pan de agua* (biscuits of the masa cooked in the oven) and one of the more popular pastries, *sopapillas* (flour tortilla dough rolled, folded once, and fried in hot lard—they tend to puff up, and are eaten with honey or other condiments). *Buñuelos,* another popular pastry, is made by frying a flour tortilla in hot grease until crisp, then sprinkling it with cinnamon and sugar.

Pan blanco (also called *bolillos* locally) is the small, fairly tough little loaves of bread that have become very popular among Anglos as well as Mexicanos in the region. Almost every bakery in Ojinaga sells them. The various sweets made from wheat flour are almost innumerable. The more common ones are *pan dulce* (Mexican sweet bread), *bizcochos* (anise cookies), and cupcakes (sometimes called mamones because of their shape). These various pastries are an integral part of most fiestas, particularly quinceañeras, weddings, birthdays, Christmas, and New Year.

A dessert eaten during Lent is *capirotada,* made from sliced, store-bought bread toasted and placed in layers in a bowl with cheese and a syrup of water, cinnamon, and *piloncillo* (raw sugar). A substitute, eaten at other times as well, is *arroz blanco con leche cocido,* a rice and milk dessert with raisins and sugar for sweetening.

Ironically, though potatoes are of New World origin, "potatoes" in La Junta means Irish potatoes. There is a possibility that potatoes were available in La Junta even in pre-Hispanic times. Potatoes are found in many dishes, some of which include the Quechuan *papa* (potato) in their names.

Asadero is very popular, but generally available only to those with a good supply of fresh milk. It is made by mixing fresh and sour milk (about half and half) with water in which *trompillo* berries (a plant of the nightshade family, *Solanum elaeagnifolium,* known as horse nettle) have been crushed. The mixture is allowed to sit and is put into a warm area (such as near a cookstove) until it curdles or coagulates. The curd is heated in a skillet, cooled, and patted into the thin patties called asaderos. Mixed with green chile, salt, and garlic, the asadero is heated and makes *asadero con chile. Sopa de Arroz* (or simply *arroz,* called Spanish or Mexican rice by Anglos) is also a common dish in the region.

Common vegetables and fruits not discussed above include green peas (*chécharos*—eaten boiled, fried with tomatoes and onions as *chícharos guisados,* or as pea soup, *sopa de chícharos*), lettuce (in tacos, chalupas, salads, hamburgers, and as garnish with a number of other dishes), cabbage (boiled as *repollo cocido* or in soups), carrots (boiled and in soups and stews), avocados (in guacamole, in salads, and eaten from the shell with salt, lemon and pepper), turnips, canned or fresh beets, and occasionally cauliflower. Canned and fresh fruits commonly eaten in the area are bananas, mangos, apples, and pears; melons include watermelons, cantaloupes, and honeydews.

SUMMARY AND CONCLUSIONS

Foodways in the La Junta region have changed considerably since the coming of the Spaniards. These changes are the result of a number of factors: improved technology; the borrowing of foods from different cultures—Spanish, Mexican, and Anglo; greater economic prosperity; greater access to a variety of foods through stores that serve the area; and improved farming practices. Clearly, people enjoy a far richer and more varied diet than ever before. And the foodways continue to change, thanks in part to changing lifestyles and the ever-greater availability of processed foods.

While there is little doubt that traditional foodways will continue to play an important role in the diet of Mexicanos in the region for the foreseeable future, fairly dramatic changes are continuing at an increasing pace. Women work outside the home far more commonly than a generation ago and have less time to put together complicated dishes. Processed foods are replacing more traditional preparations, and while there is some attempt to produce traditional foods in processed form (atole mixes are commonly found in local markets, especially in Ojinaga, and one can buy masa harina or Maseca for corn tortillas and tamales), people are more likely to eat cornflakes for breakfast than atole or pozole.

The move from the small ranches and farms—where people could raise their own plant foods and animals to butcher—is having a significant effect on the use of certain dishes and on ways of preparing others. When people cease butchering hogs, morcilla and homemade chicharrones will disappear. When no one raises goats to butcher, there will be no more sangríta or barbacoa de cabeza or burruñate. These items are disappearing from the diet of high school students in the Marfa area more rapidly than from that of their peers in Presidio.

It is apparent that the changes are accelerating. Interviews with members of the grandparental generation in Marfa and Presidio reveal that foodways were once almost uniform among them. Significant changes began in the parental generation, and as the survey results indicate, the rate of change is increasing. For example, the survey shows that among fifteen-to seventeen-year-olds, those in Presidio are about twice as likely to eat pozole, pinole, atole, and chacales as their Marfa counterparts, although all of them reported eating tamales regularly. Yet one has to marvel at the persistence of certain of these foodways, which have survived almost unaltered for centuries. In spite of these rapid changes, many traditional foodways will persist into the foreseeable future and continue to fulfill the same basic social functions they did in the past, beyond simply providing nourishment for the body.

Notes

1. "La Junta," as used in this article, refers to a broad region around the junction of the Río Conchos of Mexico and the Rio Grande at Ojinaga, Chihuahua, and Presidio, Texas.

References

Bancroft, H. H. 1886. *The Works of Hubert Howe Bancroft.* Vol. 2, *The Native Races.* San Francisco: History Company.
Bieber, R. P., ed. 1938. *Exploring Southwestern Trails, 1846–1854.* Glendale, California: Arthur H. Clark.
Bolton, H. E., ed. 1916. *Spanish Exploration in the Southwest, 1542–1706.* New York: Charles Scribner's Sons.
Emory, W. H. 1857. *Report on the United States and Mexican Boundary Survey.* Vol. 1. Washington, DC: GPO.
Farga, A. 1980. *Historia de la comida en México.* 2nd ed. México, DF: Litografica México.
Felger, R. S. 1977. "Mesquite in Indian Cultures of Southwestern North America." In *Mesquite, Its Biology in Two Desert Scrub Ecosystems,* edited by B. B. Simpson, 150–76. Stoudsburg, Pennsylvania: Dowden, Hutchinson, and Ross.
Graham, J. S. 1983. "Foodways of Pioneer Texas Mexicans." In *Texana,* edited by L. Johnson Jr., 1:11–16. Austin: Texas Historical Commission.
———. 1984. "Mexican-American Traditional Foods: Sources and Prospects." In *Proceedings of the Fourth Annual Meeting of the Popular Culture Association,*

edited by M. K. Schoenecke, 421–49. Oklahoma City: Oklahoma Historical Society.

Hawley, C. A. 1964. *Life along the Border*. N.p.: *West Texas Historical and Scientific Society* 20.

Holden, G. K., and M. W. Lamb. 1962. "Early Foods of the Southwest." *Journal of the American Dietetic Association* 40:218–23.

Jones, O. L. 1979. *Los Paisanos: Spanish Settlers on the Northern Frontier of New Spain*. Norman: University of Oklahoma Press.

Lantz, E. M., H. W. Gough, and M. M. Johnson. 1953. *Nutritive Values of Some New Mexico Foods*. [Las Cruces, New Mexico]: Agricultural Experiment Station, New Mexico College of Agricultural and Mechanical Arts.

Luxán, Diego Pérez de. (1582) 1966. "Diego Pérez de Luxán's Account of the Antonio de Espejo Expedition into New Mexico, 1582." In *The Rediscovery of New Mexico*, edited by George P. Hammond and Agapito Rey, 153–212. Albuquerque: University of New Mexico Press.

Novo, S. 1973. *Cocina Mexicana, o historia gastronómica de la ciudad de México*. 3rd ed. Mexico: Editorial Porrúa, S.A.

Pugay Parga, M. M. 1972. *La cocina practica*. 15th ed. Santiago de Compostela, Spain: Libreria Editorial Gali.

Shipman, O. L., and J. Shipman. 1933. "Savage and Successful." *Voice of the Mexican Border* 1:8–12.

Smith, Buckingham, trans. 1871. *Relation of Alvar Nuñez Cabeza de Vaca*. New York: Privately printed.

Winkler, B. A. 1932. "Wild Plant Foods of the Desert Gatherers of West Texas, New Mexico and Northern Mexico: Some Nutritional Values." MA thesis, University of Texas.

11 Naming Practices among the Black Seminole of the Texas-Mexico Border Region

Mischa B. Adams

Kenneth Wiggins Porter (1971) was the first of a succession of American scholars to focus upon the culturally and ethnically diverse Black Seminole communities of Texas and Mexico. Porter began his research in the early 1940s and continued developing his manuscript about the Seminoles throughout his professional life, although his major work on this topic was not published until after his death (see Porter 1996). Other publications, such as William Loren Katz's *Black Indians* and *The Black West* (1986, 1987), stimulated popular interest in the topic of Native American/African American heritage. Yet it was not until the publication in 1993 of Kevin Mulroy's *Freedom on the Border: The Seminole Maroons in Florida, the Indian Territory, Coahuila, and Texas* that an entire volume was devoted to this subject.

Regional historians such as Marilyn Dell Brady (2000) and Thomas A. Britten (1993) contributed to this work. The general public is gradually becoming aware that the rich multicultural and interethnic texture of life on the border is not a new phenomenon. Black Seminoles figure prominently in two motion pictures of the nineties: John Sayles's *Lonestar* (Sayles 1996) and TNT's made-for-television epic *The Buffalo Soldiers* (Haid 1997). Independent scholars and genealogists, some of whom, like Col. Isaac Payne IV (1995), are themselves descendants of Seminole Negro Indian Scouts, are attempting to trace and chronicle the complex patterns of Black Seminole heritage. The history of Black Seminole people in the border regions of Texas and Mexico lends itself to popularization; readers of this history will encounter adventure, pathos, and humor in tales of extraordinary courage and resourcefulness, charismatic leadership, daring escapes, and epic battles. Yet this particular history has remained unportrayed for generations, and has only recently begun to make its way into the canon of regional self-knowledge that we border-dwellers take for granted (Britten 1993, 67–68).

Multiethnic and cross-cultural life surrounds us, although our need to fit other human beings into unambiguous categories sometimes obscures that reality. One hundred years before a call for the incorporation of multiracial categories in US census data, the American government commissioned a military unit known as the Detachment of Seminole Negro Indian Scouts. "But did this mean Seminole Negro Indians who were scouts," Kevin Mulroy asked, "or Seminole Negroes who were Indian scouts?" (1993, 134).

Men of African and Native American descent (and later other men of color who joined this community through marriage) served as scouts for the celebrated Buffalo Soldiers. They specialized in tracking and reconnaissance missions during twenty-five years of warfare against other indigenous people, while their mothers, sisters, and daughters worked as laundresses, domestics, and child nannies on frontier army posts. The United States government conveniently changed the meaning of the scouts' racial classification several times, and with each transformation in perceived identity, the Black Seminoles' dream of finding a permanent homeland on American soil grew more and more distant (Mulroy 1993, 133–51).

Histories such as the works cited above give us the ability to imagine what the lives of ethnically mixed people might have been like during the turbulent decades just before and after the turn of the century. However, as is so often the case with historical records, the focus has been upon great battles, notable men, the meandering of governmental policy, etc., to the exclusion of what has traditionally been thought of as the private sphere, i.e., domestic relationships, kinship ties, worlds composed of "blood and marriage" (Schneider 1977, 64)—women's worlds. Clearly the scouts' descendants, however they classify themselves, whatever their cultural preferences, whether they speak English or Spanish as a first language, embody unique patterns and principles of social organization. These patterns are not only highly complex but also heavily context-dependent. It is to be hoped that an interdisciplinary approach in full collaboration with indigenous scholars and researchers can advance our collective understanding of these webs of kinship.

The purpose of this chapter is to examine Black Seminole naming practices and kinship in the border region from an anthropological perspective. This inquiry makes use of historical and genealogical data, as well as personal interviews with members of Black Seminole families. I find it significant that more extensive studies, such as those of Porter (1996) and Mulroy (1993), have characterized Seminole family relationships and names as being highly complex and often confusing to outsiders. Thus the scope of this work will be limited to the description and analysis of certain social, historical, and cultural patterns. Specifically, this investigation will look at traditional Seminole/Muscogulge[1] and African naming practices; the acquisition by Mascogo families of Spanish names and language upon immigrating to Coahuila, Mexico; and the frequent use by Black Seminole families of two and three names, dependent on context.

History of Black Seminoles

As is the case with much of African American history, the story begins with slavery. In the early eighteenth century, Spanish-ruled Florida became a refuge for enslaved people of African origin. They fled across the borders from plantations in Georgia and the Carolinas, exchanging slavery under the British for nominal freedom and virtual self-rule in Indian towns allied to Spain. After Spain lost Florida to Britain in 1763, escaped slaves continued to settle there. Mulroy observes that "whether runaways, captives, or slaves of the Seminoles, these blacks preferred to live beyond the pale and ally with Europeans and Native Americans rather than remain enslaved on southern plantations" (1993,11).

By the 1820s, the institution of slavery was well established among the Muscogulge peoples. Indians of the Creek Confederation of tribes held Africans and mixed-blood people as slaves but allowed them to live in their own semiautonomous villages, to fight under their own chiefs, and to keep most of the products of their own labor except for a small annual tribute (Mulroy 1993, 11–12). Some of the more prominent leaders among the African villages joined the Seminole tribe through marriage or adoption (Porter 1996, 29). Although he emphasized the differences between Seminole Indian and Black Seminole social organization, and concluded that the degree of intermarriage between Seminoles and African Americans may have been overstated in both historical and contemporary contexts, Mulroy (1993, 177) also acknowledged that Black Seminole family relationships retain some elements of both African and Seminole influence.

The Second Seminole War was fought from 1835 to 1843. The American government's interest in driving the Seminoles and their black allies out of Florida had as much to do with the institution of slavery as with territory, possibly even more. Slaves on Southern plantations continued to escape to join the Indians, who welcomed them as warriors and fellow resistors to white rule (Wright 1986, 73–83). Although the entire Seminole nation never officially surrendered to the US Army, a great many war-weary Seminoles finally agreed to accept relocation to the Indian Territory, taking their Black Indian slaves, allies, and, in some cases, family members with them (Wright 1986, 80). These Black Indians who remained in the Indian Territory eventually acquired a legitimate presence in tribal administration as Seminole Freedmen (Bateman 1990).

Their journey to the tough, arid region later known as Oklahoma was a death sentence to many of those who left the Florida swamps (Mulroy 1993, 40–41; Porter 1996, 116–19). Forced to board overcrowded and ill-maintained steamboats for their trip up the Arkansas River into exile, those Black Seminoles who survived to reach the Territory rallied around a charismatic mixed-blood African and Muscogulge war leader known by many names: Gopher John, John Nikla, Juan Cowaya, Juan Caballo, Capitán Juan de Dios Vidaurri, and most often in the historical record, Chief John Horse. He was a brilliant statesman, interpreter, translator, and war counselor to the Seminole Chief Coacoochee or Wild Cat (Mulroy 1993, 188).

When they reached the Indian Territory, the Seminoles and their African and mixed-blood allies discovered that the best of the arable land was already in the hands of their sometime enemy, the closely related Creek tribe. Soon after their arrival, Black Seminoles fell prey to slave-hunting gangs of Creeks who captured them and sold them back to the white-owned plantations from which some of them had recently escaped. The longer they remained in the Indian Territory, the more Istilustis (black Indians) were taken by slavers, including the family members of prominent men such as Chief John Horse, whose sister, Juana, lost two of her five children to kidnappers (Littlefield 1977, 114). This predation had the effect of drawing the followers of Chiefs John Horse and Wild Cat together in a common cause. The Istilustis stood to lose the relative autonomy they enjoyed as vassals of the Seminoles if the kidnappings continued. The Seminole full-bloods risked being deprived of status, property, the right to command a formidable fighting force of proven warriors, and possibly even members of their own families whom they had claimed "on paper" as slaves so as not to leave them behind in Florida to be sold (Wright 1986, 313; Mulroy 1993, 54–55; Porter 1996, 128–31).

In 1848 the two chiefs' factions, including some eight hundred Muscogulge/Seminole and Black Seminole people, decamped from their Indian Territory reservation, much to the surprise of the Creeks and the dismay of the US military troops whose task it was to guard them. Traveling separately to avoid capture, the two tribes fled westward through Texas to Mexico, pursued unsuccessfully by bands of slavers and US military units. On the way they were joined by a faction of Kickapoo Indians who had absconded from a reservation near Fort Leavenworth, Kansas. Wild Cat and John Horse had already reconnoitered the route to Mexico in the year since their people's relocation from Florida. After crossing the Rio Grande at Eagle Pass, the two chiefs secured an agreement with the governor of the Mexican state of Coahuila to be given land and farming implements in exchange for employing their warriors as scouts against Apache and Comanche raiders, who constituted a significant barrier to settlement along the Mexican frontier. This remarkable accomplishment of statecraft allowed the Seminoles and African Seminoles (now called *Indios Mascogos* by their Mexican hosts) to negotiate their own future as a sovereign nation. The terms of that treaty are still in effect today. The Seminole, Kickapoo, and Mascogo colony became a multiracial, antislavery enclave south of the border (Porter 1996, 132).

The Mascogo colony in Coahuila, Mexico, was not destined to deliver the bright promise of land and freedom that the Black Seminoles had struggled so long to attain. Disputes over which portions of land belonged to which of the three tribal groups caused constant friction inside the colony, while outside, wealthy Mexican families plotted with regional and federal officials to nullify the Indian and Mascogo titles to the land. A smallpox epidemic in 1856 decimated the Seminole full-blood population, although the Mascogos were somehow better able to resist the epidemic. Chief Wild Cat of the Seminoles succumbed to the disease, and most of his Seminole followers returned to tribal lands in the Indian Territory. Some of them would later take up arms for the Confederacy, since they had, after all, been slave-owners from the beginning. Meanwhile, the Mascogos, under the leadership of John Horse, and Chief Papicua's Kickapoos remained at Nacimiento and continued scouting for the Mexican army, helping to protect border settlements from raids by indigenous mountain tribes (Mulroy 1993, 84–86).

After the Civil War ended and the threat of slavery no longer hung over them, many members of the Mascogo colony in Mexico longed to return to the United States. Chief John Horse was still hopeful that his people might someday find a secure and permanent home in America. In 1870 the Mascogos were invited to return by Capt. Frank Perry, a recruiting officer from Fort Duncan (Britten 1993, 68; Mulroy 1993, 114–15). Under the rubric of an agreement less formal than that negotiated by their chiefs with the Mexican government two decades earlier, two bands of Mascogo tribespeople returned to the United States and took up residence near Texas frontier military posts at Fort Duncan and Fort Clark. There, most of the able-bodied men enlisted as scouts and were attached to units of the 9th and 10th Cavalries of the US Army, where they served with distinction as the Detachment of Seminole Negro Indian Scouts (Mulroy 1993, 114).

Most historians concur with the living descendants of the Seminole Scouts that there must have been some written record of the original terms under which they agreed to serve in the American military; however, no such document can be found today. The Black Seminoles resettled themselves in a quasi reservation adjacent to Fort Clark near the town of Brackettville, Texas. They continued to have faith, despite mounting evidence to the contrary, that the American army would eventually either grant them permanent title to the land or help them return to Seminole tribal lands in the Indian Territory (Mulroy 1993, 132). In reality, their employers held quite a different attitude toward them. A decade of waffling by various governmental entities resulted in the expulsion in 1914 of the Black Seminoles from their reservation at Elm Creek near Fort Clark. Only a few of the oldest and most infirm were allowed to live out the remainder of their lives there (Mulroy 1993, 168–70).

By this time the Mascogos were not thought sufficiently "Indian" to be welcomed back into the Seminole Nation in either Florida or the Indian Territory. Nevertheless, as "Negroes," they were not entitled to any special consideration from the US Army or American government. Seminole Negro Indian Scouts and surviving members of their families were casually abandoned by the same government that had presented them with the highest number of Congressional Medals of Honor awarded to a single fighting unit (Mulroy 1993, 117; Porter 1971, 490–91). Since immigrating to the west, they had always lived in small, close-knit clusters of related kin, loosely organized into bands, which had some similarity to Seminole clan organization. In order to survive as a people, they had to find the means to integrate themselves as best they could into small Texas communities along the border with Mexico (Porter Papers).

Some Black Seminole warriors who had been army scouts became ranch hands, adding to the legends of black cowboys in the modern West. Hardworking Black Seminole women continued to support their families as they had always done, by hiring out as maids, cooks, laundresses, and midwives, and by growing subsistence gardens and operating storefront food concessions, canteens, and other small businesses out of their homes. They relocated to the rural villages surrounding Forts Duncan, Griffin, Davis, and Clark, as well as the far West Texas outposts of Peña Colorado and Neville Spring, adapting and acculturating as they went, though always retaining their own unique cultural identity as black Indians (Mulroy 1993, 180–81; Porter Papers).

Seminole and Istilusti Naming Practices

In modern populations of Black Seminoles, we find distinctive naming conventions that hearken back to their multicultural past. The Seminole tribe (a diverse aggregate of subtribes including Miccosukees, Muskogees, Yuchis, and others) traditionally bestowed many different names upon children and adults throughout their lifetimes, so that each important rite of passage was marked by assuming a new name.

> As we know, Indian names were a source of confusion. It confounded whites that males frequently had a succession of three or more names. The first, the baby name, was derived from a physical trait, an event at the time of birth, or a clan reference. At or soon after puberty, the Indian acquired a war or hunting name at the busk: "A Seminole man might have a childhood name and later a busk or ceremonial name, which is given at the occasion of his initiation at the Green Corn Ceremony, called the *Boskida* by Florida and Oklahoma Seminoles who still follow ancestral traditions (Wright 1986, 29). During the Seminole Wars, notable Indian leaders were most often referred to by busk names in American military correspondence. For instance, the Seminole warrior Osceola's name is as well known in popular culture as that of Geronimo or Crazy Horse, yet few Anglo Americans know that Osceola is a busk name meaning "Black Drink Singer," and is composed of two Muskogee words: *assi*—a

sacred drink made from snake-button root, and *yahola*—to sing or shout. Osceola probably had another name during his childhood, and had he not died young of influenza while being held at Fort Marian as a prisoner of war, he might have acquired a different name later in life (Wright 1986, 112). The Seminole Scout and subchief Sgt. John Kibbetts added his ceremonial busk name, Chitto Tustenugge, which translates from Muskogee as Snake Warrior, when he enlisted in the American military (Mulroy 1993, 114). Scout Hardy Factor was also known by his busk name of Yaha Tustenugge (Wolf Warrior) (Porter 1996, 178). It follows that the older members of the Black Seminole community, who had a closer relationship to Seminole tribal customs, would be those most likely to have had and used multiple names. Chief John Horse, whose mother was African and whose father may have been his master, the Seminole Chief Kawaya, was known by a variety of names, including "Gopher John," a nickname left over from a prank he pulled as a young man, John Nikla ("Burnt-John" in Hitchiti), and Juan Caballo in Mexico (Porter 1996, 30, 148).

The significance of busk names when used by Black Seminole leaders has been the focus of a minor theoretical disagreement between two of the best-known historians working on the topic of Black Seminoles. Wright (1986) emphasizes the Indianness of the Black Seminole population, both during the Seminole Wars and later, after their removal to the Indian Territory; he is persuaded by historical evidence that black allies were sometimes adopted into Seminole clans and participated to some extent in the ceremonial life of the Muscogulge nation (1986, 74–80). Mulroy (1993), however, chooses to emphasize the Africanness of the same people, citing linguistic evidence that the dialect called "Seminole" still being spoken by elders in Black Seminole communities today contains elements of Gullah and perhaps of other West and Central African languages (Hancock 1980). Both Wright (1986) and Mulroy (1993), along with Porter (1996), have reported the connection between modern Black Seminole surnames and African day names such as Mundy, Cudjo, etc. For example, Hardy Factor: "Hardy (often pronounced Arty)—might be either the Seminole Artis or the African Ati, the name of a deity" (Porter Papers). Mulroy's (1993) evidence is less convincing when considering that the Black Seminole dialect (as spoken in both Texas and Mexico, and also by Freedmen elders in Oklahoma) has been analyzed only by a linguist who specializes in African languages and has little familiarity with or fluency in any of the languages spoken by the Seminole, Creek, or Miccosukee nations. E. Mario Hankerson, a Black Seminole sociologist who is fluent in both the Hitchiti (Miccosukee) and Muskogee languages and is a member of the Miccosukee Tribe of Florida, heard the Muskogee word *takoja* (ant) being used by an elderly Black Seminole woman he met in Brackettville in 1964. He is of the opinion that the "Seminole" dialect might contain more Indian elements than was previously thought (E. M. Hankerson, personal communication 1993).

While Mulroy acknowledges that busk names were appended to official documents by John Kibbetts, Abraham, and others, he discounts the importance of this fact, since "there is no evidence that the maroons ever participated in busk rituals on a large scale, adopted the matrilineal clan system of the Seminoles, or intermarried extensively with Indians" (1993, 186).

Nevertheless, the right to use a busk name is not a trivial matter to the Seminoles. Their use of such names and assumption of the rank of warrior (Tustenugge) indicates that some of the Black Seminole elders underwent initiation at a busk ceremony, which they would not have been allowed to do had they not been members of Muscogulge clans, at least by adoption. Given the inconclusive nature of the evidence, I am inclined to suspend judgment on whether Black Seminole cultural, social, and linguistic traits are more influenced by African or Native American traditions. I prefer to believe, as do many of the Black Seminole people who were kind enough to contribute to this study, that it is African *and* Seminole (as well as Mexican and Anglo American) traditions, in combination, that make the people who they are today. As has been written of the Oklahoma Freedmen, "They share in common with the Lumbees, Ramapos, Wampanoags, and others the difficulty of asserting an identity different from that which others would assign them. This self-ascribed identity is based not on skin color or cultural distinctiveness, but on the Freedmen's own perceptions of their past, of their historical relationship to the Seminole tribe, and on the strong ties to one another that have served to unite them as a group" (Bateman 1990, 17).

Chief John Horse and many of his Black Seminole followers arrived in Nacimiento with only their first names, to which had been appended the names of their Seminole (or in some cases Creek or even white) masters. It is possible that some Mascogos in this situation had been emancipated by their Indian masters or had their freedom purchased for them by family members while still in Florida or the Indian Territory, yet they retained the surnames of their Seminole protectors as a means of warding off slave catchers who often captured free people of color and sold them back into slavery (Littlefield 1977, 110).

This heritage is obvious in contemporary Black Seminole communities in both Texas and Mexico. Today Black Seminole family names such as Payne, Ferryman, Factor, Daniels, Bowlegs, Fay, Wilson, and Ward (Warrior), along with other names derived from African (and other foreign) naming patterns, link together with the names of freedmen families in Oklahoma and family names widely used among Muscogulge tribal people still living in Florida (Bateman 1990, 88; Walton-Raji 1997; Littlefield 1977, Appendix, List K; Wright 1986, 230). For example, the black Factor was a Seminole chief and entrepreneur who specialized in trade with Americans as well as other Indians. He owned merchandise, land, and a great many slaves. This man may indeed have been an African or a mulatto; however, his name may have had more to do with his area of expertise than his race. In traditional Seminole society, the color black symbolized trade, death, and commerce, just as red stood for war and communication, and white for "medicine" or spirituality (Wright 1990, 77).

The Seminole trait of using first names as surnames in succeeding generations is widely represented, both in the historical record and in present-day families. An example is the name Fay, possibly taken from the name of an African woman, Fai, who lived with the Seminoles (Porter Papers), and also perhaps from the given name of a Seminole slave, Felipe, who was removed to the Territory along with other Seminole deportees (Littlefield 1977, Appendix, List K). Fay was used as a surname by early Black Seminole families and was later turned back into a given name, as with Fay July—a male enlisted in the Seminole Scouts (Porter 1996, pictorial section). Porter (Papers) has attributed male use of feminine first names, such as those of Fay July and his brother Carolina July, to Africanisms in Black Seminole culture. He states that the Julys' family name originated with a male slave, July, who was listed as belonging to Nellie Factor, a Seminole slave owner. July's son Samson, who later became the leader of a band of Black Seminoles in Mexico, took his father's name as his surname, while some of July's other children took the name of Factor, their former master, instead (Porter Papers). This practice seems also to have derived equally from the Seminole custom of using English Christian names as surnames, as evidenced by Louis Capron's (1953) interviews with Seminole medicine men Josie Billy and Sam Tommie, and their helpers Jimmy Billy and Frank Charlie, in the 1950s.

A number of examples exist, both in the literature and in personal reminiscences of Black Seminole family members, of nicknames becoming formalized into both first names and surnames. Mascogo informants told Kenneth Porter (Papers) that Joe Coon, the son of Chief John Horse, was given that name because he was small, curious, and clever like a raccoon. This example points up the striking difference between Seminole (and by extension, Black Seminole) attitudes toward the relative importance of family names in determining status and social rank. His family or friends thought it was not important for Joe Coon to use his surname to identify himself with his father, arguably the most famous Black Seminole in history. Clearly, in this cultural context, names are transient and fame accretes to other elements of the personality instead. In a further example, a Black Seminole woman, the dependent of a Seminole Scout, who was probably born in the Mascogo colony in Mexico, appears in enlistment records at Fort Clark as Molly. She appears in other documents and was known to her family as Antonia. Community members who knew her in Nacimiento say that the name Molly was derived from the nickname "Big Tamale," by which Antonia was known because she was a large woman, while her husband was rather small in stature (Kibbet 1998).

I have detailed influences on Black Seminole naming conventions in order to portray a culture in which one must expect the unexpected when it comes to names. Mulroy (1993) has characterized the Black Seminoles as *neoteric* societies—cultural groups who have survived as a people by weaving together useful elements of their diverse cultural and symbolic history as they rapidly assimilate to conditions of extreme scarcity or pressure from the outside world. "Such groups," Mulroy says, "tended to welcome and even encourage rapid change to survive and prosper. Indeed, they might even be considered as having been created by the circumstances to which they adapted" 1993, 25).

Certainly scarcity and outside pressure were among the few constants in the lives of John Horse's "freedom seeking people." The illusion of a secure homeland was offered them countless times, yet repeatedly they were forced to watch that promise fade, just as they were forced to see their loved ones sold away into bondage after being told they were free. Full-blood Seminole traditionalists once relied upon the annual Boskida—the Green Corn Ceremony—to renew themselves in body and spirit after having engaged in war. Perhaps their Black Seminole allies, who supported themselves for more than a hundred years by means of military professionalism, cottage industries, and farming, have perfected the art of self-renewal through their system of diffuse, yet enduring kinship bonds (Schneider 1977).

Spanish Names in the Mascogo Colony Nacimiento de los Negros, Coahuila, Mexico

Soon after being resettled in their military colony at Nacimiento de los Negros near the town of Santa Rosa (now Múzquiz), Coahuila, Mexico, the Mascogos began the process of acculturation that would secure their survival in their new land. The state government of Coahuila ordered all Mascogo children to be baptized Catholic, be assigned godparents from neighboring families, and receive Spanish names. Between 1853 and 1856 this edict was carried out, spilling over to adult Mascogos as well. Chief John Horse took as his godfather Juan Nepomuceno Vidaurri, whom the governor had appointed to instruct the Mascogos in religion and to update their farming techniques. Chief John Horse is sometimes referred to in Coahuila's historical archives as Capitán Juan de Dios Vidaurri (Mulroy 1993, 81–82). Thus Mascogos (and later, by extension, Black Seminoles from Fort Clark and Fort Duncan) acquired Spanish names that many of their descendants continue to use today. In this way Thomas Factor (the son of July, who had been the slave of Seminole Nelly Factor) became Tomás González. Many of these newly acquired Spanish names were not direct translations of the colonists' original names, and probably originated with godparents who were expected to sponsor the Mascogos in their conversion to Catholicism. It did not seem to matter to their *padrinos* that the Mascogo colonists remained overwhelmingly Baptist (Mulroy 1993, 82; Porter Papers, Appendix). They also adopted the Hispanic custom of appending one's mother's family name to that of one's father.

It is interesting to note that researchers focusing on Texas and Mexico Black Seminole communities at different periods of time have produced differing accounts of the English equivalents of Mascogos' Spanish names. Kenneth W. Porter (Papers, Appendix) offered a list of name pairings in 1943. William "Dub" Warrior (1998) reported that Isaac Payne's Mexican name was Pablo Murillo, and that Adam Payne was called Valdéz in Nacimiento. And Doña Alicia Fay Lozano (1998), who has lived in both Nacimiento and Brackettville, offers yet another list of names.

Some of the apparent discrepancies in these bilingual family names derive from the interaction of a historical event—the 1853 edict requiring baptism and renaming of Mascogo children and adults, with a social custom—attaching mothers' names following fathers' names, preceded by a given name and in some cases a confirmation name. For example, historian José Guadalupe López (1996, charts from Los Vázquez) describes the marriage of Santiago Vázquez Flores to Jesusita Valdéz Wilson, which produced these children: Gertrudis Vázquez Valdéz, Sara Vázquez Valdéz, Nora Vázquez Valdéz, Lucia Vázquez Valdéz, María de Jesús Vázquez Valdéz, and Santiago Vázquez Valdéz. Col. Isaac Payne IV's (1995, 22) genealogy of the Payne family lists Adam Payne and his wife Hannah, along with their daughter Mary. Since we know from two sources that Adam Payne was known as Valdéz, we can extrapolate that the lineages of Payne, Wilson, and Vázquez come together in the union of Mary (Spanish name: Jesusita) Valdéz Wilson with Santiago Vázquez Florez. Indeed, Gertrudis Vázquez Factor (1994) of Nacimiento, a Mascoga elder and herself the sister of the current Capitan Santiago "Chago" Vázquez, confirms this. Gertrudis is related through her father's mother to the Gordon family, whose Spanish name is Florez (Factor 1994; Lozano 1993, 1994, 1998).

By tracing the "weave" of Black Seminole kinship it is possible to gain a clearer perspective on the social adaptiveness of such complex family ties. As reported by López (1996), the family Neco (of Seminole and Biloxi ethnicity) and the family Vázquez (incorporating elements of all of the various ethnic groups represented in the Kickapoo/Mascogo/Seminole Colony of Nacimiento) were able to establish hereditary rights to not only the Seminole, Kickapoo, and Mascogo lands, but also, by virtue of intermarriage with powerful Mexican families in the area, to become charter members of the neighboring *ejido*—a post-revolutionary communal ranch. Ejidos have their own governing principles, including strict rules about how the land is to be managed. Failure to comply with these regulations can result in ejidatarios being evicted from the property and their parcels of land sold off to outside interests. "Actualmente a los descendientes de los Neko, también se les considera como cuarterones, por lo que también tienen derechos en el ejido Morelos, ya que como decia Doña María Ibarra (hija de uno de los fundadores del ejido), que el nombre complete del mismo es 'Morelos y Cuarterones'" (López 1996, 4).[2]

Escalating conflicts among descendants of the multiethnic founders of the "Three Nacimientos" and the administrative officers of the ejido are mirrored in other parts of rural Mexico. As ejidatarios become unable, through a combination of economic and natural disasters, to amass sufficient operating capital to work their land, governmental policy now permits the once-protected ejidos to be forfeited and turned over to agribusiness (Monto 1994, 39–42). By establishing ties of blood and marriage to each of the land-holding entities, Black Seminole families in Mexico have been able to stave off encroachment by the same sort of unscrupulous land grafters who reduced the families of Oklahoma freedmen to the level of sharecroppers on tribal lands they once owned (Monto 1994; Bateman 1990, 116).

The Payne Family, An Example of Black Seminole Naming Practices

Living today in East and West Texas, and buried in Nacimiento and Brackettville cemeteries, are the members of a family called Payne. All of these kinspeople connect their family's history to Chief John Horse's desperate flight from the Indian Territory in search of land and freedom for his black Indian people. The Paynes comprise several different biological lineages. Theirs is not so much a family tree as a woven basket, made up of many strands: biological relationship, in-marrying affines, mother-centered families, and what Col. Isaac Payne IV (1995, iii) has so eloquently termed "adopted heritage."

Some of the Paynes who came west in 1850 with the Wild Cat party were the former slaves of a Florida Seminole chief, King Payne. King Payne owned a number of African and Black Seminole slaves who, after his death, became the nominal property and responsibility of Chief Micanopy, his successor. After they were transported to the Indian Territory, Micanopy died, leaving these people in immediate peril because of their indeterminate status under the laws of slavery. They lived in constant danger of being kidnapped by Creek slave-hunters and sold back to plantations from which some of them had already escaped. Aaron, Caesar, Titus, and Adam Payne were part of this group (Littlefield 1977, Appendix, List K). Although the exact degree of relationship between the members of the four original Payne lineages is not known, both historians and family genealogists agree that Caesar and Adam Payne probably were brothers. Titus Payne may also have been a brother or a nephew, and Eva Payne was a sister or daughter (Payne 1995). They all survived to reach safe haven in the Mascogo colony of Wild Cat and Chief John Horse.

While living in Nacimiento the Paynes clustered together in family camps near Caesar and Abby Payne Wilson Grayson, the elders of their line. In time they were joined by a former slave and Union army soldier named Isaac Paine, also known as Issum Sanders. He changed the spelling of his name to Payne, and remained in Mexico as the adopted son of Caesar and Abby Payne. He eventually married Julia Shields Wilson Payne and began raising a family. When his adopted kinsmen returned to Fort Clark to serve with the Seminole Negro Indian Scouts, Isaac Payne went with them. He distinguished himself by participating, along with two other Seminole Scouts, in the heroic rescue of his commanding officer while being fired upon by superior numbers of Comanche warriors. Payne and his fellow scouts were awarded the Congressional Medal of Honor for valor (Porter 1996, 194; Payne 1995, 1–3).

Payne (1995), Isaac Payne's descendant and biographer, believes that after his final discharge in 1901, Isaac Payne Sr. left the Black Seminole community, as well as his wife, Julia Shields Wilson Payne, and their eight children. He then traveled to Moorville in East Texas, where he married Katherine "Katie" Long and fathered four more children. After separating from his second wife, Isaac married Elizabeth Little and they had nine children. As the years passed, Isaac Payne's line intertwined with other Black Seminole lineages—some marriages joined cousins from the other strands known as Payne. Whether related to one another by blood, marriage, adoption, or the unshakable conviction that they share a common ancestor—as do members of true Seminole clans—the members of the current generation of the Isaac Payne lineage have heard his story and can partake of his fame. As Isaac Payne IV has written, "Knowing who our forebears were, when and where they lived, and what they did contributes to our own identity. Our humanity binds us to them equally as surely as the blood ties reported in this Payne family history" (1995, 93).

Meanwhile, another Payne lineage was also forming in Nacimiento. Sometime after the formation of the Mascogo colony, two men arrived. The elder, Natividad Mariscal, is believed by his descendants to have been a captive of a tribe of Indians in Mexico, possibly the Comanches or Yaquis. During the many harsh years he spent in captivity, Natividad befriended a younger man, Vidal Soria, who may also have been an Indian captive. By the time they were able to make their escape and seek refuge among the Mascogos, the two men were such close comrades that many residents of the colony believed them to be brothers. Mariscal married Antonia Gordon, the daughter of a former slave, Isaac Gordon, who was not part Native American, but who had fled to freedom in Mexico along with his two brothers (Albert and Henry). Antonia's mother's name was Sukey. She appears in some historical documents as Susan Factor (Porter Papers, Appendix), but she may have also been the young slave called Sukey who was born under the jurisdiction of Seminole Chief King Payne (Littlefield 1977, Appendix, List K). Natividad "Nato" and Antonia "Molly" Mariscal had several children, including two sons, Monroe and Juan, and two daughters, one of whom, Rafaela, eventually married Nato's close friend Vidal Soria. Rafaela and Vidal were the parents of six children, including a son named Monroe (the same as his cousin) who was often called "Mundy" (Lozano 1994).

Eventually the Mariscals and Sorias left Nacimiento and moved to Brackettville, Texas, where the two men enlisted in the Seminole Scouts. Soon after leaving Mexico the Mariscals and Sorias began to use the surname of Payne. Since they were contemporaries in military service, Mariscal and Soria have been confused (by genealogists, historians, and even some family members) with Isaac and Adam Payne. The descendants of Natividad Mariscal (and possibly also Vidal Soria) say that the Mariscals assumed the name Payne when entering the United States because "Nato Mariscal's wife was named Payne" and the American enlistment officers had a difficult time writing and pronouncing their Spanish names. Hence, it is said that the two families began to use the name Payne when in Texas and Mariscal or Soria when visiting in Nacimiento (Payne 1995, 16–17; Brady 2000; Gerron 1998). In actual fact, no one knows how Antonia Gordon/Florez Mariscal came to be known as Payne. Perhaps further study of archival materials will establish that Antonia was briefly married to Titus Payne, a Seminole Scout, and subsequently widowed before her marriage to Nato Mariscal. It is equally plausible that Payne was the slave name by which Antonia's mother, Susan (or Sukey), was known as a child in King Payne's Florida. Antonia Payne is also the Molly mentioned above who was called "Big Tamale." Whatever the empirical truth turns out to be, the reality is that four generations of Paynes trace their kinship back to this female ancestor.

The Soria branch of the Payne lineage intersects with that of Isaac Payne Sr. and Julia Shields Wilson Payne through the eventual marriage of Julia and Isaac's granddaughter Lena Blanks (who preferred to use the surname of her mother, Katie Payne) and William Soria, the son of Rafaela Mariscal (Payne) and Vidal Soria. William also used the name Payne. This couple typifies some of the distinctive elements of Black Seminole kinship in having names that change volitionally, and "adopted heritage" (Payne 1995, 34).

Since members of the Black Seminole communities in Nacimiento and the reservation in Brackettville followed prescriptive marriage customs as recently as the 1950s, preferring to choose spouses from among their own people, marriages between cousins were not unusual (Porter 1996, 181). As Bateman found with the Seminole Freedmen in Oklahoma, "A point that was emphasized over and over again by Freedmen of all ages was 'we are all kin.' I did not have to collect very many genealogies before I realized that this was no exaggeration. Until recently, the tendency for Black Seminoles to avoid marriages outside of their group and the fact that some Black Seminole communities were particularly endogamous led to the formation of a complex web of kin ties binding every Freedman to virtually every other Freedman" (1990, 21–22).

Since Col. Isaac "Ike" Payne IV's (1995) rich and careful research on his family covers every in-marrying spouse and does not leave out adopted or stepchildren, he has conclusively demonstrated the truth of this claim in regard to the Texas and Mexico communities as well.

Crossing Names

Brady (1999) documents the adaptive use of bilingual/bicultural family names by members of Black Seminole families in West Texas. Modern descendants of Mascogo families, some of whom maintain residences on both sides of the Texas/Mexico border, still use alternate versions of their names, depending upon which country (or which language, for most are bilingual in English and Spanish) they happen to be inhabiting. In 1994, I visited the Colonia Nacimiento de los Negros, located about fifteen miles south of the town of Múzquiz in Coahuila, Mexico. Joe Gordon, who also is the descendant of Seminole Scouts and Mascogo colonists, drove my host Alicia Fay Lozano and me from Del Rio to Nacimiento. To my astonishment, transforming himself into José Florez after crossing the border at Piedras Negras came as easily for Gordon as trading his baseball cap for the summer straw cowboy hat waiting for him on its spring-loaded wire holder inside the cab of his pickup truck. The conversation inside the truck, which had been mostly English, graded over into Spanish with occasional phrases in the Seminole dialect spoken by Lozano. All these transformations were most aptly summarized when Florez got out to open a gate and drove us across a cattleguard. "From now on," he said, "you're on Indian land."

During my stay at Nacimiento, Lozano told me about bicultural life in the colony. She said that since the 1950s, the Mascogos' Kickapoo neighbors had been able to come and go as they pleased across the Texas/Mexico border. The Kickapoo Capitán negotiated permission from both governments for his people to cross without restriction, since they engage in an annual migration between Nacimiento and Eagle Pass. According to Lozano, the Mascogos could have been granted the same privileges, but the Capitán of that era, Juan B. González, was not in favor of exposing the colonists to outside influences, which he felt to be corrupting and exploitative. As a result, only those Black Seminoles who are able to speak English (and some others who have long since established their dual residency with immigration officials) may cross with impunity. Some monolingual Spanish-speaking Mascogos have difficulty getting across the border to visit friends and family in Texas even today.

"All the Seminole Negroes of Brackettville, Texas, and Nacimiento, Coahuila, Mexico, have at least two sets of names, an American and a Mexican" (Porter Papers). Using English versions of their names has allowed Black Seminole families to blend in more easily with their surrounding communities in Texas, giving them better access to education, employment, and health care on that side of the border. Since Mascogos are equally comfortable using their Spanish names (and language) in Mexico, they are able to maximize whatever cultural resources become available as social and economic climates change around them. This very flexibility can be traced back to the multilinguistic, multicultural origins of the Seminole nation, as well as to the diversity and resourcefulness of the Seminoles' African allies.

Notes

1. I will refer to these Native American people as Muscogulge, as well as Seminole, as does Wright (*Creeks and Seminoles,* 5–18), to emphasize the fact that even in its earliest manifestations, their nation consisted of many tribes, spoke several different languages, and had a high degree of ethnic diversity.

2. Translation: "Today the descendants of the Neko family are also considered to be *cuarterones*—offspring of white/mulatto unions—and as such retain communal rights in the Morelos Ejido; and, indeed, Doña María Ibarra (daughter of one of the ejido founders) attested that the full name of the ejido is 'Morelos and Cuarternones.'"

References

Bateman, Rebecca Belle. 1990. "'We're Still Here': History, Kinship, and Group Identity among the Seminole Freedmen of Oklahoma." PhD diss., Johns Hopkins University.

Brady, Marilyn Dell. 1999. "The Paynes of Texas: Black Seminole Cowboys of the Big Bend." In *African American Cowboys of Texas,* edited by Sarah Massey, 255–71. College Station: Texas A&M University Press.

Britten, Thomas A. 1993. "The Seminole-Negro Indian Scouts in the Big Bend." *Journal of Big Bend Studies* 5:66–77.

Capron, Louis. 1953. "The Medicine Bundles of the Florida Seminoles and the Green Corn Dance." In *A Seminole Sourcebook,* edited by William C. Sturtevant, 159–219. New York: Garland.

Factor, Gertrudis Vázquez. 1994. Interview by author. Nacimiento, Coahuila.

Gerron, Nora Payne. 1998. Interview by author. September.

Haid, Charles, director. 1997. *Buffalo Soldiers* (film). Turner Pictures.

Hancock, Ian. 1980. "Texas Gullah: The Creole English of the Brackettville Afro-Seminoles." In *Perspectives on American English,* edited by Joseph L. Dillard, 305–33. The Hague: Mouton.

Katz, William Loren. 1986. *Black Indians.* New York: Atheneum.

———. 1987. *The Black West: A Pictorial History.* Seattle: Open Hand Publishing.

Kibbett, Mrs. Ardie. 1998. Interview by author. September 21, San Antonio.

Littlefield, Daniel F., Jr. 1977. *Africans and Seminoles: From Removal to Emancipation.* Westport: Greenwood Press.

López, José Guadalupe. 1996. *Los Neko y los Vázquez de Múzquiz.* Múzquiz, Mexico: Un Estudio de el Colegio de Investigaciones Historicas y Culturales.

Lozano, Alicia Fay. 1993. Interview by author. September, Seminole Days, Bracketville, Texas.

———. 1994. Interview by author. September, Seminole Days, Bracketville, Texas.

———. 1998. Interview by author. September 20, Seminole Days, Bracketville, Texas.

Monto, Alexander. 1994. *The Roots of Mexican Labor Migration.* New York: Prager.

Mulroy, Kevin. 1993. *Freedom on the Border: The Seminole Maroons in Florida, the Indian Territory, Coahuila, and Texas.* Lubbock: Texas Tech University Press.

Payne, Isaac. 1995. *A History of the Payne Family of Florida, Tennessee, the Indian Territory, Mexico, Texas, and Oklahoma, 1785–1995.* On file with Isaac Payne, Albuquerque, New Mexico.

Porter, Kenneth Wiggins. 1971. *The Negro on the American Frontier.* New York: Arno Press.

———. 1996. *The Black Seminoles: History of a Freedom-Seeking People.* Gainesville: University Press of Florida.

———. Papers. New York: Schomburg Center for Research in Black Culture.
Sayles, John, director. 1996. *Lonestar* (film). Columbia Pictures.
Schneider, David M. 1997. "Kinship, Nationality, and Religion." In *American Culture: Toward a Definition of Kinship in Symbolic Anthropology: A Reader in the Study of Symbols and Meanings,* edited by Janet L. Dolgin, David S. Kemnitzer, and David M. Schneider, 62–71. New York: Columbia University Press.
Walton-Raji, Angela Y. 1997. The African–Native American Genealogy Homepage.
http://www.african-nativeamerican.com.
Warrior, William "Dub." 1994. Interview by author. September 20, Bracketville, Texas.
———. 1998. Interview by author. October 8, Bracketville, Texas.
Wright, J. Leitch. 1986. *Creeks and Seminoles.* Lincoln: University of Nebraska Press.

12   *Transient Clergy in the Trans-Pecos Area, 1848–1892*

Robert E. Wright

The Trans-Pecos region of Texas extends westward from the Pecos River all the way to the El Paso district. Outside that district, where Spanish settlement began in 1682, there was no European-origin settlement until the mid-1800s. Given that great difference in their histories, this chapter does not include the El Paso district. The only Spanish missions established in the rest of the Trans-Pecos region were at La Junta de los Ríos, the confluence of the Río Conchos and the Río del Norte or Rio Grande. The missions established at La Junta on what is now the Texas side of the Rio Grande had no resident Franciscans after 1720; rather they were taken care of by missionaries stationed across the river, on what is now the Mexican side.[1] The La Junta missions were eventually displaced by the military settlement of Presidio del Norte, which was permanently reestablished at La Junta in 1773 on what is now the Mexican side of the Rio Grande.[2]

THE PRE-CIVIL WAR ERA: THE FRONTIER PARISH OF PRESIDIO DEL NORTE

At Presidio del Norte, there were a few brave Mexican families living on the northern bank of the Rio Grande when it was annexed to the United States in 1848 as a result of the Mexican-American War. Although Mexican land grants existed on that side of the river, marauding Apaches and Comanches made them dangerous.[3] A few months after annexation, US citizens Spencer, Leaton, and Burgess, who had arrived in the area along with the US Army invasion of Chihuahua, became property holders in the new Texan territory just across from Presidio del Norte. In typical border fashion, they acquired land not only through outright purchase from previous owners, but also through marriage into the local Mexican society, and in some cases through more devious means. The Spencer and Burgess ranches and "Fort Leaton," a private enterprise a few miles downriver, were the origins of what would eventually be named Presidio, Texas.[4]

The US Army established Fort Davis in 1854 at the foot of the Davis Mountains, eighty miles north of Presidio, to help protect the transcontinental route between San Antonio and El Paso, as well as the route into Chihuahua by way of Presidio. In 1859 Fort Stockton was established at the strategic Comanche Springs, about eighty miles northeast of Fort Davis on the road to the Pecos River. Both forts were abandoned soon afterward, during the Civil War, and were reoccupied only in 1867.[5] During these years of abandonment, the few civilians who had begun to settle around the two forts fled for safety from Indian attacks.[6]

The Catholic diocese of Galveston, which in principle had jurisdiction over all of Texas, was hard-pressed to care for the rapidly multiplying population in the more settled areas of the state to the east. Even if the church leaders somehow became aware of the Catholics in the new and far distant West Texas posts and the extremely remote Presidio vicinity, they did not have the resources to reach out to them immediately. Prior to the Civil War, the "western" outposts of the Galveston diocese barely reached past San Antonio to Castroville and Fredericksburg.[7]

Not that it mattered much. For the mostly Mexican Catholics from Chihuahua who settled in the Trans-Pecos region after 1848, it was only natural to continue to rely upon their accustomed clergy from the Durango diocese who staffed the old parish church of Jesús Nazareno in Presidio del Norte. For a brief period after 1843, Presidio del Norte had temporarily been without a resident priest. During those difficult years, clergy who were stationed at or near the city of Chihuahua periodically visited the town. Franciscan friar Antonio del Refugio Gómez, who in 1841–1843 had been the last resident military chaplain and pastor at the presidio, was in the midst of his three-week pastoral visit to the community in October 1848 when the Jack Hays expedition, the first to come overland from San Antonio, arrived without any provisions. Gómez helped resupply the group with mules and food.[8]

George Evans, a Protestant from Ohio who passed through Presidio del Norte in 1849 on his way to the California gold fields, reacted with disgust to the religious imagery in the homes of the people: "In each house may be seen a revolting image, representing the crucifixion of our Savior, which is worshipped instead of God. Mary, the mother of Christ, also occupies a conspicuous place at the family altar, and a rude picture of St. Wan [Juan], or St. John, and the other apostles fills up the background."[9]

The bloody reality of the passion of the scourged, nailed, and pierced

Jesus was graphically depicted—not sanitized—in Mexican religiosity, shocking many Anglo Catholics even today.

Beginning in July 1849, perhaps due to its enhanced status as an international port of entry, Presidio del Norte once again had resident pastors. Father José María Montijo was there for only a few months, possibly falling victim to a cholera epidemic. His successor was none other than Father Gómez again, who remained until 1855. It was Father Gómez who in 1850 instructed and baptized John Spencer, whose ranch was the beginning of the future town of Presidio, Texas. Gómez christened Spencer "Juan de Dios" and in January of the following year received permission from the bishop of Durango to officiate at his marriage with María de Jesús Baeza.[10] Fray Antonio impressed United States Boundary Commissioner William Emory when the latter passed through the town in 1852: "The padre who presides over the church in this district," Emory wrote, "was by nature intended for the military profession. Brave, frank, handsome, and energetic, he is the leading spirit in every foray against the Indians, and is by no means an insignificant person in the trade of the place. He bears on his person more than one wound received in battle. In the present isolated and defenseless state of the Presidio, this gentleman is nevertheless as good a spiritual and temporal adviser as could be desired."[11]

Emory also commented, like Evans before him, upon the religious imagery he found in the church and homes of the settlement: "The church . . . contains one or two paintings of a better class than are usually found disfiguring the walls of frontier churches. In almost every house is found, in addition to the cross, a figure of our Saviour, which is sometimes so very grotesque that piety itself cannot divest it of its ridiculous appearance."[12]

Father Gómez was followed by Nemesio García in late 1855, but this priest departed after July 1857, perhaps due to illness, since he died less than a year later. His successor, Luis Colomo, arrived in December 1857. Father Colomo, possibly a native of Presidio, became an institution in the vicinity. He remained the local priest for more than two convulsive decades, up until the end of 1879. It was thus to Father Colomo at Presidio del Norte that the settlers of the Trans-Pecos region turned for priestly ministrations.[13] This included the majority of the American men who settled in the Presidio district before 1870, since they married Mexican Catholic women, as was typical in other border settlements across the Southwest.[14]

The Post-Civil War Era: The Fort Stockton-Fort Davis Parish

After the reestablishment of Forts Davis and Stockton in 1867, those two places once again began to draw settlers and ranchers to their vicinity. Among them were a significant number of San Antonio Catholics of various ethnicities who, along with Mexicans from Chihuahua, figured prominently in the civilian resettlement of the region. By 1870, the Fort Stockton vicinity alone was home to four hundred to six hundred civilians.[15]

The first non-lay Catholic to visit the Trans-Pecos region during this period was apparently Sister Stephen. Her congregation, the Sisters of Charity of the Incarnate Word, had just established the first hospital and orphanage in San Antonio in 1869, and two of the sisters soon engaged in begging tours for the orphanage.[16] When the military paymaster made his trip to the West Texas forts in early spring 1870, Sister Stephen was allowed to join his party. This gave her the distinct advantage of asking for donations as the pay was being distributed. On a subsequent begging trip she took a stagecoach to the West Texas forts in the company of a Mr. Gallagher of Fort Stockton. Another fellow passenger reported the experience: "Sister St. Stephen was an entertaining traveling companion, and she made herself agreeable throughout the trip. We sometimes presumed on her sociability by making jolly remarks, but she did not resent the liberty and was always in a pleasant humor. Once I ventured to say that she could be of no service in case we were attacked by Indians. She laughed and replied that if such an event should happen her part would be attended to equally as well as ours; that we should do the fighting and she would do the praying."[17]

Even though the closest Catholic parish of the Galveston diocese was still Fredericksburg, and there were other small settlements in between (Mason, Menard, Fort Concho), the bishop decided to send priests to the Trans-Pecos region only a few years after the reestablishment of the forts. San Antonio-connected Catholics like Mr. Gallagher and the eyewitness reporter about Sister Stephen probably persuaded him. He assigned two French priests in their late twenties, Claude Jaillet and Adolphe Guichon, to Fort Stockton and Fort Davis in 1871. Both had spent their first years of ministry in the heavily Mexican San Diego district of South Texas.[18] In his memoirs Jaillet asserted that Guichon, dissatisfied with the San Diego mission, had asked the bishop for a new assignment. Little did he know what was in store for him. The bishop offered Guichon Forts Stockton and Davis, provided that Jaillet would also go. Jaillet described the stagecoach route at that time from San Antonio:

> In those days it took 7 days by stage running day and night from San Antonio to El Paso and sometimes having to fight against Indians. . . . The stage road as I took it in 1871 was passing by Boerne, Fredericksburg, Llano, Fort Masson [sic], Concho, Little Concho, the Staked Plains 80 miles without water, from Head Concho to the Pecos River. The two stages coming from above and the other from below had to water their mules, the former at the Pecos, the other at Head Concho and running the 80 miles without water. They used to meet half way for self protection and to give oats to the mules. Each stage had an escort. So Escort Driver and passengers too had to carry their Winchester.
> . . . It was rough time, rough encounters, rough mules and rough drivers.[19]

The two young priests apparently arrived in mid-1871.[20] They were the first Catholic priests actually stationed in the Trans-Pecos region since the Franciscan missionaries at La Junta before 1720. Jaillet made a quick stagecoach trip to El Paso County soon after they arrived, since he had been charged by the bishop of Galveston to ascertain the extent of the Galveston diocese's jurisdiction in the Trans-Pecos region. Arriving in the El Paso area in mid-August, he met the priests of the Mexican diocese of Durango, which for two decades had refused to surrender jurisdiction over the towns on the Texas side of the El Paso Valley. A letter was sent to the Durango bishop on the issue of diocesan jurisdiction in the Trans-Pecos region and informing him of the arrival of Jaillet and Guichon as pastors of the forts. The following month the San Elizario pastor, Father Borrajo, forwarded the bishop's response to Jaillet.[21] Borrajo also replied to the bishop's questions about church jurisdiction in the Trans-Pecos region:

> The bishop of Texas had never exercised his jurisdiction as far as that place (Presidio del Norte), even though before the Civil War there were mail stations and military forts to protect the road from San Antonio de Bexar to here. At present there is a rapid growth of population in the shadow of those forts and stations, with the majority being Mexicans (and almost the only Catholics)

coming from the Mexican border, which has been populated since before the annexation of Texas to the United States. Therefore I presume that the ecclesiastical jurisdiction continues, as before annexation, as part of the Bishopric of Durango, since it seems like a branch of the same tree which is growing and extending itself to where it finds a vacancy. The parish priest of Presidio del Norte (Mexico) should be better able than I to inform you on this point.[22]

Upon his return to the West Texas forts, Jaillet discovered that Guichon had already abandoned the district out of extreme discouragement.[23] In his memoirs Jaillet described the situation that thus confronted him:

If San Diego's mission was a poor mission, the situation at the military post was still worse. There was no chapel, no house. It was not possible for one priest to live there and still less for two. The country was a desert. Except two little settlements adjoinings [sic] the posts there was none between them on [the] west side to El Paso and east to Fredericksburg. Father Guichon realizing the true condition of affairs left two weeks after his arrival, so I remained alone for a year in complete isolation. . . . Having neither chapel nor house I had to use two old barns where I celebrated mass. I had a room among the Catholics of Stockton and Davis, boarding with their families.[24]

Jaillet also had the use of another building at Fort Stockton for a schoolhouse.[25]

Probably in fulfillment of a commitment made to the bishop if a priest was sent, on September 22, 1871, Peter Gallagher donated a three-acre tract at Fort Stockton as the site for a future church.[26] Father Jaillet described the local Catholic population at the two forts as mostly Mexican, with the soldiers consisting of the African American companies, the famous "Buffalo Soldiers," commanded by Anglo officers:

I got acquainted with some officers of the army. I visited general Merritt who was in command at Fort Stockton and among the officers there were good Catholics. Among the settlers there were very few among the English speaking people; the others were Mexicans, but generally very poor. As for the soldiers they were all Colored people, forming 4 companies at Fort Stockton and six at Fort Davis; very few of them being Catholics. Morality was at a low ebb; gambling, drinking, swearing without speaking of other evil habits were very common.[27]

Three years later the first Pecos County grand jury, whose foreman was a Mexican, declared that "in this county there is a looseness of moral conduct based upon old habits, and found in a new and somewhat uncivilized country."[28] Father Jaillet found among the "good Catholic" officers at Fort Stockton one who, although "a model Christian and soldier," for some reason was staying away from communion. The priest convinced him to come to confession and communion, and he was a regular communicant thereafter.[29]

A Visit to Presidio

At some point during his stay in the area, Jaillet made the hazardous trip to the Presidio district to ascertain the church situation there and to visit the Mexican priest, Father Colomo. By this time the old Mexican settlement of Presidio del Norte had been renamed Ojinaga. Jaillet's reminiscences of this visit were haunted by his encounters with some Indians. He departed from Fort Davis accompanied by a young Mexican, Juan García, as his companion and guide. After about an hour's fast riding, Jaillet noticed some Indians hurrying toward them. The young man advised the priest to remain calm and not show that he was afraid:

> Juan dismounted, made the sign of the Cross, and held up some bright colored beads. The Indians put their bows down and looked very attentively at Juan and the Padre. Juan started toward them on foot, still holding up his trinkets. The Indians got suspicious and took aim. Juan stooped, picked up two sticks and made a cross with them and raised it high. The Indians recognized the sign. . . . They made a sign to Juan which Father Jaillet did not understand, but which seemed perfectly clear to Juan, and then they turned around and went on their way without molesting our travelers.[30]

When they arrived at Ojinaga, Jaillet met two Mescalero Apaches passing through the town. His remarks about the event, recalled decades later, evidence both his fear and his stereotypical views of these Native Americans. But they also provide an intriguing vignette of a French missionary conversation with "wild Indians," a conversation combining both concern for personal safety and a zeal for conversion:

> Presidio was on the Mexican side [of the Rio Grande] and is called today Ojinaga. To go there was not without danger. There was no settlement between Fort Davis and Presidio and the country was overrun by Indians. The distance between the 2 places is 90 miles. I went there once only and I thank God I did it in safety.
>
> When at Presidio I met two Apache Indians of the Mescaleros tribe. While I was visiting the place I saw a squaw wrapped up in a coarse cotton blanket. Anxious to know something about wild Indians, I followed her there to a Mexican store. She looked at me as a suspicious being and would not talk to me. I inquired from the Mexican storekeeper why she was keeping mum and he told me she took me for an American. On my telling her that I was a priest, she became more tractable and promised to visit me at the priest-house the next day, which was a Sunday, in company with her nephew whom they called the Colorado, who was one of the principal [*sic*] of the tribe.

So the next day after Mass they came to the priest residence.

> The Colorado could not speak Spanish but the old squaw could make herself understood a little. The reason why they had come to Presidio was that they were going to Chihuahua on a visit to governor Terrazas in order to reclaim some Apaches detained prisoners there. It appears that some time before the Mescalero Indians had stolen horses from the people of Presidio. The Presidio people had organized a party in pursuit of the Indians but did not find the fighting young men only some women and old men. After burning their camp they took prisoners some of those who had been left and had sent them to Chihuahua. It was for that reason they passed through Presidio.
>
> Among other things I asked the Colorado through his interpreter, the old squaw, what he would do if he should find me alone on the Texas plains, and he gave me a respectful answer,

stating that he would not do me harm because I was a *totache*. When I asked him how he would know me to be a *totache* he showed me my Roman Caller [collar]. I asked the squaw if she would be baptized. She seemed to not be opposed to receive Baptism. But when I told her she would have to remain [a] few days under instruction, and when I added she should not steal and kill as the Indians did, she had no more wish to become a Christian. Still we parted good friends. I gave the Colorado some tobacco and some little things to the squaw. This was my first and last interview with the red skins.[31]

But it was not his last encounter. On the way back to Fort Davis, scarcely an hour out of Presidio, he and García suddenly came under attack by unseen assailants. An arrow knocked off Juan García's hat; another just missed Jaillet's nose. Spurring their horses, they managed to outrun two Indians after a lengthy chase, but only because the latter were both mounted on a single horse. Terror-stricken, Jaillet was somewhat calmed only by García's reassurance. Suffice it to say that the priest did not attempt to visit Presidio again.[32] "I went there but once," he later wrote, "with the firm determination of not risking my life again."[33]

Revolving Clergy—and Father Hoban

Traveling between Fort Stockton and Fort Davis, and even down to Presidio, Father Jaillet was the first "circuit rider of the Big Bend." But fearful of traveling because of Indian attacks, at a great distance from other settlements and from any other Catholic priest, discouraged by the poverty and desolateness of the area, and despairing of accomplishing any good in the face of the immorality he encountered, within a year Father Jaillet also gave up: "I saw that I could not do any good and that being alone I could not discharge my duties. I resolved to leave the posts. In consequence I wrote to Bishop Dubuis to appoint me to another mission."[34] He left before July 1872.[35] The national Catholic directories listed Father Emile Augustine Antoine, another young Frenchman whose earlier ministry had been mostly among the Mexican-American communities below San Antonio, as the pastor of Fort Stockton and Fort Davis in the latter part of 1872 and 1873.[36] He was traveling eastward through Fort Concho/San Angelo and Menard between May 18 and May 23, 1873, and was back at Fort Concho on June 1 of that year.[37]

The diocese of San Antonio was created in late 1874, assuming jurisdiction of the Trans-Pecos region from the diocese of Galveston. The clergy assignments for the San Antonio diocese in fall 1874 and 1875 listed Father Mathurin Pairier as pastor of Fort Stockton and Fort Davis.[38] In contrast to his young French countrymen who had preceded him, Pairier had already served as a priest for a quarter of a century. Unlike them, however, he had had no previous experience in ministry among people of Mexican origin. Reportedly weighing over three hundred pounds, he was nevertheless a pioneer pastor throughout the state of Texas.[39] A contemporary who knew him in the last years of his life praised him as "a man of brilliant parts, of a kind heart, who was satisfied to live and work among the poor in his vast district and sought, by his ready defense of religion and pleasant manners, to win them over to God."[40] From his residence in Fort Stockton, Pairier visited Fort Davis and La Mota and Victoria, two farming areas which had recently been started along Toyah Creek, west of Fort Stockton and north of Fort Davis.[41] It was during Pairier's time that Bishop Pellicer of San Antonio, with the protection of a military escort, in mid-1875 became the first Catholic bishop to visit the Trans-Pecos region as part of his tour of the entire diocese.[42] Father Pairier departed from the area in the latter part of 1876.[43] His successor, Father Joseph Paganini, was apparently only a temporary appointee, ministering in the area from mid-September to mid-October 1876.[44]

By October 29, 1876, Father Joseph Ferra, another young Frenchman, and the newly ordained Father Joseph Hoban had arrived at Fort Stockton.[45] Since Ferra had already been a priest for five years, ministering in the bilingual South Texas area, and Hoban had been ordained for less than two weeks, the more experienced Ferra was the pastor.[46] At that time there were six companies of black soldiers and an estimated two hundred Mexican civilians at Fort Stockton, along with a few Americans, and another hundred civilians at Fort Davis.[47] From Fort Stockton the two priests promptly extended their visits to the Toyah Valley and to Fort Davis.[48] In March 1877, Father Hoban became the first priest of the US church to extend his missionary field to the ranches such as Ruidosa along the Rio Grande in the Presidio vicinity. This visit must have convinced the two priests to divide the vast territory between them, since in July Hoban established himself in Fort Davis with responsibility for the Presidio-area ranches, while Ferra remained in Fort Stockton. The ranches along the Chihuahua Trail to Presidio included Ojo de Veranda, San Esteban, and La Cien Station (probably La Ciénaga, a Milton Faver ranch), and those along the Rio Grande included Fort Leaton and the Spencer, Russell, Indio, Borracho, and Ruidosa ranches.[49]

In Fort Stockton, Father Ferra had a school conducted in his own house while plans for a church with an arched roof and a school were being drawn up. By April construction had begun, and on August 1, 1877, the cornerstone of the church was laid. Like the buildings constructed at the fort, the church had a stone foundation and stone walls for the first few feet, with the rest of the walls made of adobe, and the flat roof (completed in 1878) formed out of mud and tule. Finances probably dictated abandoning the initial plans for an arched roof. Ferra left the parish in the midst of construction, soon after September 1877.[50] With his departure, the Trans-Pecos region was reduced to one priest again, the recently ordained Father Hoban, and the veteran Father Colomo down at Ojinaga.

Father Hoban was the first priest to stay for more than two years in the area, remaining until October 1884. He probably had a special fondness and enthusiasm for the region whose people taught him how to be a priest, as have many young priests for their first assignment. When it became clear that no one would be coming for a while to replace Father Ferra, Hoban moved back to Fort Stockton in December 1877. This was probably to oversee the completion of the church construction there. After September 1878, however, he seems to have begun traveling more regularly among the various locations in his vast mission territory.[51] An adobe church and a small dwelling for the priest were finally built in Fort Davis in 1879.[52] From mid-July through the end of August 1879, Hoban led Father Thomas Mas, an exiled Jesuit from Mexico temporarily ministering in the San Antonio area, on what was probably a revival tour (called a "mission" by Catholics) through the Trans-Pecos communities. For the following seven months, Hoban's sacramental entries were mostly in the Fort Stockton parish registers.[53]

1880–1885: Railroads, New Settlements, Clergy Fluctuations

The 1880s ushered in a new period for the Trans-Pecos region. In the year 1880, United States and Mexican troops had pacified most of the hostile Apaches, allowing travelers and settlers to breathe more easily.[54] The following year, construction began across the region on the first railroads. The Texas and Pacific railroad from Fort Worth to El Paso, which passed about fifty miles above Fort Stockton, was completed in late 1881. To the west of the Davis Mountains it made use of the tracks being laid eastward from El Paso toward San Antonio by the Southern Pacific line.[55] In 1882 this lower route, passing twenty miles below Fort Davis, reached what became Alpine, and was finally joined to the San Antonio line just west of the Pecos River in January 1883.[56] While the two events—cessation of Indian hostilities and arrival of the railroads—stimulated greater settlement and development of the region, they had a negative impact on the two forts and their civilian communities. Troops were no longer needed for protection, and neither settlement lay along the railroad lines. At Fort Stockton, which lay farthest from the railroads, the town declined as troop reduction began in 1882; troops were completely withdrawn in 1886. Fort Davis was temporarily more fortunate in that it was not abandoned by the military until 1891, but the new railroad towns of Marfa and the future Alpine soon surpassed it in importance.[57]

Father Hoban apparently absented himself from the Trans-Pecos region during the month of April 1880, perhaps taking a well-deserved break while anticipating the arrival of Father L. F. Ballay as the pastor of Fort Stockton in mid-April. The young Father Ballay came with a year and a half of experience in Mexican American ministry. When Hoban returned in May, he set out immediately for a three-week visit to the Presidio district and Ojinaga, where Father Colomo had ceased to minister in December 1879 and no one had promptly replaced him. Once back at Fort Stockton, Hoban spent a month with Ballay before guiding the new priest through the Toyah Valley settlements in mid-July. Thereafter, Ballay pastored the Fort Stockton district, including the Toyah Valley, while Hoban for the second time focused upon the Fort Davis and Presidio districts.[58]

Father Mariano Uranga, who arrived in Ojinaga in August 1880, served only until October 1881. Again the Durango diocese could not provide a replacement. Under these circumstances, the zealous Father Hoban actually agreed in November 1881 to "temporarily" add the Ojinaga parish and its mission stations in Mexico to his Big Bend district.[59] At some point he saw to the building of an adobe church in Presidio, and he may have also had the church in Ojinaga rebuilt.[60] However, less than a year after having agreed to add the large Ojinaga district to his field of ministry, Hoban was faced with the departure of Father Ballay from Fort Stockton at the end of June 1882.[61] That left Father Hoban in the daunting situation of being the only priest between the Pecos River and the vicinity of the city of Chihuahua in Mexico, at precisely the time when the new railroads were stimulating new settlements in the Trans-Pecos region.

Since Fort Stockton was by then undergoing troop reductions, Fort Davis still had a military presence, and the Ojinaga district was by far the most populous, Hoban apparently opted to divide his time between the Fort Davis and Rio Grande settlements. For the first time since 1871, Fort Stockton ceased to receive regular priestly ministry and was relegated to official status as a missionary station supposedly served out of Fort Davis. As a matter of fact, there is only one extant record of a visit to Fort Stockton by Hoban during the remainder of his time in the Trans-Pecos region.[62] In June 1883 Francisco Stratigo of the Durango diocese finally arrived to be the new pastor of Ojinaga. That relieved Father Hoban of the care of the Ojinaga parish and its missions. After only a year Father Stratigo was replaced by Rosendo Castelo, who, fortunately for the people of Ojinaga and Presidio, endured in the position.[63]

In the Trans-Pecos region itself, the new lower railroad across the top of the Big Bend enabled Father Carlos Persone to come all the way from the newly established Jesuit missionary center at Ysleta near El Paso to visit Fort Davis in 1883. Met there by Father Hoban in mid-November, Persone then made a brief missionary circuit through the Toyah Valley, Fort Stockton, and back to Fort Davis while Hoban embarked on a long visit to the Presidio district. In view of subsequent events, Persone's missionary tour may have been a scouting trip for the Jesuits, to see if they might accept pastoral responsibility for at least part of the Trans-Pecos region.[64] In March 1884 Hoban was temporarily assisted at Fort Davis by Father Heyburn, and from mid-April through mid-June Father Maury took care of Fort Davis while Hoban ministered in the Presidio district.[65] These were both Texas diocesan priests, coming by the lower railroad from the east. If the hope was to interest them in the Trans-Pecos missions, it did not work. In fact, Father Heyburn, who had originally been a Jesuit seminarian from England but had been ordained for the diocese of San Antonio in 1879, opted to go with the Jesuit priests in Saltillo, Mexico, whom he had come to know while ministering in Eagle Pass and Uvalde, Texas.[66]

At the end of October 1884, Father Hoban departed from the Trans-Pecos region that he had served assiduously for eight years. Within a year, Hoban had left the diocese of San Antonio itself.[67] To replace him immediately, Bishop Neraz of San Antonio turned first for help to the Jesuits at Ysleta, who were able to provide one person. A month after Hoban's departure, Father Persone accompanied Father José María Montenarelli, SJ (Society of Jesus, Jesuit), to Fort Davis to introduce him as the new pastor of that settlement and its far-flung missions. Montenarelli visited the Toyah Valley and Fort Stockton every three months; he toured the Presidio district in late January 1885. He also visited the nascent Murphysville (Alpine) and Marfa.[68] The Jesuit priest began building a larger adobe church at Fort Davis, which was completed under his successors in the 1890s.[69] The bishop later wrote that Father Montenarelli accomplished much good and was well liked.[70]

Bishop Neraz himself made a visitation tour in August 1885, confirming people as he traveled. The bishop was accompanied by Father Ferra, who had been the pastor of the Trans-Pecos region eight years earlier, and Father Rigomer Olivier, OMI (Oblate). Guided by Montenarelli, the bishop's entourage traveled from Fort Davis to Presidio, Ojinaga, la Plazuela (the newly opened mines at Shafter), and back through Fort Davis to Fort Stockton, finally catching the train back east at Murphysville. The bishop confirmed 4,755 people: 593 in the Fort Davis district, 483 in the Fort Stockton district, 714 in Presidio, and a whopping 2,965 in Ojinaga. How disappointing it must have been to Father Ferra to find the church he had begun at Fort Stockton already falling into ruin, only seven years after it had been completed. The bishop must have instructed Montenarelli to record in the Presidio, Texas, register the baptisms of Texas residents conducted by Father Castelo of Ojinaga, since Montenarelli did so for several such baptisms between March and October 1885.[71]

Bishop Neraz had the future in mind when he asked Father Olivier, a veteran missionary along the lower Rio Grande, to accompany him on his first episcopal visit to the Trans-Pecos region. As a young seminarian, the future bishop had come to the United States from France in 1852 on the same boat with the newly ordained Olivier and the other Oblate pioneers in Texas. Father Neraz had come to appreciate the Oblates' missionary work in East Texas and especially in the Lower Rio Grande Valley of South Texas. After he became bishop in 1881, he had finally persuaded the Oblates to take over the large mission district of Eagle Pass, which included everything between Uvalde and the future Del Rio, in 1884.[72] Father Olivier was the Oblate pastor at Eagle Pass, the nearest parish southeast of Fort Davis at a distance of 250 miles.

Hoping to get several Oblates to take over the Trans-Pecos region also, Bishop Neraz wrote their superior general in France soon after returning from his West Texas tour:

> I am writing to ask you to be kind enough to allow your Fathers
> in Texas to take care of the missions of Fort Davis, Stockton
> and Presidio del Norte, Fort Davis being the central point. All
> the population is Mexican, intermixed with Americans; there
> is much good to be done and the people are well disposed. I
> desire to entrust these missions to your Fathers, in the first place,
> since they have worked so many years among the Mexicans and
> understand their habits and manner of acting and, secondly,
> since these are missions very distant from the episcopal city and
> I fear to send young priests there. The need is urgent, and since
> it is furthermore difficult, not to say impossible, to find two or
> three secular priests who work in harmony, I have thought about
> your Fathers since the moment that God deigned to place me in
> charge of this part of his flock.[73]

Since 1873, even before becoming bishop, Neraz had been the right-hand man of previous bishops for church affairs in San Antonio and West Texas.[74] He had witnessed the coming and going of the mostly very young diocesan priests who had been sent to the Trans-Pecos region. Only Father Hoban had stayed longer than two years, and then even he had left not only Fort Davis but also the diocese itself. If he could persuade the Oblates, the bishop hoped to gain along the Mexican border a group of priests seasoned in ministry, whose religious rule called for community life and mutual support. But the Oblate leaders, already hard-pressed to provide priests for their expanding commitments in Texas and beyond, could not immediately oblige the bishop. Persisting in his hopes, however, Neraz did not definitively entrust the region to the Jesuits. Consequently, these latter ceased to provide a resident pastor.[75] Father Montenarelli ended his ministry at Fort Davis in late November 1885, and no one replaced him.[76]

Upon his departure, no priest remained within the entire Trans-Pecos region at precisely the time when several new towns, ranches, and farms were developing due to the arrival of the railroads. Like the lower railroad, the upper railroad gave rise to new settlements, such as Toyah, about twenty miles north of the Toyah Creek villages, and Pecos, located just west of where the railroad crossed the Pecos River.[77] People in the Presidio district could, and did, turn to Father Castelo in Ojinaga. But everywhere else—in Fort Davis, Fort Stockton, the Toyah Creek villages, and the incipient communities of Marfa, Alpine, and Pecos—there was no resident priest. The Trans-Pecos region was to remain in this state until 1892.

The third group to which the bishop turned for help was the German Carmelite monks who in 1882 had established a monastery and missionary center at the train stop they named Marienfeld. Marienfeld (renamed Stanton in 1890) was situated along the upper railroad 115 miles to the northeast of the Pecos River. In September 1885, thanks to their newly ordained members, the Carmelites were able to begin extending their railroad visits on a regular basis to Toyah station in the Trans-Pecos region. Most of this railroad settlement was made up of Mexican laborers, and by 1890 they had a frame chapel dedicated to St. John the Baptist.[78]

1886: Oblate Revival Preaching

While the Oblates along the Texas-Mexico border were hopefully awaiting word that their leaders in Paris had accepted the Trans-Pecos mission, Father Olivier from Eagle Pass returned by himself for an extended pastoral tour that lasted the entire spring. Making the Fort Davis-Toyah Creek-Fort Stockton circuit, he then visited all of the Presidio district, from Polvo (Redford) to Ruidosa and then up through Shafter, and once again made the upper circuit before finally returning to Eagle Pass by way of Murphysville.[79] In August of that year two other Oblates embarked on an extended three-month preaching tour in the region, holding missions, or revivals, which lasted anywhere from one day to over a week, in all the settlements below the upper railroad line. In an effort to persuade the Oblate leaders in France to send more personnel to assume responsibility for this vast missionary region without pastors, one of the priests, Father Joseph Malmartel from Eagle Pass, penned a lengthy account of the entire experience, which he sent to Paris.[80] According to an Oblate contemporary, Malmartel had an additional motive for undertaking this tour. Needing funds for the stone church that he was building in Del Rio, part of the large mission district served out of Eagle Pass, he hoped that the offerings he would receive during the trip would serve to further the project.[81]

Father Malmartel was joined on this occasion by Father Evaristo Repiso from Brownsville. When the two arrived on the westbound train at an unidentified station in the Trans-Pecos region at 2 P.M. on August 10, they were greeted by a Mexican teenager who regularly met the train to retrieve the freight for Fort Stockton.[82] The young man was expecting the priests and drove them without charge in his father's conveyance the fifty-five miles to Fort Stockton with only one brief stop. Arriving at 5 A.M., they noticed that most of the dwellings in the town itself were unoccupied, due to the very recent final withdrawal of the military. Only five or six families remained. They did not spend any time in the mostly abandoned settlement.

Rather, switching carriages, the priests were taken to a large farm three miles outside the town, where, aided by a five-hundred-pound bell, they preached their first mission. They were very impressed by the owner, a former career soldier and "excellent Catholic," who gave his Mexican sharecroppers a decent house and tools in exchange for a quarter of the principal harvest.[83] On August 18 their host and one of his sons drove them nine winding miles westward to "three villages really forming one" (undoubtedly Leon Springs), where they preached the next mission, again for nine days. On their way to this second place they had paused at a small, "very well kept" private oratory dedicated to Saint Joseph. During this second mission, when one of the priests carried the communion wafer to an infirm woman in her home, they were deeply impressed by the traditional reverence of the people, who swept the streets ahead of the procession and, bearing candles, walked along praying or in deep reflection.

Next came the long trip to Saragosa, at the northern end of the Toyah Creek settlements. On the way the priests were regaled with stories about hunting and Comanches by the Basque Frenchman and his Mexican wife who had offered to take them in their well-equipped carriage.[84] At Saragosa they saw thousands of cattle, oxen, and horses, although they were told that more than two thousand cows had died from the bad drought that year. There they stayed during the three-day mission with the "American" county sheriff, a Catholic who sported a long, graying beard, and his Mexican wife. From Saragosa they began the journey up Toyah Creek, with the sheriff giving them a ride to Indio. Along the way they admired the perfectly clear skies and enjoyed less intense heat than they were accustomed to in the Oblate missions along the Rio Grande. At Indio, where there was an abundant spring of water, they stayed with the family of Agustin Hernández, who had an immense maize field. There they were joined by a joyful old Mexican man who, hearing of the two missionaries while up in the mountains, had sought them out. He accompanied them for twelve days, from Indio to Victoria, proving to be a great help in encouraging the people of the valley to make the most of this rare spiritual opportunity.[85]

Upon their arrival at nearby La Lorna, transported by a Señor Hernández, the priests were confronted by a pastoral dilemma. The young American Catholic owner of the ranch had prepared a room as a chapel, but so had a Mexican woman. The "natural" choice, the priests opined, would be the first, as that of the owner and thus more impressive. Furthermore, the Mexican woman's room was too narrow and low, and without ventilation—but much better decorated. The solution: the Mexican woman graciously agreed to send the best of her pictures, artificial flowers, and candlesticks to the other chapel. When they left La Lorna, the priests were accompanied by a great crowd to nearby Victoria with its remarkable springs. At all of these places the two priests were kept busy, successfully urging most people to go to confession, which usually kept the missionaries up until 1 A.M. At each locality there were couples not married by the church, some of whom were convinced by the insistent missionaries to have their marriages blessed. Others who had left a previous marriage suffered through wilting sermons about the hellfire that awaited them, but refused to separate from their present partner. Practically everywhere the priests went, the people strongly lamented not having a priest regularly available to them.[86]

When it was time to continue to Fort Davis, Hernández again offered to transport them. There was still no marked-out route at the time. Approaching the canyon in the Davis Mountains, Malmartel was awed by a spectacular West Texas lightning storm in the distance: "In the twenty years I have lived in Texas, I had never seen anything so beautiful." On September 13 the priests arrived at Fort Davis, which Malmartel described as having eighteen hundred inhabitants living in "three quite distinct groupings: on one side, the garrison; on the other the Mexican families; in the center the Americans, our invading masters, the men of the future."[87] The social division evident in Fort Davis was amply reflected in a poem written the previous year by a major at the fort:

Beside a post, on the far frontier
Has grown up a village, quaint and queer,
In its straggling rows of mud jacals
With flat earth roofs, where the Mexican dwells,
Where the sun-dried bricks are the same today
As those that were made of Egyptian clay

Picturing now as it pictured then,
The rude endeavors of barbarous men.

In this frontier village in the far Southwest,
With its mud-walled homes, where even the best
Are meager and poor, lives a motley crew
Of Mexicans, Negroes, and a few
Frontier Americans here and there,
The ne'er-do-wells of a race more fair.[88]

Malmartel wondered about the healthiness of Fort Davis: a good number of people had typhoid fever, including forty of the garrison, but none were dangerously ill.[89] He was not sanguine about the place's future: agriculture appeared impossible, and the garrison, upon which the town depended, would probably disappear soon. The small adobe church was very well kept inside but miserable-looking outside. A larger one had been started but then halted due to lack of money. The two Oblate priests spent a full two weeks at the settlement, once again helped in their efforts by an old Mexican, this one a former soldier. While the response was not as enthusiastic as it had been in the smaller villages, many people came in from the surrounding ranches.[90]

When the two priests left Fort Davis, for the first and only time no one offered them a free ride. Paying to ride with some travelers, they went on to Marfa, where they spent the night and then continued southward toward Presidio in the midst of an unrelenting cold north wind and rain. Losing their paid ride at the Alamo ranch, they were fortunate that the Mexican owner of the new ranch of San José came along on his return trip from Fort Davis and begged them to visit his large family. From there they were conducted to the Refugio ranch, and they finally arrived at Presidio, Texas, on October 2. Father Malmartel described Presidio as a small village of several hundred inhabitants, Mexican, American, and Jewish. It had a post office, a customs house, and two Masonic lodges. It also had a large adobe church, whose tarpaulin roof had disappeared.[91]

The next day Father Malmartel sent a letter to the bishop in San Antonio, whose response was dated October 8. Bishop Neraz wrote that three weeks previously a Father Dowling had arrived in San Antonio, having passed through Fort Davis and having no knowledge of the whereabouts of the Oblates. Dowling had offered to go to Presidio to make arrangements for the roof of the church, since several Americans had promised to help him with this. Not knowing where Father Malmartel was, the bishop had given Dowling permission to arrange for the roof as well as to do what he could spiritually for the people. Neraz gave Father

Malmartel faculties to give any dispensations needed for any marriages Dowling might have conducted. The bishop also restated his hope that some Oblates would be able to take charge of the territory.[92]

While at Presidio Father Malmartel crossed over to Ojinaga, a town of three to four thousand people, in an unsuccessful attempt to meet the "young priest" there. Father Castelo had left on Monday and was not expected back until after the Oblates' departure. Malmartel was unimpressed by the town and its people, whom he described as excessively plain or unsightly (in French, *excessivement laids*. He attributed the large adobe church to Father Hoban and described the building as consisting of one nave, "long, narrow, high, without windows or side chapels." He particularly noted the people's great devotion to the church's principal statue, the large *Jesús Nazareno* (the suffering Christ standing as a prisoner before his crucifixion): "His figure of a notable suffering expression makes a great impression and invites reverence." The modest bell tower had two bells, suspended by iron chains.[93]

In Presidio, Texas, the appearance of the two missionaries did not cause as much of a sensation as it had elsewhere in the region. In fact, hardly anyone attended the Sunday mass offered by the priests the day after their arrival. Although Father Malmartel did not say so, this was undoubtedly because the people were all at their customary place of Sunday worship and socialization in Ojinaga, across the river. A fairly large number attended the Oblates' special religious services beginning Monday evening, with the younger people showing more interest than the older ones. The missionaries blessed the cemetery on the eleventh and then journeyed down the road along the Rio Grande, passing the abandoned former Fort Leaton and the ruins of the foundations of the old Mexican *fortín*.[94]

Spending the night at their driver's ranch, they arrived the next day at Polvo (today's Redford), where a young storekeeper extended them excellent hospitality. A while before, a customs agent had been killed by some smugglers, and their host, while not present at the time of that incident, was reputed to have had "some interests engaged in this affair." He went about always armed, fearful of being either killed or arrested. Here they found a church "fifty paces from the Rio Grande, a little too removed from the people."[95] Fairly large for the population, it was in a sorry state: the door and a window lying on the ground, all the others tightly closed, the roof full of holes, and the altar covered with bat droppings. After the building was cleaned, they gave a mission there for a week. Then they returned to Presidio and continued upriver, provided now with good Mexican wool blankets against the cold.

After spending a night on the road, the priests arrived at Ruidosa, reported as forty-five miles upriver from Presidio, on October 20. The village had been located some miles farther upriver until a flood a few years previously had destroyed the farmlands, and the people had moved. The strict European missionaries discovered it to be a village full of musicians, with trumpets, guitars, violins, and flutes, and averred that the dancing that such music usually accompanied was too immodest and provocative. Father Malmartel was implacable with those who had a previous marriage partner still alive and were in second marriages, no matter how pitiable a story he heard. The only solution he would condone—indeed, he insisted upon it—was to abandon the second marriage:

> A tall vigorous man, with a sad, dejected air, confronted me after Mass and said: "My legitimate wife abandoned me after six months of marriage, at least twenty years ago. Six years ago I took another wife, and we have a little five-year old girl whom I love more than my life. Yesterday my wife confessed to you. Afterwards she left me, taking our child with her. She does not want to leave her with me. Now, it is impossible to separate me from my dear little girl. No, no, I could never do it. My wife is leaving for———, 150 miles from here. She has brothers who are violent men; I know them. I could never show up there; they would kill me on the spot. Please, don't separate from me these beloved ones! How could I live, alone with my flocks! . . . It's easy to see, you don't know what it is to be a father! For the love of God, don't separate me from my child!" Seeing that he had not altered my position, he added: "Very well! Since everything is over, I am going to sell all that I have, give it to my little daughter, and blow my brains out."[96]

The distraught man charged out of the room before Father Malmartel could rise to see him off. All in all, the priest reported that a great revival took place in the community.

From there it was on to the Rancho Depot, accompanied by a dozen enthusiastic horsemen. There the priests were asked to dedicate the ranch in honor of Our Lady of Guadalupe. Then it was on to San José, Indio, and La Hacienda. In these upriver ranches a recent smallpox epidemic had killed the majority of the children. At Indio the old American owner, a Catholic, gave the priests an excellent dinner but did not go to hear their sermons.[97] At La Hacienda there was a very small, windowless chapel, built on an elevated site with a nice view. Returning to Indio, the Oblates then set off cross-country to the recently opened silver mines and smelter at La Plazuela (Shafter), accompanied by the old sacristan of Fort Davis. Arriving there on November 1, they found a bustling community, with new homes being built and a hotel with two young Chinese servants who could not understand Spanish and spoke very poor English. The two priests spent a week there, with many people attending their services but few going to confession.

After visiting nearby Cibolo, where they were hosted by Milton Faver,[98] they arrived back at Marfa, where they spent three days giving an unsuccessful mission, with less attendance each evening. Reaching Murphysville (Alpine) by train, they deemed this last place the worst of all they had encountered: "The sacrament of marriage is almost unknown, or at least totally ignored. Scandal in all its most hideous forms is found everywhere among these families, most of whom live in dugouts like rats. It is shocking." Spending only a day there, they took the train back to Eagle Pass on November 13, 1886.

Father Malmartel concluded his long account with an appreciative summary of the religious characteristics of the Mexican population of the Trans-Pecos:

> 1. In almost all the houses, there is a well-kept room similar to a small chapel, decorated with a very great number of images of Our Lord, the Holy Virgin, Saint Joseph, and other favorite saints.
> 2. All those who are able to obtain rosaries (and those who have them are numerous—we ourselves distributed around a thousand), men and women, elderly and infants, take pride in wearing them visibly around their neck; and their preference is not for the most precious or smaller ones, but rather for the biggest and longest.
> 3. Hundreds were enrolled in the confraternities of the scapular of Mount Carmel and of the Immaculate Conception.
> 4. All of these Mexicans are filled with the highest respect for the priest, whom they call "Christ on earth." Not a word, nor an act, nor a sign which would wound in the slightest degree this profoundly Christian respect. . . .
> 5. Their love of family is truly admirable.

6. What these poor people are lacking are good schools (hardly one-tenth know how to read) and priests according to God's heart.[99]

On a final note, Malmartel disapproved of how previous priests visiting the Trans-Pecos region had admitted young children to their first communion "with a shocking ease to which we are unaccustomed, both in consideration of their age and of their lack of instruction." An Oblate contemporary wrote that during this missionary tour the two priests heard about four thousand confessions, gave about three thousand communions, baptized a great many children—and garnered six hundred dollars to apply to the Del Rio church construction.[100]

1886–1892: Clergy Visits from Afar

The pattern of clergy visits from afar established in 1886 continued for the next six years. Father Castelo of Ojinaga remained available for the people of the Presidio district, occasionally traveling as far as Shafter.[101] In spring 1887, the Carmelite who visited Toyah journeyed for the first and only time before 1889 down to the Toyah Creek villages to the south. Although he had to pass through Pecos on his railroad trip from Marienfeld, apparently no ministry was begun at Pecos until 1890.[102] From late April through late July 1887, Father Olivier of Eagle Pass returned for an extended revival tour, duplicating the itinerary of Malmartel and Repiso the previous year. He passed through the Toyah Creek settlements only a few days after the Carmelite, Father Berthold Ohlenforst, had departed.[103]

Bishop Neraz was still hoping for the Oblate leaders in France to accept the care of the Trans-Pecos region below the upper railroad line. While on a confirmation tour of the Oblate mission territory in the Lower Rio Grande Valley of Texas, he and some of his old Oblate friends determined to try once again. At the suggestion of the head of the Oblates in the United States, Neraz wrote to Paris in October 1887, but this time to Father Martinet, an Oblate assistant general who was highly favorable toward the Texas mission:

> A few weeks ago Father McGrath replied to me that he could not place Oblate Fathers in the Davis mission, where there are more than 15,000 Catholics, mostly Mexican, since he did not have enough men available. But if I could obtain from the [Oblate] Su-

perior General the necessary Fathers, he would not be opposed. Therefore I write you . . . in order to obtain two or three more priests, a sufficient number for a few years who could take charge of the Davis mission. This mission is very populated and the few American Catholics are desolated to see that there is no resident Father in a place where there are so many Catholics and there is not yet a Protestant church. It is impossible for me to send two secular priests, in the first place because I do not have enough who speak Spanish but above all because it is very difficult to find two secular priests who can work together harmoniously in the missions. The Jesuit Fathers of New Mexico [Ysleta] have taken care of this mission for three or four years; but since I have not given it to them definitively because I was reserving it for the Oblate Fathers, they have understandably withdrawn their Father who did a lot of good and was well beloved.[104]

Actually, as previously noted, the Jesuit Fathers, in the person of Father Montenarelli, had been in charge of the pastoral care of the region only in the year 1885. By his gross exaggeration, the bishop may have been hoping that a spirit of intermissionary rivalry might goad the Oblate leaders into action. Simultaneously with the bishop, one of his old Oblate allies, the veteran missionary Father Clos, also wrote to Paris, and even added that the bishop would be willing to give the Oblates the important Rio Grande town of Laredo (requiring another three priests) if they would accept the Trans-Pecos region. This would put the Oblates in charge of the entire frontier of Texas with Mexico except for the El Paso district.[105] This letter advocating the acceptance of yet another new mission district besides the Trans-Pecos region probably did more harm than good for the bishop's cause.

Neraz probably did not receive a response from Paris until February 1888. It was not what he had hoped for. Martinet replied that he had delayed responding in an effort to come up with some extra priests, but that everywhere the needs were greater than the numbers.[106] A month later Martinet responded in the same vein to Clos. But in this letter the assistant general indirectly revealed that the real obstacle lay with the Oblate superior general: "Plead with the Lord of the harvest. Plead also with 'the lord of the house' that he send laborers. The houses of training for seminarians are full. Write directly to the Superior General. Interest him in your missions."[107] If Father Clos did write again, it did not bring about a positive response. The Oblate leaders in France never accepted the Trans-Pecos mission.[108]

In the meantime, Olivier had made a quick trip to Fort Davis during the second week of December 1887, and had promptly returned in January 1888 for a month's circuit from Fort Davis to the Toyah valley and Fort Stockton.[109] Bishop Neraz himself visited Toyah station on March 5, 1888, as one of his stops along the upper railroad line. He confirmed thirty people there, mostly Mexican (Pecos still being skipped).[110] From early May through mid-July 1888, Olivier once more followed the Malmartel-Repiso itinerary throughout the Trans-Pecos region below the upper railroad line. A curiosity in the sacramental records of Fort Davis for 1887-88 is the appearance of Father C. J. Smith, OMI (Oblate), on the final day of each of Father Olivier's pastoral tours of a month or longer. After each of the two summer tours by Olivier, Father Smith remained in the area for the month of August, doing almost no ministry in 1887 but regularly baptizing in 1888.[111] The probable explanation is that Father Smith, stationed at St. Mary's Church in San Antonio, had been sent from Massachusetts to Texas in late 1886 in the hope of restoring his failing health. The trips to the Davis Mountains must have been beneficial, since he continued in ministry for two more decades.[112]

The Texas Oblates must have surmised by mid-1888 that their and the bishop's three-year-old hope for them to take charge of the Trans-Pecos region was futile. Whereas the Oblates from Eagle Pass had engaged in an extended visit of the region every six months during that time, nearly a year elapsed between Olivier's tour in the summer 1888 and Father Malmartel's during the months of May and June 1889. This trip by Malmartel was the last such expansive Oblate visit to the Trans-Pecos region. He retraced the steps of his 1886 journey, but omitted for the first time the Toyah Creek settlements.[113] That was because in February 1889 the Marienfeld Carmelites, who had continued to visit Toyah, began to regularly include in their rounds the settlements along Toyah Creek below the upper railroad. It had been nine months since the people there had seen a priest. In March of the following year Father Albert Wagner, OCC (Carmelite), added Pecos to the railroad settlements regularly visited.[114]

The sharply declining Oblate effort was abundantly clear after Malmartel's early summer 1889 tour. When he returned in late October that year, and again in February 1890, it was only for a rapid visit of a few days to Fort Stockton by way of the Haymond train stop.[115] The waning Oblate effort brought about a return of Jesuits visiting from the El

Paso district. In the last nineteen days of April 1890, Father Ricardo di Palma, SJ (Jesuit), conducted a whirlwind visit from Fort Davis—which had not seen a priest for nine months—down to the stretch of the Rio Grande between Polvo and Presidio (but not to the villages upriver from Presidio), up through Shafter to Fort Stockton, down to Haymond, and back to Fort Davis. August and October of that year witnessed the last Oblate visits, confined to Fort Davis, Marfa, and Alpine. The first was by Malmartel, the second by Father F. X. Brule, another Oblate stationed at Eagle Pass/Del Rio.[116]

By the time Father Wagner agreed to include Fort Stockton in his Trans-Pecos itinerary in October 1890, the Carmelites had further expanded their mission territory. In this way the care of the Toyah valley settlements was once more joined to that of Fort Stockton, the whole shepherded by the Carmelites still operating out of Stanton, the new name for Marienfeld. Thereafter, Bishop Neraz of San Antonio could be happy that at least the Carmelites at Stanton had established a regular visitation of the new towns of Toyah and Pecos along the upper railroad line and Fort Stockton and the Toyah valley.[117] After Father Ballay's departure in mid-1882, the temporarily declining Fort Stockton had seen a priest only every year or so up to 1885. Thereafter it had been visited anywhere from every two to nine months, except for one stretch of fifteen months from January 1888 to May 1889. While relying on Carmelites traveling all the way from Stanton was not ideal, at least it introduced a regular pattern of visitation.

That still left the Fort Davis and Presidio districts without regular pastors from Texas. From El Paso the Jesuits Stephen Bueno, Charles Ferrari, and P. M. Pennella took turns making quick visits to Fort Davis by way of Marfa in November 1890 and February, May, and July 1891. On his May visit, Pennella also spent a week at Shafter. He was back for three weeks in October, visiting Fort Davis, Marfa, Alpine, and Shafter. In January 1892 he made the circuit of Alpine, Marfa, and Fort Davis twice within twelve days.[118] Worthy of note here is that no priest from the Texas church jurisdiction visited Presidio or the villages downriver from it after April 1890, nor the villages upriver from Presidio after June 1889. As already noted, for decades, with the brief exception of a few years under Father Hoban, the Presidio district settlements, even Shafter, continued to rely mostly on the priest at Ojinaga.[119]

When the bishop contemplated the situation in the Fort Davis district itself, now including Marfa and Alpine as well as responsibility for the

Presidio district below it, he could not have been happy that he had still not been able to establish a resident priest there since the departure of Father Montenarelli in November 1885. Yet, thanks to a succession of mostly Oblate and Jesuit priests coming from long distances, the people there had very seldom gone without seeing a priest for longer than two or three months. The longest periods of priestly absence had been during the transition from Oblate to Jesuit visitation between mid-1888 and mid-1890, when priests came only every eight or nine months.

1892: THE FORT DAVIS PARISH REESTABLISHED

Bishop Neraz finally decided that the growing Catholic population in the Trans-Pecos region could no longer be kept without resident priests. He had waited a long time, hoping somehow to obtain the Oblates for this territory. At the end of April 1892, Father Pennella returned once more to Fort Davis, but this time to orient Father John Ginier as the first resident pastor since Montenarelli. Besides Marfa and Alpine, Ginier also visited Shafter for ten days—but he was gone by early July.[120]

The bishop then turned to the only group that had been willing and able to include part of the Trans-Pecos region in its regular missionary field. He shared with a longtime Oblate friend his reluctant decision: "I have given to the Carmelites of Marienfeld the missions of Davis, Stockton and Presidio. I have waited long enough to give them to the Oblate Fathers, but seeing the continual refusal of the Superiors and the necessity of providing for these very populated missions, I have been obliged to abandon a project which I had so much at heart."[121]

On September 18 Father Albert Wagner, OCC, had visited Fort Davis, undoubtedly to check out the situation in view of the bishop's offer. Father Castelo from Ojinaga quite possibly came to meet him, since Castelo was, surprisingly, all the way up in Marfa on September 21.

Father Wagner established the second Carmelite residence in West Texas at Fort Davis on October 31. From there he and his associate, Father Brocardus Eeken, OCC (Carmelite), would care for all of the towns, villages, and ranches in the Trans-Pecos region below the upper railroad line. From Fort Davis they visited the Toyah valley regularly, Fort Stockton every two months, and the Presidio vicinity.[122] Their mission territory soon included the stations along the lower railroad line from Sanderson to Valentine: "The Missionaries travel about 900 miles while visiting these stations, 200 or 300 miles are made by train, the rest in a private conveyance over rugged roads, through swollen creeks and the burning heat of the sun.... The Catholic population is composed vastly of Mexicans and of a few American families."[123] Just recently abandoned by the military, Fort Davis and the Big Bend would have in Father "Brocardo" Eeken their most famous and long-standing Catholic circuit rider. When he began his more than forty years of ministry there, he brought to an end the twenty-year period of transient Catholic priests of the Trans-Pecos.[124]

NOTES

1. Charles Wilson Hackett, ed., *Historical Documents Relating to New Mexico, Nueva Vizcaya, and Approaches Thereto, to 1773,* 3 vols. (Washington, DC: Carnegie Institution, 1923–1937), 3:407–10.

2. Oakah L. Jones, "Settlements and Settlers at La Junta de los Ríos, 1759–1822," *Journal of Big Bend Studies* 3 (1991):52–53.

3. Carlysle Graham Raht, *The Romance of Davis Mountains and Big Bend Country,* Edition Texana (Odessa: Rahtbooks, 1963), 85; Leavitt Coming Jr., *Baronial Forts of the Big Bend: Ben Leaton, Milton Faver and Their Private Forts in Presidio County* (San Antonio: Trinity University Press, 1967), 21; Jefferson Morgenthaler, *The River Has Never Divided Us: A Border History of La Junta de los Ríos* (Austin: University of Texas Press, 2004), 27–29, 42–43.

4. Raht, *Romance of Davis Mountains,* 46, 84–85, 115, 168; Coming, *Baronial Forts,* 20–24; Ronnie C. Tyler, *The Big Bend: A History of the Last Texas Frontier* (Washington, DC: US Department of the Interior, 1975), 53, 55, 121; Morgenthaler, *The River Has Never Divided Us,* 40–48, 50.

5. Robert Wooster, *Fort Davis* (Austin: Texas State Historical Association, 1994), 4, 15, 17–21.

6. Martin Donell Kohout, "Fort Davis, Texas," *New Handbook of Texas,* ed. Ron Tyler et al. (Austin: Texas State Historical Association, 1996), 2:1097.

7. *Catholic Directory* for 1860, 124–26.

8. Morgenthaler, *The River Has Never Divided Us,* 53 and 257n18. For Gómez's ministry at Presidio del Norte, see the sacramental registers, Parroquia de Jesús Nazareno, Ojinaga.

9. George W. B. Evans, *Mexican Gold Trail, The Journal of a Forty-Niner,* ed. Glen S. Dumke (San Marino: Huntington Library, 1945), 79, cited in Morgenthaler, *The River Has Never Divided Us,* 67.

10. For the ministry of the two priests, see the sacramental records, Parroquia de Jesús Nazareno, Ojinaga. For the cholera epidemic in October 1849 (Montijo's last sacramental entries), see Morgenthaler, *The River Has Never*

Divided Us, 63–64. For Spencer, see the August 25, 1850, baptismal entry and the marriage permission by Bishop Zubiria to Father Gómez, January 14, 1851, Chihuahua, in *Libra de Defunciones 1783–1856,* Parroquia de Jesús Nazareno, Ojinaga.

11. William H. Emory, *Report on the United States and Mexican Boundary Survey* (Austin: Texas State Historical Association, 1987), vol.1, pt.1: 86.

12. Ibid., 85.

13. Sacramental registers, Parroquia de Jesús Nazareno, Ojinaga; Luis Colomo, "Inventario," December 5,1857, La Junta Church Records, box I, folder 6, Archives of the Big Bend, Sul Ross State University, Alpine.

14. Raht, *The Romance of Davis Mountains,* 162; Coming, *Baronial Forts,* 45 (Faver); Morgenthaler, *The River Has Never Divided Us,* 97.

15. Wooster, *Fort Davis,* 23; Ernest Wallace, "Fort Stockton, Texas," *New Handbook of Texas,* 2:1120 (420 civilians); Gerard Decorme, SJ (Jesuit), "Cristo en el Big Bend," pt. 2, "Especial de Fort Davis-Fort Stockton" (typescript, New Orleans Province Jesuit Archives, Loyola University, New Orleans), 16–17, 35–36; María Eva Flores, CDP, "St. Joseph's Parish, Fort Stockton, Texas, 1875–1945: The Forging of an Identity and Community," *US Catholic Historian* 21, no. 1 (Winter 2003), 13–15 (582 civilians).

16. Sister Mary Helena Finck, CCVI, *The Congregation of the Sisters of Charity of the Incarnate Word of San Antonio, Texas: A Brief Account of Its Origin and Its Work* (Washington, DC: Catholic University of America, 1925): 46–60.

17. August Santleben, *A Texas Pioneer: Early Staging and Overland Freighting Days on the Frontiers of Texas and Mexico,* ed. I. D. Affleck (New York: Neale, 1910), 121–22.

18. Jaillet was born in 1843 and ordained in France in 1866, immediately before coming to Texas and being assigned to San Diego (Sister Mary Xavier [Holworthy], IWBS, *Father Jaillet, Saddlebag Priest of the Nueces* [privately printed, 1948], 8–9, 14–40). Guichon was born in 1844 and ordained in Galveston on February 27, 1869 (*Liber Sacerdotum et Ordinationum,* 211, Houston Archdiocesan Archives); two weeks later he began assisting Jaillet in San Diego (sacramental records, St. Francis de Paula Catholic Church, San Diego). Jaillet spent most of 1870 on loan to Corpus Christi because of an accident to a priest there (sacramental records, St. Patrick Cathedral, Corpus Christi).

19. Claude Jaillet, "Historical Sketch," 7, 11–13 (quotation), Corpus Christi Diocesan Archives.

20. There are no extant sacramental records for either Fort Stockton or Fort Davis until September 1876. The last entries of the two priests at San Diego were on January 16, 1871, for Jaillet and June 12, 1871, for Guichon (sacramental

registers, St. Francis de Paula Catholic Church, San Diego). Jaillet was the only priest at Fort Stockton on July 25, 1871 (Peter Gallagher to Col. J. Y. Wade, July 25, 1871, microfilm roll 1182 #2, Letters and Telegrams Received, Fort Stockton, Texas, February 24, 1867, to December 27, 1874, National Archives, generously shared with me by Mary Williams, Fort Davis National Historic Site).

21. C. Jaillet, "Sketches of Catholicity in Texas," *Records of the American Catholic Historical Society of Philadelphia* 2 (1886–1888), 145; Jaillet, "Historical Sketch," 10–11, and additional autobiographical notes in 1922, 26, appended to the typescript of his "Historical Sketch," Corpus Christi Diocesan Archives; Antonio Severo Borrajo to Bishop of Durango, September 29, 1871, Rio Grande Historical Collections, Hobson-Huntsinger University Archives, New Mexico State University Library. The long dispute over the El Paso Valley between the diocese of Durango and church jurisdictions in the United States takes up a good amount of Paul Horgan's *Lamy of Santa Fe: His Life and Times* (New York: Farrar, Straus and Giroux, 1975).

22. Borrajo to Bishop of Durango (author's translation from the Spanish).

23. Jaillet, additional notes in 1922, 26. Guichon was still listed with Jaillet at the two forts in the national *Catholic Directory* for 1872, the first to note any priests assigned to the Trans-Pecos area (189). Since the diocesan information had to be sent months ahead of time for the directory for the coming year, these directories usually reflected the situation as known by diocesan authorities around September of the year prior to their publication. Perhaps Guichon had not arrived back in San Antonio before the report was sent in, or perhaps diocesan authorities were hoping to persuade him to return to Fort Stockton.

24. Jaillet, "Historical Sketch," 7, 10.

25. Gallagher to Wade.

26. *St. Joseph Catholic Church, Fort Stockton, Texas* (Fort Stockton: St. Joseph Catholic Church, 1975), 11.

27. Jaillet, "Historical Sketch," 10.

28. Raht, *The Romance of Davis Mountains,* 216.

29. Holworthy, *Father Jaillet, Saddlebag Priest of the Nueces,* 42–45.

30. Ibid., 49–50.

31. Jaillet, "Historical Sketch," 8–9.

32. Holworthy, *Father Jaillet, Saddlebag Priest of the Nueces,* 52–54.

33. Jaillet, additional autobiographical notes 1922, 27.

34. Jaillet, "Historical Sketch," 10.

35. Jaillet was assigned to Graytown (Elmendorf) and Las Gallinas below San Antonio in 1872 (Jaillet, "Historical Sketch," 10, 13–14). He had arrived

on the lower Medina River by July 1 (*Medina [El Carmen] Bautismos* 1:92, San Antonio Archdiocesan Archives).

36. *Catholic Directory* for 1873 (Fall 1872), 197; *Catholic Directory* for 1874 (Fall 1873), 199. Antoine was born in 1844 and ordained in November 1866 *(Liber Sacerdotum,* 199). For his previous ministry locations, see the Graytown (Elmendorf) baptismal records, November 1866–January 1867, and the *Catholic Directory* for 1870 (Fall 1869: Pleasanton).

37. Original ledger pages for the West Texas forts and towns between Fort Mason (Mason) and Fort Concho (San Angelo), sewn into Menard first sacramental register. The *Catholic Directory* listing of Antoine in Fort Stockton two years in succession, as well as the entries of travel eastward and then back westward in 1873, would seem to indicate that Pairier did indeed serve at Fort Stockton.

38. *Catholic Directory* for 1875 (Fall 1874), 198; *Catholic Directory* for 1876 (Fall 1875), 358–59. Decorme, who arrived in Fort Stockton in 1916, wrote that Pairier never kept sacramental records (*nunca llevo libro ni registro alguno*) in his frontier assignments ("Cristo en el Big Bend," 20). But Decorme cited local tradition that Pairier remained until Father Hoban (he meant Paganini) arrived in 1876 (27n1).

39. Mark Woodruff, *Sacred Heart Cathedral Parish Centennial History Project,* pt. T, ed. Larry J. Droll (San Angelo: Sacred Heart Cathedral, 1984), 5–8. Woodruff wrote that Pairier was born around 1822, ordained in 1849 in France, worked as a Marist missionary in New Zealand, and probably came to Texas around 1869. He was a pioneer priest in the Fort Worth-Dallas area before going to West Texas. It may have been on his initial trip out to the Trans-Pecos region that Father Pairier was present for the granting of the deed to the Catholic church of a block of land in the incipient San Angelo, next to Fort Concho, on September 22, 1874.

40. P. F. Parisot and C. J. Smith, OMI, comp., *History of the Catholic Church in the Diocese of San Antonio, Texas* (San Antonio: Carrico and Bowen, 1897), 199.

41. *Catholic Directory* for 1876 (Fall 1875), 358–59.

42. James Talmadge Moore, *Through Fire and Flood: The Catholic Church in Frontier Texas, 1836–1900* (College Station: Texas A&M University Press, 1992), 174, citing the bishop's 1875 *Pastoral Letter;* Assistant Adjutant General, San Antonio, to Commanding Officer, Fort Concho, May 21, 1875, National Archives Microfilm Publication MI114, Department of Texas, Letters Sent by Headquarters, Roll 2, January 2, 1873–December 31, 1875 (vols. 4, 5), 887, #548, photocopy generously shared by Mary Williams, Fort Davis National Historic Site.

43. The *Catholic Directory* for 1877 (Fall 1876), 355–56, still listed Pairier at

Fort Stockton, with Mason still being attended from Fredericksburg. Pairier was sent to establish Mason as the first parish with a resident priest between Fredericksburg and Fort Stockton. His missionary territory in Mason included Fort Concho at San Angelo (*Catholic Directory* for 1878 [Fall 1877], 365; *Acta* [Journal 186], of Bishop Neraz's administration, 3, Catholic Archives of San Antonio [cited hereafter as CASAD]). In 1884 Pairier became the first resident pastor of San Angelo; he died in San Antonio in late 1888 (Woodruff, *Sacred Heart Cathedral Parish,* 7–8).

44. Loose leaves inserted in Baptism Register 1, St. Joseph Parish, Fort Stockton. Mary Williams, Fort Davis National Historic Site, informed me of a waybill of the Texas and California Stage Company for September 27, 1876, from Concho to Davis. The waybill listed under Freight "1 package from consignee Rev. Pagarrine" and identified its source and destination: "where from: San Antonio, where to: Stockton" (negative, Fort Davis National Historic Site).

45. October 29, 1876, marriage by Ferra and November 4, 1876, baptism by Hoban, leaf inserted in Baptism Register 1, St. Joseph Parish, Fort Stockton.

46. Ferra was ordained in March 1871 by Bishop Dubuis, and Hoban, on October 17, 1876, by Bishop Pellicer (*Acta* [Journal 186], 2). While still a seminarian, Ferra spent a few weeks in the late summer of 1870 with Father Jaillet in Corpus Christi, where Ferra served as a *padrino* at several baptisms. After he was ordained, Ferra succeeded Guichon in San Diego when the latter left for Fort Stockton, but he was there only until November 1871. He then served in the San Patricio district near Corpus Christi for a year, and then in Corpus Christi itself until January 1874 (sacramental records, St. Patrick Cathedral, Corpus Christi; St. Francis de Paula Catholic Church, San Diego; San Patricio registers at Sacred Heart Catholic Church, Mathis). After that he was in Indianola (*Catholic Directory* for 1875 [Fall 1874], 198) and at San Fernando, the Spanish-speaking parish in San Antonio (*Catholic Directory* for 1876 [Fall 1875], 357 and *Catholic Directory* for 1877 [Fall 1876], 355).

47. Nathaniel Alston Taylor, *The Coming Empire; or, Two Thousand Miles in Texas on Horseback,* rev. ed. (Houston: N. T. Carlisle, 1936), 306–7, 355.

48. Baptism Register 1, St. Joseph Parish, Fort Stockton, and Book 2-A, St. Joseph Parish, Fort Davis. This Book 2-A now at Fort Davis is actually the first marriage register for Fort Stockton.

49. Baptism Register 1, St. Joseph Parish, Fort Stockton; Book 1, St. Joseph Parish, Fort Davis (records of the Rio Grande and Fort Davis baptisms and marriages); *Catholic Directory* for 1878 (Fall 1877), 364–66. For the location of the ranches along the Chihuahua Trail between Fort Stockton and Presidio, see Santleben, 102n17.

50. For the construction in April and May, see Ferra's financial records in Book 2-A, St. Joseph Parish, Fort Davis, 238–39, 254–56. For the rest, see Decorme, "Cristo en el Big Bend," 30–31, citing a document found in the cornerstone, a March 1877 article in the *Freeman's Journal* (also in the 1877 *Missions Catholiques*), and local oral history. For the fort construction material, see Wallace (n15 above), "Fort Stockton," 1119.

51. Sacramental Registers, St. Joseph Parish, Fort Stockton, and St. Joseph Parish, Fort Davis. Thus Parisot and Smith (see n40 above), 201, credit Father Hoban with the completion of the church at Fort Stockton. The *Catholic Directory* for 1880 (Fall 1879) still listed Fort Stockton, not Fort Davis, as the residence of Father Hoban (375–76). He was finally listed at Fort Davis beginning with the directory for 1881 (Fall 1880), when a different priest was assigned to Fort Stockton (*Catholic Directory* for 1881, 409; *Catholic Directory* for 1882, 430).

52. Parisot and Smith, *History of the Catholic Church*, 201, reported that an adobe chapel and a small dwelling were built in 1878. The more probable year is 1879: Mary L. Williams, "Fort Davis's St. Joseph Catholic Church and the People of the Trans-Pecos and Big Bend," presented at the annual meeting of the Center for Big Bend Studies, Sul Ross State University, Alpine, November 2002, 6.

53. Sacramental registers, St. Joseph Parish, Fort Stockton, and St. Joseph Parish, Fort Davis. Decorme, "Cristo en el Big Bend," 31, credited a Mr. Corbett, a Catholic layman from Fort Stockton, with bringing Father Mas.

54. Wooster (n15 above), *Fort Davis*, 39–40.

55. George C. Werner, "Texas and Pacific Railway," *New Handbook of Texas*, 6: 385.

56. Tyler, 120; George C. Werner, "Galveston, Harrisburg and San Antonio Railway," *New Handbook of Texas*, 3:61.

57. Ernest Wallace, "Fort Stockton," *New Handbook of Texas*, 2:1119, 1120; Wooster, *Fort Davis*, 24, 44–46.

58. Sacramental registers of St. Joseph Parish, Fort Stockton; St. Joseph Parish, Fort Davis; and Parroquia de Jesús Nazareno, Ojinaga. *Acta* (Journal 186), 2, noted that Ballay had been ordained in April 1877 by Bishop Pellicer. He was listed previously as serving at Victoria (*Catholic Directory* for 1878 [Fall 1877], 366), and then at the mostly Mexican-American Graytown and its missions from November 1878 through early April 1880 (Graytown sacramental records at St. Anthony Catholic Church, Elmendorf).

59. Sacramental registers, Parroquia de Jesús Nazareno, Ojinaga.

60. For the Presidio church, see Parisot and Smith, *History of the Catholic Church*, 201. For Ojinaga, see Father Malmartel to Father Martinet, May 24, 1887, Eagle Pass, General Administration Correspondence transcripts, South-

west Oblate Historical Archives (cited hereafter as SWOHA), Oblate School of Theology, San Antonio.

61. Sacramental registers, St. Joseph Parish, Fort Stockton.

62. Ibid; sacramental registers, St. Joseph Parish, Fort Davis (a Fort Stockton baptism by Hoban in May 1883 entered later by someone else [Book 1, 90]); sacramental registers, Parroquia de Jesús Nazareno, Ojinaga; and the new register started for the Presidio, Texas, district in December 1882, now archived as Book 2 at the Fort Davis parish. For Fort Stockton as a missionary station of Fort Davis, see the *Catholic Directory* for 1885 (Fall 1884), 296.

63. Sacramental registers, Parroquia de Jesús Nazareno, Ojinaga.

64. Sister M. Lilliana Owens, SL, *Reverend Carlos M. Pinto, SJ (Jesuit), Apostle of El Paso, 1892–1919* (El Paso: Revista Católica Press, 1951), 35–36, 55; sacramental registers at Fort Davis and Fort Stockton.

65. Sacramental registers at Fort Davis.

66. Heyburn file, CASA; *Acta* (Journal 186), 2, CASA.

67. Father Hoban had been listed as still assigned to Fort Davis in the *Catholic Directory* for 1885 (Fall 1884), 295–96. Plans must have changed soon after that listing. In 1885 he left the San Antonio diocese *(Acta* [Journal 186], 2), but he later returned to serve at other West Texas places like Mason-Brady-Menard (sacramental registers), Stanton, and San Angelo in the first decade of the 1900s (Woodruff, *Sacred Heart Cathedral Parish,* 12). Decorme ("Cristo en el Big Bend," 36), had a negative assessment of Hoban, probably highly influenced by the latter's lack of attention to Decorme's beloved Fort Stockton after 1882: "It seems that his administration was pretty disordered and not punctual (especially in the most important place, Fort Stockton) and his conduct not satisfactory. In that year of 1888 [sic] he resigned/abandoned his position and went to California. The last notice we have of him was as an apothecary in Cusihuiriachi, Chihuahua" (author's translation from the Spanish). After 1882, Fort Stockton was in steep decline compared to Fort Davis, definitely not "the most important place" as it was in the time of Decorme.

68. Sacramental registers at Fort Davis and Fort Stockton.

69. Parisot and Smith, *History of the Catholic Church,* 201.

70. Bishop Neraz to Father Martinet, 16 October 1887, Brownsville (passage cited later in this essay), General Administration Correspondence transcripts, SWOHA.

71. Sacramental registers at Fort Davis and Fort Stockton; see in particular Book 1, St. Joseph Parish, Fort Davis, 146, for the record of the bishop's confirmation tour. See Decorme, "Cristo en el Big Bend," 37 for the comment about the condition of the church at Fort Stockton.

72. Bernard Doyon, OMI, *The Cavalry of Christ on the Rio Grande, 1849–1883* (Milwaukee: Bruce, 1956), 34n9, 232; Neraz to McGrath, March 1, 1884, "Neraz, John C. (Bishop) 1884–1885" file, and McGrath to Neraz, April 2, 1884, "Oblates of Mary Immaculate" file, CASA.

73. Neraz to Oblate Superior General, October 30, 1885, General Administration Correspondence transcripts, SWOHA (author's translation from the French).

74. *Archdiocese of San Antonio, 1874–1974* (San Antonio: Archdiocese of San Antonio, 1974), 18.

75. Neraz to Martinet, October 16, 1887, General Administration Correspondence, SWOHA. In this letter (quoted later in this chapter) Bishop Neraz appears to be saying that the Jesuits continued to provide a priest for the region until 1887, which was not the case.

76. Sacramental registers, St. Joseph Parish, Fort Davis.

77. Julia Cauble Smith, "Pecos, Texas," *New Handbook of Texas*, 5:119.

78. John Benedict Weber, O. Carm., "The Carmelites of Marienfeld and the Missions of West Texas, 1882–1901," *Journal of Texas Catholic History and Culture* 6 (1996): 47–53. The first entries for Toyah in the sacramental registers at St. Joseph Church, Stanton, are a marriage on September 18, 1884 [sic] and a baptism on September 18, 1885. Parisot and Smith (206) dated the first visit in 1885 and reported the building of the church there in 1890.

79. Sacramental registers at Fort Davis and Fort Stockton.

80. The account of this extended missionary visit is taken unless otherwise indicated from Father Malmartel to Father Martinet, May 24, 1887, Eagle Pass (transcription of the original document in General Administration Correspondence, SWOHA).

81. Parisot and Smith, *History of the Catholic Church*, 161.

82. The station was Haymond, a section stop which no longer exists, about twenty miles east of Sanderson; it was there that the stagecoach from Fort Stockton met the train. I owe this information to a conversation on April 11, 2003, with J. Travis Roberts Jr., of the Brewster County Historical Commission. Haymond was listed among the places visited by the priests at Fort Davis in the 1890s (Parisot and Smith, *History of the Catholic Church*, 201).

83. This was probably Mr. Rooney, on whose ranch the bishop had held confirmations for the Fort Stockton vicinity the previous year (Decorme, "Cristo en el Big Bend," 37).

84. The Frenchman was probably Martin Peña, who had arrived in the Fort Stockton area in 1880, and became more identified with the "Mexican" people than the "American" ones (Flores, 15n7). Malmartel said he was fifty-six years old, "not too tall, solidly built," and had arrived in Mexico at the age of

eighteen. This was his second marriage, and his wife's third; her first husband was a Mexican, and upon his death she had married an Irishman who was subsequently assassinated. Malmartel called her "a real Diana," who could "see very far and shoot very accurately." The couple lived at the first ranch at which the missionaries had preached.

85. Father Malmartel to Father Martinet, May 24, 1887.

86. Ibid.

87. The remark about "our invading masters, the men of the future" is found only in the version of Malmartel's report published in *Missions de la Congrégation des Missionnaires Oblats de Marie-Immaculée* 26 (1888), 190. Wooster, *Fort Davis*, 24, notes the class and racial stratification of the settlement.

88. Barry Scobee, *Old Fort Davis* (San Antonio: Naylor, 1947), 81.

89. For the health problems at this time and their cause, see Wooster, *Fort Davis*, 44.

90. Father Malmartel to Father Martinet, May 24, 1887.

91. Ibid.

92. Bishop Neraz to Father Malmartel, October 8, 1886, San Antonio, General Administration Correspondence, SWOHA. Dowling recorded baptisms in the Fort Davis register for July 30–August 5 and August 21; he also was said to have officiated at a marriage, without recording it in the local registers, in a ranch upriver from Presidio (Book 2, St. Joseph Parish, Fort Davis, 169).

93. In his 1857 inventory of the church's possessions, Father Colomo described the two bells as *"chicas"* (small) (Colomo, "Inventario," n13 above).

94. For the small Mexican fort, see Morgenthaler, *The River Has Never Divided Us*, 29.

95. This was most probably the "Palor" chapel noted in Parisot and Smith, *History of the Catholic Church*, 201.

96. Father Malmartel to Father Martinet, May 24, 1887.

97. This was probably John Spencer: see Morgenthaler, *The River Has Never Divided Us*, 50, who states, however, that Indio was midway between Presidio and today's Ruidosa.

98. Malmartel wrote that Faver had become a Catholic in Mexico thirty-six years previously in order to get married.

99. Father Malmartel to Father Martinet, May 24, 1887.

100. Parisot and Smith, *History of the Catholic Church*, 161.

101. When the Carmelites assumed the care of the Trans-Pecos region in 1892, they noted in the Fort Davis and Presidio, Texas, registers (Books 1 and 2, St. Joseph Parish, Fort Davis) many, undoubtedly not all, of the baptisms of residents of the Presidio district conducted by Castelo from December 1885

through February 1888, and again from September 1891 through November 1892. Those records clearly indicate four visits of Father Castelo to Shafter in 1892 alone.

102. Sacramental registers, St. Joseph Parish, Stanton; Weber, 53–54. Weber dates the first visit to Pecos in 1888, but the first entries for Pecos in the Stanton sacramental registers are in 1890. Notice of a Carmelite merely passing through Pecos in 1885 is reported in Franz B. Lickteig, O., Carm., "Commissariate of the South," *Sword* 25, no. 3 (October 1965): 13. Parisot and Smith reported that St. Catherine's Church was built in Pecos in 1893, and that the town had been visited since 1895—a typographical error (206).

103. Sacramental registers at Fort Stockton and Fort Davis.

104. Bishop Neraz to Father Martinet, October 16, 1887, Brownsville, General Administration Correspondence, SWOHA (author's translation from the French).

105. Father J. M. Clos to Father Martinet, October 17, 1887, Brownsville, General Administration Correspondence transcripts, SWOHA.

106. Father Martinet to Bishop Neraz, January 10, 1888, Paris, General Administration Correspondence transcripts, SWOHA.

107. Father Martinet to Father Clos, February 9, 1888, Paris, General Administration Correspondence transcripts, SWOHA (author's translation).

108. *St. Joseph Catholic Church,* 17, mistakenly interpreted the periodic entries of visiting Oblates as meaning that they officially accepted the care of the Fort Stockton-Fort Davis-Presidio triangle, and even assumed that they assigned resident priests there from 1887 to 1889.

109. Sacramental registers at Fort Stockton and Fort Davis.

110. Sacramental registers, St. Joseph Parish, Stanton.

111. Ibid., Fort Davis.

112. Parisot and Smith, *History of the Catholic Church,* 152; J. McGrath, OMI, to Father Malmartel, OMI, November 15, 1887, General Administration Correspondence, SWOHA.

113. Sacramental registers at Fort Stockton and Fort Davis. In January 1889 a Father Charles Berwingalle spent a single week in the area. The baptisms and marriages he conducted are entered in the Fort Stockton registers (Baptism Register 1, St. Joseph Parish, Fort Stockton, and Book 2-A, St. Joseph Parish, Fort Davis), but the three marriages, all in the first days, are of residents of Fort Davis. The author has been unable so far to ascertain who Berwingalle was; his name does not appear in either the Oblate or San Antonio Diocese records.

114. Sacramental registers, St. Joseph Parish, Stanton.

115. Baptism Register 1, St. Joseph Parish, Fort Stockton; Book 2-A, St. Joseph Parish, Fort Davis (Fort Stockton marriages), 45–46.

116. Sacramental registers, St. Joseph Parish, Fort Davis. For the Oblate Brule at Eagle Pass-Del Rio, see John Jos. Gorrell, "The Catholic Church in Eagle Pass," *Mary Immaculate* 17, no. 6 (June 1934): 168.

117. Sacramental registers, St. Joseph Parish, Stanton; Weber, "The Carmelites of Marienfeld," 53–59. The Carmelites continued to enter all the baptisms and marriages in their expanding mission territory, including those of Fort Stockton, in their registers at Stanton. The original Fort Stockton registers were probably kept at Fort Davis by this time.

118. Sacramental registers at Fort Davis. There was also a Father Thomas Sheehy (provenance unknown) who passed through Fort Davis at the end of April 1891. For the Jesuits Di Palma, Bueno, Ferrari, and Pennella in the El Paso district, see Owens (n64 above), 39–48.

119. Decorme, "Cristo en el Big Bend," 38.

120. Sacramental registers, St. Joseph Parish, Fort Davis. The priest's signature is not totally clear; it appears to be "Jh. Ginie[r?]."

121. Bishop Neraz to Father Clos, December 12, 1892, San Antonio, General Administration Correspondence transcripts, SWOHA (author's translation).

122. Sacramental registers at Fort Davis; Weber, "The Carmelites of Marienfeld," 57; Lickteig, "Commissariate of the South," *Sword* 26, no. 3 (October 1966): 39–59; W. D. Smithers, *Circuit Riders of the Big Bend,* Southwestern Studies Monograph 64 (El Paso: Texas Western Press, 1981), 11–16.

123. Parisot and Smith, *History of the Catholic Church,* 201; Smithers, *Circuit Riders of the Big Bend,* 11. There were, of course, Protestant military chaplains, but their ministry did not extend beyond the immediate vicinity of the forts. For the earliest notice of a chaplain that I have encountered, see Lawrence L. Brown, *The Episcopal Church in Texas, 1838–1874: From Its Foundation to the Division of the Diocese* (Austin: Church Historical Society, 1963), 158 (D. Eglinton Barr at Fort Davis, 1872–73).

124. Smithers, *Circuit Riders of the Big Bend,* 11–16.

13 *William Rufus Shafter with the Frontier Army in the Big Bend*

Paul H. Carlson

William R. Shafter, who in 1898 led the American expeditionary force to Cuba in the Spanish-American War, served for nearly seventeen years on the Texas frontier. A lieutenant colonel of the black 24th Infantry, he was a bulky, lumbering, overweight man, but considered the most energetic man of his rank on the Texas frontier. Although Shafter was coarse and abrasive, his record in Texas, including the Big Bend country, reveals courage, zeal, and intelligence. His official explorations produced some of the most thorough early reports on the Big Bend available to the army and to settlers entering the region.[1]

A veteran of the Civil War from Michigan, Shafter served three tours of duty in the Big Bend. He was at Fort Davis with black troops of the 24th Infantry in 1871–72, he assisted briefly in the Victorio campaign in 1880, and upon promotion to colonel he led soldiers of the 1st Infantry at Fort Davis in 1881–82. His hitches in the Big Bend were among the most significant of his long military career.

While at Fort Davis, Shafter kept the post in top shape. The post medical officer reported in October 1881 that "the general police of the grounds, barracks, hospital, guardhouse, kitchen, [and] mess-rooms . . . have been very well performed." The water supply, obtained from a well about a mile away along Limpia Creek, was good, and ample for ordinary purposes. "The quality of rations," the surgeon indicated, "has been very good, the mode of cooking and serving very satisfactory." The general health of the men and officers was excellent.[2]

Shafter also drove his men hard. During his first stint at Fort Davis, May 1871 to June 1872, Shafter led his command in pursuit of Indians through the Sand Hills near present Monahans. It was a grueling expedition of over four hundred miles that has been chronicled by J. Evetts Haley in *Fort Concho and the Texas Frontier*. The expedition was a success. On the march Shafter and his black troops discovered and destroyed an abandoned Indian camp, two dozen robes, many skins, and a large supply of provisions. They captured about twenty horses and mules and an old Indian woman, who informed Shafter that Comanches and Apaches, longtime enemies, had concluded a peace in the Sand Hills. Lead he had found at the Indian camp, stamped with the trademark of a Saint Louis, Missouri, firm, provided important evidence that the Sand Hills was a place of barter for the Comancheros, traders from New Mexico. Of far more significance, the long-range results of the march lay in the successful penetration of the Sand Hills, where it had been generally believed that soldiers could not operate. The expedition not only destroyed an Indian sanctuary, but also brought back geographical knowledge necessary for future operations.[3]

Shafter believed that extensive scouting, such as in the Sand Hills, even though no major engagements with the Indians were fought, produced valuable results. "My experience has been that Indians will not stay where they consider themselves liable to attacks," he informed his superiors, "and I believe the best way to rid the country of them . . . is to thoroughly scour the country with cavalry."[4] Because his scout through the Sand Hills seemed to support his thesis, he determined to apply the technique to the Big Bend, where, it had been reported, Apaches were camping.

Accordingly, in October 1871, leading about seventy men and officers, Shafter rode southeastward to the Chisos Mountains and beyond to the Rio Grande. He struck the river below San Vicente, an old village on the Mexican side above the Great Bend. Here, near the lower end of Mariscal Canyon, he reported that because the banks were several hundred feet high, it was impossible to get down to the river with animals. Shafter and five others, however, by climbing down a ravine that ran to it, succeeded with difficulty in getting to the stream.

Because signs indicated that Indians were almost constantly in the Big Bend, Shafter and the black troops thoroughly laced the country, crossing and recrossing trails, noting important water holes, and marking the sites of old Indian camps. At San Vicente they discovered an important Apache crossing on the river. They reported abandoned Indian encampments at several locations. The grass along their line of march was excellent, but the only wood they found was a few large cottonwood trees along the streams. Where they struck the Rio Grande, there was no timber.[5]

When it returned to Fort Davis a month after departing, the expedition had covered nearly five hundred miles. Although it had seen no Indians, it found abundant evidence that Apaches used the Big Bend as a sanctuary. Perhaps more importantly, the expedition added considerably to the geographical knowledge of the Chihuahuan desert and Big Bend mountains. Indeed, the information it gained about the territory and its resources later enabled the army to maneuver more confidently in the region.[6]

No sooner had Shafter returned to Fort Davis than an Apache chief sent word that he wished to surrender. The chief, who frequented the Big Bend, had gone to Presidio del Norte to negotiate with Mexican authorities for release of some children of his band. Shafter sent Lt. Isaiah McDonald to receive the surrender. But perhaps because the Mexican residents there did not welcome complete harmony between Indians and Americans, the alcalde warned the chief that his departure to Texas would prejudice release of the children. Whatever the reason, McDonald returned to Fort Davis empty-handed. Shafter agreed with his lieutenant that "the local authorities at Del Norte do not want [the Apaches] to make or keep peace with the United States," for they gained their living largely by supplying United States army posts.[7]

Early in 1872 Shafter laid plans to continue his scouting of isolated Big Bend areas. He intended to spend a month searching the Guadalupe Mountains and another two months exploring the long stretch of broken country along the Rio Grande west of the Pecos. Through March and April, a number of small detachments and scouts combed the region southwest of the Llano Estacado, but Shafter received orders transferring him out of the Big Bend before he could lead the two extended expeditions.[8]

Meanwhile, however, Shafter had moved twice to protect his black troops from civilian authorities. The first incident was largely a routine one. One of the responsibilities his men handled in the Big Bend was guarding stagecoach lines. Duty as station guards was generally quiet work, but appreciated by the troopers because it afforded an escape from the tedium of garrison life. At the end of such a tour of duty, the men usually returned to the post on an inbound stage. Unfortunately, Shafter's black troops sometimes suffered by being kept off the stages and forced to walk back to the post. When the El Paso Mail Lines station keeper at Leon Hole, about eight miles west of Fort Stockton, refused to provide food and shelter for the station guards, Shafter warned the stage company officers against such discrimination. When the black guards were put off the stage, he wrote, they were obliged to walk to Fort Stockton and along the way to obtain their rations "by their wits." He demanded that his troops should "be fed by the company or allowed facilities at the stations for cooking their own rations." He would "be glad to furnish mail escorts as long as they are wanted," he concluded, "but they must be properly treated." Apparently his letter got results, for the records show no further complaints against the stage company.[9]

The second incident was more explosive. It involved Henry Tinkhouse, sheriff of Presidio County. The Tinkhouse affair grew out of Shafter's garrison rules. To retain a high level of morale in his commands and to encourage temperance, Shafter limited the amount of liquor post traders and sutlers could sell to enlisted men. His favorite method of restriction at Fort Davis required that noncommissioned officers and privates who wanted whiskey must get an order from their captain for the purchase of a pint, and it was to be bought in the sutler's store. Because of the rules, his men often left the post to obtain alcohol. The drunkenness that sometimes followed exposed them to mountebanks, scoundrels, and others who found a queer joy in molesting the regulars. When soldiers resisted the harassment, trouble developed.

In November 1871, after one such incident near Fort Davis, Shafter intervened. Sheriff Tinkhouse attempted to enforce a civil process for public drunkenness on one of Shafter's troopers, who had struck a civilian. Because Tinkhouse did not consult him before entering the military post, Shafter refused to allow the sheriff to perform his business, thus saving the soldier from arrest.

By interfering in this way, however, Shafter touched off the problem. He and Tinkhouse got into a bitter verbal exchange over who in this affair possessed the higher authority. The argument concluded only when Shafter had the sheriff thrown off the reservation. Tinkhouse, after he had been removed, swore that he would kill Shafter the next time they met. To protect himself and his soldiers, Shafter ordered that Tinkhouse not be allowed on the post again. On the same day he wrote to S. R. Miller, Justice of the Peace for Presidio County, stating that, although he was required upon proper demand to deliver to civil authorities any person in his command charged with a crime, Miller in this instance would have to send another constable.[10]

Shafter's second hitch in the Big Bend, August to November 1880, was no less eventful. Having been promoted to colonel, Shafter with his 1st Infantry was assigned duty in the Big Bend in late stages of the Victorio campaign. His men guarded lonely and isolated waterholes and mountain passes through the vast and empty region.[11]

Although neither he nor his troops engaged in military action against Victorio's Apaches, Shafter became involved in a complicated investment in a silver mine. John W. Spencer, a freighter and part-time prospector who had come to the Big Bend as a trader and merchant during the Mexican War, found some silver in the Chinati Mountains. In August 1880 he showed samples of the ore to Shafter, who at the time was in camp near the modern-day town of Shafter. The samples when assayed showed a small but profitable deposit of silver. Shafter, interested in securing title to as much land as possible near Spencer's discovery, encouraged Lts. Louis Wilhelmi and John L. Bullis to join him in purchasing several sections of land. They agreed that all land should be held in common and that Spencer should be taken in as a partner. They also agreed to split ownership and any profits from the land four ways—one-quarter each.

In October, accordingly, the partners applied for the right to purchase nine sections of school land in the area of Spencer's discovery, and a few months later, in January 1881, Bullis and Wilhelmi purchased four of the nine sections for which the partners had applied. Lacking the financial resources and technical skills to operate a mine, and no longer being in the Big Bend, in June 1882 the partners leased some of the property for twelve months to Daniel Cook, a San Francisco mining speculator, who sent his agents to the Big Bend. When just over a year later the agents discovered silver deposits valued at $45 per ton, Cook organized the Presidio Mining Company and started production at the mines.

Because the lease had expired, the Presidio Mining Company offered to buy the land. The company offered five thousand shares of company stock and $1,600 to each of the partners. By the end of the year, it had secured the interests of Shafter, Wilhelmi, and Spencer.[12]

Bullis held out. He refused to accept the money and company stock that awaited him at a bank in San Antonio if he would sell. In fact, this colorful leader of the Black Seminole Scouts, and Shafter's good friend, secured a court injunction to stop the mining operations and eventually brought legal action against the Presidio Mining Company.[13]

The case *Presidio Mining Co. v. Alice Bullis*, heard before a Presidio County jury at Marfa, was based largely on Bullis's argument that the two sections he had bought in January 1881, where major mining operations were under way, had been bought for his wife and never formed part of the group's community property. Therefore it was his wife's land, and the company did not have her permission to operate a mine or buy the land. The mining company denied the Bullises' assumption, saying that all lands were held in "community" by the partners. The court decided in favor of the Bullises. The company thereupon appealed the case to the Texas Supreme Court, and in 1887 the Texas high court reversed the lower court's decision, reasoning that there was no proof that Bullis had purchased the land exclusively for his wife. Thus the land in question was community property of the partners.[14]

The Presidio Mining Company prospered. It produced silver from the Big Bend until the mines were closed in 1942, when the price of silver dropped below the cost of production at its operations. The village of Shafter, Texas, grew up near the mines. Although at one time it could boast of its four thousand inhabitants, the place today is nearly a ghost town. Profits from the mining scheme made Shafter a rich man, but the court case haunted him in the 1890s when he applied for promotion to brigadier general. Moreover, he lost the friendship of Bullis, who for several years had been one of Shafter's closest military aides.[15]

Shafter's final hitch in the Big Bend, from February 1881 to April 1882, proved to be far less active, but no less significant. As Indian problems declined, Shafter saw his men settle into the monotonous routine of garrison life. As they did so, he took steps to complete construction of Fort Davis, by now a major army installation with headquarters for twelve companies. It consisted of nearly fifty buildings and several long rows of stables for horses and mules. Shafter supervised many of the fatigue duties at the post. He directed the construction of the post stables, and, when new privies were needed, he personally planned the necessary changes. Thus, by close observation of even undistinguished activities, he maintained a tight control over Fort Davis.

Out of such close supervision came an episode related by Barry Scobee in his book *Old Fort Davis*. According to Scobee, one evening in 1881 while Shafter was sitting on the porch of his home at Fort Davis, a soldier walked across the parade ground from the enlisted men's barracks holding a tin plate with a scanty supply of meat and vegetables on it. The trooper saluted. Then, trembling with anger and indignation, he displayed the food.

"Sir," he complained to Shafter, "this is my dinner!"

Shafter leaned forward in his easy chair, took a long look at the rather meager contents of the plate, and said, "Well, eat it, then; I have had mine."

Without a word the soldier saluted and returned to the barracks, presumably cursing Shafter as well as the food.

Shafter quickly took action. After the trooper had left, he sent for the captain of the company responsible for the meager rations. "Sir," Shafter demanded of the captain, "how much money have you in your mess fund?"

The captain, proud that he had been able to cut food expenses, replied, "Eighteen hundred dollars, Colonel."

"Well sir," returned Shafter, "change the eighteen hundred dollars into provisions for your company and do it damn quick."[16]

The complaining soldier never knew that Shafter had immediately taken steps to improve the food and possibly for years afterward denounced his colonel. Shafter, as long as the rations were adequate, was unconcerned whether or not his soldiers knew why the food suddenly and unexpectedly improved.[17]

Of far greater importance was the Flipper affair. When Shafter arrived at Fort Davis in February 1881, one of his first official duties was to remove Henry O. Flipper, 10th Cavalry, the first black graduate of West Point, as acting assistant quartermaster and to inform the young lieutenant that as soon as a suitable replacement could be found, he would also be removed as acting commissary of subsistence. As was army custom, Shafter apparently wanted men of his own regiment in the positions. Flipper, however, believed that his new commander removed him for personal (perhaps racial) reasons. He became alarmed at the sudden change in command, and when his friends cautioned him to beware of the colonel, he made a sincere effort to avoid trouble, stay clear of Shafter, and get along with his fellow officers.[18]

But getting along with his fellow officers proved to be impossible. One officer with whom he clashed was Lt. Louis Wilhelmi, a close friend of Shafter's, who had been at West Point briefly with Flipper. Wilhelmi had failed at West Point for medical reasons and apparently resented the presence of the successful black man. Another officer with whom Flipper had trouble was Lt. Charles E. Nordstrom, 10th Cavalry. At Fort Davis Flipper had a riding companion in Millie Dwyer, a friend whose companionship he jealously guarded. When Nordstrom arrived at Fort Davis, the relationship began to change as Miss Dwyer, a young white woman, increasingly found less time to go riding with Flipper but more time to spend with Nordstrom.

When Nordstrom and Flipper were forced "to share the same set of double quarters" with "a common hall," the situation became troublesome. Flipper resented the tall Swede and dubbed him a "brute" and a "hyena."[19] Ordinarily the nettled officer would have had periodic field assignments during which he might have decompressed, but his duties at the post kept him at Fort Davis each time his Company A left for service in the field—perhaps Shafter saw to that.

Removed from a position of responsibility, harassed by the man with whom he shared quarters, and resentful of having lost his riding companion, Flipper concluded that he was the subject of a nefarious plot to ruin his military career. Years later he recalled that Shafter, Nordstrom, and Wilhelmi deliberately went out of their way to "persecute" and "lay traps" for him. The "traps," he wrote, were "cunningly laid and [although] never did a man walk the path of uprightness straighter than I did . . . I was sacrificed."[20] He may have been set up.

But there is little evidence of a plot. Granted that Nordstrom and Wilhelmi hated the black officer and that Shafter, as historian Robert M. Utley has said, was "afflicted with barely concealed racism," it was Flipper's handling of the post commissary funds that prompted his arrest and eventual dismissal from the service. He carelessly ignored Shafter's advice to transfer all commissary funds to the San Antonio National Bank and kept them in his private quarters. He incorrectly assumed that a directive ordering the cessation of cash transmittals to San Antonio temporarily applied to all commissary funds and thus stopped forwarding weekly statements. In fact, Flipper did not resume the transfer of any funds until Shafter in July finally ordered him to send all commissary funds to department headquarters.[21]

Next, when he discovered a deficiency in the funds, Flipper reasoned that he could submit a check for the amount of the deficit and then deposit personal funds in the San Antonio bank to cover it. However, he was unable to raise the required cash—about $1,400—and rather than admit that money was missing and that he had written a bad check to cover it, he procrastinated and resorted to duplicity. He made illegal entries in the weekly accounts and reported the funds "in transit," evidently hoping that Shafter would cast no more than a cursory glance at the invoices submitted for his signature. The stratagem succeeded. Shafter, not suspecting his junior officer of any wrongdoing, remained ignorant of Flipper's situation until August, when Major M. P. Small of department headquarters informed him that no funds had arrived in San Antonio.[22]

Then Shafter launched a revealing investigation. More than $2,000 in commissary checks was found scattered on Flipper's desk. Weekly statements of funds for May, June, and July were uncovered in a trunk in his personal quarters. When clothes belonging to a servant were found in his quarters, she was called and searched. Some $2,800 in checks was removed from her person. Arrested and temporarily confined to the guardhouse, Flipper admitted the worthlessness of the check he had written to cover the deficit in commissary funds and that he had lied to Shafter. Altogether, nearly $3,800 was missing.

Arraigned on charges of embezzlement and conduct unbecoming an officer and gentleman, Flipper was tried before a general court-martial at Fort Davis. Despite circumstantial evidence to the contrary, most people, including Shafter, believed the lieutenant to be innocent. Disorder over commissary funds was not unusual in the frontier army. Flipper, evidently believing he was the victim of a vicious plot concocted by Nordstrom, Wilhelmi, and Shafter, pleaded not guilty to all the charges and specifications. In the trial that followed, he was acquitted of embezzlement, but rightfully found guilty of conduct unbecoming an officer and gentleman. In the spring he was sentenced to be dismissed from the army, a sentence far too harsh for the crime of which he was found guilty. He may have been guilty of a serious breach of military honor in lying to a superior officer, but he was not guilty of stealing commissary funds. Lucy Smith, the servant who was found with the $2,800 in checks, probably was the thief.[23]

As commanding officer at Fort Davis, Shafter played a key role in the Flipper affair. Neither the records in Shafter's personal file at the adjutant general's office nor those in the several collections of Shafter's papers even hint that he conspired with either Wilhelmi or Nordstrom. Moreover, participation in such a scheme would not be characteristic of Shafter. Although he was a martinet who sometimes badgered subordinate officers, he was not a malicious commander. On the contrary, he was an honest, thoroughly professional soldier, committed by the very nature of his calling to an aggressive attitude toward what he regarded as incompetency on the part of his officers and men.

Nonetheless, Shafter throughout his career remained one of the army's most maligned field commanders. Uninformed citizens, arrogant newspaper correspondents, malcontent men of his command, and his fellow officers, most of whom, perhaps, believed that at one time or another he had treated them in what they regarded as a cavalier manner, assassinated his character and reputation. Although the fact that he seldom cared for what Americans have come to call interpersonal relations helps to explain some of his trouble, the truth is that many who believed they knew Shafter well never penetrated past the gruff, and even grim, front he presented to soldiers and civilians alike.

Clearly, as a commander of the frontier army in the Big Bend, Shafter was tough and aggressive. Outspoken and contentious by nature, he found it difficult, at best, to be diplomatic. Although he could on occasion charm people, he really preferred to shock them. He was self-confident, abrupt, and unyielding. During the long months that he served in the Big Bend, Shafter gave the impression of being a large, forceful, indomitable man who could not be defeated. Impartial and resourceful, he possessed initiative, looked out for the welfare of his men and animals, and was utterly unafraid of responsibility. He proved to be an energetic leader whose troops were at all times well disciplined and thoroughly trained.

Shafter's experiences in Big Bend were personally and professionally significant. The venture in the silver mine, although it resulted in the loss of a good friend, made him a wealthy man. The troubles associated with the sordid Flipper affair nearly cost him promotion to the rank of brigadier general, and long afterward they continued to invite unfriendly reporting about his relationship with black troops of his command. But the success he enjoyed in command in the Big Bend and the experience he gained in service led to additional frontier assignments in the Southwest.

William R. Shafter left Fort Davis for the last time in April 1882. In his subsequent career he served in the Apache wars in Arizona, in the Sioux campaign in South Dakota following the Wounded Knee massacre, and in Los Angeles during the Pullman Strike in 1894. In 1898 President William McKinley chose him to lead the US land forces in Cuba. He did not again enter the Big Bend in an official capacity, but like many modern folk he returned to the high mountain region to hunt big game and to enjoy a few days away from modern pressures.

Notes

1. James Parker, *The Old Army: Memories, 1872–1918* (Philadelphia: Dorrence, 1929); Charles D. Rhodes, "William Rufus Shafter," *Michigan History Magazine* 16 (1932): 371–72.

2. Post Medical Reports, Fort Davis, March–April 1881, Books 7–9, 12, October 1854–May 1891, Old Records Department (ORD), Adjutant General's Office (AGO), National Archives (NA); Post Returns, Fort Davis, March 1881, Microcopy (MC) 617, Roll 297, NA.

3. J. Evetts Haley, *Fort Concho and the Texas Frontier* (San Angelo, Texas: San Angelo Standard-Times, 1952), 163–67; Shafter to H. Clay Wood, Assistant Adjutant General, Department of Texas, July 1871, Letters Sent (LS), Fort Davis, US Army Commands (USAC), Record Group (RG) 98, NA; Post Returns, Fort Davis, June–July 1871, MC 617, Roll 297, NA; Post Medical Reports, Fort Davis, June–July 1871, Books 7–9, 12, ORD, AGO, NA.

4. Shafter to Wood, February 12, 1872, LS, Fort Davis, USAC, RG 98, NA.

5. Ibid., February 1, 1872, LS, Fort Davis, USAC, RG 98, NA.

6. Ibid.; Post Returns, Fort Davis, October 1871, MC 617, Roll 297, NA; Post Medical Reports, Fort Davis, October–November 1871, Books 7–9, 12, ORD, AGO, NA.

7. Shafter to Lt. Isaiah H. McDonald, 9th Cavalry, December 8, 1871, in Shafter to Wood, January 4, 1872, LS, Fort Davis, USAC, RG 98, NA.

8. Shafter to Wood, February 12, 1872, LS, Fort Davis, USAC, RG 98, NA; Post Returns, Fort Davis, March–April 1872, MC 617, Roll 297, NA.

9. Shafter to F. C. Taylor, Agent, El Paso Mail Lines, ca. January 4, 1872, LS, Fort Davis, USAC, RG 98, NA. Also see Arlen L. Fowler, *The Black Infantry in the West* (Westport, Connecticut: Greenwood, 1971), 26–27.

10. Shafter to S. R. Miller, Justice of the Peace, Presidio County, November 6, 1871, LS, Fort Davis, USAC, RG 98, NA.

11. Regimental Returns, First Infantry, May–November 1880, MC 665, Roll 7, NA.

12. *Presidio Mining Co. v. Alice Bullis,* Court Transcript no. 5909 (now filed as M11633), filed in Texas Supreme Court at Austin, Texas, May, 1886.

13. Ibid.

14. *Presidio Mining Co. v. Alice Bullis,* 68, *Texas Reports,* 581–91 (1887). To support its decision the court also pointed to legal and technical errors made by the district court judge in charging the jury. The charge, it said, was misleading. Also see David S. Stanley, Commanding the Department of Texas, to Adjutant General, United States Army, July 2, 1887 (filed with 2220 Appoints, Commissions, Personal [ACP] 1879), LR, AGO, RG 94, NA.

15. Shafter to Bullis, November 12, 1883, in A. J. Evans, Brief for the Appellees, *Presidio Mining Co. v. Alice Bullis,* Supreme Court of Texas, Austin Term, 1887 (filed with 2220 ACP 1879), LR, AGO, RG 94, NA; Carlysle Graham Raht, *The Romance of Davis Mountains and Big Bend Country* (El Paso: Rahtbooks, 1919), 283; John E. Gregg, "The History of Presidio County, Texas" (MA thesis, University of Texas, Austin, 1933), 142–48; Virginia Madison, *The Big Bend Country of Texas* (Albuquerque: University of New Mexico Press, 1955), 168–73; *San Francisco Call,* November 13, 1906.

16. Barry Scobee, *Old Fort Davis* (San Antonio: Naylor, 1947), 86–87.

17. Ibid.

18. Theodore D. Harris, ed., *Negro Frontiersman: The Western Memoirs of Henry O. Flipper, First Negro Graduate of West Point* (El Paso: Texas Western College Press, 1963), vii, 18–19.

19. Ibid., 19–20.

20. Ibid.

21. J. Norman Heard, *The Black Frontiersmen: Adventures of Negroes among American Indians, 1828–1918* (New York: John Day, 1969), 117; Robert M. Utley, "'Pecos Bill' on the Texas Frontier," *American West* 6 (January 1969): 6.

22. Proceedings of Court-Martial, September 3, 1881, 44–54, in Records Relating to the Army Career of Henry Ossian Flipper, 1873–1883, Microcopy T 1027, Roll 1, NA.

23. Ibid. Also see Bruce J. Dinges, "The Court-Martial of Lieutenant Henry O. Flipper: An Example of Black-White Relationships in the Army, 1881," *American West* 9 (January 1972): 14–16; Donald R. McClung, "Henry O. Flipper: First Negro Officer in the United States Army, 1878–1882" (MA thesis, East Texas State University–Commerce, 1970), 86–89, 112, 115–17; Barry C. Johnson, "Flipper's Dismissal: The Ruin of Lt. Henry O. Flipper, USA, First Coloured Graduate of West Point," in *Ho, For the Great West!*, ed. Barry C. Johnson (London: English Westerners' Society, 1980).

14 Acculturation on the Rio Grande Frontier

The Founding of San José del Polvo and the Family of Lucia Rede Madrid

Earl H. Elam

It was unusually hot and dry in July 1852 when Major William H. Emory rode into Presidio del Norte, leading the American survey team that was mapping the international boundary between the United States and Mexico, as provided for in the Treaty of Guadalupe Hidalgo. The temperatures, which sometimes reach 115 degrees or more in the area, though not recorded at that date, apparently exceeded what was normal, and little rain had fallen for three years. Located on a hilltop southeast of the junction of the Rio Grande and the Río Conchos, the town was inhabited by about eight hundred people, who, Emory recorded, were in terrible shape, suffering from famine, scarcity of water, and Indian depredations.[1]

Emory described the isolated and remote community as "a miserably built mud town." It was the oldest Mexican settlement on the Chihuahua-Texas border, having been a stopping place for Spanish explorers as early as 1581, and it may have been visited by Cabeza de Vaca nearly five decades before that. The community was formally organized as a town by Spanish authorities in 1715 and was the site of one of the important frontier presidios that guarded the northern provinces of New Spain. Impressively named Presidio de Nuestra Señora de Belén y Santiago de Amarillas de la Junta de los Ríos de Conchos y del Norte when it was established in 1759, the presidio was commonly referred to as La Junta de los Ríos (sometimes just La Junta) or Presidio del Norte. After the Spanish left in 1821, it was occasionally used by garrisons of Mexican soldiers, but was mostly in ruins in 1852.[2]

Prior to 1865 the town also was generally called La Junta or Presidio del Norte. In that year Mexican president Benito Juárez changed the name to Ojinaga in honor of General Manual Ojinaga, governor of Chihuahua, who had been killed in fighting in Guerrero in 1864.[3] Ojinaga, therefore, will be used to designate the town in this chapter, whether referring to it either before or after 1865.

Ethnically, the majority of the Mexican residents of the Ojinaga area were assimilated Indian and Spanish people, descendants of early inhabitants and immigrants who had come as soldiers or camp followers to the La Junta presidio. African blood in some residents may be traced to associations with slaves who had worked in mines in southern Chihuahua and Zacatecas or to blacks in the service of the presidial garrison.[4]

Living day-to-day within the confines of a subsistence economy at the time of Emory's visit, the Ojinagans were part of a historical process of frontier development that had been initiated far to the south with the coming of the Spanish in the sixteenth century. Their culture exhibited characteristics both Indian and Spanish and was strongly influenced by Roman Catholicism. After 1848, the Ojinagans and other Mexicans who made up the population of the northern Mexican frontier began to feel the influence of people with a different cultural heritage who came, gradually and in increasing numbers, into the Trans-Pecos/Big Bend region of Texas. These people, collectively referred to as Anglo-Americans or just Anglos, were mainly of English and northern European stock.

The Anglo-American frontier has been one of the most discussed and debated subjects in American historiography. When Frederick Jackson Turner in 1893 delivered his paper "The Significance of the Frontier in American History," he focused on a subject that had not been the target of critical intellectual analysis.[5] According to the Turner thesis, the uniqueness of American democracy could be attributed to what had happened on the geographical frontiers of the United States as the country expanded westward. Turner talked about the development of institutions on the frontiers in their successive stages of advance across the continent between the Atlantic and Pacific oceans and argued that in them could be found the main and unique characteristics of American civilization. Moreover, since the human forces behind the developments were primarily English-speaking, and the political characteristics of the United States were based on English patterns, society in the frontier areas, though distinctive and uniquely American, had a decidedly English (Anglo) orientation.

Turner also wrote about the importance of geographical sections in the expansion of the United States.[6] He observed common features and patterns in the development of society in the various sections, but detected, at the same time, variety in each that made distinctive contributions to the composite whole of the country. His lifetime of work spawned a plethora of writing by scholars about frontiers and sections. Almost every region in the United States has been subjected to analysis using Turner's ideas. To date, however, the Trans-Pecos, Rio Grande borderlands frontier in Texas has not been given this treatment. One thing seems certain: historical influences have interacted in the region to create a society with characteristics that vary greatly from the stereotypical frontier that Turner described. On the other hand, many examples of human activity in the region compare favorably with the waves of activity that he noted in other sections.

A significant variation found on the Rio Grande frontier is the acculturation that occurred involving Indians, Spaniards, and Mexicans long before Anglo influences were felt in the region. The date 1848 is a convenient time to mark the beginning of the new influences, an effect of the establishment of the international boundary and the opening of much former Mexican territory to American expansion. The coming of the Anglos resulted in the meeting of two frontiers—the westward-moving Anglo phenomenon described by Turner, and the relatively stable Mexican settlements along the Rio Grande, themselves the products of the long northward-moving Hispanic frontier and of the processes of multicultural assimilation.

In the following pages, the experiences of one family, located principally in one section of the Rio Grande frontier, will be discussed with the purpose of illustrating how people with a complex cultural heritage different from that of the Anglos were instrumental in the development of society in the region. Attention is focused on the founding of the community long known as Polvo, now Redford, in Presidio County, and incidents in the lives of members of the family of Lucia Rede Madrid, a prominent citizen of the town.

For thousands of years before the coming of the Spanish, the area around Ojinaga was inhabited by sedentary Indians who made a living hunting and farming. A delta at the junction of the Rio Grande and Río Conchos below the gravel hill on which the presidio was located was a good place to raise vegetables, melons, and corn and other grain crops. Prospects were not good at this site in 1852, however, nor were they much better at other farming sites that were located intermittently for many miles up and down the floodplains of the rivers. Before Emory's visit, some citizens of Ojinaga had gone up the Rio Grande to the northwest on the Mexican side of the border to try their luck at some of these sites. In some cases they formed the nucleus of new settlements, and in the years after 1852 many new farming communities developed both above and below Ojinaga along the Rio Grande.

Apparently the only settlement on the Texas side of the Rio Grande in the La Junta region in 1852 was a small community of Americans and Mexicans at a place known as Fort Leaton, or El Fortín, located about six miles downstream from Ojinaga. Established in 1848 by an Anglo frontiersman named Ben Leaton, it had been designated the county seat of Presidio County by the Texas Legislature in 1850. A county government was not organized, however, until 1875, and then in the town of Fort Davis; no official county work was ever transacted at Fort Leaton.[7]

Leaton and the Mexican families who worked for him were engaged mainly in trading activities, but some subsistence farming was being done. The land along the river around Fort Leaton is extremely fertile when irrigated. To the north of the community, the arable land is bordered by rocky bluffs and desert. East of the fort, the extensive Bofecillos Mountains gradually encroach on the river until, after about twenty miles, no land suitable for farming exists. The last good soil of sizeable proportions along this stretch is located in the vicinity of modern Redford, an area, incidentally, where for centuries ancient native inhabitants had engaged in primitive agricultural enterprises to supplement their hunting and gathering lifestyles.

Across the Rio Grande, southeast of Fort Leaton, good farmland exists as far as the hills of El Centinela and along the floodplain down to El Mulato and Barrio Montoya, communities located near Redford. At this point, the banks on both sides of the Rio Grande become increasingly precipitous as the river passes through canyons with walls that range in height to approximately fifteen hundred feet at their eastern terminus in the "Grand Canyon" (a name often used in the late nineteenth century and early twentieth century in reference to Santa Elena Canyon). Beyond this canyon, which is fifty miles or more down the river from Redford, agricultural land again is relatively plentiful on both sides of the river.

Redford had its beginnings as one of the communities spawned by Ojinaga residents looking for land to farm for a living. In May 1876, several former citizens of Ojinaga received land grants of 160 acres each from the State of Texas.[8] One of these was Secundino Luján, grandfather of the most prominent citizen of the river region, Lucia Rede Madrid, who has spent most of her nearly eight decades in Redford. To all who will listen, she talks enthusiastically and with pride about the experiences of her family in the area. Much of what is said here about the founding of San José del Polvo is based upon her recollections of family history and her life experiences.[9]

Secundino Luján's interest in obtaining land in Texas was stimulated when he and other residents of Ojinaga talked to a representative of the Texas government, Don Luis Cardiz, who visited the area looking for persons to settle on land in Presidio County.[10] At the time, Luján was farming west of Ojinaga, but not prospering. Eager to find a better place, he and four other Ojinaga men accepted Cardiz's offer and began to look for suitable land along the north bank of the Rio Grande. The other men were Juan José Acosta, Mateo Carrasco, José María Borrillo, and Nicolás Sánchez. They, too, received grants of 160 acres each in 1876; with Luján, they became known as the "First Five" of El Polvo.[11]

Under the watchful eyes of nomadic Apaches who lurked nearby but never bothered them, the men began to clear the land of mesquite, cresote bushes, and catclaw and other cacti, and to dig a canal (*acequia*) for irrigation. For several years they went back and forth from their homes at Ojinaga.

They worked mostly in the spring of each year, beginning in March, a time when the wind blew hard and sandstorms were common. They would say, "*Va es tiempo del Indios el Polvo.*"[12] When the dust invariably would come rolling in, they would say, "*Alli viene el polvo.*" Thus, the name El Polvo began to be used for the site; it is a name still used locally by old-timers. Later, when several families moved to the site and a church was built, the more formal name of San José del Polvo, in honor of the Catholic patron saint of workers, was adopted. The name Redford, in recognition of the red clay banks at a nearby river crossing, is of early twentieth-century origin; it was first used to designate the post office that was established in the community in 1912.[13]

Sometime in 1869 Secundino Luján put his family and their belongings into a *carreta* drawn by oxen and moved to the vicinity of Fort Leaton to be nearer Polvo. Secundino, who had been born in 1837 in Ojinaga, traced his lineage back to Diego Pérez de Luján, the chronicler of the expedition of Antonio de Espejo that passed through the area in 1583. Secundino's wife was Matilde Acosta. They lived in the vicinity of Fort Leaton for two years in *jacales* constructed of tree limbs, brush, and grass, similar to those of Apaches. They also constructed *jacales* for temporary homes at El Polvo in the area where the plaza later took shape. After moving to El

Polvo in 1871, they built a permanent home of adobe. In this house in 1872 Matilde gave birth to the first child to be born in the community, a daughter named Cleofas. Matilde and Secundino had thirteen children, several of whom were born in Mexico before the family moved across the river. All the children born after Cleofas were also born in Texas. One of these was a daughter, María Antonia, who was born in January 1878. She became the mother of Lucia Rede Madrid.[14]

In February 1876, Secundino formally renounced his Mexican citizenship and stated his intention to become a citizen of the United States.[15] One tradition holds that he expressed this wish as early as 1846, but it was his application for the land grant in Texas that prompted him to formalize the process. After the grant was finalized, he and his growing family were relatively secure on their new farm at El Polvo.

Not unlike the American settlers of Turner's frontiers, the El Polvo residents banded together to do all the work that needed to be done. They helped each other in building houses, farming, and constructing and maintaining the canal. The canal turned out to require continuous attention as it was gradually extended for several miles from the Rio Grande west of Redford, through the modern town, and back to the river southeast of the site of the original El Polvo, located about one mile southeast of the present school building. A few old buildings still are in use in the area, and nearby are the ruins of a US Army post called Camp Polvo, that was in operation between 1916 and 1920.

The construction of the canal, a vital necessity to get river water to the parched desert soil, was a monumental undertaking for men without earth-moving equipment and modern explosives. They performed most of the work by hand. Luján rode to Chihuahua City on horseback to obtain sulfur, and the men extracted nitrate from bat guano found in nearby caves, enabling them to make dynamite, which was used to blast a tunnel, or canyon (locally called El Juque), about three hundred feet long through a formation that ranged from twenty to forty feet in height. A good flow of river water passed through El Juque and to the farmland that extended for several miles through the fledgling community. It took five years to complete the project.

To meet the increased need for water as more land was gradually put into service, and to maintain the canal, the First Five formed the Presidio Irrigation Company on May 29, 1876. With Juan José Acosta as president and the others as directors, the company was capitalized at $3,000, with shares of stock worth $100 each. The First Five held all the shares.

Under the provisions of the charter, additional canals to be dug by the company would be not less than six feet wide and two and one-half feet deep. The company was bound by state law regarding irrigation districts and could never make charges for water used from the canal by the El Polvo residents to irrigate their crops. Most of the land serviced by the canals was owned by the First Five and other settlers who came in the 1870s, but the availability of water was assured by these early efforts in community development. The original canal is still in use.[16]

Another example of community spirit at El Polvo was the willingness of the founders to set aside land for public purposes. Appearing before Justice of the Peace Samuel Twill at Presidio on November 6, 1877, the First Five and seven other owners of land signed a document stating their desire to set aside an area 324 varas (approximately 1,000 feet) wide and the length of Survey No. 15 to "form a town or village."[17] They agreed to call the area the Community Property and to adjust the boundaries of their land to compensate Mateo Carrasco, who owned Survey No. 15, for land that he ceded for this purpose. The Community Property provided space for the construction of a plaza, a church, a school, and a public gathering place.

Time passed, more settlers came from Mexico, and the community grew in size. Most residents were subsistence farmers, a characteristic of early frontier development, again, not unlike those about whom Turner had written, but with one major difference: the settlers were Hispanic, not Anglo.

In 1895 a severe drought caused the loss of all the crops at El Polvo, forcing the men to seek work elsewhere to feed their families. By this time silver mining was under way at Shafter, about thirty-five miles to the north. There was a need for workers, so many of the El Polvo men, including Secundino Luján, went to work at Shafter. Mining, it should be noted, was among the experiences on some of the frontiers about which Turner wrote.

Luján took his family with him to Shafter. The move was an auspicious one for Antonia, who had grown to be an attractive young lady. She met a young man named Eusebio Rede with whom she fell in love. Eusebio had been born in Ojinaga in March 1879 and had come to Shafter to live with his grandfather, Francisco Rede, a man who had lived an unusually exciting life.[18]

Francisco was the descendant of a Jewish family that had fled Spain during the Inquisition in the sixteenth century. The family split, some members going to Canada and others to Portugal. One of the Portuguese families migrated to New Spain and lived in the vicinity of Monterrey in Nuevo León, an enlightened region where many Jews were living in comparative freedom, so long as they did not openly practice the Jewish religion. Francisco's father, Jesús, grew up in the Monterrey area and married a woman named Juana Torres. By 1825, when Francisco was born, they were living near Delicias in Chihuahua.[19]

When Francisco was eight years old, he and another boy were kidnapped by four Apaches. The Indians suddenly appeared on horses, grabbed the boys, and headed for their camp in the mountains. When Francisco's friend began to cry and would not stop, one of the Apaches hit him with a lance and killed him. Frightened, but determined not to resist, Francisco kept silent.

Francisco lived with the Apaches for fifteen years, becoming, during that time, an Apache himself for all practical purposes. He gradually learned to speak the language and did what he was told. The Indians treated him well, kept him busy with chores around the camp, and used him as an interpreter when they had dealings with Mexicans. One day in 1848, he was with a large war party that launched an attack on Ojinaga. A fierce battle raged during which, in the words of Francisco's granddaughter Lucia, the young man was rescued by residents of the town:

"Of course he wasn't going to fight the Mexicans. He could speak Spanish fluently. He was a Mexican. So the first ones that he saw when he first came to fight he told them that he was a captive and that he had been living with the Indians for many years and had wanted to escape and had never had the chance until this time. He asked them to help him. He said, 'I don't want to kill any Mexicans. I am one of you. I want to be with you.' So they hid him."[20]

Suffering many men killed, the Apaches at nightfall withdrew to Cerro el Centinela. The next morning they resumed the attack and did so for several days thereafter, but their losses were severe, and they were unable to penetrate the town. If they searched for Francisco, there is no record of it; presumably they thought he was among the dead.

Francisco stayed in Ojinaga, quickly adjusting to the lifestyle of the residents, but, having spent the formative years of his youth with the Apaches, he never completely gave up all the Indian traits he had acquired. For the remainder of his life, he would arise early each morning and go to the top of a nearby hill and pray Apache style. He was a hard worker, learned quickly, and, in Ojinaga, became skilled in a number of crafts, including blacksmithing and carpentry, which enabled him to earn a living.

Not long after his arrival in Ojinaga, Francisco had the good fortune to meet a beautiful Spanish girl named Tomasa Onsurez. They fell in love and were married in the parish church of Nuestra Padre Jesús on July 19, 1848.[21] Francisco and Tomasa became the parents of five sons. The first was Nabor, born in 1849. He grew up in Ojinaga and married Dolores Bustamante. They were the parents of Eusébio. As was the custom among Catholic families in those days, the first grandson of a man was expected to spend considerable time with him. Thus Eusébio, being the first grandson of Francisco, became closely associated with his grandfather, and at age fifteen went to live with him in Shafter.

Francisco had moved to Shafter in 1880. He raised goats and became acquainted with local rancher Milton Faver. In a land deal, Faver told Francisco to find a site where he wanted to live and that he could stay there the rest of his life. Francisco selected a spot near an open space in the middle of the town. The Mexican people called the space La Plazuela and used this name in reference to the town. Francisco and his family built a rock house at La Plazuela near the bridge and lived there many years. It was here, as luck would have it, that Eusébio Rede met Antonia Luján when she arrived with her family.[22]

Antonia was a beautiful and talented young woman. She sewed, painted landscapes, and, to help with family finances, peddled milk from door to door in Shafter. One of her customers was an Anglo woman whose language, the young Spanish girl thought, was like music. She wanted to learn it, and the woman graciously began to teach her. In time, other tutors helped Antonia, too, so that she became fluent in English. And she had received the rudiments of a general education from family and friends who had tutored her in El Polvo. Antonia had an insatiable desire to learn, obtained books whenever possible, and was anxious to pass on her learning to others. In 1897 she had the opportunity to become a teacher in the one-room adobe school in Shafter that had been built on the banks of Cibolo Creek. Here she taught in both English and Spanish, becoming, so it is believed, the first teacher in the region to use bilingual methods in teaching.[23]

Antonia and Eusébio were married in the Catholic Church at Shafter by Father Luis Castelo on October 11, 1900.[24] Afterward they continued to live in Shafter, where Eusébio worked in the mines. Several years later, when Secundino Luján divided his land among his children before his death, Antonia received her share, and she and Eusébio moved their growing family to Polvo. In all, eight children were born to the couple.

Lucia was born in Polvo on January 8, 1913. Eusébio engaged in farming and a number of other occupations in the Polvo area, including hauling freight for the US Army. In 1917, Antonia was appointed postmaster, a position she held until the family moved to Marfa in 1925.[25]

The move to Marfa was stimulated by the desire of the Redes for their children to acquire a good education. In later years Lucia would say it was from her parents that she and her brothers and sisters had received a "great legacy—a commitment to excellence." Eusébio read widely, including the works of Cervantes, Victor Hugo, Alexander Dumas, Tolstoy, and Dante, and instilled in Lucia the love of reading and learning. From Antonia she learned to love the English language and was inspired to go on with her studies.[26]

During Eusébio's trips to the railroad in Marfa while freighting supplies for the army, he had found a house and several lots he wanted to buy. He did so in 1925. Lucia and her brother Edmundo went to Marfa Elementary School in 1926, starting there in the fifth grade after having gone to school earlier in Polvo. They were among the first Hispanic students to go to Marfa Elementary, a distinction that has been noted by the Institute of Texan Cultures in San Antonio in recognizing them as "pioneers" in Texas education. Lucia graduated from Marfa High School in 1932 and went on to receive a bachelor's and a master's degree from Sul Ross State University in Alpine.[27]

In fact, all of the children of Eusébio and Antonia Rede finished high school and college, and all became teachers, and their sons and daughters became teachers, collectively compiling by 1992 more than four hundred years of service in education in Texas, New Mexico, California, and Indiana. More than fifty-five academic degrees have been earned by members of the family. While all have served with distinction, Lucia has received the most recognition. She taught at several schools in West Texas, and after returning to Redford in 1942, taught seventeen years in the local school there. She became nationally known, however, for her untiring efforts to establish a library in Redford and for providing books for children on both sides of the international border.

She also became a wife and mother. On May 3, 1941, Lucia married Enrique Madrid, also of Redford. He had studied in Los Angeles to be a diesel engineer and had worked for a while in Shafter before returning to Redford. He became a prominent businessman and was active in local and county government until the time of his death in 1991. They had three children: Lydia, Jaime, and Enrique, all of whom have been involved in teaching and educational activities. Lydia is a professor of art at the University of New Mexico; Jaime, a priest, is a professor of philosophy and theology; and Enrique is a translator of regional oral histories and Mexican colonial era documents and is much involved in local historical and archeological projects along the Rio Grande in the Redford-Ojinaga area.[28]

A record of Lucia's activities, too numerous to be discussed in detail here, reads like a chapter of the American dream, a phrase she often uses. The idea of the American dream is closely associated, also, with Turner's frontier thesis: westward streamed the pioneers in search of the American dream on one frontier after another. What it meant was as subjective as the people who went were different, but there were common denominators. For Lucia Madrid, the dream is intrinsically associated with education. "Education is not only what we are told," she recently wrote. "We must learn, read, and help others to acquire great values. To me values are culture, and culture we must have in this Great Country. To me that is the American Dream."[29]

Lucia's rewards for pursuing the American dream have been numerous. They include being honored as a Texas Woman of the Year at ceremonies at the state Capitol and at the Governor's Mansion on March 27, 1990, one of five women so recognized at that time. Then, exactly one month later, she was among nineteen women from across the United States who were recognized in a ceremony at the White House in Washington, DC. She received the President's Volunteer Action Award, accompanied by a silver medal, and the Ronald Reagan Award for Volunteer Excellence, which came with a gold medal. The presentations were made by President George Bush. She displays them in her home in Redford, which she describes as "the best place in the world" and the only place she wants to be.[30]

Lucia Rede Madrid's life experiences and those of her parents and grandparents involved developments on the Rio Grande frontier in Texas that are comparable in many respects to the experiences of settlers in other frontier areas of the United States. In the geographical section where the Lujáns, Redes, and Madrids lived there were people representative of the successive waves that Turner identified who swept across many American frontiers: Indian traders, miners, yeoman farmers, ranchers, commercial farmers and businessmen, and townspeople engaged in a variety of professions and occupations. Using democratic procedures, they made homes in the wilderness (or desert), formed communities, and engaged in capitalistic ventures.

There also were significant differences in settlement on the Rio Grande frontier. Most obvious were the ethnic backgrounds of the pioneers, and their cultural heritages. Hispanic Americans were in the majority. Proud bearers of many centuries of tradition (Indian and Spanish) in the New World and with ties to a different part of the Old World than the settlers on the Anglo-American frontiers, they brought with them unique cultural institutions and folkways, which are still being incorporated into the socioeconomic-political system of the section. The founding of San José del Polvo and the experiences of the family of Lucia Rede Madrid are examples of the dynamics and diversity to be found in the processes of acculturation on this frontier.

NOTES

1. William H. Emory, *Report on the United States and Mexican Boundary Survey* (Washington: Cornelius Wendell, Printer, 1857), vol. 1, pt. 1: 85.

2. Ibid. The plan of the presidio is reproduced by Oakah L. Jones Jr. in *Nueva Vizcaya: Heartland of the Spanish Frontier* (Albuquerque: University of New Mexico Press, 1988), 46–47.

3. Francisco R. Almada, *Geografía del Estado de Chihuahua* (Chihuahua, Mexico: Louis Sandoval, 1945), 569. In 1715, the official name of the town was San Francisco de la Junta de los Ríos.

4. For a discussion of settlement throughout the area of northern New Spain, see Oakah L. Jones Jr., *Los Paisanos: Spanish Settlers on the Northern Frontier of New Spain* (Norman: University of Oklahoma Press, 1979). Also, see Jones's article "Settlements and Settlers at La Junta de los Ríos, 1759–1822," *Journal of Big Bend Studies* 3 (January 1991): 43–70; Jones concludes that racial mixing among Indians, Spanish explorers, presidial soldiers, and civil settlers occurred at La Junta "openly and frequently."

5. Frederick Jackson Turner, "The Significance of the Frontier in American History," in the American Historical Association's *Annual Report for 1893* (Washington, 1894), 199–227.

6. See, for example, Ray Allen Billington, ed., *Frontier and Section: Selected Essays of Frederick Jackson Turner* (Englewood Cliffs: Prentice-Hall, 1961).

7. Emory, *Report,* vol. 1, pt. 2, 50; Gammell, *Laws of Texas* (3rd Legislature, January 3, 1850), article 1946.

8. Presidio County, Texas, *Deed Records* A:81–91.

9. Lucia Rede Madrid, recorded interviews with the author, Redford, Texas,

March 12, 1990; May 18, 1992; August 18, 1992 (hereafter cited as Madrid interviews).

10. Cecilia Thompson, *History of Marfa and Presidio County, Texas, 1535–1946* (Austin: Nortex, 1985), 1:18–19.

11. Ibid., 1:119; Lucia Rede Madrid, unpublished notes on family history, copy in possession of the author. The land grants are recorded in Presidio County, Texas, *Deed Records,* A:81–91.

12. Madrid interviews.

13. Ibid.

14. Ibid.

15. Declaration of Secundino Luján, copy of document from Presidio County records, in possession of Lucia Madrid.

16. Presidio County Records, May 29, 1876. All the men signed their names with an "x" mark except Luján, who, presumably, was the only one who could write.

17. Presidio County, *Deed Records,* November 6, 1877, 1:30–31; also 5:94–95.

18. Madrid interviews; Lucia Madrid, "Francisco Rede," unpublished summary of Rede's life, provided for the author's use.

19. Ibid.

20. Madrid interviews, May 18, 1992.

21. La Junta Church Records, 1775–1857, Archives of the Big Bend, Sul Ross State University.

22. Madrid interviews.

23. Ibid.

24. In an interview on August 18, 1992, Lucia Madrid insisted that the marriage took place in Shafter and that the ceremony was performed by Father Castelo. Thompson, *History of Presidio County* 1:347, says the vows were exchanged in the Catholic church in Marfa with Father Franco Maas presiding.

25. Madrid interviews.

26. Lucia Madrid, notes provided the author, fall 1992.

27. Ibid.

28. Ibid.

29. Ibid.

30. She proudly displays the medals and plaques in her home. Accounts of her work have been published in newspapers in Texas and in national publications such as *Parade: The Sunday Newspaper Magazine,* May 24, 1992, 30–31, and *Reader's Digest,* November 1992, 14.

Glossary of Archaeological Terms

Robert J. Mallouf

aceramic. Lacking pottery.

archaeology. The study of past human culture based on material evidence (artifacts and sites).

Archaic period. In prehistory, the period from 6500 BC to AD 700–900, when Native Americans lived in small nomadic bands and survived by hunting and gathering wild plants and animals.

arrow point. A stone or metal projectile on an arrow shaft intended for use with a bow.

artifact. Any object made, modified, or used by humans.

assemblage. A group of artifacts recurring together at a particular time and place.

association. The co-occurrence of an artifact with other archaeological remains, usually in the same matrix.

biface. A stone artifact that is flaked on both faces.

blade. A specialized stone flake with parallel or subparallel lateral edges and a length that is equal to, or greater than, twice the width.

cache. In prehistory, a grouping of provisions or implements concealed for later recovery; a ritually placed offering of objects such as projectile points.

cairn. A typically oval to circular stack of rock placed above a human burial or cache, or used as a trail marker.

chronology. The arrangement of events or periods of time in the order in which they occurred.

complex. A related group of cultural traits in a culture area.

component. A distinctive cultural occupation, usually in buried context.

Contact period. The period from AD 1500 to 1750, which saw initial contact between Native Americans and Europeans.

core. A stone from which flakes or blades are removed to further reduce into tools.

cultigen. A plant dependent on man for its survival; domesticated foodstuffs.

cultural boundary. The geographical limits of a cultural group; the geographical zone in which multiple cultures interact.

culture. A set of learned beliefs, values, styles, and behaviors shared by members of a society.

dart point. A stone tip attached to a wooden shaft for use with the atlatl, or throwing stick.

debitage. The debris created as a result of the manufacture of stone tools.

diffusion. The spread of elements of one culture to another without wholesale dislocation or direct migration.

ethnographic analogy. Inferring the use or meaning of an ancient site or artifact based on observations and written accounts of its use by historic cultures.

feature. Any human construction or disturbance, such as a pit, dwelling, cairn, burial, or midden.

ground stone. Stone artifacts such as manos and metates made by grinding, pecking, and the use of abrasive materials.

hearth. A pit or pavement, often stone lined, constructed for a fire; campfire.

hunter-gatherers. Semisedentary and nomadic peoples who live in small groups and subsist by hunting animals and collecting wild plant foods.

indigenous. Native; produced, growing, or living naturally in a particular region or environment.

in-situ. In the location where last deposited—said of artifacts.

Jornada-Mogollon. In late prehistory, Puebloan-related farmers of the El Paso region.

La Junta phase. An archaeological construct for prehistoric (AD 1200–1400) agriculturalists along the Rio Grande and Río Conchos in Texas and Chihuahua.

Late Prehistoric. That period in late prehistory characterized by the use of the bow and arrow, ceramics, and/or agriculture.

lithic. Relating to stone.

mano. A circular to oval ground-stone implement for processing plant foods.

mesic. As relates to environment, moderately moist.

midden. An area used for the disposal of trash; a deposit of refuse.

morphology. The form and/or shape of objects, as used in describing artifacts.

Paleoindians. Early, pre-Archaic cultures; often characterized as big-game hunters of Pleistocene fauna such as mammoth.

pestle. An implement used to pulverize foodstuffs in a mortar.

phase. An archaeological construct for a cultural unit possessing traits sufficiently characteristic to distinguish it from other cultural units.
pit house. An aboriginally excavated house floor; a semisubterranean dwelling.
Pleistocene. The latest major geological epoch; known as the "Ice Age" (3,000,000–10,000 years before the present).
pluvial lake. A typically small body of water formed by rainfall.
preform. A stone blank intended for manufacture into an implement.
prehistory. The period of human history before the advent of writing; in the Chihuahuan Desert prehistory ends with the arrival of the Spanish in AD 1535.
projectile point. A pointed implement of stone or metal attached to the end of a dart or arrow.
Protohistoric period. See Contact period.
radiocarbon dating. An absolute dating method based on the radioactive decay of Carbon-14 contained in organic matter.
ramada. A small, usually rectangular or squarish, open-sided shelter constructed with poles and roof thatching.
rasp. A wood or bone noise-maker.
reconnaissance. An archaeological sampling technique involving the identification of sites in specific localities over a large area.
sedentary. Living or remaining in one area; not migratory.
semisedentary. Practicing both a sedentary and nomadic existence; often seasonal.
settlement pattern. The spatial distribution of cultural activities across a landscape at a given time.
sinker stone. A flat, notched pebble used to weight fishing nets.
site. Any locality having material evidence of human activity.
subsistence. The means of supporting life, usually referring to food and other basic commodities.
survey. Locating archaeological sites through a technique of intensive exploration.
symbiotic relationship. A mutually dependent connection between distinct cultures, evolving through trade or other interaction.
temporal. Of or relating to time.
testing. A small exploratory excavation designed to determine a site's depth, content, and integrity prior to major excavation.
typology. The systematic organization of artifacts into "types" on the basis of shared attributes.

wickiup. A type of dwelling used by nomadic Native Americans of the arid regions of the southwestern United States and northern Mexico, having an oval to circular base, a framework of poles or branches, and a covering of grass, brush, or hides.

Suggested Readings

Bruce A. Glasrud and Robert J. Mallouf

The studies we include here ought to provide both scholars and general readers with relevant secondary sources about the history and prehistory of the Big Bend region of Texas. Many of these works have proven particularly useful to us.

Alexander, Thomas E. *Rattlesnake Bomber Base: Pyote Army Airfield in World War II*. Abilene, Texas: State House Press, 2005.

Anderson, Gary Clayton. *The Conquest of Texas: Ethnic Cleansing in the Promised Land, 1820–1875*. Norman: University of Oklahoma Press, 2005.

Anderson, James G. "Land Acquisition in the Big Bend National Park of Texas." MA thesis, Sul Ross State University, 1967.

Bannon, John Francis. *The Spanish Borderlands Frontier, 1513–1821*. Albuquerque: University of New Mexico Press, 1974.

Blagg, Dennis. *Big Bend Landscapes*. College Station: Texas A&M University Press, 2002.

Brooks, James F. *Captives and Cousins: Slavery, Kinship, and Community in the Southwest Borderlands*. Chapel Hill: Published for the Omohundro Institute of Early American History and Culture, Williamsburg, Virginia, University of North Carolina Press, 2002.

———. *Confounding the Color Line: The Indian-Black Experience in North America*. Lincoln: University of Nebraska Press, 2002.

Cain, Virginia Alice. "A History of Brewster County, 1535–1934." MA thesis, Sul Ross State Teacher's College, 1935.

Campbell, T. N., and William T. Field. "Identification of Comanche Raiding Trails in Trans-Pecos Texas." *West Texas Historical Association Yearbook* 44 (1968): 128–44.

Casey, Clifford B. *Mirages, Mysteries, and Reality: Brewster County Texas, the Big Bend of the Rio Grande*. Hereford, Texas: Pioneer Book Publishers, 1972.

_____. *Soldiers, Ranchers, and Miners in the Big Bend*. [Washington, DC]: US National Park Service, 1969.

_____. *Sul Ross State University: The Cultural Center of Trans-Pecos Texas, 1917–1975*. Seagraves, Texas: Pioneer Book Publishers, 1976.

Clark, Gary, and Kathy Adams Clark. *Enjoying Big Bend National Park: A Friendly Guide to Adventures for Everyone*. College Station: Texas A&M University Press, 2009.

Corning, Leavitt, Jr. *Baronial Forts of the Big Bend: Ben Leaton, Milton Faver, and Their Private Forts in Presidio County.* Austin: Trinity University Press, 1967.

Crimmins, M. L., ed. "Two Thousand Miles by Boat in the Rio Grande in 1850." *West Texas Historical and Scientific Society Publications* 5 (1933): 44–52.

Daniel, James M. "The Advance of the Spanish Frontier and the Despoblado." PhD diss., University of Texas, 1955.

Dearen, Patrick. *Portraits of the Pecos Frontier.* Lubbock, Texas: Texas Tech University Press, 1993.

DeLay, Brian. *War of a Thousand Deserts: Indian Raids and the US-Mexican War.* New Haven: Yale University Press, 2010.

De León, Arnoldo. "Mexican Americans in the Edwards Plateau and Trans-Pecos Region, 1900–2000: A Demographic Study." *Southwestern Historical Quarterly* 112 (October 2008): 148–70.

Duncan, Dayton. "El Despoblado." In *Miles from Nowhere: Tales from America's Contemporary Frontier,* by Dayton Duncan, 217–38. New York: Viking Penguin, 1993.

Fletcher, Henry T. "From Longhorns to Herefords: A History of Cattle Raising in Trans-Pecos Texas." *Voice of the Mexican Border* 1 (October 1933): 61–69.

Frank, Ross Harold. "From Settler to Citizen: New Mexico Economic Development and the Creation of Vecino Society, 1750–1820." PhD diss., University of California, Berkeley, 1992.

Glasrud, Bruce A., ed. *African Americans in the West: A Bibliography of Secondary Sources.* Alpine, Texas: SRSU Center for Big Bend Studies, 1998.

Glasrud, Bruce A., and Charles A. Braithwaite, eds. *African Americans on the Great Plains.* Lincoln: University of Nebraska Press, 2009.

Glasrud, Bruce A., Paul H. Carlson, and Tai D. Kreidler, eds. *Slavery to Integration: Black Americans in West Texas.* Abilene: State House Press, 2007.

Gómez, Arthur R. "The Glen Springs-Boquillas Raid Reconsidered: Diplomatic Intrigue on the Rio Grande." *Journal of Big Bend Studies* 4 (1992): 97–113.

———. *A Most Singular Country: A History of Occupation in the Big Bend.* Santa Fe: National Park Service, 1990.

Gregg, John E. "The History of Presidio County." MA thesis, University of Texas, 1933.

Griffen, William B. *Culture Change and Shifting Populations in Central Northern Mexico.* Tucson: University of Arizona Press, 1969.

Guffee, Eddie J. "Camp Peña Colorado, Texas." MA thesis, West Texas State University, 1976.

Hämäläinen, Pekka. *The Comanche Empire.* New Haven: Yale University Press, 2008.

Hammond, George P., and Agapito Rey, trans. *The Rediscovery of New Mexico (1580–1594): The Explorations of Chamuscado, Espejo, Castaño de Sosa, Morlete, and Leyva de Bonilla and Humana.* Albuquerque: University of New Mexico Press, 1966.

Harris, Jodie P. "Protecting the Big Bend—A Guardsman's View." *Southwestern Historical Quarterly* 78 (January 1975): 292–302.
Hawley, C. A. "Life Along the Border." *West Texas Historical and Scientific Society Publications* 20 (1964): 7–88.
Henderson, Aileen Kilgore. *Tenderfoot Teacher: Letters from the Big Bend, 1952–1954*. Fort Worth: TCU Press, 2002.
Hickerson, Nancy Parrott. *Jumanos: Hunters and Traders of the South Plains*. Austin: University of Texas Press, 1994.
Hitchcock, Totsy N. "Representative Individuals and Families of the Lower Big Bend Region, 1895–1925." MA thesis, Sul Ross State College, 1960.
Jameson, John Robert. "Big Bend National Park of Texas: A Brief History of the Formative Years, 1930–1952." PhD diss., University of Toledo, 1974.
John, Elizabeth A. H. *Storms Brewed in Other Men's Worlds: The Confrontation of Indians, Spanish, and French in the Southwest, 1540–1795*. College Station: Texas A&M University Press, 1975.
Jones, Oakah L. *Los Paisanos: Spanish Settlers on the Northern Frontier of New Spain*. Norman: University of Oklahoma Press, 1979.
———, ed. *The Spanish Borderlands—A First Reader*. Los Angeles: Lorrin L. Morrison and Carroll Spear Morrison, 1974.
Justice, Glenn. "Englishmen, Railroads, and the San Carlos Coal Mine." *Journal of Big Bend Studies* 21 (2009): 49–72.
———. *Revolution on the Rio Grande: Mexican Raids and Army Pursuits, 1916–1919*. El Paso: Texas Western Press, 1992.
Keil, Robert. *Bosque Bonito: Violent Times along the Borderland during the Mexican Revolution*. Edited by Elizabeth McBride. Alpine, Texas: SRSU Center for Big Bend Studies, 2002.
Kelley, J. Charles. "The Historic Indian Pueblos of La Junta de los Ríos." *New Mexico Historical Review* 26 (October 1952): 257–95.
———. *Jumano and Patarabueye: Relations at La Junta de los Ríos*. Museum of Anthropology Anthropological Papers 77. Ann Arbor: University of Michigan, 1986.
———. "The Route of Antonio de Espejo down the Pecos River and across the Texas Trans-Pecos Region." *West Texas Historical and Scientific Society* 7 (1937): 7–25.
Kelley, J. Charles, Thomas N. Campbell, and Donald Lehmer. *The Association of Archeological Materials with Geological Deposits in the Big Bend Region of Texas*. West Texas Historical and Scientific Society Publication 10. Alpine, Texas: Sul Ross State Teachers College, 1940.
Langford, J. Oscar., with Fred Gipson. *Big Bend: A Homesteader's Story*. Austin: University of Texas Press, 1952.
Lehmer, Donald J. "A Review of Trans-Pecos Archeology." *Bulletin of the Texas Archeological Society* 29 (1958): 109–144.

MacLeod, William. *Big Bend Vistas: A Geological Exploration of the Big Bend*. Alpine, Texas: Texas Geological Press, 2002.

———. *Davis Mountains Vistas: A Geological Exploration of the Davis Mountains*. Alpine, Texas: Texas Geological Press, 2005.

———. *River Road Vistas: A Journey along the River Road*. Alpine, Texas: Texas Geological Press, 2008.

Madison, Virginia. *The Big Bend Country of Texas*. [Albuquerque]: University of New Mexico Press, 1955.

Madison, Virginia, and Hallie Stilwell. *How Come It's Called That? Place Names in the Big Bend Country*. Albuquerque: University of New Mexico Press, 1958.

Mallouf, Robert J. "Late Archaic Foragers of Eastern Trans-Pecos Texas and the Big Bend." In *The Late Archaic across the Borderlands*, 219–46. Austin: University of Texas Press, 2005.

———."A Synthesis of Eastern Trans-Pecos Prehistory." MA thesis, University of Texas at Austin, 1985.

Maxwell, Ross A. *The Big Bend of the Rio Grande: A Guide to the Rocks, Geologic History, and Settlers of the Area of Big Bend National Park*. Austin: Bureau of Economic Geology, University of Texas, 1968.

Miles, Elton. *More Tales of the Big Bend*. College Station: Texas A&M University Press, 1988.

———. *Tales of the Big Bend*. College Station: Texas A&M University Press, 1976.

Morgenthaler, Jefferson. *La Junta de los Ríos: The Life, Death and Resurrection of an Ancient Desert Community in the Big Bend Region of Texas*. Boerne, Texas: Mockingbird Books, 2007.

Nelson, Al B. "Campaigning in the Big Bend of the Rio Grande in 1787." *Southwestern Historical Quarterly* 39 (January 1936): 200–227.

Nelson, Barney. *The Last Campfire: The Life Story of Ted Gray, a West Texas Rancher*. Marathon, Texas: Iron Mountain Press, 2000.

Ohl, Andrea J., and William A. Cloud. *Archeological Survey of Select Boundary and Power Line Segments, Big Bend Ranch State Park, Presidio County, Texas*. Alpine, Texas: SRSU Center for Big Bend Studies, 2001.

Osorio, Ruben. *The Secret Family of Pancho Villa*. Alpine, Texas: SRSU Center for Big Bend Studies, 2000.

Parsons, Judith A., ed. *Proceedings of the Conference on Hispanics and Higher Education*. Alpine, Texas: Sul Ross State University Press, 1988.

Perttula, Timothy K. *The Prehistory of Texas*. College Station: Texas A&M University Press, 2004.

Powell, A. Michael. *Trees and Shrubs of the Trans-Pecos and Adjacent Areas*. Austin: University of Texas Press, 1998.

Powell, A. Michael, and Patricia R. Manning. *Grasses of the Trans-Pecos and Adjacent Areas*. 1994. Marathon, Texas: Iron Mountain Press, 2000.

Powell, A. Michael, and James F. Weedin. *Cacti of the Trans-Pecos and Adjacent Areas*. Lubbock: Texas Tech University Press, 2004.

Ragsdale, Kenneth B. *Quicksilver: Terlingua and the Chisos Mining Company.* College Station: Texas A&M University Press, 1976.

———. *Wings Over the Mexican Border: Pioneer Aviation in the Big Bend.* Austin: University of Texas Press, 1984.

Raht, Carlysle Graham. *The Romance of Davis Mountains and Big Bend Country: A History.* Odessa, Texas: Raht Books, 1963. First published 1919 by Raht Books.

Reséndez, Andrés. *Changing National Identities at the Frontier: Texas and New Mexico, 1800–1850.* Cambridge, UK: Cambridge University Press, 2005.

Riley, Carroll L. *Río del Norte: People of the Upper Rio Grande from Earliest Times to the Pueblo Revolt.* Salt Lake City: University of Utah Press, 1995.

Saxton, Lewis H., and Clifford B. Casey. "The Life of Everett Ewing Townsend." *West Texas Historical and Scientific Publications* 17 (19): 1–68.

Sayre, Harold Ray. *Warriors of Color.* Fort Davis, Texas: H. R. Sayre, 1995.

Scobee, Barry. *Fort Davis, Texas: 1586–1960.* El Paso: Hill Printing, 1963.

Scogin, Russell Ashton. *The Sanderson Flood of 1965: Crisis in a Rural Community.* Alpine, Texas: SRSU Center for Big Bend Studies, 1995.

Seebach, John D. "Past and Present of the Chispa Creek Folsom Site, Culberson County, Texas." *Journal of Big Bend Studies* 16 (2004): 1–30.

Shipman, Mrs. O. L. *Taming the Big Bend: A History of the Extreme Western Portion of Texas from Fort Clark to El Paso.* Marfa, Texas, 1926.

Skaggs, Jimmy M. "A Study in Business Failures: Frank Collinson in the Big Bend." *Panhandle-Plains Historical Review* 43 (1970).

Smith, Ralph A. "The Comanche Sun over Mexico." *West Texas Historical Association Year Book* 67 (1970), 25–62.

Smith, Victor J. "Early Spanish Exploration in the Big Bend of Texas." *West Texas Historical and Scientific Society Publications* 2 (1928): 55–68.

Smithers, W. D. *Chronicles of the Big Bend.* Austin: Madrona Press, 1976.

———. *Early Trail Drives in the Big Bend.* El Paso: Texas Western Press, 1979.

Smith-Savage, Sheron, and Robert J. Mallouf, eds. *Rock Art of the Chihuahuan Desert Borderlands.* Alpine, Texas: SRSU Center for Big Bend Studies, 1998.

Stillwell, Hallie. *I'll Gather My Geese.* College Station: Texas A&M University Press, 1991.

Stillwell, Hallie. *My Goose Is Cooked: The Continuation of a West Texas Ranch Woman's Story.* Alpine, Texas: SRSU Center for Big Bend Studies, 2004.

Thompson, Cecilia. *A History of Marfa and Presidio County, 1535–1946.* 2 vols. Austin: Nortex Press, 1985.

Townsend, E. E. "Rangers and Indians in the Big Bend Region." *West Texas Historical and Scientific Society Publications* 7 (1937): 43–48.

Turpin, Solveig A., and Herbert H. Eling, Jr., eds. *Dust, Smoke, & Tracks: Two Accounts of Nineteenth Century Mexican Military Expeditions to Northern Coahuila and Chihuahua.* Alpine, Texas: SRSU Center for Big Bend Studies, 2009.

Tyler, Ron C. *The Big Bend: A History of the Last Texas Frontier.* College Station: Texas A&M University Press, 1996.

Utley, Robert M. "The Range Cattle Industry in the Big Bend of Texas." *Southwestern Historical Quarterly* 69 (April 1966): 419–41.
Wagstaff, R. M. "Beginnings of the Big Bend Park." *West Texas Historical Association Year Book* 64 (1968): 3–14.
Walker, Kathryn B. "Quicksilver Mining in the Terlingua Area." MA thesis, Sul Ross State College, 1960.
Warnock, Barton H. *Wildflowers of the Big Bend Country.* Alpine, Texas: Sul Ross State University, 1970.
Wauer, Roland. *A Field Guide to Birds of the Big Bend.* Austin: Texas Monthly Press, 1985.
Webb, Walter P. "The Big Bend of Texas." *Panhandle-Plains Historical Review* 10 (1937): 7–20.
Weber, David J. *Foreigners in Their Native Land: Historical Roots of the Mexican Americans.* Albuquerque: University of New Mexico Press, 1973.
———. *New Spain's Far Northern Frontier: Essays on Spain in the American West, 1540–1821.* Albuquerque: University of New Mexico Press, 1979.
———. *The Spanish Frontier in North America.* New Haven: Yale University Press, 1992.
Weber, David J., and Jane M. Rausch. *Where Cultures Meet: Frontiers in Latin American History.* Wilmington, Delaware: SR Books, 1994.
Wilcox, David R., and W. Bruce Masse, eds. *The Protohistoric Period in the North American Southwest, AD 1450–1700.* Tempe: Arizona State University Press, 1981.
Willeford, Glenn P., and Gerald G. Raun. *Cemeteries and Funerary Practices in the Big Bend of Texas, 1850 to the Present.* Alpine, Texas: Johnson's Ranch & Trading Post, 2006.
Wood, C. D. "The Glenn Springs Raid." *West Texas Historical and Scientific Society Publications* 19 (1963): 65–71.
Wooster, Robert. *Fort Davis: Outpost on the Texas Frontier.* Austin: Texas State Historical Association, 1994.
———. *Frontier Crossroads: Fort Davis and the West.* College Station: Texas A&M University Press, 2006.
Wright, Paul. "Characteristics of Big Bend Mining Towns, 1885–1920." *Journal of Big Bend Studies* 9 (1997): 89–115.
———. "A Tumultuous Decade: Changes in the Mexican-Origin Population of the Big Bend, 1910–1920." *Journal of Big Bend Studies* 10 (1998): 163–87.
———. "Work among Anglos and Hispanics in the Big Bend, 1910." *West Texas Historical Association Year Book* 71 (1995).
Wuerthner, George. *Texas' Big Bend Country.* Oakland, California: Two Bears Press, 1989.
Yarborough, Sharon C., and A. Michael Powell. *Ferns and Fern Allies of the Trans-Pecos and Adjacent Areas.* Lubbock: Texas Tech University Press, 2002.

Contributors

Mischa B. Adams lives in Santa Cruz, California, where she pursues her career as a mystery writer. Her academic training and earlier publications are in cultural anthropology.

Paul H. Carlson is professor emeritus of history at Texas Tech University. He is a renowned scholar of the history of the West and Southwest as well as of Native American history, and his many publications include *"Pecos Bill": A Military Biography of William R. Shafter* and *The Buffalo Soldier Tragedy of 1877*.

William A. Cloud is the director of the Center for Big Bend Studies at Sul Ross State University and has extensive archaeological experience in Texas, having served with the office of the State Archaeologist, Texas Parks and Wildlife, Big Bend National Park, and the Texas Archeological Research Laboratory. He is the author of numerous publications and has an avid interest in the archaeology and history of the Big Bend. Cloud lives in Alpine, Texas.

Franklin W. Daugherty, born and raised in the Big Bend, was a geologist who taught for many years at West Texas A&M University. Upon retiring to Alpine, Texas, Daugherty maintained his strong interests in geology and history, publishing in both disciplines. He was an active and dedicated board member of the Center for Big Bend Studies.

Earl H. Elam is a retired history professor from Sul Ross State University, where he also served for many years as an academic administrator. A prolific scholar of the history of West Texas, Elam was largely responsible for the creation of the Center for Big Bend Studies and served as its first director. He lives in Hillsboro, Texas.

Luis López Elizondo is an independent scholar who lives in Ciudad M. Múzquiz, Coahuila, Mexico. He is an avid historian and has for years served as an indispensable contact for researchers working in northern Mexico.

Bruce A. Glasrud is professor emeritus of history, California State University, East Bay, and retired dean of the School of Arts and Sciences, Sul Ross State University. He lives in Seguin, Texas. Glasrud specializes in the history of blacks in the west; he is co-editor/author of more than twenty books.

Joe S. Graham was a research associate at the John E. Conner Museum, Texas A&I University, when he wrote the article included in this publication. He was a distinguished ethnohistorian and borderlands ethnologist who focused his research efforts on Mexican and Mexican American lifeways of the Rio Grande and on the Hispanic origins of the cowboy in Texas.

Elizabeth A. H. John, a historian who lived in Austin, Texas, specialized in studies of the Native Americans of the Southwest. Her prominent book, *Storms Brewed in Other Men's World's: The Confrontation of Indians, Spanish, and French in the Southwest*, was a classic example of the work of a historian at the top of her field.

Oakah L. Jones was professor emeritus of Latin American history at Purdue University before retiring in the Southwest. A highly respected ethnohistorian and the author of numerous publications on the Spaniards and Indians of the borderlands, Jones was a longstanding chairman of the Advisory Council for the Center for Big Bend Studies.

J. Charles Kelley was professor emeritus of anthropology at Southern Illinois University at Carbondale and a pioneer of archaeological and ethnohistorical research in the Texas Big Bend. Best known for his seminal research in northwestern Mexico, Kelly maintained a strong and active interest in borderlands research throughout his lifetime.

Enrique R. Madrid is a long-time borderlands researcher and archaeological steward for the Texas Historical Commission. A well-known contact for regional researchers, Madrid lives in Redford, Texas, and has played a pivotal role in historic preservation of the La Junta de los Ríos area for many years.

Robert J. Mallouf, former Texas State Archeologist, director of the Center for Big Bend Studies, and assistant professor of anthropology at Sul Ross State University, has authored numerous publications related to the archaeology and history of Texas, as well as western Kansas and northern Chihuahua. Mallouf lives in Alpine, Texas.

Stacy B. Schaefer teaches anthropology and is director of the Museum of Anthropology at California State University at Chico. He is an authority on the indigenous peoples of Mexico and is editor of the book *People of the Peyote: Huichol Indian History, Religion, and Survival.*

Lonn Taylor is an accomplished historian and curator. Following numerous curating jobs in Texas, Taylor went to Washington to serve at the Smithsonian Institution's Museum of American History. Upon retirement, he moved to Fort Davis, Texas, and for a few years chaired the Advisory Council of the Center for Big Bend Studies. The subjects of his marvelous books include furniture and the United States flag.

Solveig A. Turpin is a long-established research archeologist at the University of Texas at Austin. Turpin specializes in hunter-gatherer adaptations to the arid lands of southwestern Texas and northeastern Mexico, and in the rock art for which this region is justly famous. She is the author of many publications on the archaeology of Texas and northern Mexico.

Robert E. Wright is associate professor of systematic theology at Oblate School of Theology in San Antonio. He is a graduate of the University of St. Thomas (Rome); his interests include culture and religion, and Catholic history in the Southwest.

Index

The letter *f* following a page number denotes a figure; the letter *t* denotes a table.

acculturation, 9, 186–89, 190. *See also mestizaje* (racial mixing)
Acosta, Juan José, 292, 293
Acosta, Matilde. *See* Luján, Matilde Acosta
Adams, Mischa B., 13–14, 218–37
Adobe Walls Draw site, 40, 41f
African languages, influence on Seminole language, 13, 220, 225–28
agricultural cultures: abandonment of La Junta district, 112; cultural affiliations of, 136; La Junta cultures as, 53, 74, 98–99; in Late Prehistoric period, 8, 38; origin theories, 54–55, 119; role of climate in success of, 7–8, 119–20; village sites of, 48
agricultural practices: contemporary, 124–27; of Late Prehistoric period, 11, 120–23
Alamo Springs site, 48, 61t, 62t, 97
Alex, Betty L., 79
Alex, Thomas C., 78, 79, 85
Almada, Francisco R., 122
Alpine, Texas, 259
Alsate (Apache chief): accounts of, 12, 158–59; capture and imprisonment of, 161–63; death of, 163, 170–71; description of, 169–70; family of, 162–63, 166–68, 171–72; origins of name, 164–66; places named for, 157–58, 160–61; relations with military authorities and Mexican towns, 160–61
Alsate (Williams), 158
Alvarado, Cosme, 201–02, 206
American democracy, 289, 298
American Indians. *See* Native Americans
Amerindians, 177–79, 181–82, 185–86, 188–90. *See also* Mexican Indians; Native Americans
Anderson, Edward, 135
Anglo-Americans, 196, 199–200, 289
antelope hides, 25, 27, 27f, 28, 30
Antonia (Seminole), 228. *See also* "Big Tamale" (Seminole); Mariscal, Antonia Gordon "Molly"; Molly (Seminole); Payne, Antonia "Molly"
Antonio, Fray, 240
Apachean cultures, 52, 64, 74, 108, 112, 136–39
Apache Indians: acculturation of, 186–89, 199; baptism of children of in La Junta district, 186, 188–89; burial customs of, 70; kidnapping of Francisco Rede, 295; language of, 164; Leaton's treaty with, 160; marriage customs of, 171; military action against Victorio, 276, 279–80; pacification of, 186–89, 248, 249; relations with Comanches, 12, 147–49, 152, 154, 169, 277; relations with Mexican government,

Apache Indians (*cont.*)
278; relations with Spanish, 12, 147–49, 150–55, 179, 186–89; as threats to settlement, 14, 222, 238, 276–79. *See also* Alsate (Apache chief); Lipan (Lipane, Lipyane) Apaches; Mescalero Apaches
apaches de paz, 150–51
Archaic period, 7, 22t, 38, 40–44, 42f, 111. *See also* Early Archaic period; Late Prehistoric period; Middle Archaic period
arid-land farming, 121–24
arrowpoints: forms of, 42f; as grave goods, 71–72, 85, 87–88; Harrell, 80, 85–86, 88f, 98; Late Prehistoric, 42f, 45–48, 46f; Livermore, 42f, 45–47, 46f; private collections of, 10, 37, 38, 69; reworked, 88–89; ritual fracturing of, 87–88; stone types used for, 89, 91. *See also* Perdiz arrowpoints
arroyos, 40, 43, 44, 120
artifact collectors, 19, 25, 27, 29–30, 69–70
Arzate, Francisco, 164
asadero, 201, 204, 205, 214
assemblages: from Cielo Bravo site, 52, 53, 53f; from Cielo complex sites, 47, 56–57; of hunter-gatherers, 48, 63; and La Junta phase origin theories, 64; from La Junta phase sites, 47, 64; from Las Haciendas site, 37, 41; Perdiz points in, 47–48, 52, 53, 53f; ritual breakage in, 99–100; from Rough Run site, 85, 87f, 88f; from Toyah phase sites, 56–57; from village sites, 45–48
atlatls, 43
atole, 198, 203, 207, 215, 216

Ballay, L. F., 249, 263
barbacoa, 206, 212, 215
barbacoa de cabeza, 212
base camps, of hunter-gatherers, 48, 50, 53–54, 74
Bateman, Rebecca Belle, 226, 234
beads, stone and shell, 52
beans: arid-land farming methods for, 121–22, 123, 124, 125; as traditional food, 197–98, 201, 202, 205
Becker, Bernd, 40, 60–61t, 62t, 97
beds and mattresses, prehistoric: at Cueva Encantada site, 19–21, 20f, 22–25, 23f; materials and construction methods, 10, 27–32, 27f, 30f, 31, 31t; at Wroe Ranch site, 9–10, 19–21, 20f, 25–27, 26f, 27f
beef, dishes made from, 212–13
Bell, Robert E., 90–91
Bement, Leland C., 21
Bennett, Wendell, 139, 142
Beta Analytic, Inc., 93
Bieber, R. P., 200
Big Bend National Park, 10, 37, 48, 69, 76f
Big Bend region, 35f, 46f, 59f, 147–48, 157–58, 263
"Big Tamale" (Seminole), 228, 233. *See also* Mariscal, Antonia Gordon "Molly"; Payne, Antonia "Molly"
bison hides, 30, 31, 112
bison hunters, 56, 57, 58, 98, 136
black cowboys, 224
Black Indians (Katz), 218
Black Seminole Indians: bicultural family names of, 234–35; as ethnically diverse peoples, 13, 218–19; history of, 218–19, 220–24; Payne family names, 231–34;

Seminole and Istilusti naming practices, 224–29; Spanish names of, 229–31
Black Seminole Scouts, 170, 218, 219, 223–24, 227, 232, 233
black troops, 14, 219, 243, 247, 276, 278–79, 282–85
The Black West (Katz), 218
Blanco (General), 162–63, 166
Blanco, Victor, 166
Bolton, H. E., 197, 199
borderlands history, 4–5
Borrajo, Father, 242
bow-and-arrow technology, 8, 43
Bravo Valley aspect, 63, 73–74, 98–99, 113
breads and pastries, traditional, 204, 207, 214
Brooks, Richard H., 109–10
Brooks, Sheilagh, 109–10
Buena Esperanza pueblo, 149–50, 186–87
Buffalo Soldiers, 219, 243, 247
The Buffalo Soldiers (television), 218
Bullis, Alice, 280
Bullis, John L., 170–71, 280–81
Burgess, John D., 158, 160–61, 238
burial customs. *See also* grave goods
burial customs, prehistoric, 10, 25, 71–73, 82–83, 83f, 93, 99–102. *See also* grave goods
burial pits, 25, 27f, 28
burials, infant, 29–30, 30f
burial sites, 31t, 37, 49, 49f, 56, 69, 70–73. *See also* Las Haciendas site; Rough Run site
burro dams (*presas*), 126–27
burruñate, 200, 209, 215
busk names, 224–26

Caballo, Juan, 221, 225. *See also* Horse, John (Seminole war leader)

Cabeza de Vaca, Alvar Núñez, 7, 121, 179, 288
cabrito en su sangre, 200, 209
cactus, as traditional food, 198, 206
cairn burials, 56, 70–74. *See also* Las Haciendas site; Rough Run site
cairns, 49, 49f, 70
cairn stones, 78, 82–84, 84f, 101–02
calabaxa, 205, 213
caldillos, 203, 213
caldo (doup), 206, 207, 213
Campbell, T. N., 37, 44
Cárdenas, Juan de, 134
Carlson, Paul H., 14, 276–87
Carmelite monks, 253, 260, 262, 263, 264
Carrasco, Jesús José, 124–25
Carrizo Indians, 135, 140, 141
Casas Grandes culture, 54, 63–64, 65, 110, 111, 113
Casas Grandes site, 112, 119
Castelo, Rosendo, 250, 251, 252, 257, 260, 264
Catholicism, 122, 229, 289
cattle, 199, 202. *See also* beef, dishes made from
Cavelier, Robert. *See* La Salle, Robert Cavelier de
Celis, Alonso Rubin de. *See* Rubin de Celis, Alonso
Center for Big Bend Studies, 3, 5–6
ceramics, 8, 52, 56, 63, 111
ceremonial items as grave goods, 102
ceremonial names, 224–26
chacales, 202, 216
charcoal, 85, 93, 94f, 97, 100–101
cheeses, 201. *See also* asadero
chicharrones, 200, 210, 211, 215
chicken, dishes made from, 206
Chihuahua, Mexico: Archaic period in, 40–44; Cielo Bravo site, 50–52,

Chihuahua, Mexico (*cont.*)
51f, 53f, 54, 55; Cielo complex in, 10, 48–52, 53–58, 59f, 62–65; La Junta phase in, 10, 48, 50–52, 59f, 62–65; Late Prehistoric period in, 10, 45–48; Paleoindian period in, 38–40; study area in, 34–38, 35f; Toyah phase origin theories, 56–58. *See also* La Junta de los Ríos; Las Haciendas site; Río Conchos drainage; Rough Run site

Chihuahuan Desert: archaeological study areas in, 19, 34–36; cairn burial sites in, 70–71; environmental conditions in, 178; flora and fauna of, 2, 34, 36, 75; prehistoric fiber industry in, 10, 19, 31–32; resources and raw materials available to prehistoric peoples, 36

chile con carne, 204, 209, 212

chiles (peppers), as traditional foods, 197–98, 209, 212, 213

Chiricahua Apaches, 138, 141, 153

Chisos Apaches. *See* Alsate (Apache chief)

Chisos cultures, 44, 54, 55

Christianity, 133, 143, 188–89

chronometric data, 54. *See also* radiocarbon analysis

churches, 181, 248, 251, 256–57

Cibolo Indians, 9, 55

Cielo Bravo site: and Apachean arrival date, 64, 74; cultural affiliations of, 136; excavations of, 37, 48, 50–52, 51f, 53f, 109; radiocarbon dating of Perdiz-bearing components, 60–61t, 62t, 97; stone-based dwellings at, 54, 55

Cielo complex: base camps of, 74; cultural affiliations of, 136; investigations at sites of, 37; origin theories, 10, 53–58, 59f, 64, 74; Perdiz points affiliated with, 47, 60–61t, 62t, 73–74, 98–99; stone-based dwellings at, 48–52, 49f

clergy, itinerant, 246–53

Clos, Father, 261–62

Cloud, William A., 5, 10, 69–105

Coacoochee (Seminole war leader), 221. *See also* Wild Cat (Seminole war leader)

Coahuila, Mexico, 19. *See also* Cueva Encantada site

Coahuila complex, 41

coal mines, 3, 14

Collins, Michael B., 30

Colomo, Luis, 240, 244, 248, 249

Colorado (Apache leader), 245–46

Colorado Canyon (Rio Grande), 38, 44, 48

Comanche Indians: acculturation of, 199; burial customs of, 70; effect of arrival on native peoples, 9, 137–38; and peyote religion, 135, 143; relations with Apaches, 12, 147–49, 152, 154, 169, 277; relations with Spaniards, 12, 154; as threats to settlement, 222, 238, 253; trading and raiding activities, 140, 159, 168, 169–70

comancheros, 159, 277

Concepción phase, 64, 74, 112

Conchos cultures, 54, 107, 111, 112, 113, 181, 197

Contact period, 47, 48, 55, 73–74, 107, 177–78

Cook, Daniel, 280

Coon, Joe, 228

Cordero, Antonio, 150

corn (maize): arid-land farming methods for, 121–22, 123, 124, 125; as traditional food, 197–200, 201, 202–04

cornbread, 198, 204
Coronado, Francisco Vásquez de, 136
Cortes, José, 100
Cowaya, Juan, 221. *See also* Horse, John (Seminole war leader)
cradles and cribs, 30, 31t
Creek Indians, 220, 221, 222, 231
Cremony, John C., 164
Croix, Teodoro de, 186, 187
Cueva Encantada site, 19–21, 20f, 23f, 27–32, 27f, 31t
cultigens, 120, 122
cultural boundaries, 39, 45
Culture Change and Shifting Populations in Central Northern Mexico (Griffen), 8

dams, 120, 121, 123, 124, 126–27
dart points, 21, 39, 42f, 43
Daugherty, Franklin W., 6, 12, 157–73
debitage, 10, 85, 91, 100
democracy, American, 289, 298
desserts, 214
día de los muertos, 196, 207
Díaz, Domingo, 151, 152–53
Díaz, Porfirio, 161, 162
differential diffusion, 11, 133, 141
domesticated animals, 199–200, 207–13
Domínguez de Mendoza, Juan, 180
Dowling, Father, 256–57
Durango, diocese of, 250

Early Archaic period, 7, 21, 22t, 41, 42, 42f, 43
Eca y Músquiz family, 167–68
Eeken, Brocardus "Brocardo," 264, 265
ejidos, 230–31
Elam. Earl H., 5, 15, 288–300

El Fortin, 160, 257, 291
Elizondo, Luis López, 12, 157–73
El Polvo, Texas. *See* Polvo, Texas (later Redford)
Emory, William H., 125, 199, 200, 240, 288–89
enchiladas, 201, 203, 204, 206
"Englishmen, Railroads, and the San Carlos Coal Mine" (Justice), 14
entradas, Spanish, 106–07, 168
Espejo, Antonio de, 179, 197, 292
Espejo expedition, 7, 107, 121–22, 178, 179, 292
European contact, 8–9, 134. *See also* Spanish period
Evans, George, 239
excavation procedures, 78–80

Factor, Hardy, 225, 227
Factor, Susan, 233
Factor family, 227, 229, 230
family names, bicultural, 234–35
farming cultures. *See* agricultural cultures
farming methods. *See* agricultural practices
Farrer, Claire R., 12, 136, 137, 141, 144
Faver, Milton, 201, 247–48, 259, 296
Feature 1, Rough Run site, 79f
Feature 19, Wroe Ranch site, 25, 26f
Ferra, Joseph, 247–48, 251
fiber industry, prehistoric, 10, 19, 31–32
fire ecology, 123
First Infantry, 276
first names, as surnames, 227–28
fish, 197, 207
Flannery, Kent V., 57
Flipper, Henry O., 282–84, 285
flooding, annual, 120, 123
flood irrigation, 121

INDEX | 319

floodplain (humedad) agriculture, 120–23, 124, 125
flora and fauna, Chihuahuan Desert, 2, 34, 36, 75
Flores, Manuel Antonio, 153, 188
Flores family, 230
Florez, José, 234. *See also* Gordon, Joe
Florida, 220, 221, 224, 225
foods, traditional: brought from Spain, 207–15; of contemporary Mexican peoples, 200–202; cultural importance of, 13, 196–97, 215–16; of pre-Hispanic peoples, 197–98, 202–07; of Spanish settlers, 199–200
Fort Davis, Texas: black troops at, 14, 276–79; construction of, 281; establishment of, 160; and Flipper affair, 282–84; itinerant clergy of, 246–48; missions of, 249–52, 255–57, 260–61, 262, 263; reestablishment of parish of, 241–44, 264–65; role in Big Bend military history, 3; troop reductions at, 249
Fort Leaton, Texas, 160, 257, 291, 292
Fort Stockton, Texas: establishment of, 160; itinerant clergy of, 246–48, 249–50, 251, 252, 253–54, 262–63, 264; reestablishment of parish of, 241–44; troop reductions at, 249
frames, bed and mattress, 10, 24, 27, 28, 30, 30f, 31
Franciscan missionaries, 179, 183, 190
Freedom on the Border (Mulroy), 170, 218
French missionaries, 180–81, 251–52
frijoles, 205

The Frontier People (Riley), 178
frontier regions, borderlands as, 15, 288–99
fruits and vegetables, 215

Galveston, diocese of, 239, 241, 242, 247
Gálvez, Bernardo de, 148–49, 150, 152
Galvéz Instruction, 150–54
game animals, 197
García, Juan, 244–46
Gardinier, Russell J., 178
Garza component, 52
Garza Falcon, Mariana de la, 167
Garza points, 42f, 45, 47, 48
Genoves, Santiago C., 92
geographical sections, and development of societies, 289–90
geology of Big Bend region, 1–2
Gerald, Rex E., 179, 189
Glasrud, Bruce, 1–15
goats and goat meat, 199, 200, 201, 202, 208–09
Gómez, Antonio del Refugio, 239–40
González, José Miguel María del Refugio Sabas Músquiz, 166, 167. *See also* Músquiz, Miguel
González, María Josefa Músquiz, 166
Gopher John, 221, 225. *See also* Horse, John (Seminole war leader)
Gordon, Antonia "Molly." *See* Mariscal, Antonia Gordon "Molly"
Gordon, Joe. *See also* Florez, José
Gordon family, 232–33. *See also* Flores family
Graham, Joe S., 5, 6, 13, 196–216
grasses, for beds and mattresses, 25, 26f
grasses, for prehistoric beds, 27, 27f, 29, 30, 30f, 31, 31t
grave goods: ceremonial items as,

102; from Las Haciendas site, 37, 41, 69–72; Perdiz arrowpoints as, 10, 85–90, 87f, 88f; ritual destruction of, 99–100, 101–02; and status of deceased, 99, 101–02
Green Corn Ceremony, 224, 229
greens, as traditional foods, 206
Griffen, William B., 8, 54, 140, 179, 189, 190
Guajardo, Luis Alberto, 165–66, 169, 170
Guichon, Adolphe, 241, 242, 243
guisados, 206, 209, 211, 213

Habicht-Mauche, Judith A., 136
Hankerson, E. Mario, 226
Harrell arrowpoints, 80, 85–86, 88f, 98
Hawley, C. A., 201, 212
hearths, stone, 49, 49f
Helm, June, 100
hides and skins, 25, 27, 27f, 28, 30, 31, 112
Hinojosa site, 95, 96t
Hispanics. *See* Mexican Americans
Historic period, 22t, 38, 44, 106–07, 119, 124–27
Hoban, Joseph, 247–51, 252, 257, 263
hogs, 207–08. *See also* pork, dishes made from
Horse, John (Seminole war leader), 221, 222–23, 225, 226–27, 228–29, 231
horses, Spanish introduction of, 12, 147
Huebner, Jeffrey, 73
huevos rancheros, 206
Huichol Indians, 133, 134, 139, 140, 141, 142
human remains. *See* skeletal material
humedad (floodplain) agriculture, 120–23, 124, 125

Humpris, John, 14
hunting (busk) names, 224
hunting-gathering cultures: of Archaic period, 44; arrival in Big Bend region, 7; base camps of, 48, 50, 53–54, 74; burial customs of, 99–100; Cielo complex peoples as, 53, 74, 98–99; cultural affiliations of, 119, 136; in La Junta district, 108, 112, 123; origin theories, 54–55; Toyah phase peoples as, 56

Indians, American. *See* Native Americans
Indians, Mexican. *See* Mexican Indians
Indian Territory, 221, 222, 223, 231
infant sleeping nests, 10, 22–24, 23f, 28, 29–30, 30f, 31t
Infierno phase, 10, 53, 56
interments, 72, 93
Introductory Handbook of Texas Archeology (Suhm), 73
Iodiaga, Joseph de. *See* Ydoiaga, Joseph de
irrigation systems, 121, 122–27
Istilusti peoples, 221–22, 224–29

Jaillet, Claude, 241–46
Jesuit missionaries, 248, 252, 262–63
Jesús Nazareno church, 117, 185, 190, 239, 296
John, Elizabeth A. H., 5, 6, 12, 13, 147–56
Jones, Oakah L., 5, 6, 13, 177–95, 199
Jornada Mogollon culture, 10, 54, 62–64, 111–12, 113, 119, 121
Journal of Big Bend Studies, 4, 5, 9
July family, 227
Jumano and Patarabueye (Kelley), 178, 189

Jumano-Apaches, 74
Jumano Indians: acculturation of, 9; Apache takeover of, 136–39, 169; arrival of, 64, 112; and arrival of Spanish, 137; conversion to Christianity, 179–80; cultural affiliations of, 98, 178; as hunter-gatherers, 55, 107–08; traditional foods of, 197
Justice, Glenn, 14

Katz, William Loren, 218
Kelley, J. Charles, 106–15; *Jumano and Patarabueye,* 178, 189; and Jumano peoples, 58, 74; La Junta district excavations of, 37, 38; La Junta phase interpretations of, 52, 53, 55, 62–65, 190; and Livermore focus, 45, 47; Millington excavations of, 51; Paisano point theories of, 44; Perdiz point named by, 73; Río Concho excavations of, 11, 36–37
Kibbetts, John, 225, 226
Kickapoo Indians, 222, 230, 235
Klein, Jeffrey J., 60–61t, 62t
Kreiger, Alex D., 90

La Barre, Weston, 11, 132, 133, 134, 140, 141
La Esperanza pueblo, 149–50, 186–87
La Junta de los Ríos: acculturation in, 185–86, 188–90; agricultural practices in, 11, 119–27; archaeological investigations in, 35f, 36, 37, 178–79; disappearance of native peoples from, 190; environmental conditions in, 119–20, 178; excavations in, 36, 108–13; intermarriage in, 13, 184–86; Jumano and Patarabueye Indians in, 107–08, 136–37; location of, 36, 59f, 119, 177; origins of agricultural peoples in, 119; peacemaking efforts in, 186–89; Perdiz points from, 47–48; peyote religion in, 136–37; post-Civil War era in, 241–44; pre-Civil War era in, 238; prehistoric agricultural villages of, 74; Spanish presence in, 13, 106–07, 177–84, 238. *See also* Cielo Bravo site; Polvo site
La Junta de los Ríos (town). *See* Presidio del Norte (later Ojinaga, Chihuahua)
La Junta phase: agricultural peoples of, 48; cultural affiliations of, 74, 111–12, 136; origin theories, 10, 37, 53–58, 59f, 62–65; Perdiz-bearing components of, 47, 60–61t, 62t, 98–99
lard, and traditional foods, 207–08
La Salle, Robert Cavelier de, 180
Las Haciendas, Chihuahua (Paso de San Antonio), 35f, 38, 69–70
Las Haciendas site: description of, 71–72; projectile points from, 37, 41; skeletal remains at, 71, 99; variability of arrowpoints from, 47, 89–90, 95, 96t, 97
Late Archaic period, 8, 22t, 24, 30, 40–41, 42f, 44
Late Paleoindian period, 22t
Late Prehistoric period: agricultural practices of, 11, 120–23; and Cielo complex, 10, 48; hunter-gatherer lifestyle in, 8; Lower Pecos chronology, 22t; origins of agricultural peoples in, 119; projectile points of, 42f, 45–48, 73–74; study sites of, 21, 24, 25, 37–38, 41, 42f
Leaton, Ben, 160, 200, 238, 291

Lechon, Vicente, 186, 189
Lipan (Lipane, Lipyane) Apaches: and peyote religion, 11, 132, 133, 134–35, 138, 140, 141; relations with Spanish, 151; and Santa Rosa attack, 169–70
Livermore focus, 45–47
Livermore points, 42f, 45–47, 46f
Llano Estacado, 136, 137, 138
Lockhart, W. E., 165
Lonestar (film), 218
López, José Guadalupe, 230
López, Nicolás, 179–80
López-Mendoza entrada, 122
Los Paisanos (Jones), 13
Lower Pecos River chronology, 21, 22t, 24–25
Lozano, Alicia Fay, 229–30, 234, 235
Luján, Antonia. *See* Rede, Antonia Luján
Luján, María Antonia, 293, 294
Luján, Natividad, 158–59, 171
Luján, Secundino, 291–93, 294, 296
Luján family, 291–96
Lumholtz, Carl, 139–40
Luxán, Diego Pérez de, 197

Madrid, Enrique R., 11, 119–32
Madrid, Lucia Rede, 15, 290–93, 295, 297–98, 299
maize. *See* corn (maize)
Mallouf, Robert J., 1–15, 34–68; Cielo Bravo excavations of, 98, 109; influence of research by, 113; La Junta phase interpretations of, 136; Las Haciendas interpretations of, 94; Rough Run excavations of, 71–74, 79–80, 89
Malmartel, Joseph, 253–54, 255–60, 262, 263
Manuel Benavides, Chihuahua (San Carlos), 35f, 36, 38, 39, 41

Marfa, Texas: diet study in, 215–16; itinerant clergy of, 249, 252, 256, 259, 263, 264; Rede family in, 297
Marienfeld, Texas (later Stanton), 253, 262, 263, 264
Mariscal, Antonia Gordon "Molly," 232, 233. *See also* Antonia (Seminole); "Big Tamale" (Seminole); Molly (Seminole); Payne, Antonia "Molly"
Mariscal family, 233
marriage customs, 171, 258, 259–60
Martinet, Father, 260, 261
masa, 203, 204, 215
Mascogo people, 220, 222–23, 226–34. *See also* Black Seminole Indians
mattresses, prehistoric. *See* beds and mattresses, prehistoric
McDonald, Isaiah, 278
McGregor, Roberta A., 24, 32
melons, 197, 202, 206, 215
menudo, 200, 213
Mescalero Apaches: at Buena Esperanza, 187; effect of arrival on native peoples, 9, 137–38; and French missionaries, 244–46; New Mexico reservations of, 138; and peyote religion, 11–12, 132–33, 134, 138–44; relations with Spanish, 137–38, 148–54, 186–89; trading and raiding activities in Mexico, 159, 169–70. *See also* Alsate (Apache chief)
mesquite beans, 197, 198
mestizaje (racial mixing), 13, 177–78, 185–86. *See also* acculturation
mestizo peoples, 119, 124–27
metate and mano, 197–98
Mexican Americans, 196–97, 215–16, 289, 290, 298, 299

Mexican Indians: effect on culture of Ojinaga, 289, 299; and peyote religion, 132, 133, 134, 139–40, 141, 142, 144

Mexican peoples: acculturation of, 185–86, 188–90, 189–90; and Alsate's Apaches, 161–64; marriage customs of, 258, 259–60; of Presidio del Norte parish, 238–41; religious imagery of, 239–40

Mexico: independence from Spain, 137, 138; relations with Apaches, 138, 159, 163, 171

Micapony (Seminole chief), 231

Middle Archaic period, 7, 22t, 25, 41, 42f, 43

military history, 3, 13, 179, 181–84, 238

milk, cow and goat, 208

Millington site, 51, 52, 108, 111

mining industry, 3, 14, 280–81, 294

Minjares Sánchez, Pedro, 124

missionaries, 9, 122, 179–82, 238, 248, 251–52, 262–63

missions, 168, 181–82

Mogollon culture, 111–12. *See also* Jornada Mogollon culture

Molly (Seminole), 228. *See also* "Big Tamale" (Seminole); Mariscal, Antonia Gordon "Molly"; Payne, Antonia "Molly"

Montenarelli, José María, 251, 252, 261, 264

Mooney, James, 11, 132, 134, 135–36, 138

Moorhead, Max, 179, 189

morcilla, 200, 210, 211, 215

Morelos family, 230

mortuary customs, prehistoric, 10, 25, 71–73, 82, 83, 83f, 93, 99–102. *See also* grave goods

Mulroy, Kevin, 170, 218, 219, 220, 225–26, 228

Muñoz, Manuel, 149, 183, 186–87

Murillo, Pablo. *See* Payne, Isaac, Sr.

Muscogulge people. *See* Seminole Indians

Muskogee Indians, 224–25, 226

Músquiz, Coahuila (formerly Santa Rosa), 159, 166–67

Músquiz, José Miguel Blanco, 166, 167. *See also* Blanco (General)

Músquiz, Manuel, 162–63, 165

Músquiz, Miguel, 159, 162, 171–72

Músquiz, Pedro, 165, 166, 171–72. *See also* Alsate (Apache chief)

Músquiz family, 159, 162–63, 165–68, 171–72

Myres, S. D., 164

Nacimiento de los Negros colony, 229–35

Native American Church, 133, 135–36, 141, 143–44, 189–90

Native Americans: acculturation, 185–86, 188–90; arrival in Big Bend region, 7; effects of European contact, 8–9; and peyote religion, 11, 132, 133–36, 141. *See also specific tribes and groups*

Nava, Pedro de, 153, 186

Neco family, 230

neoteric societies, Black Seminoles as, 228

Neraz (bishop), 250–52, 256, 260–61, 262, 263, 264

New Mexico, 138, 159

nicknames, 228

Nikla, John, 221, 225. *See also* Horse, John (Seminole war leader)

Ninth Cavalry, 223–24

Nolan, Philip, 167

nomadic peoples, 38. *See also* hunting-gathering cultures
Nuestra Señora de la Buena Esperanza pueblo. *See* Buena Esperanza pueblo
Nuestra Señora de Santa Ana y San Francisco de Xavier mission, 181
Nuestro Padre Jesús Nazareno church, 177, 185, 190, 239, 296
Nueva Vizcaya, 152, 153, 182–83, 184
Nueva Vizcaya (Jones), 179

Oblate missionaries, 251, 252, 253–56, 260–65
O'Conor, Hugo, 149, 184
Ojinaga, Chihuahua (formerly Presidio del Norte), 35f, 36–37, 39, 244–46, 249, 250–51, 288–91
Oklahoma Indian reservations, 132, 135, 140, 221
Old Fort Davis (Scobee), 281
Olivier, Rigomer, 251, 253, 260, 262
Opler, Morris, 132, 134–35, 140–41, 142, 143
Ortiz (Colonel), 161, 163, 171
Osceola (Seminole warrior), 224–25

Páez, Joseph, 183
Paine, Isaac. *See* Payne, Isaac, Sr.
Pairier, Mathurin, 247
Paisano points, 42f, 43, 44, 46f
Paleoindian period, 7, 22t, 38–40, 42f, 43
pan (breads and pastries), 204, 207, 214
pan de muerto, 207
Paquimé. *See* Casas Grandes site
Parker, Quanah (Comanche chief), 143
Paso de San Antonio, Chihuahua (Las Haciendas), 35f, 38, 69–70

Paso Lajitas, Chihuahua, 35f, 38, 39
Patarabueye Indians, 55, 107, 178, 179–80, 199
Payne, Abby, 232
Payne, Adam, 229, 230, 231, 233–34
Payne, Antonia "Molly," 233. *See also* "Big Tamale" (Seminole); Mariscal, Antonia Gordon "Molly"; Molly (Seminole)
Payne, Isaac, IV, 218, 230, 231–34
Payne, Isaac, Sr., 229, 233
Payne family, 230–34
Peabody, Charles, 70–71
Pecos River burial site, 29–30, 30f, 31t
Pennella, P. M., 263, 264
Pennington, Campbell, 139
peppers (chiles), as traditional foods, 197–98, 209, 212, 213
Perdiz arrowpoints: in Cielo Bravo assemblages, 52, 53, 53f; distribution of, 46f, 47, 59f; as evidence of cultural affiliations, 73–74, 98–99; as Las Haciendas grave goods, 72; Late Prehistoric classification of, 42f; and origins of Infierno phase peoples, 56; and origins of Toyah phase peoples, 56; in private collections, 45; radiocarbon dating of components bearing, 60–61t, 94t, 97; recovered from Rough Run, 10, 69–70, 78–80, 79f, 85–91, 87f, 88f; reworking of, 88–89; ritual fracturing of, 87–88, 99–100; similarities of Rough Run points, 89–90, 94–97, 96t; stone types used for, 89, 91; variability in, 72, 89–90
"The Personal Geography of a Significant Border Region, La Junto de los Ríos" (Gardinier), 178
Persone, Carlos, 250

peyote and peyote religion: ceremonies and rituals, 142–43; diffusion from Mexico to United States, 11–12, 133–36; in La Junta district, 136–37; and Mescalero Apaches, 11–12, 138–44; overview, 132–33
pigs, 199, 200, 202. *See also* pork, dishes made from
pinole, 198, 202, 216
pit houses, 54, 108–09
pits, burial, 80–84, 81f, 84f, 101–02
Polvo, Texas (later Redford), 253, 257, 292, 293–94. *See also* San José de Polvo, Texas
Polvo site, 37, 52, 54, 60–61t, 62t, 97, 109, 112
pork, dishes made from, 203, 209–12
Porras Ruiz, Alberto, 124
Porter, Kenneth Wiggins, 218, 220, 227–28, 229, 235
post-Civil War era, 241–44
posture and orientation, corpse, 25, 71–73, 99
potatoes, as traditional food, 197–98, 213–14
pottery. *See* ceramics
pozole, 203, 215, 216
pre-Civil War era, 238–41
Prehistoric period, 22t, 120. *See also* Late Prehistoric period
The Presidio (Moorehead), 179
Presidio, Texas: archaeological sites near, 37, 39; diet study in, 204, 206–07, 211, 215–16; establishment of, 238, 239, 240; itinerant clergy of, 246, 247–48, 249, 250, 251–52, 253, 256–58, 263–64; Millington site, 51, 52, 108, 111; peyote collection site near, 139

Presidio del Norte (later Ojinaga, Chihuahua): and Alsate's Apaches, 160–61, 163, 171; history of, 182–84, 288–89; itinerant clergy of, 247–48, 260, 263–64; Mescaleros relocated to, 149, 151–54; Mexican Catholic families of, 238–41; missions of, 249, 251, 252, 253, 256, 257, 258
Presidio Irrigation Company, 293–94
Presidio Mining Company, 280–81, 285
Presidio Mining Co. v. Alice Bullis, 280–81
presidios, establishment of, 149–54, 182–84
Presidio Santa Rosa, 151–55
prickly-pear: pads used for bedding, 10, 24, 26f, 27f, 28, 31t, 75; as traditional food, 198, 206
projectile points: of Archaic period, 42f; as grave goods, 37, 69–70; private collections of, 10, 37, 38, 41–42, 43, 44, 45. *See also* arrowpoints; dart points
Protohistoric period. *See* Contact period
Puebloan cultures, 63, 65, 119
pumpkins, as traditional food, 197–98, 202, 205–06

racial assimilation. *See* acculturation
radiocarbon analysis: of bedding fibers, 25, 31t; of charcoal, 93, 94f; of Cielo Bravo site, 51–52; of Late Archaic components, 38, 40, 41f, 44; of Late Prehistoric components, 47–48, 72; and Lower Pecos chronology, 9, 21, 22t, 24–25, 30, 47; of Perdiz-bearing components, 47, 57–58, 60–61t; of Rough Run components, 93, 94t, 97

Raht, Carlysle Graham, 158
railroads, 14–15, 248–53
Ramírez, Andrés, 122
Rede, Antonia Luján, 296
Rede, Eusebio, 294, 296–97
Rede, Francisco, 294–96
Rede, Lucia. *See* Madrid, Lucia Rede
Rede family, 294–98
Redford, Texas (formerly Polvo), 257, 291–92, 297–98
Reimer, P. J., 21, 24, 25, 31t
relic hunters, 19, 25, 27, 29–30, 69–70
religious imagery, 239–40
religious traditions, 139. *See also* Catholicism; Native American Church; peyote and peyote religion
reservations, Indian, 132, 135, 138, 140, 221, 223
reworking of arrowpoints, 88–89
rice, as traditional food, 201
Riley, Carroll L., 178, 189
Rio Bravo del Norte. *See* Rio Grande River
Río Conchos drainage, 11, 36, 37, 38, 106, 107–12. *See also* La Junta de los Ríos
Rio Grande frontier, 15, 288–99. *See also* Trans-Pecos Texas
Rio Grande River: archaeological sites of, 35f, 37–40, 44, 45, 47, 48, 50, 56; and Big Bend region, 1, 11, 106; Colorado Canyon, 38, 44, 48; and diffusion of peyote religion, 132–38; as early exploration route, 106–07. *See also* La Junta de los Ríos
rites of passage, 196, 229
ritual fracturing of arrowpoints, 87–88
robes and bed covers, 25, 27, 27f, 28, 30, 31, 112

rock shelters, 21–22, 24. *See also* Cueva Encantada site; Wroe Ranch site
Rodríguez, Augustín, 179
Rodríguez-Chamuscado expedition, 107, 121, 179
Rough Run site: arrowpoints and tools recovered from, 85–91, 87f, 88f, 94–97, 96t; cultural affiliations, 10, 70, 98–99; description of, 77f, 80–85, 81f, 83f; discovery and excavation of, 10, 69–70, 78–80; environmental setting, 74–75; evidence of burial customs, 10, 99–102; radiocarbon analysis of charcoal at, 93, 94t, 97; regional context of, 70–74; skeletal material recovered from, 91–93
Rubin de Celis, Alonso, 183
Ruidosa ranch, 247, 253, 258

Sabeata, Juan, 179, 180
salsas, 203, 204
San Carlos, Chihuahua (Manuel Benavides), 35f, 36, 38, 39
San Carlos Coal Company, 14
Sanders, Issum, 232. *See also* Payne, Isaac, Sr.
San José de Polvo, Texas, 292–97, 299
Santa Rosa, Coahuila (later Músquiz), 161–63, 169–70, 188. *See also* Músquiz, Coahuila (formerly Santa Rosa); Presidio Santa Rosa
sausage, as traditional food, 200, 210, 211, 215
Sayles, John, 218
Schaefer, Stacy B., 6, 11, 132–46
Scobee, Barry, 281
scrapers, 52, 56, 57
Seminole Freedmen, 221, 226, 234

INDEX | 327

Seminole Indians, 220–21, 222, 223, 224–29, 230
Seminole-Negro Indian Scouts. *See* Black Seminole Scouts
Seminole Wars, 221, 224, 225
seviche, 207
Shackelford, William J., 109
shade ramadas, 48, 49f, 51
Shafer, Harry J., 30
Shafter, Texas: itinerant clergy of, 253, 259, 260, 263, 264; mines at, 251, 259, 294; Rede family in, 290–91, 296, 297
Shafter, William Rufus: with 24th Infantry at Fort Davis, 276–79; military career of, 14, 276, 281–82, 284–85; role in Flipper affair, 282–84; and silver mining scheme, 280–81
shamanism, 142, 143–44
sheep, introduction of, 199
Sierra el Virulento, Chihuahua, 35f, 38, 41
silver mines, 3, 280–81, 294
skeletal material: from Las Haciendas, 71–72; from Rough Run, 70, 80, 82–83, 83t, 85, 91–93; and status of deceased, 99, 101–02
slaves and slavery, 220–23
sleeping accommodations, prehistoric. *See* beds and mattresses, prehistoric
Smith, C. J., 262
Smith, Victor J., 71, 108
Sociedad de Agricultores, 127
Soria family, 233–34
sotol: for prehistoric beds, 10, 24, 30, 31, 31t; as traditional food, 198
Southern Pacific Railroad, 14, 249
Southern Plains hypothesis, 57–58, 64

Spain, Mexican independence from, 137, 138
Spaniards: accounts of native farming practices, 121; effect on culture of Ojinaga, 289, 299; effect on native peoples, 7, 8–9, 112, 132, 134, 137, 177–79, 190; exploration routes of, 106–07; and Jumano and Patarabueye Indians, 55, 136, 137; Mascogo children named by, 229–31; military presence, 13, 179, 181–84, 288; missionaries, 9, 122, 179–82, 238; and peyote religion, 134, 141; relations with Apaches, 12, 137–38, 147–49, 150–55, 186–89; relations with Comanches, 12, 154; settlement by, 13, 119, 179–82, 189–90
Spanish names, for Black Seminoles, 229–31
Spanish period, 177–78. *See also* Contact period
Spanish Presidios of the Late Eighteenth Century in Northern New Spain (Gerald), 179
Spencer, John W., 189, 200–201, 238, 240, 280
Spicer, Edward H., 185
squash: arid-land farming methods for, 121–22, 123, 124, 125; as traditional food, 197–98, 202, 205–06
Stanton, Texas (formerly Marienfeld), 253, 263
Stephen, Sister, 241
Stewart, Omer, 132, 134–35, 138, 140, 143
stone-based dwellings, 48–51, 49f, 51f, 54, 55, 56; of Cielo complex peoples, 74
stones, cairn. *See* cairn stones

stone types for projectile points, 89, 91
Storms Brewed in Other Men's Worlds (John), 12, 13
Stuiver, Minze, 21, 24, 25, 31t, 40, 60–61t, 62t, 94t, 97
Suhm, Dee Ann, 90, 91
Sukey (slave), 233. *See also* Factor, Susan
surnames, first names as, 227–28

tabular stones, 78, 80, 83, 84, 101–02
tacos and tostadas, 203, 204, 206, 213
Talma, A. S., 94t
tamales, 198, 201, 203, 206, 209, 215
Tamarón y Romeral, Pedro de, 184
Tarahumara Indians: farming methods of, 121, 125; and peyote religion, 12, 133, 134, 138, 139–40, 142, 143–44
Taylor, Walter W., 41, 43
temporal farming, 122, 124–25
Tenth Cavalry, 223–24, 282–84
Texas and Pacific Railroad, 248–49
Texas Rangers, 138
The Romance of Davis Mountains and Big Bend Country (Raht), 158
Thompson, Cecelia, 171
Tinkhouse, Henry, 279
tomatoes, as traditional food, 197–98
tools, stone, 38–40, 52, 56–57, 89. *See also* projectile points
tortillas, 198, 201, 203, 204, 207, 215
Toyah cultures, 10, 53, 56–58, 73, 98
Toyah points, 42f, 45, 91
Toyah Valley, Texas, 247, 249, 250, 251, 252, 260, 262, 263

trade centers, Casas Grandes as, 112
Trans-Pecos Texas: Fort Davis parish, 241–44, 264–65; as frontier region, 288–99; itinerant clergy of, 246–48; location of, 76f, 238; Oblate missionaries in, 253–64; pre-Civil War era in, 238–41; railroads and settlement in, 14–15, 248–53; study areas in, 45–47, 46f
Trasviña y Retis, Juan Antonio, 181
Trasviña y Retis expedition, 122
Treaty of Guadalupe Hidalgo, 288
Trotter, Mildred, 92
turkeys, as traditional food, 206
Turner, Frederick Jackson, 289–90, 293, 294, 298
Turpin, Solveig A., 9–10, 19–33
Twenty-fourth Infantry, 14, 276–79

Ugalde, Juan de, 151–52, 153
Ugarte y Loyola, Jacobo, 150–51, 152, 153, 186, 188
Utley, Robert M., 283

Valdéz, Adam, 229. *See also* Payne, Adam
Valdéz family, 229, 230
vandalism of architectural sites, 19, 25, 27, 29–30, 69–70
Van Valkenburg, Alan, 78
Vásquez de Coronado, Francisco. *See* Coronado, Francisco Vásquez de
Vásquez family, 230
Vásquez Valdéz family, 230
vegetables and greens, 215
Victorio (Apache war chief), 276, 279–80
Vidaurri, Juan de Dios, 229. *See also* Horse, John (Seminole war leader)
village sites, 50–51, 51f
Vogel, J. C., 94t

Wagner, Albert, 262, 263, 264
war (busk) names, 224
Warrior, William "Dub," 229
Weddle, Robert S., 168
wheat and wheat flour, 122, 125, 199–200, 213–14
wickiups, stone-based, 49f, 50–51, 51f, 54, 56
Wild Cat (Seminole war leader), 221, 222, 223, 231
Wilhelmi, Louis, 280, 282, 283, 284
Williams, Oscar W., 158–59, 163, 164, 166, 171
Wilson family, 230
Winkler, B. A., 198

women, role in prehistoric and historic societies, 10, 32, 224
Wright, J. Leitch, 225
Wright, Robert E., 14–15, 238–75
Wroe Ranch site, 19–21, 20f, 25–27, 26f, 27f, 31t

Yarrow, H. C., 70, 99
Ydoiaga, Joseph de, 122, 123, 124, 182
Ydoiaga expedition, 7, 122, 123
Ysaguirre, Fernando de, 185–86

Zingg, Robert M., 109, 139, 142

www.ingramcontent.com/pod-product-compliance
Lightning Source LLC
Chambersburg PA
CBHW020352080526
44584CB00014B/993